D. Z. PHILLIPS' CONTEM
PHILOSOPHY OF REL

This collection presents a critical discussion and exploration of the late D.Z. Phillips' contemplative approach in the philosophy of religion. What are the main characteristics of this ground-breaking approach, which is inspired by thinkers like Kierkegaard and Wittgenstein and meant as a serious, critical alternative to the mainstream way of doing philosophy of religion? What is its aim, if it is deliberately avoiding apology and defence of faith? How does Phillips' approach relate to systematic, historical and empirical theology and is it really as 'neutral' as he claims it to be? Or is he, perhaps, a certain kind of theologian? What are the implications of his contemplative philosophy for central issues of religious life today, such as petitionary prayer, the hope of 'eternal life' and radical religious diversity? The essays of six distinguished scholars from five different nations critically and sympathetically address these questions and are responded to by Phillips in essays of his own, written briefly before his sudden death in July 2006.

In memory of D.Z. Phillips (1934–2006)

D. Z. Phillips' Contemplative Philosophy of Religion
Questions and Responses

Edited by

ANDY F. SANDERS
University of Groningen, The Netherlands

Routledge
Taylor & Francis Group

LONDON AND NEW YORK

First published 2007 by Ashgate Publishing

Published 2016 by Routledge
2 Park Square, Milton Park, Abingdon, Oxon OX14 4RN
605 Third Avenue, New York, NY 10017

First issued in paperback 2021

Routledge is an imprint of the Taylor & Francis Group, an informa business

Publisher's Note
The publisher has gone to great lengths to ensure the quality of this reprint but points out that some imperfections in the original copies may be apparent.

British Library Cataloguing in Publication Data
D.Z. Phillips' contemplative philosophy of religion : questions and responses 1. Phillips, D. Z. (Dewi Zephaniah) 2. Religion – Philosophy
I. Phillips, D. Z. (Dewi Zephaniah) II. Sanders, Andy F.
210

Library of Congress Cataloging-in-Publication Data
D.Z. Phillips' contemplative philosophy of religion : questions and responses / edited by Andy F Sanders.
    p. cm.
Includes bibliographical references and index.
ISBN 978-0-7546-6285-3 (hardcover : alk. paper) 1. Religion–Philosophy. 2. Phillips, D. Z. (Dewi Zephaniah) I. Sanders, Andy F.

BL51.D22 2007
210.92–dc22

2007007964

ISBN 13: 978-1-03-209968-2 (pbk)
ISBN 13: 978-0-7546-6285-3 (hbk)

Contents

Notes on Contributors   vii

Introduction: Questions for Contemplative Philosophy of Religion   1
Andy F. Sanders

I   Wittgenstein's Temple: Three Styles of Philosophical Architecture   13
Stephen Mulhall

II   Locating Philosophy's Cool Place – A Reply to Stephen Mulhall   29
D.Z. Phillips

III   Philosophy, Theology and Heresy: D.Z. Phillips and the Grammar of
Religious Belief   55
Mario von der Ruhr

IV   Pictures of Eternity – A Reply to Mario von der Ruhr   75
D.Z. Phillips

V   Internal Realism: A Joint Feature by Dewi Z. Phillips and Paul Tillich?   95
Tage Kurtén

VI   Philosophy and Theology – Too Close for Comfort.
A Reply to Tage Kurtén   111
D.Z. Phillips

VII   A Friend of Demea? The Meaning and Importance of Piety   125
Walter van Herck

VIII   Philosophy, Piety and Petitionary Prayer – A Reply to Walter van Herck   139
D.Z. Phillips

IX   Religions in a World of Many Cultures: Conflict, Dialogue,
and Philosophical Contemplation   153
Ingolf Dalferth

X   Philosophy, Theology and Cultural Conflicts – A Reply to I. Dalferth   167
D.Z. Phillips

XI   Philosophy of Religion in a Pluralistic Culture   181
Henk Vroom

XII   Philosophy's Radical Pluralism in the House of Intellect –
      A Reply to Henk Vroom   197
         D.Z. Phillips

In Retrospect   213
         D.Z. Phillips

Bibliography   216
Index   223

Notes on Contributors

Ingolf Dalferth is Professor of Systematic Theology, Symbolics and Philosophy of Religion in Zurich, Director of the Institute of Hermeneutics and Philosophy of Religion and Research Fellow at the Collegium Helveticum in Zurich. His major research areas are systematic theology in the nineteenth and twentieth centuries, philosophical and theological hermeneutics in the twentieth century; ecumenical theology (Lutheranism and Anglicanism), analytical and phenomenological philosophy of religion in the twentieth century, religion and emotion, and evil. He is author of many books in German and English, including *Religiöse Rede von Gott. Studien zur Analytischen Religionsphilosophie und Theologie* (1981), *Die Wirklichkeit des Möglichen. Hermeneutische Relgionsphilosophie* (2003), *Theology and Philosophy* (2002), *Becoming Present. An Inquiry into the Christian Sense of the Presence of God* (2006), and *Das Böse. Essay über die kulturelle Denkform des Unbegreiflichen* (2006).

Tage Kurtén is Professor of Systematic Theology, Theological Ethics and Philosophy of Religion at Åbo Akademi University, Turku, Finland. The focus of his current research is on issues of religious morality in a multi-cultural and multi-religious society. Apart from many articles in Swedish, Finnish and English on issues at the intersection of axiology, epistemology and social and feminist ethics, he is author of *Foundations of a Contextual Theology* (1987) and *Trust, Reality and Value* (1995), and co-editor of the anthology *Homo Moralis* (2005). He has been chief editor of *Studia Theologica* and director of two larger, cross-disciplinary research projects on morality, law and legitimacy.

Stephen Mulhall is a Fellow and Tutor in Philosophy at New College, Oxford. He was previously a Reader in Philosophy at the University of Essex, and a Prize Fellow at All Souls College, Oxford. His most recent publications include *Philosophical Myths of the Fall* (2005), *Heidegger and 'Being and Time'*, 2nd edn. (2005) and *Wittgenstein's Private Language* (2006).

D.Z. Phillips (24 November 1934–25 July 2006) was educated at the Universities of Wales and Oxford. After a three-year ministry (Fabian Bay Congregational Church, Swansea), he was appointed Lecturer in Philosophy at the University of Andrews (1961–1963) and, next, at the University of Wales at Bangor and Swansea until 1970. From 1971, until his retirement in 2001, he was Professor of Philosophy at the University College of Swansea. From 1992 to 2006 he was Danforth Professor of Philosophy of Religion, Claremont Graduate University and from 1996 to 2001 Rush Rhees Research Professor, University of Wales, Swansea. The endowed lectures he has given include the Marett Memorial Lecture (Oxford, 1983), the Riddell Lectures (Newcastle, 1986), the Aquinas Lecture (Oxford, 1987), the Cardinal Mercier Lectures (Leuven, 1988), the Vonhoff Lectures (Groningen, 1999–2000) and the Suarez lecture (New York, 2006). Author of more than twenty books, his publications of the past fifteen years include *From Fantasy to Faith* (1991, 2nd edn. 2006), *Wittgenstein and Religion* (1993), *Philosophy's Cool Place* (1999), *Recovering Religious Concepts* (2000), *Religion and the Hermeneutics of Contemplation* (2001), *Religion and Friendly Fire* (2004), *The Problem of Evil and the Problem of God* (2004) and *Wittgensteinian Fideism?* (with Kai Nielsen, 2005). He was editor of numerous volumes of the *Nachlass* of his teacher Rush Rhees and of more than fifteen other volumes, of which the most recent ones (co-edited with Mario von der Ruhr) are: *Language and Spirit* (2004), *Biblical Concepts and Our World* (2004), *Religion and Wittgenstein's Legacy* (2005), *Whose God? Which Tradition?* and *Religion Without Metaphysics?*(both forthcoming). He was Editor of the journal *Philosophical Investigations* (1982–2006) and General Editor of the series *Studies in Ethics and the Philosophy of Religion* (1968–1974), *Values and Philosophical Inquiry* (1976–1986), *Swansea Studies in Philosophy* (1990–2006), *Claremont Studies in the Philosophy of Religion* (1993–2006) and *Wittgensteinian Studies* (2003–2006).

Mario von der Ruhr is Lecturer in Philosophy at the University of Wales, Swansea, and an Associate Editor of the journal *Philosophical Investigations*. He is the author of *Simone Weil – An Apprenticeship in Attention* (2006), and has published articles on ethics, religion and philosophical anthropology. Together with D.Z. Philips, he co-edited several volumes of the series *Claremont Studies in the Philosophy of Religion*, and is serving on the editorial board for the monograph series *Existential Themes in Contemporary Philosophy of Religion*. He is also the Director of the Rush Rhees Archive in Swansea, and Chairman of the Welsh Philosophical Society.

Andy F. Sanders is Professor of the Philosophy of Religion at the University of Groningen and, since 1994, a member of the Centre for Theological Inquiry (Princeton, NJ). His research areas are religious epistemology, hermeneutical philosophy of religion and religion and public reason. Among his publications are *Michael Polanyi's Post-critical Epistemology* (1988), *Theology and Philosophy of Science* (1990, in Dutch) and the systematic bibliography *Fifty Years of Philosophy of Religion* (2007). He is co-editor of *Concepts of Person in Religion and Thought* (1990) and *Belief in God and Intellectual Honesty* (1990).

Walter van Herck is Senior Lecturer at the Philosophy Department of the University of Antwerp and Editor of *Bijdragen. International Journal in Philosophy and Theology*. Among his publications are *Religion and Metaphor* (1999, in Dutch), and the first Dutch editions of Hume's *A Natural History of Religion* (1999) and Kant's *Religion within the Boundaries of Reason Alone* (2004). He is also co-editor of the volumes (in Dutch): *Rationality and Religious Trust* (1999), *Holy Places* (2002), *Religion and Death* (2004) and *Religion and Emotion* (2006).

Henk Vroom is Professor of the Philosophy of Religion at the Vrije Universiteit Amsterdam. His research areas are religious hermeneutics, religious pluralism and society, comparative philosophy of religion and inter-religious dialogue. Among his more recent publications are *Religions and the Truth* (1990), *No Other Gods* (1996) and *A Spectrum of World Views* (2006). He is co-ordinator of a research group that has edited volumes such as *Religion, Conflict, and Reconciliation* (2002), *On Sharing Religious Experience* (1992) and *Human Rights and Religious Values* (1995). He is co-editor of the series *Studies in Interreligious Dialogue* and currently co-ordinating the establishment of a program in Islamic theology at the Vrije Universiteit.

Introduction:
Questions for Contemplative
Philosophy of Religion

Andy F. Sanders
University of Groningen

In the present volume, six philosophers and theologians are presenting their critical essays in honour of the Welsh philosopher D.Z. Phillips' work in the philosophy of religion. Special is that the collection also offers six extensive responses by Phillips, each of which may count as an essay in itself. As a result, the collection is a paradigmatic example of, and contribution to, the ongoing discussion in the Wittgensteinian tradition of philosophy of religion. In this tradition Dewi Phillips has been a major builder; without him it would not be what it is today. Over the past forty-five years, Phillips has developed, 'with constant reference' to Wittgenstein, Rhees, Winch, Kierkegaard and Simone Weil, a mature philosophy of religion in a substantial *oeuvre* of more than twenty books and countless articles. As in the case of his great exemplars, Wittgenstein and Kierkegaard, most of this was achieved against the tide. After all, the dominant 'paradigm' or 'school' in the Anglo-American philosophy of religion has been, and still is, what could broadly be called 'metaphysical' or 'philosophical' theism.

As all the essays show, there are vast differences between the methods, aims and styles of reasoning of metaphysical theism and those of contemplative philosophy of religion. A major difference is that the latter distances itself far from the quest for justification by jettisoning the often tacit assumption that the central aim of philosophy, vis-à-vis religion, is the defence of, and continuation of, theology in philosophical terms and by philosophical means. Instead, the aim of Phillips' philosophy of religion is to do conceptual justice to religious life in all its variety and to give a 'perspicuous' representation of it. He refuses to represent it as mere building blocks for abstract metaphysical theories, which are hovering high above actual human life. This alone makes contemplative philosophy of religion a serious alternative to philosophical theism.

The authors of the essays are all to a greater or lesser extent sympathetic to Phillips' Wittgensteinian approach. In spite of this family resemblance, the essays show a rich variety of concerns, critical questions and examples. Phillips' rejoinders greatly enhance the dialogical character of the volume. Concerns that are shared by all are: (a) Phillips' conception of contemplative philosophy, in particular its aims, neutrality and authority, and its place within the family of other Wittgensteinian approaches (Chs. I–II); (b) the relation between contemplative philosophy of religion and theology (Chs. III–XII); (c) the fruits of contemplative philosophy, in particular

Phillips' accounts of religious conceptions of eternal life (Ch. IV) and petitionary prayer (Ch. VIII); (d) some consequences of contemplative philosophy of religion, in particular for realism (Ch. VI) and pluralism (Chs. X and XII). Trying not to disrupt the voices in discussion, and leaving most of what is discussed for the reader to find out, let me briefly introduce these issues.

1. Contemplative Philosophy

In an important sense, Stephen Mulhall's essay 'Wittgenstein's Temple' sets the stage for the other essays. One of his main questions is where Phillips' contemplative philosophy should be located within Wittgensteinian philosophy and whether it should exhibit the kind of neutrality that Phillips regards as essential to it. That this issue has serious implications for contemplative philosophy in regard to theology and religion can be gathered from nearly all of the other essays. Recalling three different readings of Wittgensteinian philosophy – a 'cold' or deficient version, a 'hot' or passionate version and Phillips' own 'cool' version as set forth in the latter's *Philosophy's Cool Place* (1999)[1] – Mulhall argues that these three conceptions are 'far less easily distinguishable than he [Phillips] appears to think' (Ch. I, p.27).

Elucidation. According to the 'cold' version, philosophy has a negative task, namely to unmask metaphysical conceptions as confusions to be dissolved by returning the words in question to the ordinary language-games in which they have their home ('therapy'), noting grammatical differences between language-games and to give perspicuous representations of them ('elucidation').[2] Phillips' objection to this 'underlabourer conception of philosophy' is that it disregards one of Wittgenstein's major concerns with regard to the multiplicity of language games, viz., the fundamental problem of the possibility or intelligibility of discourse and the unity of language. The concern for this problem is an essential characteristic of 'contemplation' that is not exhausted by 'therapy' or 'elucidation' (see Ch. II, section 3). Mulhall, however, is not convinced that philosophy must go 'essentially beyond the familiar Wittgensteinian business of perspicuously representing the grammar of everyday words' (Ch. I, p.20). After all, it is precisely this version that grounds the neutrality that Phillips finds so important (see Ch. I, p.21).

Neutrality. The 'passionate' version, for Phillips, according to Mulhall, confuses the distinctive philosophical 'wondering interest in the dialogical unity of language' with the passionate interest 'that every human being has in finding some way of … making sense of … that dialogue' (Ch. I, p.21). Calling this 'the distinction between the philosophical and the personal', Mulhall then embarks on an elaborate defence

---

1   *Philosophy's Cool Place*, Ithaca, NY, and New York: Cornell University Press, 1999. According to Mulhall, this book exhibits a substantial change in Phillips' position (see Ch. I, p.13). Phillips denies this (see Ch. II, pp.53–54 and Ch. VI, p.111).

2   This is near to Phillips' early statement that 'philosophy is neither for nor against religious beliefs. After it has sought to clarify the grammar of such beliefs *its work is over.*' See D.Z. Phillips, 'Religious Beliefs and Language Games', *Ratio* 12 (1970), 26–46; also in *The Philosophy of Religion*, ed. B. Mitchell, London: Oxford University Press, 1971; and in D.Z. Phillips, *Wittgenstein and Religion*, Basingstoke: Macmillan, 1993 (italics editorial)

of the Wittgensteinian philosophers James Conant and Stanley Cavell against Phillips' charge that they are conflating the philosophical and the personal. This charge, he argues, exemplifies a failure to recognize both Kierkegaard's reminder 'that philosophers are human beings too' and the obvious point that discourse about the possibility of discourse is itself engaging in discourse. In brief, Phillips' account of philosophy's distinctive interests and authority is unduly restrictive in that it fails to acknowledge philosophy's participation in, and its human significance for, broader cultural intercourse (see Ch. I, p.26).

Arguing that 'the lure of a philosophy for living' that is inherent in the 'passionate' version of Wittgensteinian philosophy should be resisted, Phillips admits that practising contemplative philosophy is in an important sense personal because it makes certain ethical demands of the philosopher, such as 'purity of attention to the world' or 'a passion for clarity.' In this sense, there is an internal relation between them (Ch. II, p.39) and the demand is as personal as it is philosophical (Ch. II, p.50) What Phillips resists, however, is to extend the connection between philosophy and ways of living to cases in which there no such internal relation because then things become 'far more complicated' and one embarks on a 'precarious journey' (Ch. II, p.43, p.48).

2. Philosophy and Theology

Philosophy of Religion. Paying attention to the question of how contemplative philosophical enquiry into religion is practised, and what its goals are, inevitably evokes background ideas and assumptions about the nature and aims of philosophy of religion. The textbooks on that issue provide neat classifications illustrated by historical examples and surveys of the changes that the discipline went through. Is philosophy of religion a branch of philosophy, of theology or, perhaps, of both? If it is a branch of both, how do the philosophy and the theology hang together, especially in the current cultural situation of the West? As a branch of theology, it is normally, and properly, called 'philosophical theology.' Since it involves a fusion of philosophical and theological interests in which the emphasis might be on either one of them, this label is hardly illuminating. Moreover, philosophical theology can be practised in many different ways. If the emphasis is on theology, for example, it can be conceptual analysis of religious language, or a hermeneutics aiming at understanding the meaning of particular religious practices and conceptions. Aligning itself closely to the apologetic concerns of theism, it can also strive for a defence or demonstration of the intellectual credibility, plausibility or rationality of faith by (re)constructing the propositional contents of religious beliefs into a rationally justified or warranted system. If the emphasis is on philosophy, it can be a philosophy for living, a guide to life, inspired by more or less explicit religious beliefs and aims. On Phillips' view of the internal relation between the (philosophical) theologian and his or her beliefs, philosophical theology cannot be a contemplative philosophy 'of religion'.

What about the philosophy of religion as branch of philosophy? Clearly, this is where contemplative philosophy of, or 'about', religion is located. The same goes for Ingolf Dalferth's conception of philosophy of religion which is '*about* religion, not a move *within* a religion or a better alternative to it' (Ch. IX, p.159). However, he implicitly criticizes Phillips' conception of contemplation not because it is too neutral or detached, but because it is only one of the options in the broad range of resources in the philosopher's arsenal. Next to, e.g. criticism, polemics, apologetics, imaginative invention or direction, 'contemplation is often but not always the appropriate way to respond' (Ch. IX, p.160). Contemplation in the sense of Wittgensteinian description, then, cannot be the whole story. Moreover, the point of philosophical contemplation, according to Dalferth, is that it is inevitably 'an exercise in … self-transformation', 'changing one's way of seeing things' on the part of the philosopher (Ch. IX, p.160). Phillips disagrees (see Ch. X, p.172) for, on his view, a contemplative philosopher of religion does not engage in apologetics. That is not a task of the philosopher but of the theologian as 'the custodian of faith'.

According to Henk Vroom, Phillips 'wants to look and see, and describe religion as it really is' (Ch. XI, p.183). What that means vis-à-vis systematic theology, however, is not quite clear. Vroom wonders whether the practitioners of contemplative philosophy of religion are 'theologians in disguise or wolves clothed as philosophical sheep' (Ch. XI, p.186). Acknowledging that Phillips' contemplative theology is neither a confessional theology nor a dialogical or comparative theology, he suggests that it strives to be a meta-theory, a place 'outside or above any school of thought and community of worldview ideas' (Ch. XI, p.189). After a detailed and interesting comparison between twentieth-century phenomenology of religion and contemplative philosophy of religion, Vroom concludes that both 'are very close indeed' (Ch. XI, p.193). Phillips agrees that there might be some similarities between the phenomenologists and Wittgenstein.[3] As for Vroom's conclusion that contemplative philosophy of religion is trying to understand and describe what is really going on in religion, Phillips emphasizes that the kind of description involved is different from what counts as such in history or the sciences. More on this below.

Neutrality. Philosophy of religion is, as practised, not necessarily 'neutral' for it can be a philosophy for life, whether religious or secular. Examples can be found of 'Christian', 'Jewish' or 'humanistic' philosophy. Neither is it necessarily a-theological or atheistic, though as a matter of fact it often is. In any case, one cannot just say, as is often done, that unlike theology, philosophy is neutral in the sense that it does not in fact propound a religious or secular view of human life. But Phillips wants to emphasize that philosophy of religion is neutral in the sense that it is neither for, nor against, religion. Obviously, the neutrality in question is not the neutrality of a 'view from nowhere', or of an 'ideal observer' because philosophical commitment to neutrality is itself a certain kind of advocacy.

It seems then that the boundaries between philosophy of religion *qua* philosophy and *qua* theology are quite fuzzy and therefore hard to draw. A theologian may be engaged in clarifying religious concepts as part of the larger theological enterprise

---

3   There might be a parallel between Phillips' contemplative neutrality and the so-called phenomenological reduction or *epochè*, which requires that one avoids all abstraction, theorizing and generalization in approaching a certain phenomenon in order for it to show itself. See for example http://www.phenomenologyonline.com/inquiry/13.html, last accessed 3 July 2007.

of transmitting, conserving and renewing the tradition. This may seem neutral, but on Phillips' view such a theologian is still internally related to the language and the life he or she is clarifying. Hence, a theologian cannot be neutral. With the exception of, say, specifically Christian philosophers, however, a philosopher of religion need not be related in the same way to the theological enterprise at all, no matter what his or her confessional background or personal convictions, religious, moral, political or otherwise may be. That is precisely what makes him or her a contemplative philosopher. As Phillips points out, discarding its neutrality, would discard the contemplative character of his philosophy as well.

Precisely at this point theological puzzlement and worry crop up. From a certain theological perspective, philosophy is mainly instrumental; a 'handmaiden of theology' as the saying goes. This is why philosophers of religion are sometimes viewed with suspicion by confessional theologians who are inclined to think, not always wrongly, that philosophers of religion are furthering an intellectual agenda that is quite close to secular thought and thus too distant from a certain orthodoxy. But philosophers may be suspicious as well. They might surmise, sometimes rightly, that philosophers of religion might be theologians who are working on some hidden theological agenda with which they do not wish to have anything to do, whether professionally (as philosophers), or personally (as persons who may or may not be religious believers), or both.

According to Phillips, contemplative philosophy of religion is *neither* a branch of theology *nor* a philosophy for living. In view of the remarks just made, however, this is not as crystal clear as it seems. What is this purely philosophical interest in religion? Surely, there must be some tacit religious motivation for that interest even if the philosopher in question denies it?

These are no mere theoretical questions as can be gathered from the essays of such sympathetic commentators as Tage Kurtén, Walter van Herck and Henk Vroom. Kurtén, for example, ends his essay with the apparently open question of the personal involvement of the philosophers of religion: 'to what extent can they maintain a detached and neutral approach?' (Ch. V, p.110) Clearly, he is questioning Phillips' claim that the contemplative philosopher of religion is, or should be, neutral. Similarly, Vroom wonders whether 'Phillips and his comrades are theologians in disguise – or wolves clothed as philosophical sheep' (Ch. XI, p.186).

In spite of the fact that Phillips has always emphasized that he is a philosopher, there are theologians who are inclined to take his philosophical account of religious concepts as covert *theological* attempts at conceptual renewal and reform. After all, they might say, by advancing elucidations of conceptions such as eternal life, God's reality, petitionary prayer, divine love, he is operating on theological home ground. As a consequence both Phillips' denial that he is not a theologian and his plea for critical discussion, are disregarded. Moreover, the autonomy that he claims for philosophical contemplation is swept under the carpet. By now, confusion is spreading widely (he says he is a philosopher but he is really a theologian in disguise) and repetition sets in (no, I'm not a theologian). Would it be an exaggeration, one wonders, to consider this as a way of doubting the integrity of the philosopher in question?

So why is Phillips, the contemplative philosopher, so often accused of, or at least conceived of, as being *a certain kind* of theologian? One reason might be that some theological readers take his philosophical aim as a mere personal gloss on his work; a first-person report of what motivates him. They might also say: No matter *what* he says about the possible sense of religious pictures and conceptions, that is surely not only assessable on *his* (philosophical) terms, but also independently of them, on *our* (theological) terms. Phillips, one may assume, would not disagree, especially because this creates possibilities for an exchange with his theological critics. He would, I suppose, also agree that if a particular theologian would accept his account of, say, eternal life or of divine love, this would not, as such, make that theologian a contemplative philosopher. The acceptance would rest, rightly or wrongly, wholly on theological grounds.

Another reason for taking Phillips as a theologian might be that certain critics simply assume that he must be propounding 'theological' views in philosophical disguise. He is voicing, unwittingly or not, his own personal views shaped by the roots of his upbringing in Wales, his confessional stance, etc. This reading seems to turn Phillips into a man of straw, a quasi-theologian and quasi-philosopher all rolled into one. In its wake, questions about the authority with which (he thinks) he is speaking, follow as a matter of course. What appears to be massively underestimated or at least overlooked, however, is Phillips' point of departure in the Wittgensteinian–Rhees philosophy of logic and its account of language and meaning. (see Ch. II, section 3).

More *in concreto*, consider Phillips' 'pictures of eternity' (Ch. IV) or his account of petitionary prayer (Ch. VIII). Born out of philosophical puzzlement and wonder, they are meant to be reminders of certain possibilities of religious sense. Reading Phillips, theologians may be reminded of those senses by grasping that they are so intended. But they may equally well be understood differently, say, as mere exercises in a certain philosophy, which are proposals for renewal and reform, or even as threatening warnings that one may well be deeply 'confused' in one's religious convictions. The hermeneutical point that may be suggested here is that how the reminders are understood is in an important sense up to the readers, their background knowledge, stances, expectations and so on. For a religious believer or theologian, a certain possibility may, so to speak, get a life of its own by showing itself as 'real' to him or her. But the possibilities that are presented may just as well be merely interesting, boring, repugnant or not quite right. In that case theological readers might launch an enquiry of their own, or start a discussion if they think a particular possibility is at odds with their tradition. As 'guardians of the grammar of faith' they practise their trade from within their personal religious commitment, rooted in that tradition. 'The theological' fully includes 'the personal' in virtue of the internal relation between the theologian and his or her subject matter. In contrast, the contemplative philosopher stays in his or her 'cool place' in the hope not to be saddled with a theological interest in reforming religious concepts or in offering alternative interpretations of religious language in order to meet the needs of religion in modern culture. In that place he or she is, according to Phillips, 'interested in *what is there to be seen*' (Ch. IV, p.82).

Description or prescription?   There is more to the issue of the neutrality and autonomy of contemplative philosophy of religion than its differences with systematic or philosophical theology may show. For example, what about religious studies, history, sociology and so on, which the practitioners also claim, describe, even explain, what is there to be seen in human life? This line of questioning easily leads to the charge that Phillips, contrary to what he says, is not merely *describing* but in fact *prescribing* when he is elucidating religious conceptions. The tacit assumption underlying this charge, it seems, is that 'describing' is the sort of thing that historians and sociologists, etc., are engaged in. That assumption, however, is mistaken because, according to Wittgensteinian philosophy of logic, 'description' is not recording what can empirically be ascertained but a matter of showing the logical space that concepts have in language and (thus) in human life. As Phillips points out in his replies to von der Ruhr, Van Herck and Vroom, to describe religious beliefs 'is not to offer an interpretation of them, but to show the conceptual space they occupy in religious life' (Ch. IV, p.78; see Ch. VIII, p.147; Ch. XII, p.201). This kind of description is a matter of 'doing conceptual justice' to that life and putting the findings forward is putting forward possibilities of sense, reminders that things may be significantly different. Whether or not readers will appropriate (in the hermeneutical sense) such a possibility is entirely up to them. Surely, one would not be far amiss to hear one of Kierkegaard's many voices in the background here.

Mario von der Ruhr's remark that Phillips' allegedly neutral elucidations of key religious concepts, instead of being applauded often lead to major interpretive disagreements with religious believers, points to a special version of the charge of prescription (see Ch. III, p.60). The argument appears to be that if the descriptions were truly neutral, they would be acceptable to the majority of believers but, as they are clearly not acceptable, they cannot be neutral. Phillips rejects this conclusion because, on his view, the first premiss is wrong. Showing the conceptual space that religious concepts have in human life is different from showing what believers may think that place is. Finding out about the latter can be done by poll-taking, the former requires philosophical investigation.

Vroom criticizes Phillips' claim to neutrality in the context of theology and religious studies. He does not believe that Phillips is neutral at all (see Ch. XI, p.186). The point appears to be hermeneutical because, according to Vroom, the practice of philosophy of religion is shaped throughout by the philosophers' stance on religion and by his or her culture. Even though philosophers can keep certain conceptions 'at arms length' while trying to understand them, they may subscribe to one of them, for example, the world as creation (or the world as cosmos).

In sum, given the special meaning of 'description' in contemplative philosophy, the charge of prescription, reform and renewal seems less serious than is often thought. In any case, Wittgensteinian philosophy of logic will have to be taken into account in further debates on this issue.

Autonomy. Is contemplative philosophy autonomous? The question is important to Phillips because he devotes the first section of his reply to Kurtén on it. According to Van Herck, contemplative philosophy should to be supplemented by 'an historical interest in religious practices ... or with an anthropological interest in the culture of religion' (Ch. VII, p.138). According to Vroom, philosophy of religion must take the results of religious studies into account because the meaning of religious conceptions can only properly be understood in their historical, social and communal contexts.

'Philosophical analysis of religious concepts without a deeper knowledge of the traditions in which they are rooted, makes no sense' (Ch. XI, p.185).

Leaving Van Herck's suggestion for what it is, Phillips considers Vroom's remark a 'bold claim'. Philosophy and theology predate religious studies, and the methodologies of the latter can themselves be guilty of conceptual confusion because they sometimes distort the religious practices they are studying or neglect important features of them (see Ch. XII, p.200).

3. Fruits of Contemplative Philosophy of Religion

Eternal life.   Taking the conception of eternal life as his example, von der Ruhr shows how Phillips analyzes the various ways in which one can be confused about the grammar of that conception. He then presents as a test-case 'the orthodox Catholic' for whom the promise of life after death is insolubly linked to Christ's resurrection. According to von der Ruhr, Phillips' descriptive elucidations are partly congruent, partly in conflict with Catholic faith and that it would 'be hasty to dismiss [this conflict] as the result of philosophical confusion' (Ch. III, p.65).

Taking von der Ruhr's point head on, Phillips acknowledges that his early account of belief in eternal life may have given rise to the idea that it 'is no more than *an attitude to this present life*' (Ch. IV, p.79). However, he rejects the suggestion that he has ever advocated this reductionist view. In the final section of his response Phillips elaborates his earlier account of eternal life in a conversation with an imaginary 'discontented believer'. With reference to Rhees, Weil, Winch, Kierkegaard, the poet R.S. Thomas and St. Paul, Phillips takes his readers on a journey that should enable them 'to see, philosophically, pictures of eternity' (Ch. IV, p.93). Readers will have to decide for themselves, but if this reader is to be honest, he would admit that if a discontented believer would claim that something is still seriously missing from that picture or that something has been reduced, he or she would be both intellectually and existentially at a great distance from him.

Von der Ruhr concludes his paper with a plea for 'a satisfactory account of the relation between religion and science' (Ch. III, p.74). Since Phillips does not respond to it, it makes one wonder what difference his contemplative approach would make in the thriving field of 'science and theology'. Von der Ruhr is no doubt aware of the fact that the massive literature on that issue is mostly couched in the idiom of the various brands of (supernaturalist) theism and versions of (naturalist) scientism.[4] Clearly, this is a further topic to explore for contemplative philosophers.

Petitionary Prayer.   Walter van Herck criticizes Phillips' account of petitionary prayer in the latter's *The Concept of Prayer* (1965) for being 'one-sided' and, worse even, for turning 'the majority of the believers in the world into superstitious people' (Ch. VII, p.130). Arguing that there is petition and that there is nothing wrong with believing in divine intervention, Van Herck sides with William James's 'crass supernaturalism' claiming that it corresponds to the theological doctrine of particular

---

4   For an approach that is neither theistic nor scientistic see, for example, J. Wentzel van Huyssteen, *Alone in the World? Human Uniqueness in Science and Theology*, The Gifford Lectures 2004, Grand Rapids, MI/Cambridge: Eerdmans Publishing Company, 2006.

providence. This possibility should be kept open because 'it is the door that piety uses all the time' (Ch. VII, p.134).

In his response, Phillips elaborates his account of *what it is* that may actually happen in petitionary prayer. Briefly, the central idea is that a change occurs in the one who is praying and that 'a gift is given' when a request is fulfilled because – on the condition that it is received as a gift – God is in it (Ch. VIII, p.151). Rather than an attempt to influence God, petitionary prayer is a participation in God. It is not God who is changed by the prayer, but the one who prays is changed by God in the praying. In that sense it could be called an intervention in the life of the believer.

Phillips also points out that in any account of petitionary prayer a crucial role is played by a certain conception of God's power. On a widespread view, of philosophical theists for example, that power consists in the ability to do anything that is not logically impossible. However, if that were the case, even the most horrendous evils might be attributed to God.and that, as far as Phillips is concerned, is not false, but senseless.

4. Some Consequences of Contemplative Philosophy of Religion

Ordinary Realism.　Tage Kurtén sets out to show that there are significant similarities between Phillips' work and the ideas of Paul Tillich, in particular on the issue of God's reality. Phillips' idea that there is an internal relation between the theologian and his or her religious beliefs may be seen as a parallel to Tillich's notion of 'the theological circle', the hermeneutical space in which theological understanding proceeds. According to Kurtén, Tillich should be taken as an existential thinker rather than as a builder of metaphysical systems. The former construes God's reality as something that can only be encountered and understood 'in the concrete lives of religious men and women'. Like Phillips, he holds that religious language is distorted when it is understood as mirroring the divine reality 'out there' (see Ch. V, p.99).

Appreciating Tillich's attempts to address a culture in which religion is waning, Phillips argues that in spite of the similarities, Tillich's ontological absolute 'being itself' and the related anthropological absolute 'ultimate concern' as a *necessary* feature of human existence, makes a joining hands with Tillich 'too close for comfort' (Ch. VI, p.121). He rejects 'internal realism' because it perpetuates metaphysics in the service of apologetics. 'Internal realism' should be replaced by 'ordinary realism' (Ch. VI, p.112) which on Phillips' view is neither an alternative 'grand scale' theory nor a 'no-theory' theory, but a matter of paying a certain kind of (philosophical) attention to how reality shows itself in language and in human lives.

Radical Pluralism.　In the last two essays, the focus shifts from the Christian religion to the plurality of religions and to the complex issue of the place of philosophy of religion and theology in our current culture, in which tensions and conflicts are all too evident. A prelude to this issue can already be found in the final section of Phillips' response to Kurtén, in which he summarizes his ideas on the relation between religion and culture expounded in his *Belief, Change and Forms of Life* (1986).

Ingolf Dalferth begins his essay by distancing himself from the idea that understanding religions is not a matter of a fideist 'moving in closed circles of religious meanings'. Understanding religions requires that the role they play in human life and culture should be taken into account as well. His question is whether Phillips' contemplative hermeneutics has anything interesting to contribute to that issue. Dalferth points out that religions may relate very differently to cultures and that they should not be conceived as means to a particular cultural end. In the case of conflict between a religion and its culture, religions survive only by 'being practised as a way of life that convinces by the orientation it provides and by the example of those whose lives it informs and transforms' (Ch. IX, p.159).

According to Phillips, he and Dalferth agree on a host of things (see Ch. X, pp.174–6) but he also discerns disagreement in the way in which the relation between cultures and religions should be elucidated (see Ch. X, section 4). Dalferth is charged with 'subliming' some of the conceptions he employs, such as (social) stability, peace, tolerance and 'readiness to change one's view' as a precondition of entering into discussion with others. In this way, Phillips wants to show the relevance of contemplative philosophy to the 'practical issues of conflict resolution in a culture' (Ch. X, p.179).

In the final chapter, Phillips gives an extensive account of the *radical pluralism* that is implied by his contemplative philosophy. The starting point is, again, Wittgensteinian philosophy of logic and its concern for the 'big question of the possibility of discourse' and, hence, of the intelligibility of discourse in the hubbub of voices. This radical pluralism, Phillips maintains, 'is essential if discussions of the nature of reality are to be rescued from confusion' (Ch. XII, p.204).

Distinguishing between theological pluralism and radical pluralism, Phillips says that, unlike the latter, the former is a specific attitude to (other) religions that has no particular interest in doing conceptual justice to them. In contrast, radical pluralism would try to do conceptual justice even to terrible rituals of human sacrifice by accounting for the possibility that what gives rise to them might be 'awe at the terrible' rather than, say, the wish to appease supernatural powers.

Briefly, these are the main features of Phillips' radical pluralism. First, it should not be confused with quietism ('Live and let live'). It emphatically aims at letting the disputes, criticisms and value-clashes involved in rival positions 'to be themselves' (Ch. XII, p.205). Second, it does not imply a radical relativism that has it 'that all religions are equally valid'. Obviously, this would be self-contradictory. Whether this means that some religions might be more equal than others, however, is a question that Phillips does not address, presumably because such a question is too general (valid in what respects, for what purposes and in what contexts?) or confused (are religions comparable with, and assessable in the same way as, scientific theories? who is raising the question?). Third, radical pluralism does not imply jettisoning truth in favour of notions of power, coercion, oppression, exclusion and the like. It will not ignore these notions, wherever they might be in play, but recognizes that they are 'parasitic on some conception of something being distorted or evaded' (Ch. XII, p.206). Fourth, radical pluralism does not lead to a 'schizophrenic existence', as if the contemplative philosopher was to retreat from the life he or she has to live. Fifth, radical realism is able to deal with 'single-mindedness' or dogmatism because recognizing and elucidating possibilities of meaning is wider than personal appropriation. Sixth, acknowledging the enormous discord in human life, radical pluralism allows of no *a priori* answer to the question whether such discord is avoidable.

Clearly, the implications of this radical pluralism for the religious and political issues that Western societies are currently facing will yet have to be explored. Rather than aiming at general solutions, it may at least be expected to do justice to the concepts that are used by people in grappling with those issues in the lives they are living.

The discussion between Phillips and his interlocutors will now have to begin. Phillips' decease, on 25 July 2006, is a great loss to us all. His voice, though, will not be silenced but carried on in and through our conversations. Thanks are due to Stephen Mulhall, Tage Kurtén, Mario von der Ruhr, Walter van Herck, Ingolf Dalferth and Henk Vroom for their contributions and, I should add, their patience. Thanks, most of all, to D.Z. Phillips for his efforts to give the discussions in this volume all the characteristics of a genuinely productive dialogue. It is to the memory of him that we dedicate this volume.

Chapter I

Wittgenstein's Temple: Three Styles of Philosophical Architecture

Stephen Mulhall
Oxford University

Introduction

In his book, *Philosophy's Cool Place*,[1] D.Z. Phillips attempts to characterize his own Wittgensteinian conception of philosophy by distinguishing it from two other ways in which Wittgenstein's writings have been received amongst those similarly inclined to do philosophical work in the light of their example. This strategy of self-description conveys the impression that Phillip's contemplative conception of the subject is a kind of Aristotelian mean: it locates itself between one variety of Wittgensteinianism that exhibits a certain deficiency or lack (failing to appreciate one of the deepest dimensions of Wittgenstein's interest in language), and another variety that exhibits a certain excess (reading a dimension of significance into Wittgenstein's philosophizing that simply is not there).

In Phillips' view, the contemplative Wittgenstein is not only, as it were, the true Wittgenstein – or at least the reading of Wittgenstein that is true to his most profound moments of self-understanding; it is also a conception of philosophizing after Wittgenstein that returns the subject to one of its perennial, and certainly to one of its originating, concerns. Indeed, in a manner strangely reminiscent of the early Heidegger's self-presentations, Phillip's contemplative Wittgenstein appears to represent a kink in the history of the subject, but one that in fact returns it to the defining moment of its emergence from a pre-Socratic horizon. On Phillips' account, Wittgenstein and Plato's Socrates must be understood as conversation partners, as not only having something important to say to one another about reality, discourse and philosophy, but as sharing a sense of wonder at the very possibility of intercourse about these, or indeed any other, topics – at the possibility of discourse as such.

It would hardly be an exaggeration to say that this is not the conception of Wittgenstein or of philosophy, that most of Phillips' readers would have been inclined to attribute to him before the publication of *Philosophy's Cool Place*. At the very least, it seems clear that Phillips' intensive and extensive labours on the Rush

---

1   *Philosophy's Cool Place*, Ithaca, NY, and New York: Cornell University Press, 1999.

Rhees *Nachlass* have deeply influenced his present understanding of his own work, and I hope that one consequence of my discussion of this matter will be to underline and clarify the nature of this influence. But my primary concern is to understand in more depth and detail exactly what Phillips thinks is at stake in his discrimination of his contemplative conception of philosophy from its deficient cousin (what lack is he making good, and why?), and exactly why he thinks that, having remedied this lack, he can continue to discriminate his own position from its transgressive cousin (what excess is he thereby avoiding, and why?). To put the matter in the terms provided by the epigraph to Phillips' book: when Wittgenstein tells us that 'My ideal is a certain coolness. A temple providing a setting for the passions without meddling with them', exactly what temperature does he think is appropriate to any properly philosophical contemplation of these passions?

1. Catching a Chill: Repressing Philosophy's Passion?

Phillips believes that there is a common way of reading the later Wittgenstein that omits a fundamental dimension of his concern with philosophical problems and their dissolution. In effect, this deficient or cold conception amounts to conceiving of Wittgenstein's later philosophical method in the terms provided by his early, Tractarian specification of what he called 'the strictly correct method in philosophy' – that of saying only what can be said, and demonstrating to those who fail to respect this condition on speech that they have failed to give meaning to some portion of their putative utterance. Expressed in more familiar terminology, the picture is that specifically philosophical or metaphysical utterances amount to violations of grammar, instances of language idling or going on holiday – cases in which words have been unmoored from the contexts of their ordinary use; and the task of the philosopher is to identify these violations or instances of emptiness in speech, and to return the words thus abused to their home in our everyday life with language.

This picture can be linked without much difficulty, sometimes via other familiar remarks of Wittgenstein, with a number of more or less objectionable conclusions. For example, if metaphysics exiles us from the ordinary, and is to be overcome by returning to the ordinary, then the metaphysical and the ordinary must surely stand in simple opposition to one another. This means not only that the realm of the ordinary must be conceived of as absolutely pure, as free of metaphysical confusion or bewitchment; it also means that the realm of the metaphysical must be conceived of as utterly impure, as the manifestation of confusion pure and simple. Hence the philosophical tradition as a whole appears to be utterly valueless. More precisely, the only positive value of philosophy as Wittgenstein understands it is in fact negative; it resides in its ability to cure those diseases of thought with which other philosophers and philosophies infect us.

One might well wonder: why not simply avoid catching the disease in the first place? Here, of course, one must recall that Wittgenstein himself traces the source of our metaphysical bewitchments to language itself, to our captivation by the pictures embedded in our life with words, and hence concludes that infection by philosophical confusion is no more to be avoided than is life with language.

However, this concession offers little succour to those who might wish to think of philosophical impulses as having any human significance; for metaphysics remains, even on this modified picture, exclusively the settled cultural expression of confusion, illusion and emptiness. We may not be able to avoid the impulse to set up camp within its precincts; but our intellectual health depends upon mastering the impulse to remain there in each instance in which it finds expression or, more precisely, upon coming to see that there is no 'there' in which to remain, no space suitable for human habitation.

What concerns Phillips more immediately, however, is another conclusion that might be drawn from this deficient conception of philosophical endeavour. For Wittgenstein precedes his remark about returning words from metaphysical emptiness to everyday use with the following advice: 'When philosophers use a word... one must always ask oneself: is the word ever actually used this way in the language–game which is its original home?'[2] This might naturally be read as suggesting that everyday language is essentially a collection or agglomeration of language-games. At the very least, it is the kind of remark that has led many commentators to assume that the key to Wittgenstein's conception of language is his famous analogy between uses of words and games. Indeed, the pervasiveness of this analogy, perhaps when taken together with the equally famous characterization of 'game' and 'language' as family resemblance concepts, has led even very sympathetic commentators to suspect that Wittgenstein thinks of language as a family of language-games.

According to Phillips, if one were to allow such a picture of language to guide one's philosophical practice, then one will no more expect to find a common thread linking the various specific language-games to which one must return our words than one will expect to find one linking the various things we call 'games'. In effect, since philosophical confusions arise when words are removed from their home language-game, perhaps most typically when one language-game is confused with another, one should not expect the dissolution of those confusions to involve the Wittgensteinian philosopher in anything more than the task of perspicuously representing the structure of the relevant games, and the grammatical differences between them. Since there is no reason to think that language manifests any kind of unity, the philosopher can have no responsibility to identify or characterize that unity. Putting the matter more strongly: even to raise the question whether language as such might exhibit a unity of some kind is to fail to appreciate that 'language-game' and 'language' are family resemblance concepts. It is to share in the assumption of the interlocutor in *Philosophical Investigations* §65, whose confusion the very idea of family resemblance is designed in the first instance to reveal – the assumption that language has an essence. It is, in short, to engage in metaphysical thinking.

Phillips plainly, and rightly, thinks that many philosophers influenced by Wittgenstein operate in accordance with just such a conception of philosophy. Peter Winch – at least the Winch of *The Idea of a Social Science*,[3] with its emphasis upon rules and its declaration that what counts as real is always internal to a practice

---

2   Ludwig Wittgenstein, *Philosophical Investigations*, trans. by G.E.M. Anscombe, Oxford: Blackwell, 1953, p.116.
3   Peter Winch, *The Idea of a Social Science*, 2nd edn., London: Routledge, 1990.

– might plausibly be held to fit the bill; and Phillips has acknowledged elsewhere that his own early work in the philosophy of religion was prone to a similar set of emphases.[4] But his ever-deeper conviction that such a conception of Wittgensteinian philosophy is ineluctably impoverished is Phillips' most explicit, and fateful, debt to Rush Rhees.

For Rhees devotes his famous article 'Wittgenstein's Builders' to elaborating the suspicion that Wittgenstein himself is tempted by this conception of language, and hence of philosophy, and to articulating an alternative (in Rhees's view, no less Wittgensteinian) conception of both; and these are matters that are further developed and contextualized in the posthumous publication *Wittgenstein and the Possibility of Discourse*,[5] edited by Phillips himself, and published in 1997. In essence, Rhees sympathizes with Wittgenstein's critical motive for developing this picture of language as a family – his desire to contest the view that language has the coherence or systematicity of a calculus or a formal system. However, he believes that it is itself likely to encourage another, equally profound misapprehension, and thereby to betray Wittgenstein's own deepest insights into the nature of language and speech – insights encapsulated in his remark that to imagine a language is to imagine a form of life.

For example, Rhees believes that it is the analogy between language and games that leads Wittgenstein to suggest that a primitive language-game such as that of the builders in *Philosophical Investigations* §2 might be the whole language of a tribe – a suggestion Rhees regards as unintelligible. For a language is something one speaks; and if the builders are to speak to one another, and to understand what is said, they must be able not only to give and receive orders, but to comprehend and discuss the place or point of any specific order in the broader activity of building, and the purpose or significance of building in the broader context of a recognizably human life. Wittgenstein's builders cannot exchange words with one another about their building project, or about building in general, or about its relation to other non-building activities in their lives. They have nothing to say to one another, about building or anything else, because their building activities are not taking place in the context of a life that they are living together, and in which their various activities (and their capacity to converse about those activities) interlock intelligibly with one another. For Rhees, in the absence of such a context, they emit only signals and reactions to signals.

The image of a conversation, of intercourse or dialogue, is here doing work at two inter-related levels. Most straightforwardly, it is meant to suggest that linguistic interaction cannot be properly pictured on analogy with making moves in a game. Moves in a game, Rhees claims, are determined by the rules of the game, and have no significance outside it; whereas knowing how to say something (to say something worth saying, something worth another's hearing) is not a matter of mastering rules, and does involve being responsive to the significance of matters outside the conversation itself (both the topic of the conversation, and the relation of that

---

4   See, for example, 'Religious Beliefs and Language Games'.
5   Rush Rhees, *Wittgenstein and the Possibility of Discourse*, ed. D.Z. Phillips, 2nd edn., Oxford: Blackwell, 2005.

conversation to other modes of human discourse about other topics). On another level, Rhees means us to picture the various different forms or aspects of human discourse and practice as relating to one another in the way that various contributions to a conversation relate to one another. In other words, the unity of language is the unity of a dialogue; the various modes of human discourse about things interlock intelligibly with one another, and the sense that each makes is both constituted by and constitutes the sense of these interconnections. In short, for Rhees language makes sense insofar as living makes sense; the generality or unity of language is the generality or unity of a form of life.

On Phillips' view, in refusing to acknowledge the intelligibility of any attempt to characterize the unity or generality of language, proponents of the deficient version of Wittgensteinian philosophy are in fact occluding a precondition of their own, more restricted, enterprise. For the business of clarifying the grammar of a specific language-game, and of its differences from other language-games, can be carried out only on the assumption that parties to the enterprise already speak the language concerned. In fact, a version of this thought is plainly central to Wittgenstein's opening discussions of language and games (*Philosophical Investigations* §31):

> I am explaining chess to someone; and I begin by pointing to a chessman and saying: 'This is the king; it can move like this... and so on'. In this case we shall say: the words 'This is the King'... are a definition only if the player already knows what a piece in a game is. That is, if he has already played other games, or has watched other people playing 'and understood' – *and similar things...*
>
> We may say: only someone who already knows how to do something with it can significantly ask a name.

As this quotation suggests, there is an aspect of the analogy between language and games that works for, rather than against, the thought that to imagine a language is to imagine a form of life (and that might accordingly raise suspicions about Rhees' imputation to Wittgenstein of the impoverished conception of language and philosophy that he sees as inherent in this very analogy).[6] For the guidance it offers us here is that, just as knowing how to play a specific game presupposes a grasp of what it is to play games, so knowing how to do something specific with words presupposes a more general or basic awareness of what it is to do things with words – in short, of what it is to speak. Hence, the possibility of engaging in grammatical clarifications of specific philosophical confusions about words makes manifest the very unity or generality of speech that its proponents overlook or deny. In Phillips' favoured terms, the possibility of discourse about discourse makes manifest the unity of discourse, and hence makes the task of attempting properly to characterize that unity unavoidable.

As this vocabulary is partly intended to suggest, such a way of conceiving philosophy's fundamental business aligns one dimension of Wittgenstein's work with that of Plato. Phillips traces back to the pre-Socratic the thought that philosophy's

---

6   For a more detailed defence of Wittgenstein against Rhees's charges, see sections 15–18 of Part I of my *Inheritance and Originality*, Oxford: Clarendon Press, 2001.

distinctive concern is with reality in general: its aim is not to account for the existence of one state of affairs or mode of reality rather than another, but to show how it is possible for anything to be real. The difficulty with any answer that might be given to such a question is, however, obvious; if Thales tells us that all things are water, we will naturally ask what account is to be given of the water? More generally, it will always be possible to ask, of any putative measure of the real, what account is to be given of the measure.

One response to this would be to accept the irreducible plurality of our measures of reality – to declare that whilst there might be particular measures of this or that kind of reality, there is no measure of all things. Any attempt to favour one of those measures as *the* measure amounts simply to subliming that measure – to giving it a wholly spurious authority over its peers. Such a perspective (common, in Phillips' view, to Protagoras, J.L. Austin and the deficient version of Wittgensteinian philosophizing) amounts to the denial that philosophy has any legitimate positive subject matter; it must content itself with the purely negative task of exposing the pretensions of a metaphysics that has no genuine subject matter.

On Phillips' account, Plato saw the difficulties to which this conception of philosophy was a response, but refused to respond in a like manner. For first, he saw, in the acceptance of a mere plurality of measures of reality, the impending threat of a general scepticism about the human capacity to claim genuine knowledge of the real. For example, when the sophists saw that there was and could be no such thing as 'reality' (as the pre-Socratic had understood it) into which philosophy might inquire, they concluded that the idea of our being capable of attaining knowledge – justified true beliefs about the world – was empty, and argued that we must evaluate our opinions about reality purely in terms of their effectiveness. Plato showed us how Socrates could demolish such sophistry, by showing that their supposedly self-sufficient art of rhetoric was in fact parasitic on the claims to knowledge and truth embodied in the various existing human modes of inquiry and creation. But he also portrayed Socrates as accepting that we must be content as philosophers with the various differing conceptions of reality that each such human art embodies; and here Plato dissents from his teacher. For on his view, this leaves us with a view of our modes of discourse as something essentially arbitrary. On Socrates' conception of the matter, the particular arts we have are just the ones we happen to have; they have no external grounding and no internal or necessary relation to one another, and hence the various conceptions of reality internal to each art need not stand in any intelligible relation to each other, and need make no authoritative claim upon our allegiance.

Plato is not prepared to accept this fundamental lack of intelligibility in our ways of making sense of the world. According to Phillips, Plato claims that human arts and activities stand in a dialogic relation to each other, and that each has its logos; in other words, each gives us something substantial to comprehend, and the substance of each art stands in intelligible relations to the substance of the others. However, Plato is also strongly tempted to account for this mode of unity in our discourse by positing an essentially unified reality to which our discourse is responsive; and here he verges upon an error that he is elsewhere committed to avoiding (the inter-related problems of measuring the measure, and of subliming one measure).

What Phillips sees in Rhees, and in Wittgenstein's moments of deepest insight, is an attempt to recover and reformulate Plato's image of the dialogue without succumbing to his intermittent temptation to hypostatize Reality. Indeed, one might say that for Rhees's Wittgenstein, all that can be milked out of the idea of reality as such, Reality as essentially one, is the proposition that our modes of discourse are dialogically inter-related, and hence can themselves be the object of intelligible discourse. The only thing that can show that there is any genuine reality in the different ways in which we talk to each other is our being able to give some account of how those different modes of discourse are themselves in dialogue with one another. It is to this task that Phillips' contemplative conception of philosophy is essentially devoted.

Even if we are convinced by these claims, however, it is important to note that there are grounds for doubting Phillips' repeated assertion that, in taking on this task, the contemplative philosopher is moving into an area in which the resources of the deficient conception of philosophy are of no relevance whatever. For, recall, the mark of the deficient conception is its restriction to the task of noting grammatical differences, of distinguishing one language-game from another; and Phillips gives us the following reason for thinking that such an approach can have precisely nothing to say when one's interest is in the possibility of discourse as such (*Philosophy's Cool Place* p.48–49):

> If one is confused about the use of a concept and if someone then attempts to clear up that confusion, *it will be assumed that one already speaks the language*...There is no question of marking off language as such, or speaking, from anything else. That is why this fundamental question cannot be answered by means of providing perspicuous representations, for what would it mean to speak of the whole language as confused or to give a perspicuous representation of the whole of language to clear up the confusion?

I do not wish to deny that Wittgenstein is sensitive to the anxiety that Phillips expresses here; in section 120 of the *Investigations*, he puts it as follows:

> When I talk about language (words, sentences etc.) I must speak the language of everyday... In giving explanations, I already have to use language full-blown (not some sort of preparatory, provisional one); this by itself shows that I can adduce only exterior facts about language... [T]hen how can these explanations satisfy us?' But he answers his own question immediately: 'Well, your very questions were framed in this language; they had to be expressed in this language if there was anything to ask!'

The relevance of this exchange to Phillips' argument is as follows. From the point of view of the purportedly deficient conception of philosophy, Phillips' question about the possibility of discourse is, in effect, a question about the concepts of 'language', 'speaking' and 'saying something'. If clarity is to be attained about the concept of language, we do not have to give a perspicuous representation of the whole of language; we simply have to give a perspicuous representation of the ways in which we use the word 'language'. In so doing, we will, of course, be presupposing our ability to speak, to use words to say something; but there is nothing paradoxical or self-defeating about this – any more than there is in the thought that orthography can study the word 'orthography' along with any others (see *Philosophical Investigations* §121). After all, the very same presupposition informs the raising of the question in the first place: even to ask 'How is discourse possible?' is to assume one's mastery of discourse. But if everyday language is, for all this, an adequate medium in which to frame the question of the possibility of discourse – if the everyday words 'discourse', 'language', 'speaking' signify the phenomena in which we are interested – why is it not an adequate medium in which to answer it, and specifically by clarifying the grammar of those everyday words? In fact, what else are Rhees and Phillips doing when they discuss the dialogic relations between language-games and linguistic practices than engaging in perspicuous representations of aspects of the grammar of 'language' that are otherwise hidden from us by their very familiarity?

In short, whilst Phillips may have succeeded in identifying a dimension of Wittgenstein's interest in language that relates it to a perennial preoccupation of the Western philosophical tradition since Plato, he does not appear to have succeeded in showing that its further exploration must involve going essentially beyond the familiar Wittgensteinian business of perspicuously representing the grammar of everyday words.

2. Overheating: Unphilosophical Passions?

Where Phillips thinks of the deficient interpretation of Wittgenstein's philosophy as condemned by its impoverished conception of method to failing to appreciate an essential dimension of Wittgenstein's interest in language, he thinks of his own contemplative interpretation as avoiding an error or confusion that is embraced by those who offer what he thinks of as an excessive or transgressive interpretation. The latter amounts to an over-extension of philosophy's rightful authority; as Phillips expresses it: 'It is easy to think that philosophy can do more than show that language is not prior to dialogue between people, that it can show what dialogue *should* be' (*Philosophy's Cool Place* p.52). Phillips' picture is that the transgressive conception of Wittgensteinian philosophy goes beyond the perfectly legitimate thought that philosophy must attend not only to the differences between distinct uses of language but also to the ways in which our linguistic practices hang together. For whilst this thought licenses the conclusion that philosophy is responsive to, and indeed is obliged to cultivate, its own distinctive sense of contemplative wonder at the dialogical unity of language – a wonder at the fact that people do speak to one another, that their words and ways of living are capable of being genuinely responsive both to the words and ways of living of others, and to reality – it forbids the thought that the philosopher can or should look to provide foundations for that unity, or to intervene in the progress of the dialogue that constitutes it.

The problem is not that such interventions are not possible, or not perfectly legitimate in themselves; it is rather that they can have no distinctively philosophical authority behind them. On Phillips' conception of the matter, our life with language makes sense insofar as the various modes of discourse that make it up are dialogically unified; hence, in that life, we can avail ourselves of a number of perspectives or stances from which we might wish to say something worth saying to other speakers. We might speak as practitioners of a specific art or activity – for example, history, mathematics, science; or from the perspective of a mode of discourse which articulates a certain way of making sense of our lives as a whole, perhaps by articulating a certain way of seeing other specific modes of discourse as hanging together with one another – for example, from within a specific religious, political or ethical tradition. But a distinctively philosophical perspective on our life with language must not be confused with any of these possible ways of speaking. For its concern is to explore the very possibility of there being such ways of speaking – to investigate and clarify the conditions for discourse; and the task of thus engaging in discourse about discourse is completely distinct from that of making a substantive contribution to such discourse. To wonder at the fact that such contributions can be made is not to make one more contribution; it is rather to lay stress on the multiplicity of ways in which it is possible to do so. Hence, while the contemplative conception of philosophy can arrogate to itself a certain kind of passionate, wondering interest in the dialogical unity of language, and thereby at least purport to distinguish itself from what it sees as the essentially dispassionate conception of philosophy as a matter of providing perspicuous representations of grammatical difference, it must not run that distinctively philosophical passion together with the passionate interest that every human being has in finding some way of inhabiting, making sense of and hence participating in that unifying dialogue.

In effect, then, Phillips is here attempting to stress that his contemplative conception of philosophy maintains a certain kind of neutrality, despite its rejection of the deficient conception's understanding of what grounds that neutrality. Another, perhaps more familiar, way of articulating the issue would be to say that Phillips is anxious that the realm of the philosophical should continue to be sharply distinguishable from that of the personal. We must continue to distinguish the business of clarifying a particular grammar or form of life from endorsing it; we must remember that philosophical problems and puzzles concerning how it is possible for us to find sense in living are distinct from the problems and puzzles generated by the desire or need to find a way of making sense of life that we can accept or even respect; and we must acknowledge that the difficulties of doing philosophy are intrinsic to philosophy itself, and hence essentially separable from the difficulties of living one's life in a humanly satisfying way.

It is not my concern to question Phillips' claim that at least some ways of failing to respect these distinctions would be philosophically damaging; there is certainly an important truth registered in Wittgenstein's claim that a philosopher should not be a citizen of any community of ideas – that that, indeed, is what makes him a philosopher. I am, however, less convinced by Phillips' attempts to argue that Stanley Cavell and James Conant are Wittgensteinians who exhibit a culpable version of this failing; so I propose to examine in more detail some of Phillips' reasons for asserting that they do.

I shall begin by focusing on two claims made by Conant as part of a comparative discussion of the philosophical methods of Wittgenstein and Kierkegaard, to which Phillips takes great exception. The first emerges from Conant's account of the business of clarifying grammatical differences between religious terms, in despite of our tendency to overlook those differences:

[F]ailure of attention to how we speak cannot be separated from a failure to attend to the various ways in which we act... [S]ince it is the heart of Wittgenstein's teaching... that these words draw their meaning from the way in which they figure in our lives, the task of struggling to avoid such confusions cannot be separated from a form of vigilance which is directed towards how we live.[7]

Phillips first responds by pointing out that conceptual clarification has no necessary connection with any specific change in the direction of one's life. Since, however, he goes on immediately to acknowledge that Conant does not suggest that there is such a connection (in fact, Conant emphasizes that, for example, someone who is helped by Wittgensteinian [or even Kierkegaardian] philosophy to become unconfused about what it means to become a Christian may or may not go on to become one), this point cuts little ice. Neither, as far as I can see, does Phillips' subsequent charge that Conant neglects to discuss the case of someone who remains a Christian throughout their passage from philosophical confusion to clarity on this issue. Phillips tells us that such 'neglected cases show the important *independent* source of philosophical confusion' (*Philosophy's Cool Place* p.44); but it is hard to see how.

To begin with, it is unclear how someone who really was confused about what it means to become (and hence to be) a Christian could be said to have been living the life of a Christian before the advent of the relevant philosophical clarification; she may well have been going to church and giving to charity, but that is hardly enough to merit the description. Perhaps Phillips rather has in mind someone who is living a genuinely Christian life, one in which Christian religious concepts have their full and mutually implicating place, but who is inclined to reflect on her life in a philosophically confused manner (say, by responding positively to a philosopher who asks her whether her God is a kind of entity). But is not an alteration in one's way of reflecting upon one's own life an alteration in one's life? After all, engaging in philosophical reflection is not something one does outside or apart from one's life. It is a (perhaps momentary and infrequent) part of one's life; and a religious life that includes confused modes of self-understanding is significantly different from one that does not. Furthermore, what shows that such forms of self-reflection are an expression of confusion, if not the life that the reflecting person leads outside the contexts of such reflection? In other words, it is precisely vigilant attention to how such a person lives her life that can show her the way to avoid such confusions – which is exactly the claim Conant is making.

Elsewhere, Phillips makes another attempt to clarify what he means by independently philosophical sources or kinds of confusion, when he responds to a second claim Conant makes – one in which he aligns the difficulties involved in engaging in Wittgensteinian grammatical investigations with the difficulties of self-knowledge in life. Here, Conant is referring to such familiar remarks of Wittgenstein's as: 'Nothing is so difficult as not deceiving oneself', 'You cannot write anything about yourself that is more truthful than you yourself are', and

---

7   James Conant, 'On Putting Two and Two Together', in *Philosophy and the Grammar of Religious Belief*, eds. Timothy Tessin and Mario von der Ruhr, London: Macmillan, 1995, p.280. In fact, Phillips misquotes this passage, thus making it incomprehensible; but no part of his ensuing critical discussion turns upon this inaccuracy.

'Working in philosophy is really more like working on oneself'. Phillips' response is brusque (*Philosophy's Cool Place* p.46):

> Wittgenstein is referring to difficulties in *doing philosophy*, difficulties in giving the problems the kind of attention philosophy asks of us. And this is missed if one equates the difficulties with *personal* difficulties. The analogy between working on philosophical problems and working on moral problems come from the fact that, in both cases, a resistance of will has to be overcome. In philosophy, we resist having to give up certain ways of thinking. But the hold these ways of thinking have is not personal, nor is the source of their temptation. They are ways of thinking to which *anyone* can be susceptible, because their power is in the language that we speak.

This is a strange argument. Phillips seems to think that if a problem is one to which any human being is susceptible, it cannot be a personal problem; but by parity of reasoning, since the tendency towards sinful acts is one shared by all human beings, committing a sin is not a personal problem. Furthermore, there is a certain ambiguity in Phillips' implicit attribution to Conant of the wish to *equate* philosophical and personal difficulties. What Conant in fact asserts is not an equation but a connection or alignment; Conant's thought is that the philosophical difficulties are a species of personal difficulty, one kind of way in which an individual might confront the difficulties of achieving self-knowledge in her life. There are, of course, other ways in which we might encounter such difficulties, ways which are not distinctively philosophical in character; but that does not make the ones which *are* philosophical any less personal – and of course, it does not make that species of personal difficulty any less philosophical. Once again, then, Phillips does not succeed in giving us any reason to accept his suspiciously absolute, subliming dichotomy between the philosophical and the personal; he simply presupposes it.

Perhaps, however, I am making things rather too easy for Conant (and Cavell) by focusing on philosophical clarifications of specifically religious concepts; perhaps, as Phillips also claims, this amounts to restricting ourselves to a one-sided diet of examples. Could we think of the business of clarifying the concepts of science or logic as equally dependent upon 'a vigilance directed towards how we live', or as generating difficulties that might be deemed personal as well as philosophical? Here, everything turns upon the way in which Conant and Cavell understand Wittgenstein's general characterization of philosophical confusions. Central to this understanding is the thought that, under philosophical pressure, otherwise competent speakers are driven to emptiness, to utterances that are not false or imprecise but rather nonsensical, unmoored from the contexts in which they might mean something in particular or hovering between various possibilities of making sense without ever alighting upon one in particular. Some Wittgensteinian philosophers think of such utterances as violations of grammar; Cavell calls them ways of repudiating criteria. And the question that interests him is: what human need does the satisfaction of that general impulse serve? What is it about criteria or grammar as such (rather than, say, specifically religious or psychological or scientific criteria) that sometimes compels otherwise competent speakers to refuse them?

Cavell's answer to this question has many facets; but one is this: since, on Wittgenstein's conception of the matter, criteria constitute the limits or conditions of the human capacity to know, think or speak about the world and the various things that are in it, they are in effect that without which human claims to knowledge of reality would not be possible.

Nevertheless, it is fatally easy to interpret limits as limitations, to experience conditions as constraints. And this temptation can maintain (or, at least, endlessly renew) itself even after it is pointed out that it would only make sense to think of the conditions of human knowledge as limitations if we could conceive of another cognitive perspective upon the world that did not require them, when in reality the absence of the concepts or categories in terms of which we individuate objects would not clear the way for unmediated knowledge of reality but rather remove the possibility of anything that might count as knowledge. Hence, Cavell interprets the repudiation of criteria as an inability or refusal to acknowledge the fact that human knowledge – the knowledge available to finite creatures, subjective agents in an objective world – is necessarily conditioned; and he perceives Wittgensteinian philosophizing as an attempt to overcome that repudiation, to acknowledge our finitude. But, he reminds us, nothing is more human than the desire to deny the human, to interpret limits as limitations and to repudiate the human condition of conditionedness or finitude in the name of the unconditioned, the transcendent, the inhuman.

If I were to recharacterize the desire to deny the human as the desire to be God, then it should be evident that this Wittgensteinian understanding of the philosophical impulse is internally related not only to certain 'Continental' interpretations of philosophy and of human beings (such as those of Heidegger and Sartre), but also to a broad, familiar and deeply influential range of religious and ethical – say, spiritual – interpretations of the human condition. But to recognize and acknowledge such analogies and alignments is not to equate these various philosophical and spiritual traditions or modes of discourse; one can detect family resemblances between distinct phenomena without conflating or collapsing them into each other. Indeed, Cavell's conception of the matter is rather that his understanding of Wittgenstein's conception of philosophy makes possible the recognition of certain literary, cultural, ethical, religious and psychoanalytical traditions as other to that philosophy – that is, as requiring acknowledgement as much for their differences from, as for their resemblances to, a distinctively philosophical perspective. When, for example, Cavell claims that what is taken up in philosophy as skepticism is taken up in (certain forms of) literature as tragedy, the very terms of this suggested alignment simultaneously incorporate an acknowledgement of the distinctive resources and presumptions that literature and philosophy can bring to bear on their common inheritance. Such claims and suggestions no more threaten to repress an awareness of philosophy's distinctive contribution to our culture than they presage a collapse of the distinction between the philosophical and the personal.

The depth of Phillips' resistance to this purportedly transgressive conception of philosophy becomes even harder to comprehend if we note just how easily the basic articulations of that conception can be given expression in the terms constitutive of his own, Rhees-inspired, contemplative reading of Wittgenstein. To begin with, in Cavell's conception of Wittgenstein's philosophy, the fundamental issue is the repudiation of criteria and the overcoming of that repudiation; Cavell calls this the issue of skepticism, and characterizes it as a matter of finding a way properly to acknowledge the capacity of our words to reach out to, to make contact with, an independent reality. But this fundamental anxiety about language is exactly the problem that Phillips sees at the heart of debates between the pre-Socratics, the sophists and Plato, and that he finds Rhees taking up again under the label 'the possibility of discourse': how is one to account for our capacity to word the world, for the ways we talk being genuinely responsive to the real? Furthermore, as we have seen, Phillips takes Rhees' idea of comparing language to conversation or dialogue to open up a fruitful way of answering this question; he suggests that it is only insofar as the various ways in which we discourse about things have the unity of a dialogue that we can avoid splintering and relativizing our conception of the real to that of specific language-games or practices. But of course, when Conant and Cavell identify analogies and alignments (as well as disanalogies and misalignments) between philosophical, psychoanalytic, literary, ethical and religious traditions, and go on to explore the ways in which participants in those traditions might fruitfully converse with one another, what better way is there to describe their achievement than as one of making manifest the fact that our various modes of discourse are not an arbitrary assemblage but rather possess an essentially dialogical unity? Against this background, one might say that, far from transgressing the limits of the contemplative conception, the Cavell–Conant conception is in fact a working out of its implications. Hence, by refusing to acknowledge the legitimacy of their philosophical practice, Phillips is prohibiting an elaborate and sophisticated working out of the very model of discourse of which he and Rhees have provided only the barest sketch in their own writings.

However, even if he does acknowledge this much degree of congruence between Cavell's reading of Wittgenstein and his own, Phillips may continue to feel that something fundamental continues to separate them. For whilst it might be consistent with the contemplative conception of philosophy to attend to, and perhaps even to highlight, the various ways in which our modes of discourse relate dialogically to one another, we transgress that conception as soon as we move – as philosophers – to participate in the conversations that these dialogic relations exemplify and make possible. In other words, Cavell's transgression consists in his refusal to respect the absolutely critical distinction between engaging in discourse and contemplating the possibility of discourse; for Phillips, this transgression amounts to the obliteration of philosophy's distinctive claims on our attention and interest, the misuse of the specific cultural authority philosophy acquires precisely from its willingness to hold back from the conversations of mankind.

I wonder, however, just how easy it can be, from the perspective of Phillips' own, Rhees-inspired account of those conversations and their preconditions, to draw the very distinction upon which he places so much weight. For in the terms of that account, as Phillips elaborates it through his introductory discussion of Socrates, philosophy is to be characterized as discourse about (the possibility of) discourse; but then, of course, it follows that philosophy is itself a mode of discourse. To be sure, it has its own distinctive subject matter or at least its own distinctive kind of interest in any given subject matter; but then, exactly the same can be said of any other mode of discourse that has its place in our life with language. And if philosophy must itself be seen as one of the various ways in which we talk about things, it must stand in dialogical relations with other modes of discourse. In other words, philosophy cannot simply think of itself as standing outside the dialogical unity of discourse that is its distinctive subject matter; it must simultaneously recognize that what it has to say about that subject matter is itself a contribution to a dialogue. After all, if it were not such a contribution, how would it hang together with the other dimensions of our life with language – how could it have a non-accidental or contingent, an intelligible, relation to the rest of our form of life?

What Cavell and Conant recognize is that other modes of discourse have something to say about matters in which philosophy has a rightful interest: matters such as our capacity to lose (and re-find) faith in our ability to word the world, to lose (and recover) touch with our natural responsiveness to the humanity of others, to lose (and restore) our orientation in the business of living. What grounds could we conceivably have for saying, in advance of dialogue with the relevant traditions, that the discoveries and claims of Freudian psychoanalysis, Romanticism and Christianity could have no bearing on our distinctively philosophical interests in such matters?

To put matters slightly differently: it is an inevitable part of philosophy's interest in the possibility of discourse that it be interested in the possibility of discourse about the possibility of discourse. In short, philosophy must attend to the conditions of its own possibility. Hence, a dialogue about how philosophical discourse is best to be pursued is an inevitable part of philosophical discourse; and that internal dialogue can uncover presuppositions governing any particular conception of philosophical discourse that will themselves stake out the ground for an external dialogue with non-philosophical modes of discourse. Even a conception of philosophy such as the contemplative one, which rightly prides itself on a certain kind of neutrality, may find that it can only account for that claim to neutrality by invoking conceptions of language, human beings and reality that are themselves far from neutral – that are, at the very least, legitimate topics for conversation. It is to the furtherance of that kind of conversation – one which involves philosophers in dialogue with nonphilosophers, but for reasons that are entirely internal to, and hence respectful of the distinctive character of, philosophy – that the work of Conant and Cavell is directed.

It seems to me that Phillips' resistance to developing his contemplative conception of philosophy in the directions adumbrated by Conant and Cavell's purported transgressions exemplifies a failure to recognize the pertinence of Kierkegaard's repeated and pointed reminder that philosophers are human beings too – that philosophy cannot arrogate to itself a perspective upon the human condition that is external to it. Those who discourse about the possibility of discourse are engaging in discourse, hence inevitably occupying a position within the broader web of human discourse that is at once distinctive and intelligibly, dialogically related to other such positions. If that were not the case, if philosophical discourse were not so related to nonphilosophical modes of discourse, then according to Phillips' own understanding of our life with language, the very possibility of making sense of our capacity to word the world is threatened, and so thereby is the possibility of our making sense of our existence as such. Hence it cannot be the case that a proper acknowledgement of philosophy's distinctive interests and authority involves a refusal to acknowledge its participation in broader cultural intercourse. This does not amount to a conflation of the philosophical and the personal; it merely reminds us that philosophical discourse is at once part of human life with language, and part of individual human beings' attempts to make sense of their own modes of inhabiting that distinctive form of life.

Conclusion

The result of this analysis of Phillips' most recent and most detailed attempt to characterize his contemplative conception of philosophizing after Wittgenstein is that is far less easily distinguishable from its two purportedly erroneous competitors than he appears to think. It remains unclear why his (and Rhees's) attempts to give an account of the possibility of discourse should not be thought of as contributions to the task of perspicuously representing the grammar of 'language', 'speech' and 'saying something'; and the purportedly transgressive conception of philosophy represented by the work of Conant and Cavell appears in fact to be a further elaboration of Phillips' own view that it is philosophy's distinctive business to discourse on the possibility of discourse. Perhaps, then, in the task of building Wittgenstein's temple, Phillips is not as much opposed by his fellow Wittgensteinians as he seems to believe. Perhaps, in reality, the philosophical site on which such a setting for the passions is to be erected also provides a setting for a genuinely productive dialogue about the possibility of discourse about the possibility of discourse – in short, for a fruitful conversation about philosophy between Wittgenstein's builders.

Chapter II

Locating Philosophy's Cool Place – A Reply to Stephen Mulhall

D.Z. Phillips

What is of most importance ... is Phillips' strategic goal – that of articulating a Wittgensteinian conception of philosophy that is sensitive to its distinctive contribution to the human project of making sense of our existence, and yet capable of preserving the neutrality from which its peculiar authority grows. He thus attempts to place himself between those Wittgensteinians who can see only a negative task for philosophical investigations, and those who see the human significance of philosophy as rendering its autonomy deeply questionable.[1]

So wrote Stephen Mulhall in a review of *Philosophy's Cool Place* published in 2001. Those who emphasize philosophy's negative task see the philosopher as an underlabourer (to borrow Locke's phrase), who has no subject of his own, but who has a technique for clearing up conceptual confusions on other people's sites. Those who emphasize philosophy's human significance see it as providing a philosophy for living, a guide for human life. The first conception does too little, while the second attempts too much. By contrast, a contemplative conception of philosophy, in seeking to do conceptual justice by the world in all its variety, does so in the service of philosophy's central concern with the very possibility of such a world. In relation to this contemplative conception of philosophy, as Mulhall points out in his contribution to the present volume, I see the other conceptions as transgressive cousins, one defective, and the other excessive. In *Philosophy's Cool Place*, I criticized Stanley Cavell and James Conant for joining, *at times*, the family of transgressors. In his review, Mulhall thought my discussions of them 'develop criticisms that merit serious attention'.[2] By combining the transgressive conceptions of philosophy, Cavell and Conant have been extremely influential in promoting a *therapeutic* reading of Wittgenstein's philosophy.

In 'Wittgenstein's Temple', Mulhall's view has changed somewhat. In his review, he had been frustrated by what he took to be a sparse account of what exactly philosophical contemplation of reality comes to, and urged me to say more. Now, he doubts whether there is a 'more' to say, since he has difficulty in locating philosophy's cool place. Anything it wants to achieve, he argues, can be achieved by the underlabourer conception of philosophy, in a way which shows us, at the same

1   Stephen Mulhall, Review of Phillips, *Philosophy's Cool Place*, *Philosophical Quarterly* 51:202 (2001), p.104.

2   Mulhall, Review *Philosophy's Cool Place*, p.104.

time, a philosophy for living. In short, Mulhall is deeply attracted by a therapeutic reading of Wittgenstein. So far from seeing the work of Cavell and Conant, in this context, as meriting serious critical attention, he is now 'less convinced by ... attempts to argue that [they] ... exhibit a culpable version of this failing'.[3] In my reply I'll try to show why Mulhall's change of heart is not a change for the better.

1. The Lure of a Philosophy for Living

Wittgenstein had grave doubts whether, if published, his work would be understood. This was not snobbishness or arrogance on his part, but a realistic assessment of the spirit of his and our age. It is an age concerned with progress, problem-solving, skills for personal relationships and making the world a better place. Such dominant interests are likely to be impatient with, and even uncomprehending of, a contemplative interest in the world. Béla Szabados is capturing the attitude of many philosophers in describing the reaction of Kai Nielsen to Wittgensteinian contemplation:

> Wittgenstein's philosophical outlook is ethically and politically irresponsible, since his attitude of quietism leads us to a pernicious disengagement from the world and robs us of the critical tools to assess our culture and change it for the better. To put it bluntly, a philosophy that leaves everything where it is hinders the struggle for social justice, peace and human flourishing. It is an obstacle to human solidarity.[4]

In fact, Nielsen thinks I am simply deceiving myself in thinking that I am engaged in philosophical contemplation. This is how he begins his last chapter in our recent encounter:

> D. Z. Phillips and I are, to put it mildly, at loggerheads. We both think of each other, at least on the issues before us, as a philosophical disaster ... I see Phillips as at least in effect as a preacher mounting the pulpit to preserve religion from any fundamental criticism, while thinking of himself as a neutral contemplator of the actual and the possible in a cool place, and he sees me as a fervent atheist riding the hearse proclaiming that God is dead and a good thing too.[5]

In her review of my book, Alison Denham thought I was advocating a cool philosophical way of rising above the cares and troubles of ordinary mortals. Given this misunderstanding, it is no surprise that she wondered whether I could keep that cool in the dance![6] Even in his review, Mulhall is prone to speak of 'the human project of making sense of our existence', and in 'Wittgenstein's Temple' he sees my

---

3   All quotations from Mulhall are from 'Wittgenstein's Temple' in the present volume, unless otherwise indicated.

4   Béla Szabados, 'Introduction' Kai Nielsen and D.Z. Phillips, *Wittgensteinian Fideism?*, London: SCM Press, 2004.

5   Nielsen and D.Z. Phillips, *Wittgensteinian Fideism?*, Ch. 14, p.290. I had accused Nielsen of falling to the lure of a philosophy of life.

6   Alison Denham, 'How Long Can You Stay Cool at the Dance?', *Times Literary Supplement*, 23 June 2000, n.p.

refusal to indulge in Wittgensteinian therapy as 'a failure to recognize the pertinence of Kierkegaard's repeated and pointed reminder that philosophers are human beings too' (p.999). Kai Nielsen, Alison Denham and Stephen Mulhall differ, as philosophers, in all sorts of ways, but their remarks exemplify the therapeutic spirit which Wittgenstein thought was a barrier to an understanding of his contemplative task. Rush Rhees captures that spirit as follows:

> The people who argued with Socrates and Plato may have thought that language was just a collection of techniques, and that that was what understanding is: 'knowing the technique ...' Is understanding just competence? Is language a skill? Whether speaking is a technique, whether thinking is a technique; whether living is. Again: whether life has the unity of a skill ... You might even think of methods of producing it to order then. This is the question whether virtue can be taught. It is all a matter of the method. That is what it comes to. And that would be the same as solving problems of life by calculation. Reaching an understanding of life by calculation.

> Solving philosophical problems by calculation. 'Philosophy as just a matter of sorting out various grammars that have got mixed up.' Helping you to see where things go so that you do not get into a snag.

> And so with understanding life: understanding the business of living. Knowing how to live effectively. Being a success. Doing it better than anyone else. The question of what it is to understand life. Or simply: of what it is to understand.[7]

I have not forgotten that Mulhall says of his three conceptions of philosophy (p.21),

> It is not my concern to question Phillips's claim that at least some ways of failing to respect these distinctions would be philosophically damaging; there is certainly an important truth registered in Wittgenstein's claim that a philosopher should not be a citizen of any community of ideas – that that, indeed, is what makes him a philosopher.

The question is whether, in discussing Cavell and Conant, Mulhall retains this 'important truth', or recognizes, in their work, some of the 'philosophically damaging' ways of ignoring it. I shall begin to discuss this question with reference to Cavell. I regret that, in doing so, I shall have little to say about what I take to be his excellent contemplative discussion of scepticism in his early work,[8] or about the way in which Mulhall has helped us to understand it.[9] My brief, here, is to discuss the concerns voiced in 'Wittgenstein's Temple'.

In reaction to the accusation of quietism in Wittgenstein, Szabados replies: 'It may strike some as ironic that one of the deepest critics of our culture, concerned

---

7   Rush Rhees, *Wittgenstein and the Possibility of Discourse*, ed. D.Z. Phillips, 2nd edn., Oxford: Blackwell, 2005, pp.3–4.

8   Stanley Cavell, *Must We Mean What We Say?*, Cambridge: Cambridge University Press, 1976, and *The Claim of Reason*, Parts 1 and 2, Oxford: Oxford University Press, 1979. For my appreciative discussion see *Philosophy's Cool Place*, pp.87–94.

9   See Stephen Mulhall, *Stanley Cavell: Philosophy's Recounting of the Ordinary*, Oxford: Clarendon Press, 1994.

with its animation, is charged with complacency and quietism.'[10] Commenting on Szabados' remark I said:

> The irony Szabados refers to consists in the fact that one of the concepts in our culture which Wittgenstein reanimates is *the concept of criticism*. Criticism is rescued from what philosophy tries to make of it. By reflecting on contexts where *real* criticisms have their life, these criticisms, including the most radical, are allowed to be themselves. So far from advocating quietism, Wittgensteinian contemplation allows real battles to be themselves.[11]

Mulhall wants to remind me that one can only have philosophical contemplation if there is something other than philosophy to comprehend. True enough, but that, in itself, does not threaten the autonomy of the subject. Neither does the fact that a philosopher, like any other human being, lives at a certain time and place, with particular concerns, troubles and aversions. The point is that the philosopher is related to these surroundings in a contemplative way; his questions arising from the central concerns of his subject. The vital question is whether this relation has been transgressed in Cavell's ambition to be a reappraiser of his culture:

> 'To imagine a language is to imagine a form of life' ... In philosophizing, I have to bring my own language and life into imagination. What I require is a convening of my culture's criteria, in order to confront them with my words and life as I pursue them and as I imagine them; and at the same time to confront my words and my life as I pursue them with the life my culture's words may imagine for me. This seems to me a task that warrants the name of philosophy.[12]

This activity rightly turns its back on a transcendent metaphysics. But post-Wittgensteinian philosophy, in the course of doing so, has simply continued to search for a measure of 'all things'. As Michael Weston has pointed out, *it has simply turned to our historical situatedness to provide materials for a renewed search for such a measure.* On this view, to imagine a language is to imagine a form of life one approves of after due reflection. As Weston points out, Cavell's overriding commitment to a search for community leads him to use Wittgenstein's philosophy to show that 'adherence to absolute values in ethics and religion [are] products of inadequate understanding'.[13] For whom is Cavell speaking when he says that God is dead? Or for whom is he speaking, politically, when he says,

> Society ... is what we have done with the success of Locke and the others in removing the divine right of kings and placing political authority in our consent to be governed together. The essential message of the idea of a social contract is that political institutions require

---

10 Mulhall, *Stanley Cavell*.

11 Mulhall, *Stanley Cavell.*, Ch. 17, p.350.

12 Cavell, *The Claim of Reason*, p.100.

13 Michael Weston, Review of *Philosophy's Cool Place*, *Philosophical Investigations* 23:3 (2000), p.262.

justification ... there are laws or ends, of nature or justice, in terms of which they are to be tested. They are experiments.[14]

Mulhall admits that what Cavell is propounding is a form of contract liberalism,[15] but Cavell takes himself to be arriving at the political conditions for speech and agency *tout court*. Whatever of that, Cavell is certainly not exercising a contemplative enquiry in political philosophy. Had he been doing so, he would have wanted to show that recognition of the divine right of kings can itself be a form of political consent. When Locke criticized other parties, he did so in terms of political values to which he adhered. In *Philosophy's Cool Place*, I argued (p.106),

> Political institutions are not experiments but are constitutive of certain ideas in terms of which discussion is carried on ... The contemplation of political agreement and disagreement needs to acknowledge that fact and not try to get behind the phenomena to some basic set of interests or ideas that they are supposed to serve.

In the light of the pronouncements we have seen Cavell make with respect to ethics, religion and politics, not to mention his views on Romanticism and Emersonian perfectionism, Mulhall makes two surprising claims in 'Wittgenstein's Temple', particularly since he does not attempt to meet the specific criticisms I made in *Philosophy's Cool Place*.

First, Mulhall claims 'how easily the basic articulations of [Cavell's] conception can be given expression in terms of [my] own, Rhees-inspired contemplative reading of Wittgenstein' (p.24). But how can Cavell's advocacy of specific values relating to ethics, religion and philosophy be rendered compatible with contemplation of the variety of values to be found in these contexts?[16] Mulhall asks how we can say 'in advance of dialogue with the relevant traditions, that the discoveries and claims of Freudian psychoanalysis, Romanticism and Christianity could have no bearing on our distinctively philosophical interests in such matters' (p.26). But there is no question of saying anything *in advance* of a contemplative dialogue with these traditions. One cannot legislate about the insights or confusions which may emerge.[17] By contrast, the influence of psychoanalysis on Cavell's thought leads him to speak of certain philosophical confusions as 'the denial of the human'. Further, the denial of a philosophical insight is seen as the repression of what we need to acknowledge.

---

14 Stanley Cavell, *The Senses of Walden: An Expanded Edition*, San Francisco, CA: North Point Press, 1981, p.82.

15 Mulhall, *Stanley Cavell*, pp.69–74.

16 See Cavell's political pronouncements, for example with a superb example of contemplative philosophy in Peter Winch's paper, 'How is Political Authority Possible?', *Philosophical Investigations* 25:1 (2002), 20–32.

17 For my criticisms of psychoanalysis see Ch. 8 of my *Religion and the Hermeneutics of Contemplation*, Cambridge: Cambridge University Press, 2001. For my criticisms of romanticism see 'Winch and Romanticism', *Philosophy* 77:300 (2002), 261–79. For my most recent criticism of accounts of Christianity see *Recovering Religious Concepts*, Basingstoke: Macmillan and St. Martin's Press, 2000; *Religion and Friendly Fire*, Aldershot: Ashgate, 2004; and *The Problem of Evil and the Problem of God*, London: SCM Press, 2004.

The danger is obvious: critics of Cavell may find themselves characterized as the repressed deniers of what they need to acknowledge.[18]

Second, Mulhall claims that in Cavell, we see an 'elaborated and sophisticated working out of the very model of discourse' for which, he claims, Rhees and I have only provided 'the barest sketch in [our] own writings' (p.25). This claim is indeed surprising, since surely one obvious contrast between Cavell and Swansea's contemplative philosophers is the selectivity of the former's texts, compared with the wide variety of examples discussed in the work of Rhees, Peter Winch, R.F. Holland and, dare I say, myself. How can such examples be called 'the barest sketch'? Furthermore, Mulhall recognizes the selectivity of Cavell's texts and offers a curious defence of it:

> anyone who understands the acknowledgement structure underlying Cavell's model of reading would expect him to search for and to use texts which participate in his own attitude and approach to reading ... only texts motivated by the thoughts and feelings that are crystallized in Cavell's own conception and practice of reading could provide words capable of testing and drawing out the full potential of that practice.[19]

A contemplative conception of philosophy, by contrast, would wait on texts which would challenge any already crystallized conception. It would wait on criticisms and counter-criticisms to see the conceptual character of disagreement in contexts such as these. For example, I suggested that Cavell should put the texts of Flannery O'Connor alongside those of Emerson.[20] As I keep telling my students, contemplative acknowledgement is wider than what we appropriate personally.

In his later work, and in the work of those influenced by him, Cavell and others seem to be on journeys of self-discovery. According to Richard Eldridge, life is to be lived in a creative tension between a recognition of our finitude, and the desire to transcend it.[21] According to Richard Fleming, life must be lived in a realistic acceptance of our finitude.[22] According to Timothy Gould, we must go beyond our finitude in an endless search for a common humanity. He concludes his book thus: 'Each may find the other wanting and each might try to suppress what the other is seeking to say. But each is made for –and by the other.'[23]

I do not deny that one may find insights of all kinds, along with confusions too, in the accounts of journeys of self-discovery. All I am insisting on is that they are far removed from a contemplative philosophy. The latter is found in the way Rhees emphasizes the hubbub of voices in our culture, some in close proximity, others passing each other by. They are not engaged in one big conversation or enterprise.

---

18 See *Philosophy's Cool Place*, p.109.

19 Mulhall, *Stanley Cavell*, p.194.

20 See *Philosophy's Cool Place*, p.112.

21 Richard Eldridge, *Leading a Human Life*, Chicago, IL: University of Chicago Press, 1997. See Edward Minar's review in *Philosophical Investigations* 23:1 (2000), 73–81.

22 Richard Fleming, *The State of Philosophy*, Lewisburg, PA: Bucknell University Press, 1993. For my review see *Philosophical Investigations* 19:4 (1994).

23 Timothy Gould, *Hearing Things*, Chicago, IL: University of Chicago Press, 1998. For my review see *Philosophical Investigations* 22:4 (1999), 349–53.

But they are thrown together in the language they speak. Rhees's contemplation of them is born of wonder at that fact.

Mulhall, on the other hand, wonders how easy it is to maintain a distinction between a contemplative interest in the dialogical relations between people's conversations, and one's own particular stance within them. I hope to have shown in my work, for example, in *From Fantasy to Faith*, differences and proximities between religious belief and atheism. The aim is not resolution, but an understanding of what is at issue.

Wittgenstein did not say that a philosopher *should not* be a citizen of any community of any ideas, as Mulhall has him saying, but that he *is not* such a citizen. He is not recommending, but arguing, critically, from a certain conception of philosophy and its relation to its subject matter, including the wider culture in which it finds itself. It is this latter relation that separates Cavell's therapeutic conception from Wittgenstein's philosophy. Having seen, rightly, that our forms of life are not founded on a metaphysical foundation external to themselves, Cavell jumps to the confused conclusion that, therefore, human beings are responsible for their maintenance, as though we were their managers, and they were our projects. A form of life is maintained, of course, by participation in it, but its maintenance is not the reason for our participation. Thinking otherwise leads Cavell to think of our philosophical confusions as a refusal to accept the responsibility of maintenance. This is not an advance on Wittgenstein's philosophy, but a violation of its contemplative character. A conception of language as a set of techniques or skills[24] facilitates this external and instrumental way of thinking.[25] My most recent criticism of these tendencies was expressed as follows:

> We are not 'minders' of our lives; we are *in* our lives: we are our lives. Concern may be expressed about the deterioration of a movement. But that concern is itself an expression of the movement, not an external, technical problem in handling it. We are not the technicians of culture (the tool-box analogy again).[26]

This is one of the central insights of Wittgenstein's great work, *On Certainty*, and of his emphasis on world-pictures. Wittgenstein is not trying to *establish* these world pictures, or trying to prove that we can know them. Even less is he trying to determine which world-picture is the right one. These endeavours, given what he means by a world-picture, have no messages or guidance for us in seeking a philosophy for living. Mulhall notes, as we saw at the outset, that to seek such a 'human significance' for philosophy, renders 'its autonomy deeply questionable'.[27] It is no surprise, therefore, to find confirmation of this fact in a recent pronouncement where Cavell says,

---

24 For a tendency to link speaking with mastery of a technique, see M. McGinn, *Sense and Certainty: A Dissolution of Scepticism*, Oxford: Blackwell, 1989.

25 For fuller criticisms see *Philosophy's Cool Place*, p.96.

26 D.Z. Phillips, 'The Case of the Missing Propositions', in *Readings of Wittgenstein's 'On Certainty'*, eds. Danièle Moyal-Sharrock and William H. Brenner, Basingstoke: Palgrave, 2005, p.27.

27 Review of *Philosophy's Cool Place*, p.104.

when fragments of Wittgenstein's thought continue to appear in my texts, they are not meant to authorise my methods or conclusions but often to serve as periodic checks that I am continuing to grasp the thread of philosophy, leading to some form that my contemporaries might approve. That the claim to philosophy has become inherently questionable is part of my conviction about philosophy.[28]

Wittgenstein was not concerned with whether his contemporaries approved of his contemplative endeavours. As we have seen, he was all too aware that they would not. For my part, all one can do is to show what a contemplative conception of philosophy involves, and how it differs from others. To show, for example, that in Wittgenstein, world-pictures 'are constitutive of how people think, act and live'.[29] I am, therefore, glad to have *Philosophy's Cool Place*, in its criticisms of modes of contemporary thought, and in its attempt to elucidate a contemplative conception of philosophy, described as an attempt 'to keep alive a Wittgensteinian voice in a hostile environment'.[30]

2. The Philosophical and the Personal

Remaining with a discussion of the desire for a philosophy for living, I turn now to Mulhall's defence of James Conant against the criticisms I had made of him in *Philosophy's Cool Place* concerning the methodologies of Kierkegaard and Wittgenstein.

Conant had claimed that the confusions Wittgenstein wants us to avoid 'cannot be separated from a form of vigilance which is directed towards how we live'.[31] *In this context*, I thought it worth making certain distinctions between 'the philosophical' and 'the personal'. I emphasize *the context*, since if it is ignored, we soon become embroiled in an *abstract* argument about these terms which throws little light on anything. I find such an abstraction in some of Mulhall's replies to my criticisms. For example, he writes (p.23):

> What Conant in fact asserts is not an equation but a connection or alignment; Conant's thought is that the philosophical difficulties are a species of personal difficulty, one kind of way which an individual might confront the difficulties of achieving self-knowledge in

28   Stanley Cavell, 'On Wittgenstein', *Philosophical Investigations* 24:2 (2001), p.94.

29   *Philosophy's Cool Place*, p.55.

30   Weston, Review of *Philosophy's Cool Place*, p.263. Weston's own book, *Kierkegaard and Modern Continental Philosophy*, London: Routledge, 1994, shows, with reference to Nietzsche, Heidegger and Derrida, how difficult it is not to provide substantive alternatives to a metaphysical world well lost.

31   Conant, 'On Putting Two and Two Together', p.280. Since then Conant has also published 'Philosophy and Biography', in *Wittgenstein: Biography and Philosophy*, ed. James C. Klagge, Cambridge: Cambridge University Press, 2001, and 'On Going the Bloody *Hard* Way in Philosophy', in *The Possibilities of Sense*, ed. John H. Whittaker, Basingstoke: Palgrave, 2002. I cannot reply to all Conant's points in this paper, but I shall endeavour to discuss those most pertinent to the points Mulhall raises, without assuming that Mulhall would or would not want to defend Conant on all the matters I raise.

her life. There are, of course, other ways in which we might encounter such difficulties, ways which are not distinctively philosophical in character; but that does not make the ones which *are* philosophical any less personal – and of course it does not make that species of personal difficulty any less philosophical ... Phillips does not succeed in giving us any reason to accept his suspiciously absolute, subliming dichotomy between the philosophical and the personal; he simply presupposes it.

I agree that I do not succeed in getting anyone to accept a sublimed distinction between the personal and the philosophical. That is because I was not trying to draw one. All I am saying is that the distinction is worth making, given what Conant, *at times*, wants to make of it. Ironically, it is Mulhall who sublimes the distinction. In saying that philosophical difficulties are no less personal than non-philosophical difficulties, he seems to be saying that one kind has as much of 'the personal' as the other. But what is this personal 'something' which appears no less in one context than the other? Perhaps I have financial difficulties. The bills show that they are pretty personal. But another may relieve me of my burden. My philosophical difficulties are personal, but even though I may benefit from the philosophical insights of others, they cannot, in the same sense, relieve me of my difficulties. I still have to work through them for myself. In face of these differences, no illumination is gained, and much is obscured, by saying that though not all difficulties are philosophical, this does not mean that those that are, are any less personal than financial difficulties. Again, I may have religious difficulties concerning the ways in which my self comes between me and God. I may have had philosophical difficulties in seeing that distance from God is not his consequential punishment for sin, but come to see that sin *is* the distance. I write an article about it, and feel very proud of it. As a result, the pride comes between me and God! Nothing is illuminated, and much is obscured, by saying that one set of difficulties is no less personal than the other, giving as one's justification, as Mulhall does, that a gain in philosophical clarity is, after all, 'an alteration in one's life' (p.22). To speak of all these difficulties as no less personal than each other, is to forget Mulhall's own insistence that all Conant does is not to equate, but to align or connect the philosophical and the personal. All I do is to criticize *some* aspects of those alignments and connections. It is these that Mulhall fails to address.

What of Conant? At times, he shows a commendable reticence and restraint about these matters. For example, in discussing the complex relations between philosophy and biography, the extent to which philosophical work is integral to an assessment of character, or the extent to which an assessment of character is integral to an assessment of philosophical work, he insists, at the outset, that these questions do not admit of a general answer: 'they are the sorts of questions we must each answer for ourselves and on a case-by-case basis'.[32] Conant promises not to trade in generalities concerning them. The issue is whether, in his various discussions, he sticks to this promise.

Conant identifies generalities to be avoided in two views of the relation between the philosophical and the personal. According to *reductivism*, the real explanation of a philosophical work is to be found in the personal details of the philosopher's life

---

32 Conant, 'Philosophy and Biography', p.17.

which are the external causes of the philosophy and which it subserves. According to *compartmentalism*, on the other hand, the philosophical and the personal are entirely separate from each other. Compartmentalism preserves the truths that philosophical work cannot be reduced to the merely personal, or assessed purely in terms of it. Nevertheless, its central claim can be attacked while preserving these truths.[33] Conant takes me to be a compartmentalist. He thinks I am right in thinking that philosophical difficulties are not merely personal, but wrong in thinking that they are not personal in any sense.[34] Conant argues that I want to insist on this latter point, in order to avoid saying, as he does, 'that a shoddiness in how we speak is, at the same time, a shoddiness in how we live'.[35] On the other hand, Conant also says:

> Phillips is certainly right that the wrong kind of insistence on the (idea that the sorts of *difficulty* with which Wittgenstein, in his philosophical work, is concerned are) 'personal' can lead to a disastrous misinterpretation of Wittgenstein's work.[36]

Clearly, further sorting out is required on my part to make clearer what I do and do not want to say about relations between the philosophical and the personal.

The first thing to be said is that I do not want to deny, for a moment, that practising a contemplative conception of philosophy is, in an important sense, personal. The reason why is obvious: the enquiry makes ethical demands of the enquirer. It calls for a certain purity of attention to the world which shows character. This is the natural context for the kind of remark by Wittgenstein that impresses Conant and Mulhall:

> You cannot write anything about yourself that is more truthful than you yourself are.[37]

> Nothing is so difficult as not deceiving oneself.[38]

> If anyone is *unwilling* to descend into himself ... he will remain superficial in his writing.[39]

> Working in philosophy ... is really more a working on oneself.[40]

> That man will be revolutionary who can revolutionise himself.[41]

---

33   Conant, 'Philosophy and Biography', pp.17–19.
34   Conant, 'On Going the Bloody *Hard* Way in Philosophy', p.88.
35   Conant, 'On Going the Bloody *Hard* Way in Philosophy', p.119, n.21, quoting from *Philosophy's Cool Place*, p.46.
36   Conant, 'On Going the Bloody *Hard* Way in Philosophy', p.88.
37   Wittgenstein, *Culture and Value*, Chicago, IL: University of Chicago Press, 1990, p.33.
38   Wittgenstein, *Culture and Value*, p.34.
39   *Ludwig Wittgenstein: Personal Recollections*, ed. R. Rhees, Oxford: Blackwell, 1981, p.193.
40   Wittgenstein, *Culture and Value*, p.16.
41   Wittgenstein, *Culture and Value*, p.45. Those passages are quoted by Conant on p.86 of 'On Going the Bloody *Hard* Way in Philosophy'.

Conant agrees with what I say about the relation of such remarks to the demands of philosophical attention. He also quotes, with approval, the following comments by Rhees about what philosophy meant for Wittgenstein,

> 'Go the bloody *hard* way.' I have said that for him philosophy was this. And this was not just a personal matter: it was not just the spirit in which he happened to pursue philosophy … If you see the kind of difficulty that is raised in philosophy, you will see why there cannot be a simplified way of meeting it … And this means: take the *difficulties* seriously: 'unless you recognise that they *are* difficulties; unless you recognise that they are difficult – unless they make things difficult.'[42]

In these philosophical contexts, therefore, it would be misleading to make a distinction between the philosophical and the personal. They are internally related. In *these* contexts, I agree entirely with Conant when he emphasized that the ethical demands of enquiry are no less present, for example, in the *Tractatus*, when Wittgenstein is discussing logic, than when he is discussing ethics. The ethical is present on every page of the work. What is more, Wittgenstein's different assessment of Frege and Russell, in their discussion of issues in logic, cannot be understood without bringing in the difference in the way they treated philosophical difficulties. That difference will itself involve ethical difficulties in the sense in which we are not referring to 'the ethical'.[43]

The second thing I want to say is that I do not want to deny that there are internal relations between contemplative philosophy and a way of living, but am extremely wary and dubious of attempts at connecting philosophy and ways of living beyond these internal relations.

The insight and the confusion I want to preserve in this context can be brought out by comments made by Rush Rhees in this connection. On the one hand, Rhees is clear about the kind of demand philosophy made on Wittgenstein:

> Not letting it become a way of asserting or regaining his prestige … not racing for the credit of being 'the discoverer of so and so'. As though he might say: 'Keep your attention on philosophy; …' For this kind of purity and discipline, you need purity and discipline in the rest of your life as well … And in the midst of a long discussion of some philosophical question in some notebook, you will find an isolated single remark like: 'I am always in love with my talent. This is dangerous.' The patience needed to guard against this sort of danger must go on outside philosophy as well.[44]

Rhees also gives an example of what would be surprising to find outside philosophy in the life of a contemplative philosopher. He says 'we should be surprised to find

---

42   Rush Rhees, 'The Study of Philosophy', in *Without Answers*, ed. D.Z. Phillips, London: Routledge, 1969, reprinted 2005, p.169.

43   Conant discusses these issues in great detail, but with a considerable overlap of material in 'On Going the Bloody *Hard* Way in Philosophy'; 'Philosophy and Biography'; and in 'What "Ethics" in the *Tractatus* is *Not*', in *Religion and Wittgenstein's Legacy*, eds. D.Z. Phillips and Mario von der Ruhr, Aldershot: Ashgate, 2005.

44   Rush Rhees, 'On Wittgenstein IX', *Philosophical Investigations* 24:2 (2001), p.161.

anyone who is a serious philosopher, and was at the same time a playboy or a man about town', and goes on to say:

> And this is not just because of the tradition of the Stoic 'sage', nor is it just because certain philosophers who come to mind (Socrates or Spinoza, for instance) have lived that way. We may feel that there is something more like an internal connexion between what you are engaged on in philosophy and the sort of life you lead.[45]

When Rhees speaks of the demands of a contemplative philosophy, he sees them as internally related to the kind of philosophical activity involved. This does not mean that the demands are always met, of course, otherwise Wittgenstein's cautionary reminders to himself would not be needed, but deviations from the demands of philosophy could not predominate. One would not expect to find the kind of attention to, and wonder at the world involved in philosophical contemplation of the world in a playboy, but here Rhees is not dogmatic. He says it would be surprising, not impossible, and speaks of something *more like* an internal connexion between philosophy and the life one leads.

On the other hand, in the same context, Rhees emphasizes that his central concern is with the character of the philosophical enquiry, and warns against underemphasising *the independence* of philosophical problems. Philosophy is not simply the means of removing obstacles in other fields, for example, the advancement of science, even if, on occasion, it succeeds in doing so. He would say the same of any suggestion that philosophy is the means to a better way of living. Speaking of Hume's discussion of causality, Rhees says:

> it was with problems in *philosophy* that he was most concerned. And if he is a great philosopher, it is because of what he did about *them* … A great deal has been said – in ancient times more than in modern – about 'the philosophical life'. Some of this seems to me very important. But it may lead to silly misunderstandings. I think it would have to be presented rather differently today than it was in Plato's time, and it would need someone of unusual calibre.[46]

The difficulty which confronts us, then, is one of doing justice *both* to what Rhees says about internal relations between contemplative philosophy and a way of living, and to what he says about the independence of philosophical problems and their sources. When this balance is disturbed, in certain ways, there may be an occasion for distinguishing between 'the philosophical' and 'the personal'. Since writing *Philosophy's Cool Place* and reading Conant's more recent essays I do not think these occasions have disappeared. For example, Conant, in order to show us how there can be an intimate relationship between the philosophical and the personal, calls to our attention the aims of Hellenistic schools of thought:

> The spiritual disciplines internal to each of the Hellenistic schools of philosophy seeks to promote a certain kind of existential *telos* – for the Skeptics, the telos is *ataraxia*: for the

---

45   Rush Rhees, Preface: 'The Fundamental Problems of Philosophy', in Rhees, *Wittgenstein and the Possibility of Discourse*, p.xii.

46   Preface to Rhees, *Wittgenstein and the Possibility of Discourse*, pp.x–xii.

Neo-Platonists, it is ecstatic union with the cosmos, and so forth – and the telos in question is not a merely theoretical (as opposed to practical) matter: it is a matter of successfully giving a certain sort of shape to one's self and this is achieved in part by giving a certain sort of shape to one's life.[47]

Conant admits that there is a difference between these ancient concepts and modern conceptions of philosophy, but he puts this by saying that 'the relation between philosophy and life is no longer as perspicuous as it once was'.[48] He also tells us that Kierkegaard and Nietzsche were nostalgic for this aspect of ancient philosophy.[49] Could we find such nostalgia in Wittgenstein? I do not think so. Whereas Conant wants to deny that there is a difference *in kind* between modern philosophy and the schools he mentions, I think that, in certain respects, Wittgenstein would say there was. I know Rhees would, since he spoke often of the way Stoicism had led to popular expectations, still with us today, that philosophy should provide a philosophy of life. Think of the way contemporary moral philosophy is dominated by advocacy, and the way in which contemporary philosophy of religion is dominated by apologetics. In this latter context, the dominance of advocacy and apologetics are forms of confusion, stemming from the thought of philosophy as a guide to living. Such a thought seems to be present in Conant's readiness to talk of 'shaping the self' and 'shaping one's life'. Peter Winch has shown that morality, not to mention moral philosophy, is not a guide to conduct, if only because moral considerations are already partly constitutive of the situation in which we have to conduct ourselves.[50] Any suggestion of the philosopher as the sage who points us in the right spiritual or moral direction would be anathema to Wittgenstein and wholly repugnant to Rhees and Winch. Nevertheless, Rhees would not say that the ancient schools were confused. In their notion of philosophy as a spiritual exercise, he would say that we have a different *conception* of philosophy. That is why it is misleading to speak of a modern conception as a *less* perspicuous representation of the relation between philosophy and life. On the other hand, this is not to deny important continuities between contemplative philosophy today and ancient philosophy.[51] Wittgenstein insisted that his problems were those of Plato. Conant says of modern philosophy:

> there is no longer ... any such thing as *the* relation between philosophy and life – there are as many species of this relation as there are conceptions of philosophy, and, across these conceptions, widely varying degrees and kinds of intimacy among the relata.[52]

I hope it is clear that I am concerned with a certain conception of philosophy as I find it in Wittgenstein. I believe it to be present throughout the history of philosophy.

---

47   Conant, 'Philosophy and Biography', p.21.
48   Conant, 'Philosophy and Biography', p.23.
49   Conant, 'Philosophy and Biography', p.21.
50   See Peter Winch, 'Moral Integrity', in Peter Winch, *Ethics and Action*, London: Routledge and Kegan Paul, 1972. See also my 'What Can We Expect from Ethics?', in *Interventions in Ethics*, Albany, NY/London: SUNY Press/Macmillan, 1992.
51   See Rush Rhees, *In Dialogue with the Greeks*, vol. I: *The Presocratics and Reality*, and vol. II: *Plato and Dialectic*, ed. D.Z. Phillips, Aldershot: Ashgate, 2004.
52   Conant, 'Philosophy and Biography', p.23.

It is in that context that I think it is important to distinguish, for certain purposes, between the philosophical and the personal. I shall try to illustrate some occasions on which I think making the distinction is necessary. Speaking of the Hellenistic schools of philosophy, and their notion of philosophy as a spiritual exercise, Pierre Hadot says:

> This is not only to say that it was a specific type of moral conduct ... Rather it means that philosophy was a mode of existing-in-the-world, which had to be practised at every instant, and the goal of which was to transform the whole of the individual's life.[53]

In the context I am concerned with, once we go beyond the internal relations between philosophy and life I have discussed, the attempts to make connections between philosophy and 'the whole of an individual's life' become extremely precarious and dubious undertakings. Consider, for example, the following comments by Conant:

> When Wittgenstein remarks about A. J. Ayer, 'He has something to say but he is incredibly shallow', this is, in the first instance, of course, a remark about the quality of Ayer's philosophy. But it is not *merely* a remark about the quality of Ayer's efforts at philosophizing, and as such wholly without bearing on an estimate of the shallowness or depth of the sensibility of the person whose philosophizing it is. Similarly, when Wittgenstein says about James Frazer: 'Frazer is much more savage than most of these savages',[54] this is a comment on both the man and his thought. It is a comment on something that shows itself in Frazer's writing about the forms of life and the modes of thought of the primitive peoples he studies – where part of what shows itself is something about what sort of possibilities of thought and life are (and are not) closed to Frazer himself.[55]

Conant does not actually show us an internal connection between the shallowness said to be in Ayer's philosophy, and the shallowness said to be in his life. It is supposed to show us 'something' about Ayer's sensibility in the latter context. But it is important to spell out what that 'something' is supposed to be. This becomes more apparent in Conant's remarks on Frazer. We are told that Frazer's comments on primitive practices show *something* about what possibilities of thought and life are closed to Frazer himself, but again what that 'something' is, is rather important. There are certain internal relations between the philosophical and the personal, in this context, which makes one spelling out of that 'something' fairly obvious (which is not to say obvious in our technological culture). These internal relations are elucidated in Rhees's remarks on the wonder which is characteristic of philosophy, which he says is also found 'in the thinking of less corrupted peoples':

> Wonder at death – *not* trying to escape from death; wonder at (almost: reverence towards) madness; wonder that there should be the problems that there are, and that they should

---

    53   Pierre Hadot, *Philosophy as a Way of Life*, ed. Arnold Davidson, Chicago, IL: University of Chicago Press, 1995, p.265. Quoted by Conant in 'Philosophy and Biography', p.21.

    54   'Remarks on Frazer's *Golden Bough*', in *Wittgenstein: Philosophical Occasions*, eds. J. Klagge and A. Nordmann, Indianapolis, IN: Hackett, 1993, p.131.

    55   Conant, 'On Going the Bloody *Hard* Way in Philosophy', p.89.

have the solutions that they do ... Wonder at the beauty of human actions ... And in the same way, wonder at what is terrible and what is evil ... Wonder – treating as important – what is terrible just *because* it is terrible; as primitive peoples may celebrate it in rites: the burning of human figures, perhaps of children, in effigy; treating what is terrible as a sacrament. If someone can think of those practices only as 'morbid' or as 'perversions' – or if he can think of them only as methods designed to *ward off* the terrible things they celebrate – this means he cannot imagine how people might wonder at terrible events because of what they are (as opposed to wondering what neglect should have allowed them to happen, how they might be avoided, etc).[56]

What Frazer's sensibility lacks is the ability to imagine that human life can be like that. This lack of imagination can, and usually does, lead to condescension in thought and deed towards primitive peoples. Here, there is an internal connection between the philosophical and the personal. But things are far more complicated once we go beyond these internal connections. Sometimes, of course, it wouldn't make sense to do so. For example, the opposite of saying that the primitive rituals were closed to Frazer, is not to say that they could be open to him. Their practices *could not* be his. As Rhees says, 'If there were a group of people in Dundrum today who began to practise child sacrifice – that would be something different.'[57]

But suppose that there is no misunderstanding about a primitive practice, and that a philosopher, by giving it contemplative attention, provides an illuminating account of it in an attempt to dispel confusions such as Fraser's. Where is the ethical continuity between this philosophical clarity and its connections with a person's way of life? Internal relations will not make these connections for us. In the course of a letter to Rush Rhees, Elizabeth Anscombe wrote:

> An irreligious man *rejects* certain *conceptions*; he is not innocent of them. Don't misunderstand me: there are forms which such conceptions can take, such that a man is better off if he rejects them than if he retains them in these forms. I would rather a man were like Bertrand Russell than that he were a worshipper of Dourga. (I rather believe that Wittgenstein would not: he'd certainly have me up for thinking I could say anything about a worshipper of Dourga.)[58]

Rhees comments, 'I am sure she is right in thinking Wittgenstein would react in that way.'[59] But why? Rhees writes:

> I know next to nothing about the religion of Moloch. I have heard that it included child sacrifice in certain of its rituals. And it may have included other practices which people in Western countries today would call cruel or worse. I never heard Wittgenstein speak of this. But if he had heard someone condemn such a religion because it includes child sacrifice, he would certainly have objected. He would have said that you would not know for your life what the state of mind of the people was who practised that religion and

---

56 Preface to Rhees, *Wittgenstein and the Possibility of Discourse*, pp.xii–xiii.

57 Rush Rhees, 'Picking and Choosing', in *Rush Rhees on Religion and Philosophy*, ed. D.Z. Phillips, Cambridge: Cambridge University Press, 1997, p.308.

58 Rhees, 'Picking and Choosing', p.309.

59 Rhees, 'Picking and Choosing', p.309.

sacrificed the children. And you could not begin to apply the standards by which you may judge actions in the society in which we live.[60]

Here, Wittgenstein is condemning judgements based on misunderstandings. But we see in the writings of Wittgenstein and Rhees that they *do* have insights into rituals which treat the terrible as a sacrament. What one cannot do is to show that there is an internal relation between these insights and one's moral reactions to the rituals. For example, Wittgenstein, it seems, would not intervene to stop them, and would not condemn them. But even if Anscombe *had* understood the rituals, she might still be horrified by them and want to put a stop to them given the opportunity. Rhees himself writes:

> When I am discussing as we are now, I feel I can see why Wittgenstein spoke in that way. If it affected some practical decision I had to make, perhaps I'd waver. I cannot be sure.[61]

So here we have *the same* philosophical insight leading to three *different* moral reactions. One could not show that there are internal relations between them. Moreover, as Rhees points out, it may be difficult, sometimes, to go along with what Wittgenstein says because he makes connections in a way that many people would not. For example, Rhees writes:

> When I said his view can lead to consequences that are hard to take, I meant first that in a form of worship like the worship of Dourga should have the respect due to a form of *worship*, and should not be judged as though it were a depraved practice in our own community. But I meant also that it led Wittgenstein sometimes to view certain actions – which on first view are horrible and repulsive – to view them as *tragic*; and this means that they are seen in a different way, not just as morally abominable ... When you view it as 'tragic' – then you have moved away from the question whether the policy was the right conclusion to draw from such and such deliberations, or whether it was the prudent course to take in view of the circumstances, or even (and this is where I'm less certain of my interpretation) to ask whether it showed the consideration for other men that it might have shown.[62]

What we have seen, in these examples, is that sharing the clarity Wittgenstein may be said to achieve with respect to primitive rituals, does not lead, necessarily, to shared moral reactions to such rituals. Philosophers will have different personal moral views about them which cannot be internally related to their philosophical conclusions. Thus there will be good reason to distinguish, in this context, between what one appreciates philosophically, and one's personal moral reactions to what one sees. Indeed, part of a contemplative attention to the situation will involve doing conceptual justice to this variety of moral reactions.

It is interesting in this context to compare Conant's discussion of Russell in 'On Going the Bloody *Hard* Way in Philosophy' and in 'Philosophy and Biography'. In

---

60   Rhees, 'Picking and Choosing', p.308.
61   Rhees, 'Picking and Choosing', p.309.
62   Rhees, 'Picking and Choosing', pp.309–10.

the former, the emphasis is on Wittgenstein's judgement that Frege was a deeper philosopher than Russell; a judgement which rests on *the character* of Frege's treatment of central issues in logic. That character can be elucidated by what we have called the ethics of enquiry. Whether one agrees with his conclusion or not, Conant makes an excellent case in support of Wittgenstein's judgement. In 'Philosophy and Biography' there is a far more ambitious attempt, with reference to Ray Monk's biography, to co-ordinate Russell's changes of heart in philosophy, with fluctuations in his personal relationships, and his frenzy of political and educational activities. Conant thinks that these aspects of Russell's life both trigger and are triggered by each other. What emerges in Monk's biography, he claims, is that:

> Many elements of the whirl become expressions of Russell's fluctuating philosophical aspirations, and of the restless oscillation between the poles of yearning and disenchantment that characterize both his philosophy and his life as a whole.[63]

Monk himself is worried by the adverse reaction of many to his biography of Russell. Unlike his biography of Wittgenstein, they claim that, in this instance, his dislike of Russell has led to his entering the frame which should simply reveal his subject. Whereas Monk and Conant see the fluctuations in Russell's life as an adverse comment on him, others may say he was unlucky in being surrounded by so many unstable characters. Monk writes:

> I can say 'Look at it like this and you will see that everything fits', but if I am met with, 'No, look at it like this and you will see that it all fits together in quite a different way,' then the opportunities for reasoned debate look rather slender.[64]

Monk is puzzled by what kind of disagreement that is. I do not think it can be met by saying that a more perspicuous representation should clear it up. Wittgenstein, rather, would say that the important thing is to accept that these differences are what one can expect in such cases; that they are part of the indeterminacy in human relationships. One further question is pertinent here. Monk speaks of different readings of Russell's life as differences in seeing how 'everything fits'. But why must everything fit? Surely there are biographies which show lives in which it is essential to see that everything does not fit. Russell's various fluctuations might be seen in that light. What is more, reactions to that life may emphasize different aspects of it as what is of lasting importance. Conant sees Russell's life as falling into a pattern. He writes:

> Contrary to what the compartmentalist urges, what strikes one as one reads first Monk's biography of Wittgenstein and then his biography of Russell, is not how Wittgenstein's life is relevant to an understanding of his work, whereas Russell's life is not relevant to an understanding of his work, but rather how differently relevant the life is to an understanding of the work in each case.[65]

---

63 Conant, 'Philosophy and Biography', p.36.

64 Ray Monk, 'Philosophical Biography: The Very Idea', in *Wittgenstein: Biography and Philosophy*, ed. James C. Klagge, Cambridge: Cambridge University Press, 2001, p.13.

65 Conant, 'Philosophy and Biography', p.37.

Conant has been chiefly concerned, philosophically, with Russell's fluctuations of thought since his acquaintance with Wittgenstein. But what about *Principia Mathematica*? At the outset of his article, Conant warns us against reductionism with respect to the relation between Russell's personal relations and that work; a reductionism which says: 'You only have to consider the way Russell treated his many lovers to see that *Principia Mathematica* cannot be the work of a great mind.'[66] I remember Rhees commenting on the kind of interest many people would have in the personal details of Russell's life. He regarded that interest itself as a low form of curiosity. He said to me, 'If they really wanted to know what Russell had in him, I'd tell them that he had *Principia Mathematica* in him.' Speaking of what he takes to be the boring autobiographies of Ayer and Quine, Conant says that they reveal, with an unintended sublimity, 'only surfaces all the way down'.[67] Conant thinks that writing a biography relating the poverty of a life to the poverty of thinking would demand 'tremendous talent and tact', and is 'far better left unattempted by those of us who possess a merely average prospect of success'.[68] But, for others, there would be no topic, so described, to require talent or tact, for they would refuse to describe the life of any human being 'as surfaces all the way down'. Again, a contemplative philosophy would ask what *kind* of disagreement confronts us here.

What accounts for what I take to be a too easy transition from the philosophical to the personal in some of Conant's arguments? It begins with a proper emphasis on the ethical demands of philosophical enquiry; demands that are as present when Wittgenstein is discussing logic as they are when he is discussing moral questions. Conant emphasizes, quite rightly, that Wittgenstein was opposed to dividing philosophy into distinct subjects,[69] but wrong in thinking that this amounts to saying that there are no distinctive moral subjects in philosophy.[70] What is true is that, insofar as Wittgenstein's interest, from first to last, is in what it means to say something, discussions of moral, political and religious questions are different if seen from that perspective, from what they are when treated as separate fields from which a philosophical underlabourer removes confusions. When contemplative attention is paid to moral matters, we see the heterogeneity involved. Just as Wittgenstein abandoned his view of the general form of a proposition in the *Tractatus*, so he gave up the search for the essence of 'the ethical' seen in his 'Lecture on Ethics'. In his later discussions with Rhees, he emphasized the variety in moral points of view and how one should not try to get behind this variety in the search for a spurious unity.[71] Given this variety, it is not surprising that philosophical clarity may still lead to very different moral reactions to what one has become clear about. As Mulhall points out, there are times when Conant acknowledges this,[72] but I am concerned with

---

66   Conant, 'Philosophy and Biography', p.18.

67   Conant, 'Philosophy and Biography', p.47, n.46.

68   Conant, 'Philosophy and Biography', p.48, n.46.

69   See Conant, 'On Going the Bloody *Hard* Way in Philosophy', p.87.

70   Conant, 'On Going the Bloody *Hard* Way in Philosophy', see p.90.

71   Rush Rhees, 'Some Developments in Wittgenstein's Views on Ethics', in Rhees, *Moral Questions*, ed. D.Z. Phillips, New York: St. Martin's Press, 1999.

72   As when Conant insists that after benefiting from Kierkegaard's clarification of Christianity, a person may become a Christian, remain a Christian or remain an atheist. See

other contexts where this possibility is obscured. For example, given the examples I have been discussing, we have the distinct impression that Conant would resist the view that a person may be philosophically confused about something while being clear about it in his own life. This is because he holds, as we have seen, that 'One's philosophical sensibility is not independent of one's sensibility *tout court*.'[73]

Consider the following example. In the course of a letter to M. O'C. Drury concerning the latter's doubts about whether he had done the right thing in becoming a doctor, Wittgenstein says, 'I think in some sense you don't look at people's faces closely enough'.[74] Winch says that Wittgenstein expresses a concern with Drury's spiritual welfare in language that is 'poised on the edge of the religious'.[75] The discussion as a whole illustrates what Conant means by the moral or spiritual importance of philosophical clarity. The language of *Philosophical Investigations* is very different, but, here, too, Winch thinks that a spiritual dimension can be found, for example, in the following remarks:

> But isn't it absurd to say of a *body* that it has pain? – And why does one feel an absurdity in that? In what sense is it true that my hand does not feel pain, but I in my hand?

> What sort of issue is: Is it the *body* that feels pain? - How is it to be decided? What makes is plausible to say that it is *not* the body? - Well, something like this: If someone has a pain in his hand, then the hand does not say so (unless it writes it) and one does not comfort the hand, but the sufferer: one looks into his face.[76]

Winch reacts to these remarks as follows:

> The last sentence gives me a wonderful sense of a fog suddenly lifting; the confused shapes that loom up and disappear again in the familiar philosophical discussion of 'mind and body' vanish and I am left with a clear view of something very familiar of which I had not noticed its importance. Its 'importance' lies in the first instance in its relation to the philosophical discussion. At the same time in attending to this minute detail that plays such an enormous role in our relations to each other, my sense of the dimensions of those relations is both transformed and enriched: when comforting someone who has been hurt, I look into the sufferer's eyes.[77]

As far as I can see, nothing in these remarks excludes *any* of the following possibilities: that the clearing of the philosophical confusion was, at the same time, a liberation from a personal deficiency; that the philosophical clarification enriched an already sensitive relation to the sufferings of others; that the philosophical clarification releases one from one's philosophical confusion about an already rich sensibility in

---

'On Putting Two and Two Together', p.279.

73   Conant, 'On Going the Bloody *Hard* Way in Philosophy', p.124.

74   Peter Winch, 'Response', in Norman Malcolm, *Wittgenstein – From a Religious Point of View?*, Ithaca, NY: Cornell University Press, 1994, p.126.

75   Winch, 'Response', p.126.

76   Wittgenstein, *Philosophical Investigations*, §286.

77   Winch, 'Response', p.130.

one's personal life. In the last context, the lifting of the philosophical fog is not, at the same time, a lifting of a personal fog. There was no personal fog to lift.

Sometimes, Mulhall takes me to be saying that a person who is confused in his or her religious life could nevertheless be leading one. Put in that general way, the claim would be absurd. But I do not think one can lay down rules about the extent to which one can have occasion to pray, 'Lord I believe – help thou my confusions', and still be a believer. But Mulhall goes on to recognize the obvious when he says (p.22):

> Perhaps Phillips rather has in mind someone who is living a genuinely Christian life, but who is inclined to reflect on her life in a philosophically confused manner (say, by responding positively to a philosopher who asks her whether her God is a kind of entity).

But, then, Mulhall tries to connect this philosophical confusion to 'the personal' by saying (p.22):

> what shows such forms of self-reflection are an expression of confusion, if not the life that the reflecting person leads outside the context of such reflection? In other words, it is precisely vigilant attention to how such a person lives her life that can show her the way to avoid such confusions – which is exactly the point Conant is making.

These remarks beg the question being discussed. Consider the case of a non-believer. Plenty of philosophers think that if the word 'God' does refer to an entity it is unintelligible, but they are convinced that religious belief requires that it does. One cannot ask them to reflect on their lives when not philosophising. They have no religious inclinations to reflect on. What they need to reflect on is the language of worship, whether they can make that language their own or not. Here, the contrast between the philosophical and the personal is obvious.

What of the genuine believer who is philosophically confused? Mulhall says she should be more vigilant about her life. But what is in dispute is the character of the vigilance. The lack is not religious vigilance. On Mulhall's own admission, that is already present. What is more, the primary language of their faith may be what leads a person into philosophical confusions. This is a common phenomenon. What is needed is a revealing of the path from the philosophical confusion to the genuine belief. Again, a distinction between 'the philosophical' and 'the personal' is important.

One may share a religious belief with someone who gives a confused philosophical account of it. When I hear some of the views of my contemporaries in the philosophy of religion, I confess to wondering whether we are talking of the same God. But in order to even try to answer that question, I'd have to know *them* far better than I do. To infer so much from their philosophical accounts would be a highly dubious undertaking on both philosophical and religious grounds. I have been suggesting that a passage from 'the philosophical' to 'the personal' which goes beyond internal relations between them is an equally precarious journey.

A final word in this section of my reply: given the emphasis on 'the ethical' in the writings of Conant and others, it is important to remember that Wittgenstein said that although he was not a religious man, he could not help seeing *every* problem from a religious point of view. Even in his earliest remarks on ethics, the *kind* of ethics he refers to is clearly related to religious conceptions. Conant may point out in reply, that Wittgenstein said that the point of the *Tractatus* is an ethical one. In a discussion he says:

> Wittgenstein is talking about an ethical point here, but not about religion. So the ethical, as a kind of passion for clarity runs through the whole in a way in which the religious or aesthetic does not.[78]

There are a number of points to be made about these remarks, but at this point in my reply, I must be brief. First, Wittgenstein still speaks about 'the ethical' in very general terms. Nothing he says precludes a certain religious sense. On the contrary, it seems to include it, as when he says, 'The mystical is not *how* the world is, but that it is' (6.44). As Malcolm says, this remark is connected with wonder at the existence of the world, which, as I have suggested, is connected with philosophical contemplation of it.[79] If Conant sees the ethical demand running all through Wittgenstein's work as a passion for clarity – a demand for purity in that sense – then one can say equally well, and perhaps better, that a religious-like demand for purity runs all through his work. Is not this suggested by the following?

> I have had a letter from an old friend in Austria, a priest. In it he says he hopes my work will go well, if it should be God's will. Now that is all I want: if it should be God's will. Bach wrote on the title page of his *Orgelbüchlein*, 'To the glory of the most high God, and that my neighbour may be benefited thereby'. That is what I would have liked to say about my work.[80]

If indeed his work could be 'to the glory of God', then certain concerns would be impure:

> Is what I am doing really worth the labour? Surely only if it receives a light from above. And if that happens – why should I worry about the fruits of my work being stolen? If what I am writing is really of value, how could anyone steal the value from me? If the light from above is *not* there, then I cannot be any more than clever.[81]

Furthermore, in a remark about purity which impressed Conant, the context is a religious one:

> I would like to say: 'this book is written to the glory of God', but nowadays this would be the trick of a cheat, i.e. it would not be correctly understood. It means the book was written in good will, and so far as it was not but was written from vanity, etc., the author

---

78   In a discussion of 'What "Ethics" in the *Tractatus* is *Not*', p.95. Conant is Voice B.

79   Norman Malcolm, *Wittgenstein – A Religious Point of View?*, Ithaca, NY: Cornell University Press, 1994, p.10.

80   Rush Rhees, *Ludwig Wittgenstein: Personal Recollections*, pp.181–82, quoted by Malcolm, *Wittgenstein*, pp.13–14.

81   Quoted by Malcolm, *Wittgenstein*, p.18.

would wish to see it condemned. He can not make it more free of these impurities than he is himself.[82]

As we have seen, I do not dispute that this demand for purity is as personal a demand as it is a philosophical one. I agree that philosophy, for Wittgenstein, was a religious-like vocation. Yet, he feared that if he really gave himself to religion, the bending of the knee required of him would conflict with the commitment philosophy asked of him. And for all his passion for philosophy, he never, as Winch points out, speaks of it in a remotely similar way to that in which he speaks of religious passion: 'when he spoke of religion as a "passion" through which one's life must be "turned around" he was speaking of something different'.[83] There is a good reason, therefore, to distinguish, in this context too, between 'the philosophical' and 'the personal', instead of being content with a generic notion of 'the personal'. As Winch says:

> Kierkegaard believed religious belief to stand at an 'infinite distance' from philosophical clarity. He did not believe that such clarity could by itself bring anyone one whit closer to religious faith. I think that Wittgenstein would have taken the same view.[84]

3. Beyond Language Games

So far, in my reply to Mulhall, I have been commenting on what I take to be the inadequacies of two conceptions of philosophy which have been combined to give a therapeutic reading of Wittgenstein's philosophy. In *Philosophy's Cool Place* I contrasted this reading with what I take to be Wittgenstein's contemplative conception of philosophy, one that is concerned with the possibility of discourse. Mulhall thinks that such a contrast is unnecessary, since, for him, while I have succeeded (p.20)

> in identifying a dimension of Wittgenstein's interest in language that relates it to a perennial preoccupation of the Western philosophical tradition since Plato [I have] not [appeared] to have succeeded in showing that its further exploration must involve going essentially beyond the familiar Wittgensteinian business of perspicuously representing the grammar of everyday words.

In my reply I hope to show that this conclusion misses the character of philosophy's perennial preoccupation with the possibility of discourse. From first to last, Wittgenstein's preoccupation is with the possibility of discourse, with what it means *to say something*. The earliest form of this preoccupation in the *Tractatus* is the question of the sense in which a proposition pictures reality. The early form of an answer is the emphasis on the method of projection within which the proposition has its sense. These logical concerns are missed in Mulhall's therapeutic reading of the *Tractatus* in which it is simply seen as an attempt to specify (p.14)

---

82   Wittgenstein, Preface to *Philosophical Remarks*, quoted by Winch in his 'Response' to Malcolm, *Wittgenstein*, p.131.

83   Malcolm, *Wittgenstein*, p.128.

84   Malcolm, *Wittgenstein*, p.129.

'the strictly correct method in philosophy' – that of saying only what can be said, and demonstrating to those who fail to respect this condition on speech that they have failed to give meaning to some portion of their putative utterance.

On this view, the only major difference between the *Tractatus* and the later works is that forms of language and the sources of our confusions about them are more varied than the early work presupposed. The concern with logic drops out of this account. In wanting to determine the general form of the proposition, Wittgenstein was giving a structural account of language, and he criticized himself later for doing so. By the time he has introduced the analogy between games and language, of course, Wittgenstein has given up the idea that language has a general form. But in the emphasis on games, and 'following a rule', Rhees sees 'the structure of the proposition' being replaced by 'the structure of the language game'. But Wittgenstein has not given up the question of the nature of language. It is difficult to see how he could since it is raised by the notion of a language-game itself. There is an obvious disanalogy between games and language-games. All the games we play do not constitute one big game. Thus, it is misleading to say, as Mulhall does, that 'knowing how to play a specific game presupposes a grasp of what it is to play games' (p.17), since it is the latter that is parasitic on the fact that games are played. But the language-games are played within *the same* language, by which we do not mean English or Welsh. The question of the unity of that language, therefore, remains an issue. Wittgenstein's answer to that question is in terms of family resemblances. No language-game possesses a feature common to all uses of language-games, but *some* have features in common with some others, while they share different features with those others. In this way, Wittgenstein was able to avoid the idea that language has a common form. Language has the unity of a family of language-games. Mulhall denies that Wittgenstein actually says this, but it would be difficult to avoid accepting that, at the very least, he offers it as an illuminating analogy. As such, it still offers a structural account of language. Rhees argues that it is not an account of language at all, and that, were it true, it would be impossible to *say* anything. Mulhall, on the other hand, thinks that Rhees' misgivings about the analogy between language and games are misplaced.

Mulhall argues that in many games the rules allow for a great deal of innovation and creativity. Everything is not strictly determined by the rules. There is room for self-expression.[85] Rhees's reply is to point out that there is no difference between what a move means in a demonstration game and what it means in a real game, whereas this cannot be said of the distinction between a rehearsed conversation and a real one; it is not 'internal' as a game is.[86] And when Mulhall reminds us that the significance of games in people's lives can be connected with character and understanding in all sorts of ways, that simply begs the question of whether those 'other ways' can be understood by analogy with playing games.

Rhees is interested in what kind of puzzle a puzzle about language is. He argues that it is not like being puzzled about a game, where one would explain by reference

---

85 Mulhall elaborates this point in *Inheritance and Originality*, §16 and 17.
86 See Rhees, *Wittgenstein and the Possibility of Discourse*, p.98.

to other games. But if one is puzzled about language itself, there is no 'other' something to go to, since that, too, would be an example of language and, hence, of what puzzles one. Mulhall has some curious responses to this issue. First, he says that in learning what a game is, much that is presupposed is not simply a matter of other games. Fine, but the question, once again, is whether the 'much else' that is presupposed is illuminated by the analogy between language and games.

Mulhall does not discuss some of the most powerful disanalogies Rhees presents. He argues that although Wittgenstein gave up the analogy between language and a calculus in the *Tractatus*, it continued to influence him in the *Investigations* in the discussion of 'following a rule', 'going on in the same way', and the importance of 'and so on' in learning a language. The same would apply to emphases on 'training', 'function', and 'mastering techniques'. Rhees recognizes the importance of these considerations in the context of learning the meanings of words, and of the agreements in use which show themselves in that we naturally take such-and-such as the *same* use of the world. On the other hand, he does not think that these emphases throw much light on what it means to *say* something. How does a child come to ask a question? Rhees's answer is: by coming to an appreciation of what it makes sense to say; something the child picks up by the conversations that surround it. And these conversations would be oddly described indeed in terms of 'following a rule', or 'going on in the same way'. Similarly, it would be odd to speak of speaking to another person as the mastery of a number of techniques; still less to talk of mastering them in this context. Mulhall is tempted to speak in this way:

> That mastery of specific language-games presupposes that speaking- the general impulse and capacity to do things with words – is part of the natural repertoire of human beings, and so lies beyond the reach of any philosophical accounting of the kind Rhees imagines.[87]

But when we speak with each other, are we 'doing things with words', or displaying our natural repertoire in this respect? Our words are not the instruments by which we do things, but are constitutive of what we do. That is why Rhees insists that we do not *use* language. That is why 'following a rule' cannot account for *saying* anything. As David Cockburn points out in her perceptive review of Rhees' work, a person could reel off 'the colours of all objects in his field of vision', without having anything to say about colours. As he says,

> Rhees ... introduces a clear distinction between 'knowing what is permissible' and having something to say. We can, perhaps, imagine someone who has mastered the moves (at least up to a point) – who knows, for example, that 'She is in serious pain' is to be followed by 'We must get help' – and yet has no sense of the bearing of the one remark on the other: for whom, perhaps, this is simply a response one must make if one is to move reasonably smoothly through life in this community.[88]

---

87 Mulhall, *Inheritance and Originality*, pp.75–76.

88 David Cockburn, 'Critical Notice of Rhees' *Wittgenstein and the Possibility of Discourse*', *Philosophical Investigations* 25:1 (2002), p.81.

The bearing that one remark has on another is shown in the life we share with one another. Not that our shared life *enables* remarks to have the sense they do – that, too, would be an *external* explanation – but that that sense *shows* itself *in* the lives we share. That is why Rhees keeps repeating that *language makes sense if living makes sense*. Thus, Rhees is not, as Mulhall thinks, seeking a philosophical *accounting* of language. Rather, he is engaged in a philosophical *contemplation* of it. The contemplation takes the form of the kind of discussion I have been engaged in, not of comparing one perspicuous representation of a form of discourse with another. Thus it will not do *at all* to respond, as Mulhall does, by saying (p.19):

> We do not have to give a perspicuous representation of the whole of language; we simply have to give a perspicuous representation of the ways in which we use the word 'language'.

Rhees does not say, as Mulhall thinks, that language has the unity of a dialogue. He recognizes that all language is not conversation, but that if we take conversation as a centre of variation, it throws light on those parts of language which are not conversation. Here, Rhees is indicating the kind of unity that language has – that of a hubbub of voices in all sorts of relations to each other. When Wittgenstein gave up the analogy between language and a calculus, he gave up, wrongly, one of its important aspects. He was right to reject the view that different aspects of language are related to each other formally, but wrong to underplay the interlocking intelligibility of language. It is with the nature of that interlocking that Rhees grapples, and which I tried to elucidate in *Philosophy's Cool Place*.

It is in some ways understandable that Mulhall should think that this is a recent emphasis in my work. That work, for the most part, he thinks, has been dominated by making distinctions between religion and other activities by bringing out the different rules which govern them – an emphasis which he thinks also governed Winch's *The Idea of a Social Science*. But Mulhall is wrong about Winch, who wrote in that early work:

> To ask whether reality is intelligible is to ask about the relation of thought and reality. In considering the nature of thought one is led also to consider the nature of language. Inseparably bound up with the question whether reality is intelligible, therefore, is the question of how language is connected with reality, of what it is to *say* something. In fact the philosopher's interest in language lies not so much in the solution of particular linguistic confusions for their own sakes, as in the solution of confusions about the nature of language in general.[89]

Winch's work was published in 1958. He acknowledged his indebtedness to Rhees. Even at this stage, Winch is emphasising the important difference between understanding what language is and explaining it. What he regrets, in his preface to the second edition, is that he elucidated that understanding too much in terms of rule following. In later writings, he becomes far more influenced by Rhees's

---

89   Peter Winch, *The Idea of a Social Science*, pp.11–12.

'Wittgenstein's Builders' and the kind of issues I have been engaged with in my reply to Mulhall.

Mulhall acknowledges that, in 'Religious Beliefs and Language Games', published in 1970, I was aware of the dangers in treating religious beliefs as distinctive language-games cut off from the interlocking intelligibility of life, dangers which led to the accusation of fideism.[90] But, by and large, Mulhall thinks I have been concerned with clearing up the confusions between the grammars of religious beliefs and other grammars. It would be wrong to assume, however, that I have ever embraced Mulhall's therapeutic conception of philosophy. It is easy to miss that fact because for much of the time I *have* been responding to what I take to be grammatical confusions in contemporary philosophy of religion. But that task is intimately related to the question of the nature of language, since it is the subliming of particular grammars that leads, so often, to the over-simplification of the character of that interlocking intelligibility, resulting in the case of religion, in assigning a wrong place to it in our language, or denying that it has an intelligible place at all.

Even before 1970, I was partially aware in my undergraduate years, 1952–1956, of the importance of a contemplative conception of philosophy.

> I gleaned, however vaguely, that philosophy was not a collection of specialisms; it was one subject, and its central theme was the nature of reality ... We were vaguely aware, through Oxford linguistic philosophy, that perhaps one should drop any ambition to give a general account of reality. Philosophy was a matter of logical geography, a clearing up of linguistic muddles about different uses of language. There is no 'reality' as such, only the reality of this, that, and the other thing. Through the way we were taught at Swansea, I had a sense, early on, that this was somehow an evasion of philosophy's central concerns.[91]

What is undoubtedly true is, as Mulhall says, that my editing of 'the Rush Rhees *Nachlass* have deeply influenced [my] present understanding of [my] own work' (p.13). I hope it has also deepened my understanding of Rhees. But this is not a new departure. That *Wittgenstein and the Possibility of Discourse* should have this effect on me is not surprising, since, as Cockburn says, it is 'clearly one of the most important books on the philosophy of language to have appeared since the *Philosophical Investigations* and *The Blue and Brown Books*'.[92]

---

90   See Kai Nielsen and D.Z. Phillips, *Wittgensteinian Fideism?*
91   Phillips, 'On Wittgenstein', pp.148–49.
92   Cockburn, 'Critical Notice', p.93.

Chapter III

Philosophy, Theology and Heresy: D.Z. Phillips and the Grammar of Religious Belief

Mario von der Ruhr

University of Wales, Swansea

1. Prelude – Heine's Advice to Believers

In his essayistic fragment *Religion and Philosophy in Germany*, the writer Heinrich Heine provocatively notes:

> From the moment that a religion solicits the aid of philosophy, its downfall is inevitable. Trying to defend its elf, it merely prattles itself ever more deeply into destruction. Religion, like every absolutism, must not seek to justify itself. Prometheus is bound to the rock by a silent force, and Aeschylus does not allow personified power to utter a single word. It must remain silent. The moment the religious venture to print a catechism supported by argument, the moment political absolutism releases official state documents, both are near their end. But therein consists our triumph: we have managed to get our opponents to talk, and now we can hold them to account.[1]

At first sight, Heine's advice to the advocates of religion appears implausible, for how can something as significant in human life as religion remain 'silent' and, especially hen faced with sceptical challenges, not seek to defend itself? And would not such a defence require, among other things, 'a catechism supported by arguments', both theological and philosophical? Critical attacks on religion, so it is tempting to argue, are not rebutted by stubborn recitations of its central doctrines, but through serious argumentative engagement, and here the sophisticated exegetical and explanatory endeavours of theologians and their philosophical friends must surely play a crucial role. Religious faith involves, after all, a comprehensive *Weltentwurf* and existential perspective which not only claims to be *true*, but which *commends* itself to those who have not (yet) embraced it. Hence, and as with anything that pledges for our cognitive and affective allegiance, religion, too, must give a plausible account of itself and justify its constitutive beliefs and practices – both to those who do not understand them and to those who, while claiming to understand, nevertheless reject

---

1   Heinrich Heine, *Religion and Philosophy in Germany. A Fragment*, trans. by John Snodgrass, New York: State University of New York Press, 1986, p.88. The translation is a revised version of Snodgrass's.

these beliefs and practices as false, confused, superstitious or dangerous. Silence, so the argument goes, would be tantamount to admitting defeat and conceding to the sceptic what he has always suspected, viz., that the religious form of life is seriously lacking in intellectual credentials and hence unworthy of our assent.

The trouble with this response to Heine's remark is that it is based on the very presupposition that he wants to call into question, viz., that the religious form of life *does* stand in need of a rational legitimation, and one to which philosophy may make a major contribution. Heine is rightly sceptical at this point, both because philosophical pronouncements are essentially contestable and because there is considerable controversy over the nature and proper method of philosophical enquiry itself. Clearly, a logical positivist conception of philosophy is likely to yield a different analysis of religious belief from, say, a transcendental idealist one, and neither may in the end prove satisfactory. Heine's comment thus raises interesting and important questions about the nature of religious belief on the one hand, and about the roles which philosophy and theology can play in its elucidation, on the other. If, as Heine suggests, philosophy and theology may be distortive, even destructive, of religious belief, then both disciplines must embark on critical self-reflection and ensure that they *do* deliver a fair account of religious faith.

In this connection, the ability to resist certain interpretative temptations will be of central importance. Philosophy, for one, must guard against the temptation to infer from the surface grammar of religious utterances that they *must* be either false empirical statements or metaphysical pseudo-propositions that may readily be dismissed as nonsense. Heine's remark would then be just as much directed against a hasty, positivistic analysis of religious belief, as it would caution against a certain kind of theology. As for the systematic exposition of religious faith in a catechism, Heine does not mean to reject it *per se*. But he is doubtful of the form – doctrinal postulates supported by 'rational' argument – in which it is typically presented, viz., one that is all too reminiscent of the structure of scientific theory, and thus of a radically different framework of thinking. Both approaches, philosophical positivism no less than its theological counterpart, tend to trivialize religion by couching it in the language of facts and propositions, or super-facts and super-propositions, except that, while the theologian may think such a grammatical *rapprochement* appropriate, his positivist critic either takes it at face value and rejects it as wrong, or sees it as the result of a semantic schizophrenia that vainly struggles to utter the unintelligible. Hence Heine's warning against the pitfalls of a certain kind of philosophical theology, and his exhortation not to say too much in defence of the faith, since one's 'justifications' are likely to be either misunderstood or adapted to a conceptual framework that is intrinsically inimical to religious belief. It is a dialogical context in which the adage, 'When in Rome, do as the Romans do', would be advice better not heeded.

Another way of putting the difficulty would be to say that a positivistic stance in philosophy and theology can only obscure the difference between religious belief and unbelief, as well as the nature of the disagreement between the religious and the non-religious. The difference between religion and atheism is not properly captured in terms of a disagreement about 'matters of fact and existence' in Hume's sense, nor yet in terms of the contrast between common sense and metaphysical nonsense. What is at issue, rather, is the expression of different, though by no means disconnected, ways of conceptualizing human experience, which manifest themselves in distinctive modes of thought, action and language, and which co-exist in the absence of an Archimedean vantage point from which they could be assessed or, even more absurdly, ranked according to cognitive value, evidential support, probable utility or the like.

The temptation to postulate such a universal standard of assessment is difficult to overcome, as it is rooted in certain habits of thought – the craving for generality, precision, systematicity, explanatory completeness; wanting to say such-and-such, even against one's better judgement, etc. – that are hard to shed. If it is true that philosophical thinking, in particular, gravitates towards such intellectual ills, then a certain *prophylaxis* against them is of the utmost importance. One consequence of this is that, if one wants to say anything illuminating about religion – and this applies to its advocates and critics alike –, one will have to wield a finer interpretive pen than the philosophers and theologians whom Heine holds responsible for the demise of religion. A sensitive analysis of religious discourse involves charting the religious terrain, not with the aid of an independent grammatical compass, but through careful attention to the grammatical signposts to be found on that terrain itself, to the linguistic expression of religious concepts and their role in the believer's life. This leads me to D.Z. Phillips' work in the philosophy of religion, which attempts to provide a sustained and deep grammatical exposition of the religious *Weltentwurf* without falling into positivist or other kinds of reductivism, or saying more than its linguistic and non-linguistic manifestations warrant.

2. D.Z. Phillips on Philosophy and Theology

The philosopher's task, as Phillips understands it, 'would be … a *descriptive* one: that of bringing out the kind of language involved in religious belief and the notion of reality embodied in it'.[2] This teasing-out of 'the kind of thing religious belief is', is, however, not an exercise in apologetics or a mode of advocacy, since the results of the enquiry can be seen to be just as relevant to an understanding of atheism as they are to an understanding of religious belief.[3] Unlike the theologian, who acts as a direct custodian of the faith which he expounds, the philosopher – i.e., the kind of contemplative philosopher who serves as Phillips' ideal – is merely a *disinterested* and attentive chronicler of the diverse ways in which that faith expresses itself, and a careful expounder of the rich conceptual tapestry that surrounds it. The primary methodological *desideratum* is that the philosopher be sensitive to the object of his enquiry, whatever *personal* attitude he may have towards it:

> What he must have is respect for the belief he is investigating. He may want to oppose it, proclaim it or simply note it as a serious point of view, but he cannot dismiss it as a product of confusion.[4]

---

2   D.Z. Phillips, *Religion without Explanation*, Oxford: Blackwell, 1976, p.4. My emphasis.

3   Phillips, *Religion without Explanation*, p.7.

4   Phillips, *Religion without Explanation*, p.189.

What Phillips is suggesting here is that, for the purposes of providing an illuminating account of religion, the philosopher's personal affiliations are neither here nor there, nor should they make any difference to the character of his enquiry – at least if he is sufficiently conscientious about his task.

The suggestion has implications that may sound problematic. One is that a philosopher with strong personal leanings towards atheism could be at least as perceptive an expositor of religious belief as a fully involved member of a religious community. Another is that fervent, personal advocacy of religious belief need not get in the way of a disinterested enquiry into religious phenomenology. Surely, so the objection goes, a believer would hardly turn to an atheist for enlightenment about the central articles of his own faith, any more than an atheist would consult a devout Catholic over the meaning of life and death. The conceptual frameworks seem to stand in such radical opposition to each other that fruitful dialogue, let alone mutual illumination, can hardly be possible. Moreover, isn't there a serious tension between Phillips' demand for philosophical impartiality on the one hand, and his admission that this impartiality may go hand in hand with deep devotion to a particular religious creed, on the other?

Now, both objections seem to me misguided, at least in their present formulations. First, while it is true that a believer would gain little spiritual edification from the writings of someone like Karl Marx, say, atheism covers a wide spectrum of thinkers and attitudes, and there is no *a priori* reason for thinking that, on a number of issues, a properly sensitive atheist philosopher may not be able to speak more deeply about life and death, say, than a religious believer, including theologians authorized to expound the matter in an official catechism. One would need to look at concrete examples, of course, but Phillips' discussion of Feuerbach's work in *Religion and the Hermeneutics of Contemplation* could serve as an illustration here.[5] None of this is to deny the obvious truth that there are occasions where it may matter for one's impression that an interlocutor 'really understands', that there be a shared experiential background. But this is not invariably so, nor would it be plausible to reject claims to genuine understanding or insight, simply on the grounds that such a background was missing. A Catholic priest, for example, may have no experience of married life but it does not follow that he is *ipso facto* unable either to understand, or to speak deeply, about what a marital relationship involves. Being married is not the only route to gaining insights into married life.

As for the second point, there is, of course a danger – already noted by Schopenhauer and Nietzsche – that the philosopher may present as the result of impartial and disinterested enquiry what is really his own personal attitude, propped up with an array of 'rational' arguments. Naturally, philosophical thought is not exempt from, and may indeed be particularly prone to, gravitating towards the ego's predilections – hence Wittgenstein's apt observation that the avoidance of philosophical confusion is primarily a matter of overcoming certain obstacles in one's own *will*. But Phillips is well aware of this danger, and it is no objection to his view to point to cases where philosophers self-deceptively mistake their conclusions for the product of impersonal enquiry and present it to their readers as a paradigm

---

5   Phillips, *Religion and the Hermeneutics of Contemplation.*

example of 'merely' following an argument where it leads. Not that there is anything
wrong with the attempt to produce a sophisticated argument in support of a view to
which one is deeply sympathetic, but the measure of a good *philosophical* enquiry
as Phillips understands it, is its sensitivity to the *complexity* of the issues, including
the critical charges that might be levelled by those who take a wholly different
view of the matter. The central question is always whether the enquiry in question
does justice to its subject matter, and on Phillips' view it can only do so under the
constraints of a certain detachment, one that promises illumination to believers and
atheists alike. This, I take it, is part of what is meant by saying that, in making
explicit the logic or grammar of religious beliefs, 'philosophy neither adds anything
to them nor takes anything away from them'.[6] The philosopher's detachment, in
other words, shows itself in the extent to which he honestly describes what lies open
to view, without giving in to reductivist or other kinds of interpretive temptation: 'As
far as the character of religious belief or atheism is concerned, philosophy leaves
everything where it is.'[7] The question of the personal dimension in grammatical
expositions of the faith is one that will keep surfacing, especially in connection with
Phillips' remarks on immortality and Eugen Drewermann's theological exegesis of
the mysteries of faith, and I shall return to it below.

Given what has been said so far, it should not come as a surprise that what
Phillips claims for philosophy, viz., that its proper task is attentive and disinterested
description rather than partisan apologetics, also holds for his conception of what a
properly sensitive theology should look like:

> Theology can claim justifiably to show what is meaningful in religion only when it
> has an internal relation to religious discourse ... Theology cannot impose criteria of
> meaningfulness on religion from without.[8]

The remark bears directly on Heine's worry that, if religion attempts to provide a
rational justification of its own subject matter, it is bound to fail, since there is no
external vantage point from which its truth could be demonstrated. The criteria of its
meaningfulness are 'given by religious discourse itself',[9] so they are *internal* to the
religious form of life itself, and Phillips has repeatedly shown how an assimilation
of religious language to the language of facts, propositions, hypotheses, predictions
and so on, may result in a construal of the divine that is both unspiritual and, if
one thinks of the argumentative contortions through which some philosophers and
theologians have gone to deal with the so-called problem of evil, morally repugnant.
The theologian should articulate the faith in a way that deepens the believer's
understanding of it, and this can only be accomplished if the distinctive character of
religious life and its non-theoretical foundations are permanently kept in focus:

6   Phillips, *Religion without Explanation*, p.190.
7   Phillips, *Religion without Explanation*, p.190.
8   D.Z. Phillips, 'Philosophy, Theology, and the Reality of God', in *Wittgenstein and Religion*, Basingstoke: Macmillan, 1993.
9   Phillips, *Wittgenstein and Religion*, p.3.

The theological system is often constructed to answer certain questions and problems which may arise. But the foundation of a theological system is based on the non-formalised theology which is within the religious way of life carried on by the person who is constructing the theological system.[10]

Religious sentiments, beliefs and practices do not, in other words, have their origin in a formalized system of assumptions, but constitute a primitive attitude that is both expressed in, and deepened by, subsequent reflection, including theological exegesis. And, as such exegesis is always undertaken by a concrete individual with his own spiritual *anamnesis*, it follows that, in this sense at least, 'theology is personal, since it is based on one's own experience of God'.[11] Thus, the personal aspect noted in connection with philosophical analysis has a natural correlate in theological exegesis, except that the theologian is also answerable to the strictures of an *imprimatur* from which Phillips' contemplative philosopher is exempt because, unlike the theologian, he is not commending one particular *Weltentwurf* over all others. What matters is that religious concepts be examined in the contexts from which they derive their meaning and that, in this regard, theology be just as impartial as philosophy.

3. 'Descriptive' Philosophy – The Case of Immortality

If this – still fairly general and programmatic – sketch is a fair characterization of Phillips' approach, then it seems to me not only plausible, but a helpful elaboration on Heine's comment with which I began. Even so, further questions need to be asked about the descriptive dimension of philosophical analysis, and about the relation between philosophico-theological expositions of religious belief and the ordinary believer's reactions to these expositions. For if, by virtue of providing (internal) illumination rather than (external) justification, a properly impartial account of religion 'leaves everything where it is', then it seems that, at least as far as the key religious concepts are concerned, there should be no major interpretive disagreements between philosophers or theologians and ordinary believers. What one finds is, of course, exactly the opposite, as Phillips himself admits. Towards the end of *Death and Immortality*, for instance, he notes:

> Of course it may be true, and probably is true, that at the moment only a small number of people derive sustenance from the pictures of immortality we have been discussing.[12]

The assessment is a sobering one, for if Phillips has been faithful to his own methodological guidelines, would one not expect the result of his enquiry to be applauded by more than just a few? It is tempting to think so, but the inference is unwarranted. On Phillips' account, unfavourable reactions to his grammatical endeavours may show, not so much that these endeavours are unsatisfactory, as that 'philosophical clarification may open or bar the way to religious belief or atheism for

---

10 Phillips, *Wittgenstein and Religion*, p.6.
11 Phillips, *Wittgenstein and Religion*, p.6.
12 D.Z. Phillips, *Death and Immortality*, London and Basingstoke: Macmillan, 1970, p.78.

a person', and that, in this particular case, 'what was barred or kept open previously did rest on philosophical confusion'.[13] Thus, it is the believer's conception of immortality that may be confused, not Phillips' philosophical account of it. In what, then, does the confusion consist? Phillips summarizes it in the following remark:

> Eternity is not an extension of this present life, but a mode of judging it. Eternity is not *more* life, but this life seen under certain moral and religious modes of thought. This is precisely what seeing this life *sub specie aeternitatis* would amount to.[14]

Immortality, in Phillips' view, does not involve continued personal existence beyond the grave, but a way of viewing *this* life, and the promise of eternal life in Christ is not to be understood predictively, as a future event, but evaluatively, as an admonitory picture that reveals human action to fall under a certain kind of (timeless) judgement – 'in turning away from the temporal to the eternal, the believer is said to attain immortality and overcome death'.[15] The alternative construal, which Phillips takes to be prominent among many believers and most contemporary philosophers, typically postulates the existence of soul-substances and some kind of bodily resurrection, and turns out to be little more than a 'transcendentalized' version of 'see you later!' It not only cheapens the significance of death and dislocates soul-talk from the practices in which it is typically embedded, but involves quite unintelligible assumptions about buried corpses leading to new bodies rising from the dead.[16]

Consonant with his conception of immortality, Phillips also rejects as misguided a certain reading of the common religious belief that we shall meet again beyond the grave:

> It has been said with good reason that the hope of life after death is often connected with the hope of seeing loved ones again, of taking up broken relationships, of righting wrongs committed long ago, and so on.[17]

The hope of a post-mortem reunion with our beloved must not be construed predictively, as the expectation of a future event, but constitutes a normative *picture* which, if properly interpreted, shows something about the essential equality of all human beings before God:

> Such a picture may itself be an expression of the belief that people should act towards each other, not according to the status and prestige that people have acquired or failed to acquire, during the course of their lives, but as children of God, in the equality which death will reveal.[18]

---

13 Phillips, *Religion without Explanation*, p.189.
14 Phillips, *Death and Immortality*, p.49.
15 Phillips, *Death and Immortality*, p.50.
16 D.Z. Phillips, 'Dislocating the Soul', in *Can Religion Be Explained Away?*, ed. D.Z. Phillips, London: Macmillan, 1996.
17 Phillips, 'Dislocating the Soul', p.16.
18 Phillips, 'Dislocating the Soul', p.66.

While Phillips is aware that many believers will reject this reading of their hopes vis-à-vis their (dead) loved ones, he nevertheless insists that 'these things cannot be restored',[19] and that sober philosophical analysis must not defer to the confusions generated by a deep-rooted desire for an endless temporal existence. That analysis is not, after all, conducted in a vacuum, but informed by insights already articulated in the very religious tradition on whose conceptual inventory the ordinary religious believer also draws. One such insight is that:

> *the life which is said to exist after death is said to be beyond all change.* Yet all the relationships we have mentioned depend upon change for their very meaning. Mortality is not a limitation in human relationships. On the contrary, it is a precondition of their being the kind of relationships they are.[20]

Consequently, Phillips' remarks on immortality can be understood as grammatical reminders that draw attention to ideas towards which the faith gravitates as it deepens, and the procedure may be called 'descriptive', not because it simply and naively reiterates what believers may be inclined to *say* in response to (philosophical) questioning, but in the sense that it elaborates on those aspects of the religious tradition which throw into relief the distinctive nature of its own subject matter. It is in the preservation of grammatical differences, in other words, that depth and illumination are to be found. Hence Phillips' repeated insistence that 'it is a grammatical confusion to think that this [religious] language is referential or descriptive. It is an expression of value. If one asks what it says, the answer is that it says itself.'[21] Now, Phillips is right in urging the believer, whatever his religious persuasion, to pay attention to the conceptual subtleties of his own faith, and to keep distinct grammars distinct. And it is also true that a straightforwardly *literal* interpretation of belief in such things as immortality – and is it even clear what 'straightforwardly literal' would *mean* here? – apart from being spiritually unedifying, ignores those dimensions of the faith that explicitly caution against such a reading. Clearly, Christian hope for eternal life in Christ is not (grammatically) analogous to the wish for a never-ending holiday on the Costa del Sol, and it is important to become clear about why not. Nor is the *point* of belief in immortality captured by talking, as quite a few philosophers do, about necessary and sufficient conditions of personal identity post mortem, or by speculating on the physical possibility of a resurrection 'event' sometime after death, and Phillips deserves great credit for exposing the grammatical confusions that generate such discussions.

So far, so good. On the other hand, can one not also imagine an orthodox Roman Catholic who, while agreeing with the general tenor of Phillips' approach, nevertheless finds his account of immortality unsatisfactory because it isolates belief in eternal life from other beliefs with which it is intimately connected, including that in Jesus' resurrection and ascension after his death and burial? The charge against Phillips might then be that he is guilty of an ironic *tu quoque*: his philosophical pronouncements on what can, and on what cannot, be 'restored', are themselves

---

19   Phillips, *Religion without Explanation*, p.135.
20   Phillips, *Death and Immortality*, p.17.
21   Phillips, *Death and Immortality*, p.147.

examples of how 'positivism still exercises an enormous influence over our thinking about religion'.[22] But the criticism may be unfair and requires elaboration, perhaps along the following lines. Turning to *Article 11* of his new Catholic Catechism – 'I believe in the resurrection of the body' –, our Catholic believer reads:

> We firmly believe, and hence we hope that, just as Christ is truly risen from the dead and lives for ever, so after death the righteous will love forever with the risen Christ and he will raise them up on the last day ... Belief in the resurrection of the dead has been an essential element of the Christian faith from its beginnings.[23]

The profession of faith is followed by a familiar quotation from St. Paul's *Letter to the Corinthians*, in which the Apostle poses the rhetorical question:

> How can some of you say that there is no resurrection of the dead? But if there is no resurrection of the dead, then Christ has not been raised; if Christ has not been raised, then our preaching is in vain ... But in fact Christ has been raised from the dead, the first fruits of those who have fallen asleep. [24]

The promise of eternal life, then, is inextricably linked with the resurrection of Christ, itself the culmination of a spiritual narrative that incorporates, as essential elements, the mysteries of the Incarnation, the Virgin Birth and the Immaculate Conception. As for the idea of a bodily resurrection, the Catechism is by no means blind to the conceptual difficulties it involves:

> From the beginning, Christian faith in the resurrection has met with incomprehension and opposition ... It is very commonly accepted that the life of the human person continues in a spiritual fashion after death. But how can we believe that this body, so clearly mortal, could rise to everlasting life?[25]

The notion of a disembodied spirit raises (philosophical) problems of its own, but the catechetical exposition is not concerned to address these. Instead, it proceeds to deal with the issue of bodily resurrection by asking, 'What is rising?', 'Who will rise?' and 'How?', respectively.[26] In answer to the first question, we are told:

> In death, the separation of the soul from the body, the human body decays and the soul goes to meet God, while awaiting its reunion with its glorified body. God, in his almighty power, will definitively grant incorruptible life to our bodies by reuniting them with our souls, through the power of Jesus' Resurrection.[27]

A philosopher familiar with Platonic/Cartesian dualism and the forceful objections that have been levelled against it, may find this passage 'uneven', but our Catholic believer need not have any such thoughts, and whether the picture of a separation of

---

22 Phillips, *Death and Immortality*, p.147.
23 *Catechism of the Catholic Church*, New York: Doubleday, 1995, pp.279–80.
24 1 Cor. 15:12–14.
25 *Catechism of the Catholic Church*, p.281.
26 *Catechism of the Catholic Church*, p.282.
27 *Catechism of the Catholic Church*, p.282.

the soul from the body prompts him to hold a confused or superficial belief in Christ's resurrection, is still an open question that can only be answered – if indeed it can be answered at all – in the light of what he does with it, of the ways in which it enters his thoughts and actions. As Peter Winch has rightly noted, '[a] picture can be an essential aspect of a form of representation without itself *constituting* the representation', [28] and while it is true that certain pictures easily lend themselves to confused or shallow interpretations, whether they do so is also a function of the preconceptions and ideas that are brought to it. Phillips' contemplative philosopher may find the Catechism's remarks on the resurrection conceptually unhappy and spiritually unedifying, but then our Catholic's belief in the afterlife is not a philosophical conviction, nor need he be interested in a philosophical analysis of what his faith amounts to. Similar things could, *inter alia*, be said about the common belief in a reunion with dead loved ones. A woman who has just lost her son in a terrible accident may believe that she will be reunited with him in death, but of course she need not think of that reunion as being wholly analogous to a reunion in life. Indeed, it is not even clear what would decide that she *does* think of it in that way. [29]

Now, Phillips may grant all this and contend that, whatever personal reservations he may have about the terms in which the Catechism speaks of the resurrection, he does not want to legislate in advance that they must lead to a confused or (spiritually) superficial understanding of the concept. Much will depend, for instance, on whether the believer takes talk of a personal resurrection to be little more than the expectation of a straightforward temporal existence post-mortem. Here, Phillips would rightly insist that (a) there is nothing *religious* about such an expectation *per se*, and (b) resurrection talk may be taken up into a believer's life in ways quite different from and deeper than, a belief in some future event. This insight is also acknowledged in the Catholic Catechism:

> Christ will raise us up 'on the last day'; but it is also true that, in a certain way, we have already risen with Christ. For, by virtue of the Holy Spirit, Christian life is already now on earth a participation in the death and Resurrection of Christ ... United with Christ by Baptism, believers already truly participate in the heavenly life of the risen Christ. [30]

The *concrete* implications of the resurrection mystery for the Christian life are pursued in the paragraphs immediately following the above quotation, in Sections 1005–14 (*Dying in Christ Jesus*) of the Catechism. Largely revolving around the idea of dying to the self as a way of living in Christ, they also come rather close to the kind of grammatical elucidation Phillips himself would be inclined to give. There is no indication in the Catechism that these elaborations are of lesser significance than the earlier, more stipulative, pronouncements on the resurrection, nor does the catechetical exposition invite further speculation on *how* a resurrection might be possible. On the contrary, the reader is explicitly exhorted not to ask too many questions in this regard, as 'this "how" exceeds our imagination and understanding;

---

28 Peter Winch, 'Picture and Representation', *Tijdschrift voor filosofie* 49:1 (1987), 10.
29 Winch, 'Picture and Representation', 5. The example is Peter Winch's.
30 *Catechism of the Catholic Church*, p.283.

it is accessible only to faith'.[31] The same exhortation applies to questions about the character of the afterlife:

> This mystery of blessed communion with God and all who are in Christ is beyond all understanding and description. Scripture speaks of it in images: life, light, peace, wedding feast, wine of the kingdom, the Father's house, the heavenly Jerusalem, paradise: 'no eye has seen, nor ear heard, nor the heart of man conceived, what God has prepared for those who love him.'[32]

What the Catholic faith entails, then, – and this is where Phillips' account diverges from what our Catholic believer would want to say – is that, quite independently of any possible moral or spiritual *aggiornamenti* in *this* life, the hope for a continued personal existence beyond the grave is an essential feature of belief in immortality. Phillips plausibly insist that religious utterances are much more akin to expressions of attitude than they are to hypotheses or predictions, but there does seem to be a predictive dimension to belief in eternal life that is clearly not captured by the claim that 'eternity is not *more* life, but this life seen under certain moral and religious modes of thought'.[33] For our Catholic believer, the promise of eternal life is conceptually tied to belief in Christ's own resurrection and subsequent appearance to the Apostles, and flows from a Scriptural tradition in which the writings of Luke – 'See my hands and my feet, that it is I myself'[34] – and Paul occupy a prominent place. Our believer grants that Christ was not resurrected to more of his earthly life, but neither does he think that the resurrection narrative could simply be reduced to a mode of ethico-religious judgement. 'Most philosophers', Phillips correctly notes in *Death and Immortality*, 'would say that belief in the possibility of survival after death is a necessary precondition of any kind of belief in immortality',[35] and he rightly shows that there is a belief in immortality for which that stipulation does not hold, viz., the kind expounded in his book. But while Phillips' analysis is congruent with *one* aspect of Catholic belief, it also conflicts with another, which it would be hasty to dismiss as the result of philosophical confusion.

It seems that, at this point in the debate, what is said about immortality becomes very much a personal affair, with some philosophers finding the very idea of a resurrection and afterlife either hopelessly obscure or spiritually unedifying, and others insisting that it is part and parcel of the Christian tradition and essential to its very identity. Thus, Phillips' former colleague Rush Rhees writes: 'I do not say that there can be no sense in speaking of eternal life or an afterlife. But I hardly understand what this sense may be.'[36] Elsewhere, reflecting on St Peter's transformation after Christ's resurrection, Rhees can only confess: 'I do not understand the conception

31 *Catechism of the Catholic Church*, p.283.
32 *Catechism of the Catholic Church*, p.290.
33 Phillips, *Death and Immortality*, p.49.
34 Luke 24:39.
35 Phillips, *Death and Immortality*, p.1.
36 Rhees, *Rush Rhees on Religion and Philosophy*, ed. Phillips, p.265.

of the Resurrection',[37] but he is also careful not to dismiss the idea as a piece of conceptual confusion:

> I have missed the importance of the resurrection, in some way. The story of the Passion, and especially of the words of Jesus on he cross, does make me want to think of him as divine, in some sense. But the resurrection does not seem to me to add much. I know that this shows there is some big defect in my conception of his life, and even of his Passion. But I do not know how to correct it. I can see, for instance, that the resurrection gives a special force and importance to Jesus' promise of eternal life (and resurrection of the body) to those who believe in him.[38]

To some, like our Catholic believer, the resurrection narrative adds a lot, if not everything, to thoughts of Christ's divinity and God's unconditional love. To Rhees, it adds little and might as well have been left out. Simone Weil, whose reflections on religion inform much of what Rhees and Phillips have to say on the subject, could not have put the point more succinctly when she confessed, in her 'heretical' *Letter to a Priest*: 'If the Gospel omitted all mention of Christ's resurrection, faith would be easier for me. The Cross by itself suffices me.'[39]

It is not hard to see what may have prompted this personal confession. Belief in a resurrection to eternal life can easily turn into an escapist refusal to accept the reality and significance of mortality, and appear like an egocentric expectation of post-mortem compensations for opportunities missed or happiness denied in this life. Moreover, it seems that such beliefs block from view very different – and in some respects deeper – perspectives on the significance of death, such as the idea that, in light of our fallenness and ineradicable sinfulness, death should not be seen as an evil, but as a gift. Indeed, so the argument might continue, isn't the entire Biblical narrative – from the creation myth in *Genesis* to the New Testament account of Christ's Incarnation, Passion and Resurrection – a paradigmatic example of *renunciation*? And shouldn't a life *in imitatio Christi* emulate that renunciatory and self-sacrificial dimension, even to the point of abandoning all expectation of a personal existence after death? But our Catholic believer may well acknowledge this deep and important self-renunciatory aspect of his faith and yet insist that, precisely because Christ's suffering and ascension *are* manifestations of God's unconditional love for his creation, the belief in immortality is not so much the product of selfish desire, but an expression of faith in a salvific love that assigns to human lives a role more substantial than that of fleeting episodes in an unfathomable divine dramaturgy.

Now, is there an independent vantage point from which one of these views could be judged to be the deeper? It is hard to see what it could be. In fact, the very dichotomy seems to me a false one. On close inspection, each perspective is rooted in an important feature of the Scriptural narrative and, as Peter Winch rightly says, 'there are no general rules in all this which philosophy somehow has the authority to

---

37   Rhees, *Rush Rhees on Religion and Philosophy*, p.284.
38   Rhees, *Rush Rhees on Religion and Philosophy*, p.348.
39   Simone Weil, *Letter to a Priest*, London: Routledge and Kegan Paul, 1953, p.55.

prescribe'.[40] What Rhees's frank admission shows is that there comes a point where the contemplative philosopher has completed his disinterested grammatical work and begins to speak for himself, and that he, too, must know when to fall silent, even if he thinks that our Catholic believer is walking on crutches that had better be kicked away.

As for Phillips' construal of immortality, it is quite possible that the reason why 'only a small number of people derive sustenance from ... [it]',[41] is that many believers are still suffering from grammatical confusions, and thus from a naive and superficial understanding of their own faith. On the other hand, even (unconfused) believers who applaud Phillips for providing a fine philosophical illumination of the concept of immortality *as far as it goes*, may still think it inferior to a theological treatment that offers different, and in their view more adequate, conceptions of divine love and omnipotence. The resulting disagreement, it seems to me, would be just as irresolvable as that between those who think that active euthanasia could be an expression of neighbourly love, and those for whom it is a serious violation of the Fifth Commandment.

The problem – or blessing – is that, unless the complex conceptual interconnections are forced into a formal system where such interpretive dissonances are artificially eliminated, the Christian outlook will always be ragged enough for a distinctly personal response to enter, irrespective of whether it receives an official *imprimatur*. Fortunately for Phillips, the contemplative philosopher lives in a grammatical Switzerland where the charge of heresy has no application, but the theologian's predicament is more precarious, since she is not merely a clarifier but a defender of the grammar of his faith. For her, the question of the relation between personal conviction and official Church doctrine becomes a particularly pressing one. The case of Eugen Drewermann provides an interesting illustration in this connection, not only because much of his scriptural exegesis is conducted in the spirit of Phillips' own approach, but because it confirms Simone Weil's impression that 'if the Church does not work out a satisfactory doctrine concerning so-called miraculous facts, a good many souls will be lost through its fault because of the apparent incompatibility between religion and science'.[42]

---

40 Winch, *Picture and Representation*, p.13.
41 Phillips, *Death and Immortality*, p.78.
42 Weil, *Letter to a Priest*, p.56.

4. Drewermann and Scripture as Mythology[43]

Drewermann, described by the German weekly *Der Spiegel* as 'the most popular and controversial theologian in the German-speaking world',[44] was suspended from his priestly and academic offices in 1991, primarily on account of his 'unorthodox' Scriptural exegesis and fervent criticism of institutionalized Catholicism. His condemnation revolves around the charge of theological reductivism and his refusal to give intellectual and verbal assent to particular interpretations of such key religious doctrines as the Virgin Birth, the Resurrection and the Ascension. The question, then, is whether Drewermann *is* guilty of distorting the grammar of religious belief, or whether his opponents' criticisms do not themselves constitute a *reductio* of any adequate attempt to guard the faith against positivist distortions. Since his oeuvre is extensive – Drewermann has written over forty books in which moral theology, psychology, philosophy, literature and Scriptural exegesis combine into an intricate and often densely argued analysis of religious belief –, and since a fair appraisal of Drewermann's position would require a separate paper, I shall confine myself to an illustration of his view and some excerpts from the official transcripts of his conversations with the Bishop of Fulda and other representatives of the Catholic Church.

It seems to me that the Church's condemnatory reaction to Drewermann's writings only confirms the appropriateness of Heine's warning that those who most vehemently defend the doctrinal elements of religious belief must also be the most careful not to lapse into positivist assumptions about meaning and truth. The official transcripts of Drewermann's defence – featuring also his superior, the Archbishop of Fulda, and the theologian Professor Eicher – reveal the nature of the dispute, and deserve to be quoted at some length.

On the issue of the Virgin Birth, the discussion proceeded as follows: [45]

---

43   Eugen Drewermann (1940–) studied philosophy, theology and psychoanalysis, before taking up his priestly vocation in Paderborn (Germany), where he also lectured on moral theology and worked as a church counsellor, until he was suspended from all these offices in 1991–1992. Drewermann's research record contains a commentated translation of the gospel of St Mark, a multi-volume work on psychoanalysis and moral theology, as well as depth-psychological interpretations of the gospel of St Luke, all of Grimm's fairytales, and Antoine de Saint-Exupéry's *Petit Prince*. The Catholic Church's disagreements with Drewermann began in 1983, when, in response to his criticisms of the Church's environmental policies, he was prohibited from training prospective teachers of religious studies, and were further exacerbated in 1996, when he advocated that divorcees be allowed to remarry in church. Drewermann emerged as a major figure in the public debate about the Catholic Church in the early 1990s, when his *Kleriker* (Munich: DTV, 1991) was published and became a bestseller, and when he became a familiar face on television chat shows and at religious conventions across the country.

44   *Der Spiegel* No. 52, 23 December 1991, p.61.

45   The extracts that follow are taken from Eugen Drewermann, *Worum es eigentlich geht. Protokoll einer Verurteilung* (Munich: Kösel-Verlag, Random House Group, 1992). Reproduced by permission. I have modified the structure of the conversation in such a way that the participants' contributions are strictly on the issues in question, and appear in crystallized form. As a consequence, the order of the contributions reproduced here does not necessarily

Archbishop: In the confession of faith, it is said: 'Conceived through the Holy Spirit, born of the Virgin Mary.' This statement is also about Mary's body. I'm not saying that we are just dealing with biological facticity, but affirmation of faith and biological fact are so intimately connected here, that, if I dissolve the connection and argue that this is not at all about Mary's body, or about whether Jesus was born without the contribution of a man, then – this is my conviction – this is irreconcilable with the Catholic faith.[46]

Drewermann: By a miracle *sensu strictu*, then?

Archbishop: Yes.

Drewermann: But there are passages in the New Testament, such as Mark 6, according to which Jesus had brothers and sisters.[47]

Archbishop: Catholic means ... that Mary had no other children. This must be made quite clear.[48] ... She did not have sexual intercourse with another man, so could not have had any other children. Jesus is Mary's only child. I think that, in the Catholic realm, this is uncontroversial.

Drewermann: And the virginity applies just as much to the process of giving birth as it does to the time before?

Archbishop: For me, that is a mystery. I don't know how the details are to be elaborated upon.[49] ... The decisive consideration is not biological virginity, but what it signifies and what the gospels, too, are out to proclaim, viz., that the Son of God comes into this world as a gift from God, not through human action, not by human procreation.[50]

The Archbishop's argumentation is curious. For if the decisive consideration is *not* a biological fact, then why insist that Drewermann must, nevertheless, affirm it in his teachings? Indeed, the point may be pressed even further, as Professor Eicher does when he says, in defence of Drewermann's position, that

> we have here a conceptual confusion between two different things. It is Catholic teaching that it is not an external event. According to Catholic dogma, the negation 'not an external event' is not false, and this is what Drewermann is saying here: no external event. Nobody involved in Catholic teaching is going to object to that. It is not an external event but an act of God.[51]

The Archbishop is not happy with this construal, however, because it denies that 'the Virgin Birth is, of course, also an external event, which takes place outside the

---

reflect the order in which they were originally made, though this has been indicated by the appropriate page references. All translations by the author unless otherwise specified.

46 Drewermann, *Worum es eigentlich geht*, p.127.
47 Drewermann, *Worum es eigentlich geht*, p.128.
48 Drewermann, *Worum es eigentlich geht*, p.129.
49 Drewermann, *Worum es eigentlich geht*, p.141.
50 Drewermann, *Worum es eigentlich geht*, p.131.
51 Drewermann, *Worum es eigentlich geht*, p.134.

soul'.[52] The problem with this view is that it introduces the language of external justification, proof, and evidence into a context in which it does not seem to belong. As Drewermann and Eicher point out:

> *Drewermann*: Is it a part of Catholic belief that any old physician, any Pharisee could have determined Mary's virginity, that even her husband would, in principle, have been able to do so? Is that a part of Catholic belief?[53] When Matthew affirms that Joseph himself can only learn about his wife's condition by means of a dream, then I conclude from this that it is the kind of virginity that can only be confirmed through an angelic messenger in a dream. In this sense, the virginity is real, but it is not corporeal, bodily, confirmable by this or that gynaecologist; this, I still maintain. But now you want to say that, in the Catholic understanding, the virginity is gynaecological, too.[54]

> *Eicher*: No, it's not that, if a physician had been there, he would have determined, with absolute certainty, that the hymen was intact, so this is the foundation of our faith. This would be absurd, as we are here at the level of God's actions, where the virginity reveals to us a mystery that cannot be grasped with the eyes of an unbeliever, of those who do not believe. That is what is at issue here.[55] ... One can find out that someone has been crucified, but it is impossible to find out that someone has been fathered by God. That is impossible, completely impossible. For it would mean that a physician could prove God's actions, and that is not possible.

> *Archbishop*: Agreed.[56]

Once again, the Archbishop's response is puzzling. On the one hand, he seems to admit that a physician could not show God to be at work in the world, in the way in which a scientist could confirm that electrostatic charges are at work in lightning. On the other hand, he also insists that Mary *was* a virgin in the gynaecological sense. In order to avoid the charge of self-contradiction, the Archbishop might now argue that his view has been misrepresented, that all he tried to say was that the *religious* significance of Mary's virginity was independent of what a physician might have said at the time, since not every extraordinary occurrence is *ipso facto* of religious relevance. However, this move would also ground an important article of faith on the occurrence of an event that, as Roy Holland has argued, could only be described as 'empirically certain and conceptually impossible',[57] and prompt a host of questions about the relation between religion, science and superstition.

In addition, there is the equally problematic issue of the alleged *uniqueness* of the events in question. As Drewermann has convincingly argued elsewhere that, far from being unique to the Christian faith, the idea of a virgin birth permeates the history of folklore and religious belief from Ancient Egyptian times onwards:

---

52   Drewermann, *Worum es eigentlich geht*, p.135.
53   Drewermann, *Worum es eigentlich geht*, p.138.
54   Drewermann, *Worum es eigentlich geht*, p.140.
55   Drewermann, *Worum es eigentlich geht*, p.137.
56   Drewermann, *Worum es eigentlich geht*, p.152.
57   Roy Holland, 'The Miraculous', in *Against Empiricism*, Totowa, NJ: Barnes and Noble, 1980, p.185.

in folktales from all over the world the appearance of an 'angel' so often introduces *the birth of a divine child.* In the language of myths, fairy tales, and dreams the symbol of the 'child' always stands for the basically religious permission to get a fresh start in life.[58]

The same holds for the concept of the Son of God, which appears to have an equally long history:

> The whole concept of the Son of God, who is born of a virgin, overshadowed by spirit and light (by Amun-Ra), born into the world was, as we see, completely worked out in ancient Egypt *as an idea* thousands of years before Christianity ... Only when the ancient religion died did people begin, for example, to write down the Osiris myth. Every cult that has to be propped up with explanations, because it isn't self-explanatory, is on its last legs ...

> Hence we must gratefully acknowledge the fact that the theology of divine sonship was not originally developed by Christianity but borrowed from Egypt.[59]

The Archbishop might, of course, acknowledge this genealogy of the concepts of the Virgin Birth and divine sonship, without having to give up his conviction that the gospel narratives are unique, since earlier employments of these concepts might simply be regarded as prophetic intimations or conceptual premonitions of God's incarnation in the historical Jesus. Even so, the insistence that such-and-such occurrences must have taken place as described, seems to place the faith on a weaker foundation than it deserves, since the falsity of the corresponding 'actual' reports would *ipso facto* undermine the credibility of Christian belief.

Parallel problems arise in connection with the Ascension narrative:

> *Drewermann*: Are we to think, in line with the old theological fundamentalism that the fishermen of Nazareth and Galilee were biologically healthy, not taken in by hallucinations or visions? So, if they say that he actually ascended into heaven, they must be right? But must we believe that? And is that the essence of the ascension narrative, in your opinion?

> *Archbishop*: I would, in any case, have no objection to understanding it that way.

> *Drewermann*: But do we have to – that is my question – do we have to understand it that way?[60]

> *Eicher (to Archbishop)*: You, too, would agree that scepticism is appropriate in regard to the suggestion that we now have to believe that he slowly took off from the Earth, or something like that?

> *Archbishop*: Yes, I am sceptical about that.

---

58 Eugen Drewermann, *Discovering the God Child Within*, New York: Crossroads, 1994, p.50.

59 Drewermann, *Discovering the God Child Within*, pp.73–74.

60 Drewermann, *Worum es eigentlich geht*, p.93.

Drewermann: If we put the matter positively now, we can take it that the ascension was no historical event, determinable in space and time, but still believe that Jesus is sitting to the right hand of the Father, and add a special day of celebration to the Church calendar.[61] ... It is impossible to determine historically, nor is it necessary to know or to assume as a fact, that something took place in space and time, and that it could have been photographed. That is unnecessary.

Archbishop: I cannot say whether the ascension could have been photographed.

Drewermann: In that case, the Ascension is not historical in the relevant sense.

Archbishop: That is the conclusion you are drawing!

Drewermann: What is yours, then? If it could not have been photographed, is that to do with the chemical coating on the film?

Eicher: Come now, the Bishop is not saying that. It cannot be photographed. Otherwise our salvation would depend on physical motion.

Drewermann: ... If something cannot be photographed, then it cannot be perceived by the human retina, either. For the physics that structures the chemical coating of an Agfa film and our eyes ...[62]

Archbishop: I don't know what to say, exactly, whether it could have been photographed or not, and shall leave that open. I am convinced, however, that the apostles really experienced, saw, etc. a fact.[63]

The Archbishop's remarks reveal a curious tension between his reluctance to view Christ's ascension as an occurrence susceptible to the techniques of scientific measurement, on the one hand, and his agnosticism on whether it could have been photographed, on the other. As Drewermann is quick to point out, if one is prepared to couch Christ's ascension in the language-game of photography, then neither should one hesitate to admit that what Wittgenstein calls 'the proof-game' *does* apply to religious belief, after all. If we play the photography game, in other words, we must play the evidence game as well. Indeed, given the Archbishop's conviction 'that the apostles really experienced, saw, etc. a fact', it is hard to see how the grammar of the language of facts could be excluded from consideration.

In response to this objection, Archbishop Degenhardt might, however, say that his insistence on the historicity of the ascension and resurrection narratives is by no means an idiosyncratic violation of the grammar of faith, but, on the contrary, the application of an interpretive hint provided in the gospel narratives themselves. For doesn't John (20:24–31), for example, tell us that the apostle Thomas's doubts about Jesus' resurrection were conclusively dispelled after he had, quite literally, touched the Jesus' wounds? If so, then, contrary to Phillips, Drewermann and Professor Eicher, the notions of proof and evidence do not only have a foothold in religious

---

61   Drewermann, *Worum es eigentlich geht*, p.94.
62   Drewermann, *Worum es eigentlich geht*, p.94.
63   Drewermann, *Worum es eigentlich geht*, p.97.

faith, but are an essential part of its grammar. That this is so, appears to be further confirmed by the seemingly unambiguous ending of John's gospel, according to which

> there were many other signs that Jesus worked and the disciples saw, but they are not recorded in this book. These are recorded so that you may believe that Jesus is the Christ, the Son of God, and that believing this you may have life through his name.[64]

But now, are we seriously to say that John 20:24–30 betrays a proto-positivist attitude in its depiction of a man's journey from doubt to certainty? A closer look at the text reveals that John's story of Thomas's reconciliation with the faith is not as clear-cut as the hypothetical riposte suggests. For one thing, there is Jesus' critical addendum: 'You believe because you can see me. Happy are those who have not seen me and yet believe',[65] which suggests a reading of the story in which Thomas – and to some extent the author of the gospel himself – is portrayed as the kind of believer who needs certain sorts of experiences in support of an otherwise vague and uncertain religiosity, and thus also as an example of belief that is always conditional – 'unless I see the burning bush ...', 'unless the statue weeps ...', 'unless the Pope walks on water ...', 'unless I see the risen Christ with my own eyes ...', and so on.

Thomas's reaction to his fellow disciples' claim that they have encountered the risen Christ is not the response of a cautious believer like Theresa of Avila, who is aware that mystical experiences which seem to be of the divine may in fact be the work of the devil. It is, rather, the response of a sceptic whose faith is weak, since he cannot follow Christ except on crutches that he does not really need. And if it is objected that Thomas's encounter with Christ must, after all, have been *real*, then more will have to be said about what a 'real' encounter with the divine amounts to. Saul's encounter with God on the road to Damascus was certainly real, not least because of Saul's transformation and conversion in word and deed. But should we, in deference to Archbishop Degenhardt, leave it an open question whether that encounter could have been photographed? And how important for belief in Christ's ascension is it that the question *is* left open? Drewermann plausibly asks:

> But what did we theologians accomplish when over the centuries we kept choosing an increasingly rational and 'realistic' language for interpreting religious symbols? The more this language progressed, the more people it had to exclude from the circle of believers.[66]

Drewermann's concern to save the spirit of religious texts from the distortions of a certain kind of realism is easily mistaken for a reductivist analysis of religion, in which the sacred writings are simply elliptical for a grand metaphor of human existence, with no other authority to support them than the vision of a worthy moral ideal. But this would be a serious misconstrual of Drewermann's position, since his approach to Scriptural exegesis rejects the very terms in which the Archbishop

---

64 John, 20:30–31.

65 John, 20:29.

66 Drewermann, *Discovering the God Child Within*, p.19.

is couching his objection, and regards the literal and the metaphorical as a false dichotomy:

> For us moderns there is no longer any direct access to the ways mythical narratives think and speak: Whenever we suppose to take them 'literally' we misunderstand them. And whenever we try to read them 'symbolically,' we risk deflating the seriousness of their claims on us and flattening their unconditional validity into something arbitrary and aesthetic.[67]

But there is another reason why it would be hasty to condemn Drewermann's interpretation of the Gospel message as a blatant distortion of its 'real' meaning: it is just as deeply anchored in the Christian exegetical tradition as the Archbishop's claim that the Ascension story must not be reduced to a metaphor of Jesus' righteousness. This interpretive disagreement about the Ascension narrative seems to me not only parallel to the earlier one between Phillips and his Catholic 'opponent' on the issue of immortality but, in the final analysis, just as intractable. Concerned to defend the faith against Drewermann's 'reductivism', the archbishop gravitates towards a spiritually impoverished positivism; while Drewermann, justifiably concerned to preserve the distinctive nature of religious narrative, moves in the opposite direction and, like Phillips, can see in the historicization of biblical imagery little more than 'absurd superstition'.[68] What the dispute throws into relief is not only the urgent need – rightly identified by Weil – for a satisfactory account of the relation between religion and science, and the insight expressed in Heine's warning against a certain kind of argumentative garrulity in these matters, but Augustine's observation that it is better for ordinary religious believers not to trouble themselves too much with what philosophers and theologians may have to say about the various aspects of their faith.

In Ch. 6, Bk 1 of his *Confessions*, Augustine concludes his own reflections on God's infinity and changeless nature with the following comment:

> Need it concern me if some people cannot understand this? Let them ask what it means, and be glad to ask: but they may content themselves with the question alone. For it is better for them to find you and leave the question unanswered than to find the answer without finding you.[69]

At this point, many will be tempted join Peter Winch in asking the further question, 'Where does philosophy end and religion begin in such a case?'; and there would be nothing wrong with the question, so long as it was also answered in the spirit of Heine's and Augustine's admonitions. Winch himself, I am pleased to say, does so answer it when he soberly concludes: 'That is a question better not asked',[70] and I think Phillips would agree.

---

67 Drewermann, *Discovering the God Child Within*, p.32.
68 Drewermann, *Worum es eigentlich geht*, p.35.
69 Augustine, *Confessions*, trans. by R.S. Pine-Coffin, Harmondsworth: Penguin, 1976, p.27.
70 Winch, 'Picture and Representation', p.13.

Chapter IV

Pictures of Eternity –
A Reply to Mario von der Ruhr

D.Z. Phillips

1. Pictures and Logic

In my reply to Stephen Mulhall, I insisted that Wittgenstein's philosophy is misrepresented if it is seen as simply a therapeutic technique for clearing up confusions between the grammars of different uses of language. Wittgenstein has not given up on the central question of philosophy concerning the nature of reality, the intelligibility of things. In Rhees's work, as I tried to show, this leads to an emphasis on what he called 'the interlocking intelligibility of language'. This is not to deny the intimate relationship between this wider concern and grammatical clarification, because a subliming of a specific form of discourse can lead to a distorted view of the interlocking intelligibility: the place of a certain form of discourse in it may be distorted or denied altogether. Religious beliefs have suffered at the hands of believing and non-believing philosophers in this respect, and much of my work in the philosophy of religion has been an attempt to rectify this situation or, at least, to get it recognized. In the view of many philosophers, my efforts have led to a reductive analysis of religious belief. Mario von der Ruhr does not share this general criticism, but does have questions about my discussions of belief in eternal life, or, as he prefers to put it, belief in an afterlife. He puts that '*after*' in italics, but would agree that that does not settle anything. We must ask what such talk amounts to. He grapples, in an interesting way, with what I have to say. This, I suspect, is partly because he is grappling with difficulties of his own at the same time. The difficulties can be expressed thus: how do we picture eternity?

Many have thought that after his own criticisms of the so-called 'picture theory of meaning' in the *Tractatus*, the notion of a picture simply drops out of Wittgenstein's philosophy. This is not so. He has much to say about pictures in his 'Lectures on Religious Belief'. He discusses, in his *Philosophical Investigations*, the distinction between representational pictures and genre pictures, and its importance in language. In his last work, *On Certainty*, the notion of a world-picture is central to its concerns. Although Wittgenstein's treatment of the notion of a picture develops and changes enormously in these works, it never goes away. This suggests that it is of some importance.

When one first encounters the *Tractatus*'s claim that a proposition pictures reality, it is natural to suppose that the picture does so when true, but fails to do so when false. But that would be a misunderstanding of the kind of reality which is said to show itself in the picturing relation. What a proposition shows us when it pictures reality, is a possible state of affairs; it shows us what the possibility of truth and falsity amounts to. So there is just as much reality in the proposition 'It is raining', when it is false, as there is when it is true. In the *Tractatus*, we are told that what shows the picturing relation between a proposition and the world is a method of projection. This is thought to be similar to the way in which a map depicts the surface of the earth. It has been claimed that whereas the *Tractatus* account is adequate for fact-stating propositions, Wittgenstein, in his later work, came to realize that propositions are more varied and, therefore, have to be analysed differently. As Peter Winch has pointed out, this misrepresents the radical criticisms Wittgenstein makes of his earlier view. Little is said, in the *Tractatus*, about the nature of the method of projection. It is as though its application can be taken for granted. It is as though the proposition, when true, reaches out to a state of affairs, as in the case of 'The cat is on the mat'. But as we can see with the proposition, 'The cat was on the mat yesterday', matters are far more complicated even in the context of factual propositions. But in Wittgenstein's later philosophy, the notion of a method of projection gives way to an emphasis on different uses of language.[1] One cannot assume that these uses have a common form or that they all picture reality in the same way. Certainly, that assumption cannot be made where religious pictures are concerned.

Von der Ruhr recognizes that the difference between a believer and a non-believer is not like the difference between one who asserts, and one that denies that cats exist. If I come to believe that unicorns exist, I admit to the existence of an *additional* kind of animal. I consider whether unicorns exist within a wider conceptual category with which I am already acquainted. But if I come to believe that there is a God, into what wider category do I place him? There is none. Instead, I come to recognize a new *kind* of reality, the reality of the divine. With God, divinity and reality are one.

Von der Ruhr says that, as between the believer and the non-believer, 'What is at issue … is the expression of different, though by no means disconnected, ways of conceptualizing human experience' (p.56).[2] It would be better to say that what is at issue are different *kinds* of experience. As von der Ruhr says, what is important is to recognize the categorial differences between them, and to combat the temptation to submit them to 'a universal standard of assessment [which] is difficult to overcome' (p.57). Wittgenstein's discussions of 'pictures' is an attempt to overcome it. With respect to religious pictures, he discusses the complaint that, with pictures of God, in contrast to pictures of aunts or plants, we never see that which the picture pictures, and replies, 'The absurdity is I've never taught him that technique of using this picture.'[3]

---

    1   I have benefited enormously from Peter Winch's discussions in 'Language, Thought and World in Wittgenstein's *Tractatus*' and 'Wittgenstein: Picture and Representation', in *Trying to Make Sense*, Oxford: Blackwell, 1987. In 'On Really Believing' in *Wittgenstein and Religion*, pp.33–55, I did not do justice to how radical Wittgenstein's criticisms of his earlier view are, preferring simply to insist that there are a multiplicity of methods of projection.
    2   All quotations from von der Ruhr will be from 'Philosophy, Theology and Heresy' in the present volume, unless otherwise indicated.
    3   Ludwig Wittgenstein, *Lectures and Conversations on Aesthetics, Psychology, and Religious Belief*, ed. Cyril Barrett, Oxford: Blackwell, 1966, p.63.

Consider Michelangelo's *The Creation of Adam*. Wittgenstein says that no one would take the near-naked old man to be a portrait of God.[4] Does that mean that Michelangelo did not portray God in the picture? No. God is in the picture, but does not enter it *as a picture*.

To see God in the picture, one would have to mention the significance of the fact that the old man in it is almost naked, not robed in the pomp of kingship. It is an expression of creation as an act of self-emptying, rather than as a demonstration of power. Similarly, the nakedness of Adam is an expression of a creaturehood involving casting off the vain apparels of this world. The picture is not a representational picture, but a genre picture.[5] When asked what it says, Wittgenstein wants to say that it says itself;[6] that the 'whole weight is in the picture'.[7] The same could be said of Michelangelo's painting *The Last Judgement*.

Philosophically speaking, these pictures contribute to the concept-formation of our idea of God. Von der Ruhr sees my work as an attempt to give a non-reductive analysis of such pictures. The difficulty is that we can be easily misled, since although the picture is in the foreground, its actual application is in the background. The surface grammar of religious belief may hide its depth grammar from us.

Compare a picture of a kettle boiling on a fire with steam coming out of its spout, with Michelangelo's picture of God. Our common understanding tells us that it is a picture of water boiling, although we do not see the water. The water is represented in the picture, but does not enter it *as a representation*. But this is a contingent fact. The kettle in the picture could have been transparent, in which case we would see the boiling water. With God, matters are very different. God's representational absence from the picture is not a contingent or unfortunate fact. God *cannot* be in the picture *as a picture*. But that does not mean that Michelangelo failed to paint a picture of God. To appreciate this, one must understand the logic of the picture. Von der Ruhr is correct in thinking that I strive in my work to make that appreciation available to believers and non-believers alike.

2. My Analyses and Their Reception

So far, I have been rehearsing features of my work which will be familiar to readers of it.[8] But what of the way it has been received? This question is the starting point of von der Ruhr's misgivings. If, as I claim, my analyses 'leave everything where it is', von der Ruhr argues (p.60):

> then it seems that, at least as far as the key religious concepts are concerned, there should be no major interpretive disagreements between philosophers or theologians and ordinary believers. What one finds is, of course, exactly the opposite, as Phillips himself admits.

---

4   Wittgenstein seems to have forgotten about philosophers.
5   See Wittgenstein, *Philosophical Investigations*, Part I, para. 522.
6   Wittgenstein, *Philosophical Investigations*, Part I, para. 523.
7   Wittgenstein, *Lectures and Conversations*, p.72.
8   For a more detailed discussion of these features see 'On Really Believing' and 'Religious Beliefs and Language Games' in *Wittgenstein and Religion*.

There are three comments I want to make about these remarks.

The first comment concerns the importance of making a distinction between von der Ruhr's reference to warring interpretations, and the notion of 'description' in Wittgenstein's philosophy. To 'describe' religious beliefs, for him, is not to offer an interpretation of them, but to show the conceptual place they occupy in religious life. But one cannot take a short-cut in this matter, simply by asking believers for their descriptions in this sense. The ability to give a philosophical account of one's belief is not the same as the ability to believe. So the account given by a believer has no *automatic* philosophical warrant. It, too, must be conceptually faithful to the belief. If we say, 'Who better to ask than the believers?', we should reflect on the fact that if we asked 'thinking people' to tell us what they mean by 'thinking', a confused Cartesianism would be returned with a thumping majority. We cannot do philosophy by Gallup poll.[9] Religion, like 'thinking', can be the victim of widespread friendly fire.

My second comment concerns von der Ruhr's view that I could say, whenever anyone disagrees with me, philosophically, that they are talking about *confused*, not genuine religious beliefs. That is too hurried. In the work to which von der Ruhr refers, it does indicate that as one possibility. I'll return to it in a moment.[10] But far more often in my work, I am discussing what I take to be confused philosophical accounts of genuine religious beliefs. After all, it is the surface grammar of those beliefs, among other things, which may mislead us in the first place. On the other hand, the possibility to which von der Ruhr refers is a corrective to the view that confusions about religion are always parasitic on the genuine form they distort. That is why I emphasized, recently, that there is a kind of religion which is, by nature, superstitious, and makes an independent contribution to that condition. This is the religion which offers us a 'somewhere over the rainbow' where 'dreams really do come true'.[11] As I said in my reply to Mulhall, one would have to know a person really well in order to judge whether a confused philosophical account of religious belief reflects a confused religious belief in that person's life.

The third comment which needs to be made, concerns von der Ruhr's application of his misgivings to the belief that concerns him most in his paper, namely, belief in an eternal life. Near the end of *Death and Immortality* I say:

> Of course it may be true, and probably is true, that at the moment, only a small number of people derive sustenance from the pictures of immortality we have been discussing.[12]

Von der Ruhr takes me to be referring *to the few who accept my philosophical account of belief in eternal life*. He writes (p.60):

---

9   See my *Religion and Friendly Fire*, p.3.

10   See my *Religion without Explanation*, p.189–90.

11   See 'Just Say the Word', section II: 'Confused Practices' in *Religion and Wittgenstein's Legacy*, ed. D.Z. Phillips and Mario von der Ruhr, Aldershot: Ashgate, 2005, pp.174–78. See also essays in *From Fantasy to Faith*.

12   Phillips, *Death and Immortality*, p.78.

The assessment is a sobering one, for if Phillips has been faithful to his own methodological guidelines, would one not expect the result of his enquiry to be applauded by more than just a few?

But I am not referring at all to the philosophical reception of my work, but to the religious belief itself. I believe, rightly or wrongly, that the belief itself is on the wane, and that few derive sustenance from it. Hence the ending of the book:

> If one looks at the pictures of immortality which once were strong from the point of view of the lives people lead now in our society, what they consider to be important, and what they are afraid of, there may be good reason to describe the future by an ironic use of the words of St. John and say that we see 'a new heaven and a new earth … for the former things are passed away'.[13]

3. The Charge of Reductionism

Von der Ruhr and I agree about certain confused conceptions of eternal life: (a) it does not involve belief in 'soul-substances' (p.61); (b) it is not a 'transcendentalized version of "see you later"'; it is not a matter of buried corpses which rise from the dead leading to new bodies (p.61); it is not a matter of post-mortem reunion of human beings after death (p.61); it is not a matter of making changing things changeless (p.62); it is not like 'a never-ending holiday on the Costa del Sol' (p.62). Like me, von der Ruhr thinks it is important to be clear about these matters. He and I also agree that many philosophers, on the basis of one or more of these denials, have accused me of giving a reductive account of eternal life. What of von der Ruhr himself? He thinks that a Catholic believer, who is in sympathy with the general tenor of my criticisms, may, nevertheless, feel disconcerted with at least one aspect of my account, namely, that I seem to suggest that belief in eternal life is no more than *an attitude to this present life*, and, as a result, have not said enough about the religious realities of an *after*life. This Catholic would not be alone in his view. Many of my critics share it. Von der Ruhr, too, appeals to the passage my critics never fail to quote in support of their view:

> Eternity is not an extension of this present life, but a mode of judging it. Eternity is not *more* life, but this life seen under certain moral and religious modes of thought. This is precisely what seeing this life *sub specie aeternitatis* would amount to.[14]

Von der Ruhr's own comments suggest that I would be happy to concur with the judgement that, for me, belief in eternal life is to be construed as an attitude to *this* life.

Immortality, in Phillips's view, does not involve continued personal existence beyond the grave, but a way of viewing *this* life, and the promise of eternal life in Christ is not to be understood predictively, as a future event, but evaluatively, as an admonitory picture that reveals human action to fall under a certain kind of (timeless)

---

13   Phillips, *Death and Immortality*, p.78.
14   Phillips, *Death and Immortality*, p.49.

judgement – 'in turning away from the temporal to the eternal, the believer is said to attain immortality and overcome death' (p.61).[15]

What is to be made of this charge of reductionism? Before tackling it directly, there is one retraction I should like to make. As a result of my analysis of the language of belief in eternal life, I concluded that:

> It is a grammatical confusion to think that this language is referential or descriptive. It is an expression of value. If one asks what it says, the answer is that it says itself.[16]

These claims had unfortunate results, namely, a dispute over the words 'reference' and 'description' which reduced them to contextless labels. I was asked, 'Doesn't the belief in eternal life refer to *something*?', and so on. I do not want this kind of war over words. So by all means say that the belief refers to or describes something, as long as you realise that no clarificatory work has been done by saying this. Are religious pictures of the Last Judgement representational pictures? Could they be? Is the only alternative to say that the picture simply expresses an attitude to *this* life? I deny that this last alternative expresses my view, and that to think that it does, ignores certain aspects of my work. I shall try to establish these conclusions in the last section of my paper. Before doing so, however, we will be helped on our way by seeing why von der Ruhr thinks that a famous dispute between a Catholic theologian and his church throws light on my situation.

4. My Friend, Eugen Drewermann?

In 1991, the Catholic theologian Eugen Drewermann was suspended from all his priestly and academic offices by the Church. Von der Ruhr quotes from the official transcripts of the conversations between Drewermann, on the one hand, and the Archbishop and Bishop of Fulda, and the theologian, Professor Eicher, on the other.[17] Drewermann's views were deemed to be heretical. Von der Ruhr sees similarities between my views and Drewermann's method of scriptural exegesis. The implication is obvious: I claim to leave everything where it is, but what if, in fact, my views are as heretical as the Church thought Drewermann's to be? After all, plenty of philosophers are prepared to call my views reductive, prescriptive and subversive. How are we to move beyond this disagreement?

For von der Ruhr, the disagreement cannot be settled by a simple appeal to a catechism. On the one hand, he is attracted to the idea that a catechism plays a crucial role in the concept-formation of a belief in God. Wittgenstein says, 'The word "God" is amongst the earliest learnt – pictures and catechisms, etc.'[18] On the other hand, von der Ruhr thinks there is good reason to heed Heine's warning against a catechism

---

15 Phillips, *Death and Immortality*, p.50.

16 Phillips, *Death and Immortality*, p.147.

17 I am not acquainted with Drewermann's work. My argument should be taken to apply only to the quotations provided by von der Ruhr.

18 *Lectures and Conversations*, p.59. I doubt whether we can still say that the word 'God' is amongst the earliest learnt.

that imports bad philosophical arguments in an effort to justify religious beliefs. What is more, he finds such importations in the arguments of the Archbishop in his discussions with Drewermann. For example, the archbishop is clearly in something of a muddle in discussing the Ascension. It is impossible to reconcile (p.72)

his reluctance to view Christ's ascension as an occurrence susceptible to the techniques of scientific measurement, on the one hand, and his agnosticism on whether it could have been photographed, on the other.

The following exchange occurs in the conversation (p.71):

Eicher (to Archbishop): You, too would agree that scepticism is appropriate in regard to the suggestion that we now have to believe that he slowly took off from the Earth, or something like that?

Archbishop: Yes, I am sceptical about that.

Drewermann: If we put the matter positively now, we can take it that the ascension was no historical event, determinable in space and time, but still believe that Jesus is sitting to the right hand of the Father ... It is impossible to determine historically, nor is it necessary to know or to assume as a fact, that something took place in space and time, and that it could have been photographed. That is unnecessary.

Archbishop: I cannot say whether the ascension could have been photographed.

Drewermann: In that case, the ascension is not historical in the relevant sense.

Archbishop: That is the conclusion *you* are drawing!

I was in a discussion where a philosopher had no difficulty whatsoever in talking of Christ, in his Ascension, moving off from the surface of the earth. 'After all,' he argued, 'how else can one get from A to B?' A voice from the audience interjected: 'And then?' The philosopher replied, 'I don't know. Maybe he disintegrated.' What on earth has any of this to do with a religious belief in Christ's Ascension?

On the other hand, however badly the archbishop argued, von der Ruhr asks whether it is not possible to say that he is right in seeing that 'the historicity of the ascension and resurrection narratives is by no means an idiosyncratic violation of the grammar of faith' (p.72). Didn't Thomas allay his doubts by touching the wounds of the risen Christ? Didn't Christ appear to many others before his ascension (p.72)?

If so, then contrary to Phillips, Drewermann and Professor Eicher, the notions of proof and evidence do not only have a foothold in religious faith, but are an essential part of its grammar.

But no sooner does he say this, than von der Ruhr doubts whether these narratives should be read in such a proto-positivist way (see p.73).

Clearly, von der Ruhr is pulled in different directions. What is his final verdict on Drewermann? He shows how Drewermann has been misunderstood. There are clear parallels with misunderstandings of my own analysis of belief in eternal life (p.73):

Drewermann's concern to save the spirit of religious texts from the distortions of a certain kind of realism is easily mistaken for a reductionist analysis of religion, in which the sacred writings are simply elliptical for a grand metaphor of human existence, with no other authority to support them than its vision of a worthy moral ideal.

Von der Ruhr says that this is a serious misconstrual of Drewermann's view. What he is trying to do is to break down the dichotomy between the literal and the metaphysical in certain contexts. I, too, can avail myself of this defence, since I have insisted that if 'literal' meaning is standard meaning, then religious pictures which say themselves, express their literal meaning in doing so. Why assume that 'the literal' is confined to what is empirically factual? That could only be so if the empirically factual were, in all contexts, the standard meaning of our discourse; something which is clearly not the case. Given these parallels between Drewermann and myself, can I accept him, without reservation, as a philosophical friend? That acceptance may be premature. Drewermann says (p.74):

> For us moderns there is no longer any direct access to the ways mythical narratives think and speak: Whenever we suppose to take them 'literally' we misunderstand them. And whenever we try to read them 'symbolically, we risk deflating the seriousness of their claims on us and flattening their unconditional validity into something arbitrary and aesthetic.

There are a number of unresolved questions about Drewermann's description of our predicament and his response to it. Does he see himself as a reformer or reformulator of religious language to meet modern needs? I have always resisted any suggestion of being such a reformer. If Drewermann is going to offer alternative interpretations, I am not. I am interested in *what is there to be seen.*[19] To talk, as he does, of the mythological character of religious language runs the danger he is aware of, namely, to suggest that it can be put in some other way without loss.[20] More generally, if, as Drewermann claims, we have no direct access to religious narratives, how does he know whether or not 'the seriousness of their claims' is being deflated, or that they once enjoyed an 'unconditional validity'?

For these reasons, I am not sure to what extent Drewermann is a philosophical friend. In this respect, I have no hesitation in recognizing a kindred spirit in von der Ruhr, and yet, I cannot be content with his own reaction to the disagreement between

---

19 The question of the availability of the sense of religious belief *to anyone* is a complex one, but I think it has to be an ideal for a contemplative philosophy. For disagreements on this issue, which I cannot discuss here, see H.O. Mounce, 'The Aroma of Coffee', *Philosophy* 64:248 (1989), 159–73, and my reply, 'From Coffee to Carmelites' in *Wittgenstein and Religion*. For different aspects of the disagreement see John T. Edelman, 'Pointing Unknowingly: Fantasy, Nonsense and "Religious Understanding"', *Philosophical Investigations* 21:1 (1998), 63–87, and my reply, 'An Audience for Philosophy of Religion?', in *Philosophy of Religion for a New Century. Essays in Honour of Eugene Thomas Long*, eds. J. Hackett and J. Wallulis, Dordrecht: Kluwer Academic Publishers, 2004.

20 Mario von der Ruhr has warned against this danger. See 'Is Animism Alive and Well?', in *Can Religion Be Explained Away?*, ed. D.Z. Phillips, Basingstoke: Macmillan and St. Martin's Press, 1996.

Drewermann and the Church. Arguing that what both emphasize is to be found in Catholicism, and that the disagreement between them is intractable, he gives two reasons, one weak, and one extremely complex, for letting matters rest in silence there.

Von der Ruhr's weak reason is to remind us of Heine's warning about an 'argumentative garrulity in these matters' (p.74). The reply is simple: argue philosophically in another way. One cannot and should not be silent about the fact that, *on the basis of what he has given us*, von der Ruhr has not shown that the archbishop has a case.

Von der Ruhr's second reason is extremely complex. Following Augustine, he says that 'ordinary believers' should not 'trouble themselves too much with what philosophers and theologians may have to say about the various aspects of their faith' (p.74). I agree that religious believers are not obliged to be interested in philosophical questions, or to be able to give a philosophical account of their faith. When Socrates equated 'understanding' with 'giving an account', he was combating the philistinism of the Sophists. Nevertheless, the claim cannot be justified. A believer is not obliged to give such an account.[21] Augustine, recognising that the attempt to do so can be dangerous, concludes: 'it is better for them to find you and leave the question unanswered than to find the answer without finding you'.[22]

The matter is complex. It is not as easy, as it was for Augustine, to distinguish between intellectuals and ordinary believers. Also, much depends on the urgency and seriousness of the questions being asked. It may be impossible to put the questions aside. People do not choose to have such difficulties; they simply find them arising. There is also the danger of Augustine's advice descending into condescension. It is as well to remember that there are other voices, within the Catholic tradition, acutely aware of this danger. Here is one of them:

'I don't want to study pathology', said one coward to me. 'I don't even want to know where my liver is or what it is for; I'd be imagining I had the disease I happened to be reading about. What's my doctor for and what do I pay him for if it isn't to cure me? I turn over my responsibility to him, and if he kills me, that's his look-out. And so with the priest; I'm not going to dabble in thoughts about my origin and my destiny; the whence and the whither and the wherefore, and whether there is a God or isn't, and the nature of God, and what the life hereafter is like, if there is one; all those things only give me a headache and rob me of the time and energy I need for earning my children's bread. Let the priest look to it: that's his business to find out all about it, and celebrate the mass, and absolve me when I confess my sins on my death-bed. And if he deceives himself and me, that's his look-out; he will answer for himself. As for me, there's no deception in believing.'[23]

Unamuno's verdict on the character he is depicting is unequivocal.

---

21   I owe this point to Rush Rhees. See *In Dialogue with the Greeks*, vol. II: *Plato and Dialectic*, p.22.

22   Augustine, *Confessions*, p.27.

23   Allen Lacy, *Miguel de Unamuno: The Rhetoric of Existence*, The Hague: Mouton Press, 1967, p.107.

Holy ignorance – what is that? Ignorance is not and cannot be holy. What is the meaning of that about enjoying the peace of one who has never caught a glimpse of the supreme mystery, never looked beyond life or beyond death? Yes, I know the old song. I know the one about 'How soft a pillow is the catechism, my son: sleep and believe; here in bed is heaven gained'. Coward race …[24]

Many may find that voice too strident, swinging too much to the opposite extreme from a version of Augustine's advice deemed to be condescension. But one couldn't say that of the following remarks by my teacher, Rush Rhees:

> Priests are wont to say that there are no new sins and no new difficulties. I know what they mean. But in a sense this is wrong. For the problems and difficulties of *everyone* to whom religion is more than a formality are new difficulties. And – for what my opinion is worth – they should be treated so.[25]

5. The Case of the Discontented Catholic

Von der Ruhr thinks that a Catholic, who is generally sympathetic to my work, may nevertheless be discontented with my alleged reduction of belief in eternal life in an attitude to this life. Von der Ruhr's own view is that 'Phillips plausibly insists that religious utterances are much more akin to expressions of attitude than they are to hypotheses or predictions' (p.65). But that is not my view. I think that equating the belief in eternal life with an attitude to this life is a reductive account of the belief. Wittgenstein thought so too. Winch shows that while he talked of religious pictures dominating the lives of believers,

> it's also true that he opposed an 'reductive' account of religious belief of a kind that would attempt to eliminate the believer's 'picture' as inessential and talk simply about him as having a certain 'attitude'.[26]

That much is clear from the following example:

> Suppose someone before going to China, when he might never see me again, said to me: 'We might see one another after death' – would I necessarily say that I don't understand him? I might say [want to say] simply, 'Yes I *understand* him entirely'.
>
> Lewy: 'In this case, you might only mean that he expressed a certain attitude'.
>
> I would say 'No, it isn't the same as saying 'I'm very fond of you' – and it may not be the same as saying anything else. It says what it says. Why should you be able to substitute anything else?[27]

---

24 Lacy, *Miguel de Unamuno*, p.105.
25 Rush Rhees, 'Christianity and Growth of Understanding', in *Rush Rhees on Religion and Philosophy*, p.384.
26 Winch, 'Picture and Representation', p.62.
27 Wittgenstein, *Lectures and Conversations*, pp.70–71.

Von der Ruhr could still point out that Wittgenstein's example has a *predictive* form, and that it is this aspect of belief in eternal life that I fail to deal with satisfactorily. He points out that thinkers who have influenced me also have difficulties in understanding Christ's Resurrection. Simone Weil, for example, says that she would find it easier to believe without it.[28] Moreover, she thinks that it is a harmful belief precisely because it involves belief 'in the prolongation of life (which) robs death of its purpose'.[29] Isn't this my view too? If so, the discontented Catholic would say that belief in the resurrection 'has been an essential element of the Christian faith from its beginnings' (p.63).

The discontented Catholic's view seems to be this: belief in eternal life entails survival after death. Because I cannot accept this, I reduce the belief to an attitude to this life. But the predictive form of the belief *shows* the entailment I reject. It is clear, however, that one would face a major difficulty in applying this argument to Wittgenstein. Without doubt, the language he refers to has a predictive form, but it does *not* entail belief in survival after death. That is clear from the following remarks:

> Not only is there no guarantee of the temporal immortality of the human soul, that is to say of its eternal survival after death: but in any case, this assumption completely fails to accomplish the purpose for which it has always been intended. Or is some riddle solved by my surviving for ever? Is not this eternal life as much a riddle as our present life?[30]

The predictive form of language does *not* simply entail survival after death. The latter notion, according to Wittgenstein, actually *obscures* what the language has always meant. An example from Winch's own experience makes the same point. It concerns a child who was suffering from a terrible degenerative disease of the nervous system who was certainly going to die in the near future. The child, Winch tells us, 'was in constant distress, incontinent and already virtually without the normal functions of human intelligence and perception'.[31] In a conversation with the child's mother, she said:

> That she firmly believed that one day, after death, the whole family would be together again and that her afflicted child would be there as a whole, normal human being – in full possession of the developed faculties which he had never had and never, in life, would have.[32]

If one understands the mother's words as a prediction of what will happen *in a prolongation of life after death*, obvious difficulties would have to be found.

> After infancy the child had never been a person with sound human faculties. Yet it was crucial to what his mother was saying that she would be reunited with *this child with*

---

28 Weil, *Letter to a Priest*, p.55.
29 Weil, *Gravity and Grace*, London: Routledge and Kegan Paul, 1963, p.33.
30 Ludwig Wittgenstein, *Tractatus Logico-Philosophicus*, London: Routledge and Kegan Paul, 1961, 6.4312.
31 Winch, 'Picture and Representation', p.65.
32 Winch, 'Picture and Representation', p.65.

normal human faculties. But since the child had never existed as a normal human being, it is unclear what it would mean to meet *him* as a normal human being – with no possible conception of how he might become one. Such a possibility is cut off by death, quite apart from the purely *medical* impossibility of recovery in such a case.[33]

To say that God will transform the child by methods unknown to us, is simply to sweep these difficulties under the carpet by using words without a contextual application. Our misunderstanding is in thinking that we have to overcome these difficulties if we are to understand what the mother is saying. Winch's point is that *if we do raise them, we never will.*

What, then, is the mother saying? She is not talking about anything that is going to happen in this life, since she says it is going to happen *after death*. It cannot be denied that her language has a predictive form. Winch points out that the mother used this language quite unselfconsciously, and was not interested in giving any kind of philosophical account of it. Von der Ruhr says that a Catholic may speak of God reuniting our souls with our bodies through the power of Christ's resurrection, in that same unselfconscious way. He may not give a thought to philosophical theories about mind–body dualism. Von der Ruhr says that the Catholic Catechism admits that people may have difficulties with this belief, but it does not invite 'further speculation on *how* a resurrection might be possible' (p.64). Is this because that speculation would betray a misunderstanding, or because the 'how' of it is simply beyond us as finite creatures? When we are told that the Catechism says that such matters are only accessible to faith, the 'how' of it being beyond our imagination and understanding (p.64), I would say that the retention of 'the unknown "how"' is the intrusion of an alien grammar, one which is not 'food for the soul'. With Winch's example, things are different. He writes of the mother's words:

> Her words are, of course, an expression – a wonderful expression, it seems to me – of her love for her son. They are the words she needed to express her relation to him and his terrible condition ... I am not saying that her words are *reducible* to anything like 'I love you from the depths of my heart' ... the impact of her words derives in part from their relation to other uses to describe reunitings between human beings after painful separations. But that does not mean that the words here 'mean the same' as words used in those other circumstances. It is not my understanding of her love that helps me to understand her words: on the contrary, it is in understanding her words (*these* words *so* used in *this* context) that I see something of the nature of her love.[34]

The predictive form of the mother's words is important because her love concerns, in *these* words, thought of her son's life as *a completed whole after death.*

What would be the reaction of von der Ruhr's discontented Catholic? Would he now be content? Probably not. I could imagine him saying,

> Nothing is *actually going to happen* to the child, but in the Resurrection, things are different. My Catechism tells me: 'We firmly believe, and hence we hope that, just as

---

33   Winch, 'Picture and Representation', p.65.
34   Winch, 'Picture and Representation', pp.66–67.

Christ is truly risen from the dead and lives for ever, so after death the righteous will live for ever with the risen Christ and he will raise them up on the last day.'[35]

Von der Ruhr agrees that the reference to 'the last day' is not to a day on the calendar, any more than the Last Judgement is one that simply happens to be last, the one after the penultimate one. Wittgenstein points out that 'the last things' are supposed to refer to 'the end of time', yet people keep speaking of it in temporal terms. A temporal eternity would serve no religious purpose. Any particular event after death, of the kind envisaged, would itself await to be given significance in a wider whole, whereas 'the last things' refers to that wider whole – to what matters in the end.

In my work, I have discussed religious fantasies. These can easily fill the void created by the death of loved ones. Flannery O'Connor's short story, 'The Lame Shall Enter First' culminates in the tragic hanging of a young boy who has launched himself into space in the hope of an all-too-real reunion with his dead mother.[36] This kind of case is partly why I cannot accept von der Ruhr's advice 'To fall silent, even [when] our Catholic believer is walking on crutches that had better be kicked away' (p.67). Living in tragic illusions is too important for that. All confusions are not merely grammatical. Von der Ruhr recognizes that the Catechism itself wants to emphasize the nature of 'life in the risen Christ':

> Christ will raise us up 'on the last day'; but it is also true that, in a certain way, we have already risen with Christ. For, by virtue of the Holy Spirit, Christian life is already now on earth a participation in the death and Resurrection of Christ … United with Christ by Baptism, believers already truly participate in the heavenly life of the risen Christ.[37]

'But', our discontented Catholic will ask, 'what of participating in the resurrection of Christ *after* death?' Augustine has pointed out that there are no acts of volition among the dead, but wants to say, at the same time, that the dead pray for us.[38] How can he say both? In my work, with the help of Kierkegaard,[39] I tried to explore the religious idea that those who have truly participated in the life of the resurrected Christ, in *this* life, *after* death, become transfigured wills worthy of contemplation. In this sense, the dead, simply by being who they are in Christ, can intercede for the living, as indeed Christ himself is said to do. Critics have paid little attention to this aspect of my work, but I agree that it needs greater emphasis to allay the fears of our discontented Catholic, who suspects one of saying that *nothing really happens after death*.

Von der Ruhr may be surprised, at this point, to find me turning to Rush Rhees for further illumination, since he quotes Rhees, saying that he does not understand

---

35 *Catechism of the Catholic Church*, pp.279–80.

36 See my 'Perspectives on the Dead', in *Religion without Explanation*, Ch. 8.

37 *Catechism of the Catholic Church*, p.283.

38 See Eugene I. van Antwerp, 'An Abstract of a Dissertation on St. Augustine's "The Divination of Demons and Care of the Dead"', Washington, DC: Catholic University of America Press, 1955.

39 See my *Death and Immortality*, Ch. 3: 'Eternal Life and the Immortality of the Soul'. See also Kierkegaard's discussion of the transfigured will of the dead in Søren Kierkegaard, *Purity of Heart*, London: Fontana Books, 1961.

talk of an afterlife, or the notion of the Resurrection (p.63). All I can say is that such remarks by Rhees should be treated with extreme caution, since they may well be expressions of his well-known self-deprecation. On many occasions, before giving an excellent lecture, he would say that he didn't know why we had turned up, since he had nothing to say. More to the point, one can find, again and again in his work, excellent discussions of what, elsewhere in his work, he has said he does not understand.[40] I aim to show that this is true of our troublesome topic. Five points worthy of attention can be detected in Rhees's discussions.

First, it is clear that he is against any attempt to reduce religious beliefs to attitudes to life:

> It would be ridiculous to suggest that religious language was concerned with calling forth certain attitudes. Religious language is concerned with God, with thanking God, praying to God and praising God. It will not do at all to say that this is directed towards attitudes.[41]

Second, it is clear that Rhees thinks it is confused to hold that belief in eternal life entails a belief in survival after death:

> A rather stupid theology student once asked me, 'What do you think is going to happen to you when you die?' In one sense certainly nothing will 'happen to me' after I have died – whatever may happen to my body. If I could suffer or be inspired, I should not be dead. 'I won't know anything after I am dead' can be confusing if it is thought of as parallel to 'when I am asleep' or 'when I am unconscious' – as though 'when I am dead' meant 'when I am in a certain state – as 'when I am unconscious'. I shall not be in any sort of state. I shall not be at all.[42]

Third, it is clear, that it does not follow, for Rhees, that since 'to be dead' is not to be 'in a certain state', it follows that the idea of being subject to the Last Judgement, after death, is nonsense. On the contrary, he writes:

> I *can* see, though vaguely, something of how one comes to believe in a Last Judgement: as though this were part of the sense of the life I ought to lead, of what it is to fail as I do, and so on ... it would be hard to express what this is except in the thought of standing before a judge: standing, as Wittgenstein put it 'with a queer sort of body': by which he meant whatever Christianity speaks of as a 'glorified' body – I can understand how someone might say there'd be nothing of meaning in life unless one held to something like this.[43]

Fourth, it is clear that Rhees recognizes that beliefs in eternal life vary, but that in some, their predictive form of language is important. They form a family of cases.

---

40 This does not mean, of course, that there weren't religious notions, such as that of the Second Coming, for instance, that he could make little of. See *Rush Rhees on Religion and Philosophy*, Section IV of 'Difficulties with Christianity', p.356–57. I regard this collection as head and shoulders above anything in contemporary philosophy of religion; in fact, as superior to anything I know since Kierkegaard.

41 *Rush Rhees on Religion and Philosophy*, 'Belief in God', p.61.

42 *Rush Rhees on Religion and Philosophy*, 'Death and Immortality', p.206.

43 *Rush Rhees on Religion and Philosophy*, 'Difficulties with Christianity', p.356. I have corrected the misprint 'within a queer sort of body'.

Obviously, a Viking conception of eternity is very different from a Christian one. There could also be ethico-religious demands on life, where the distinction between life and death, a 'now-and-then', plays little importance. But we should not try to eliminate the distinction in contexts where it is *so* important; where there are internal relations between the demands and what one can say of a person *after* death.

> 'Eternal damnation (of this man's soul) may be realized in a moment[44] of time without any duration at all.' – Wittgenstein used to say this was one way, and a very *real* way of speaking of it. Cf. the notion of *signing a pact with the Devil* – in this life. Lenau's *Faust*: As soon as he has signed, his soul is utterly abandoned, cut off from God. – On the other hand I think he would have said that the 'future form' – 'I *shall* stand naked before my Judge' – was *generally* the more natural. I want to suggest that we should *not* treat these two ways of speaking as incongruous or inconsistent.[45]

Fifth, Rhees thinks that in Christianity there *is* an internal connection between the fate of the soul and the redemptive power of Christ's resurrection. Rhees writes:

> The resurrection has its importance as part of the general idea of Christ as redeemer. I suppose that is in many ways the most important idea in Christianity ... If I think of Christ as God, I think of him as redeemer. It is as redeemer that he comes so close to being creator. If he is my redeemer, then it is in him that I live and move and have my being. Apart from him, I am nothing. (Apart from him, we might say, I have no soul.)[46]

Rhees makes all these points while saying, at the same time, that he is only grasping the fringe of these matters, that he needs to see things more clearly, and that he has 'already said more than the Church would sanction'.[47]

But our discontented Catholic may still not be satisfied. He may take Rhees's remarks to refer to the significance of the resurrection, rather than telling us what the resurrection is, *in itself*, as it were. And that seems to be crucial for him as, along with von der Ruhr, he wants to remind us of the words of St Paul:

> How can some of you say that there is no resurrection of the dead? But if there is no resurrection of the dead, then Christ has not been raised; if Christ has not been raised, then our preaching is in vain ... But in fact Christ has been raised from the dead, the first fruits of those who have fallen asleep.[48]

Is this the foundation the discontented Catholic is looking for? If so, he will be disappointed, since, as Peter Winch points out, the form of St Paul's remarks is not as follows:

> 'You say that there is no such thing as resurrection of the dead, but since we know that Christ rose from the dead, you are wrong', but rather: 'You say there is no such thing as resurrection of the dead, but our religion requires belief in Christ's resurrection, and it

---

44 Not 'movement' as misprinted.
45 *Rush Rhees on Religion and Philosophy*, p.359.
46 *Rush Rhees on Religion and Philosophy*, p.349.
47 *Rush Rhees on Religion and Philosophy*, p.349.
48 1 Cor. 15: 12–14.

is only through that belief that you can be saved from sin; so, since believing there is no resurrection of the dead entails not believing in Christ's resurrection, such a belief stands in the way of your being saved from sin.'[49]

We can see from the form of St Paul's remarks that it is *not* at attempt to provide an historical foundation for the Resurrection. If it were, it would be an extraordinary argument. As Winch says, it would be like saying to a despairing Nazi, 'Go on, believe that Hitler did not die in the bunker, but escaped to South America; you will feel much better for it (as opposed to trying to cure him of his despair by convincing him by – good or bad – historical arguments that Hitler survived).'[50]

But since that is so, what becomes of our discontented Catholic's conviction that the Resurrection of Christ is an event in history, a conviction shared, I think, by von der Ruhr? The first thing to note is that Winch is *not* saying

> That the Gospel story should not be taken as an account of what happened in Palestine two thousand or so years ago. Of course it is. But it is a *religious* account, not what we nowadays with our understanding of historiography, would call an historical account.[51]

The second thing to note is that Winch is *not* saying that we cannot say when the Resurrection is said to occur. We can. But the notion of 'something happened', in this context, is not an historical one, nor could it be verified by historical means. Rowan Williams has made the same point in relation to the claim that Jesus is the Messiah. Jesus' life and death are *the historical occasion* for accepting or rejecting him, but he is not *an historical object* of faith.[52] Is not the same point made by Eicher in the discussion with Drewermann, and doesn't the archbishop assent to it (p.70)?

> One can find out that someone has been crucified, but it is impossible to find out that someone has been fathered by God. That is impossible, completely impossible. For it would mean that a physician could prove God's actions, and that is not possible.
>
> *Archbishop*: Agreed.

The same point can be made about a verification by a disinterested observer of the Resurrection or of the past-resurrection appearances. Neither Lessing nor Winch speculates about what happened to Jesus' body, since that would be a seeking of that very confirmation. Lessing does ask, however, whether, if the disciples had solemnly removed the body, to fulfil the prophecy, we would have to regard them as deceivers and temple-robbers.[53] As for the post-resurrection appearances, our

---

49   Peter Winch, 'Lessing and the Resurrection', in *The Possibilities of Sense*, ed. John H. Whittaker, Basingstoke: Palgrave, 2002, p.193.

50   Winch, 'Lessing and the Resurrection', p.194.

51   Winch, 'Lessing and the Resurrection', p.194.

52   Rowan Williams, 'Looking for Jesus and Finding Christ', in *Biblical Concepts and Our World*, eds. D.Z. Phillips and Mario von der Ruhr, Basingstoke: Palgrave, 2004. See 'Voices in Discussion', pp.163–64. Rowan Williams is Voice Q.

53   Winch, 'Lessing and the Resurrection', pp.194–96. Needless to say, I am not even trying, let alone succeeding, in conveying Winch's excellent account of the complex twists

historical sense does not allow us to think of them as we would of Hitler walking around South America.[54] It would be absurd, for example, to ask what Jesus was doing between his post-resurrection appearances, as though it made sense to say, 'Well, he must have been *somewhere*.' Winch certainly agrees that the disciples and others had strange religious experiences, but that is what he thinks they were: experiences which needed the language of resurrection to express them. St Paul wants to put his experience on the road to Damascus on a par with them, whereas if the latter are understood in a straightforwardly historical way he could not, since his occurred *after* the Ascension.[55] On the other hand, Walford Gealy has put it to me that the post-resurrection appearances do *not* lead to a spiritual discernment of the Resurrection. After what is said to be the last of them, the disciples are still asking, 'Lord, dost thou at this time restore the kingdom to Israel?' (Acts 1:6). Gealy argues that there is no spiritual appropriation of the Resurrection prior to Pentecost.

Winch's main point is that the Resurrection is not the foundation or presupposition of the Gospel story, but *an integral part of it*.[56] In that story, the resurrected bodies of the faithful are celestial bodies, which is, of course, a religious conception. They are raised up in Christ. Here, Rhees's emphasis on Christ as Redeemer is absolutely central. For the Christian, Christ is the way to God, and the Crucifixion shows what love of God is – a soul utterly naked before God. The way of the Cross is one which asks that the self does not come between one and God.

But I can imagine our discontented Catholic responding. 'Yes, yes, I'm with you. I accept what you say about "the way of the Cross", the way the Christian must follow *in this life*, but is he not promised something *after* death? I'll be crude to be clear: *Is something going to happen to him then or not?*' What are we to say to him? Here is an attempt by the poet R.S. Thomas.

Face to face? Ah, no
God; such language falsifies
the relation. Nor side by side,
nor near you, nor anywhere
in time and space.[57]

Discontented Catholic: Agreed, not in time and space, but what about *afterwards*, isn't there another dimension for us all? Can't you tell me something about *that*?

Something to bring back to show
you have been there; a lock of God's
hair, stolen from him while he was
asleep; a photograph of the garden
of the spirit.
...
And always in one

---

and turns in Lessing's discussion.

54 Winch, 'Lessing and the Resurrection', pp.190–91.
55 Winch, 'Lessing and the Resurrection', pp.192–93.
56 Winch, 'Lessing and the Resurrection', pp.192–93..
57 R.S. Thomas, *Collected Poems 1945–1990*, London: Dent, 1993, 'Waiting', p.347.

another we seek the proof
of experiences it would be worth dying for.[58]

R. S. Thomas also elaborates on these matters in prose:

> But I firmly believe this, that eternity is not something out there, not something in the
> future, it is close to us, it is all around us and at any given moment one can pass into it;
> but there is something about our mortality, the fact that we are time-bound creatures, that
> makes is somehow difficult if not impossible to dwell, whilst we are in the flesh, to dwell
> permanently in that, in what I could call the Kingdom of Heaven.[59]

But I can still imagine our discontented Catholic pressing me about Thomas's saying that it is difficult to live in the eternal whilst on earth. But what of *after* death? What of eternity itself? But we have to ask our discontented friend: What sort of concern is *that*? In his essay 'Death and Immortality', at times, highly personal, but always philosophically illuminating, Rhees gives the best answer I know of to the question we are being asked.

What is his concern for eternal life? First, it is a concern that, in this life, the eternal has not been sufficiently present in his life:

> What I wish came more deeply from my heart were a thanks for this life of innocent
> defilement and degradation: since otherwise the majesty of death – lachrymosa, dies illa
> – would have no meaning. My tendency to write *melius fuerit non vivere*[60] is the same
> *unwillingness to know* – which – if it masters me – will keep me from seeing death as the
> sole beauty and majesty; as the centre of 'Thy will be done'.[61]

Second, it is in *this* context that death is seen, by Rhees, as *hope*, not as an easy way out, or even a way of bringing his sins to an end, but as an opportunity to become part of the eternity that is God and, in that way, become something other than himself. The concern, throughout, is for God, and for his judgement on one's life. Remarkably, Rhees writes, 'I know that with death I shall reach something not myself. That – saving possible nonsense in this – even my damnation will have something divine about it.'[62]

What if someone after reading Rhees and Thomas were to react like this: 'What a relief! So nothing is actually going to happen to me after death.' That might be the reaction of Archelaus if he understood that when Socrates said that an evil man is necessarily punished, he meant that he is an object of pity – 'What! only that? Pity as much as you like, it can't touch me.' Quite so.

Philosophy cannot answer these questions for anyone, but it can point to those that need to be asked. So to our discontented Catholic who wants to know whether anything actually happens to him after death, we can ask, 'Do you think anything

58 Thomas, *Collected Poems*, 'Somewhere', p. 293.
59 R.S. Thomas, 'Priest and Poet', *Poetry Wales*, Spring 1972, p. 56.
60 'It would have been better not to live' (trans. by the editor).
61 Rhees, 'Death and Immortality', pp.236–37.
62 Rhees, 'Death and Immortality', p.236. See his whole discussion, but particularly pp.235–37.

actually happens to a soul that is damned for all eternity?' – 'Do you think anything actually happens to a soul that is raised to life eternal in Christ?' In other words, we ask him to reflect on what is to count as something actually happening.

Philosophy may also comment on attempts at such reflection. Von der Ruhr quotes one from the *Catholic Catechism*:

> This mystery of blessed communion with God and all who are in Christ is beyond all understanding and description. Scripture speaks of it in images: life, light, peace, wedding feast, wine of the kingdom, the Father's house, the heavenly Jerusalem, paradise: 'no eye hath seen, nor ear heard, nor the heart of man conceived, what God has prepared for those who love him.[63]

I find a tension in these remarks, which makes me uncertain in my reading of them. Read in one way, they can be seen as a series of illuminating grammatical remarks: the mystery of communion with God after death is not a matter to be described or understood; something to be confirmed by the eye seeing, the ear hearing or by humans conceiving. The mystery of communion with God through the resurrection of Christ, is not the mystery of *how* it happens, but *that* it happens.

Read in another way, however, the Catechism seems to say that there is a 'how' to all this, but that we, finite mortals, cannot conceive of it. True, the Scripture speaks of communion with God in terms of various images, but they are presented, on this reading, as a second best, a temporary makeshift conquered with the unknown 'how' of it all. But is that what they are? Aren't they rather pictures which say themselves? Don't we have everything we need in them? Isn't this what Kierkegaard is trying to tell us when he says:

> Eternity is not like a new world, so that one who had lived in time according to the ways of time and the press of busyness, if he were to make a happy landing in eternity itself, could now try his luck in adopting the customs and practices of eternity. Alas, the temporal order and the press of busyness believe that eternity is so far away. And yet not even the foremost professional theatrical producer has ever had all in such readiness for the stage and for the change of scenes, as eternity has all in readiness for time: all even to the last detail, even to the most insignificant word that is spoken: has all in readiness – although eternity delays.[64]

Scripture speaks of it in images, pictures which say themselves – 'eternity has all in readiness'. Thus we are taken back to where we began, to the logic of pictures. The journey we have undertaken should enable us to see, philosophically, at least, pictures of eternity.

---

63 *The Catholic Catechism*, p.290.
64 Kierkegaard, *Purity of Heart*, pp.106–107.

Chapter V

Internal Realism:
A Joint Feature by Dewi Z. Phillips and
Paul Tillich?

Tage Kurtén
Åbo Akademi

Introduction

As a young scholar in the late 1970s and early 1980s I worked on my thesis on scientific theology and its relation to Church and society. I then became absorbed by, among other writers, the thought of Paul Tillich. Parallel to my thesis work, I became more and more interested in the work of Ludwig Wittgenstein. Through that interest I turned to the writings of Dewi Z. Phillips. I wrote a book on a Wittgensteinian approach to theology in comparison with the paths to theology staked out by the Swedish theologian Anders Jeffner.[1] Ever since that time, I have been of the opinion that there are some central thoughts by Tillich and Phillips which bring them close to each other, despite the very different languages they use. My intention is to show that this is true at least concerning the question of realism in religion and some important traits of their views on the theological enterprise.

The last decade has seen an ongoing discussion of realism and non-realism (anti-realism) in Anglo-Saxon philosophy of religion. Phillips has argued for a position which says 'yes' to realism in religion, but 'no' to the way realism is understood by most philosophers who argue for realism in relation to religious beliefs. Most of his colleagues have not accepted his position. One could ask why. Is it perhaps because it is not properly understood?

In an attempt to understand Phillips' position and, hopefully, to make it more understandable to others, I will examine to what extent there could be a resemblance between Phillips' position and some central traits in the thoughts of Paul Tillich. The assumption is of course that such a comparison is worthwhile. My thesis is that in Tillich's way of arguing around some of his key concepts 'Being-itself', 'the protestant principle', 'ultimate concern' and his concept of religious symbols, one can find arguments which come close to some main points in Phillips' way of understanding realism in religion.

---

1   Tage Kurtén, *Grunder för en kontextuell teologi. Ett wittgenstienskt sätt att närma sig teologi i disussion med Anders Jeffner*, Åbo: Åbo Akademis Förlag, 1987.

I want to underscore that I am not sure that Phillips will find Tillich's use of words very helpful in making his own points clearer. But I do think that he can understand the conceptual problems Tillich tries to resolve and also follow the latter's arguments to some extent. For my own part I think that an understanding of Phillips' main points can help a reader better understand Tillich. In addition to this, I hope that my comparisons between the two can help someone who is better acquainted with Tillich than with Phillips to see the points that the latter makes more clearly.

1. Modernity – A Common Background

Phillips has, as is well known, built on the thoughts of the later Wittgenstein. To a large extent it is a question of using Wittgenstein's philosophical method. Phillips does not build on a philosophical theory, thought to be 'the theoretical outcome of Wittgenstein's thoughts'. Wittgenstein did not intend to develop any theory, and Phillips very much accepts this, both when it comes to Wittgenstein and to his own philosophical work.

One important feature is that Phillips, following Wittgenstein, does not want to build upon previous philosophical results. There is no accumulative feature in philosophical thought according to either. Philosophy only tries to settle conceptual confusions in our use of language. Phillips has recently used the expression 'a contemplative conception of philosophy' of his striving to reflect on 'our discourse, our understandings of the real world, endeavouring to let them be themselves in face of deep tendencies to confuse them'. He explicitly says that he wants to go nowhere. Philosophy's task is, according to him, to bring clarity where there is confusion, not to get things done in any kind of way.[2]

Although Phillips, in this way, wants to get rid of much of the ballast of modern philosophical thinking, he (and Wittgenstein) are of course children of their own age, and are to be understood partly in relation to the situation in the history of ideas in which they live. The twentieth century was one in which many of the central ideas of the Enlightenment thinkers were very much alive. I take this to be a central feature of modernity. To the whole of the modern philosophical understanding of religion, Immanuel Kant's critique of metaphysics has been of utmost importance because it not only influenced the philosophical discussion of religion but also the religious reflection and the self-understanding of religious people. Phillips has, for example, pointed to Søren Kierkegaard's wrestling with religious thought.[3] According to Phillips, Wittgenstein differs from Kierkegaard in being a pure philosopher. Wittgenstein 'wants to contemplate the world without meddling with it' whereas Kierkegaard's 'desire for clarity is not rooted in the wonder at reality and the possibilities of sense that comes from philosophy. Kierkegaard is a religious thinker whose main concern is with clearing away confusions about Christianity.'[4]

---

2   Phillips, *Philosophy's Cool Place*, p.166.

3   Phillips, *Philosophy's Cool Place*, pp.13–40; Phillips, *Religion and the Hermeneutics of Contemplation*, p.319.

4   Phillips, *Religion and the Hermeneutics of Contemplation*, p.318.

In the wake of the Kantian critique, we can speak of an anthropological turn both in the philosophy of religion and in theology and religious thinking. This characterized most of the nineteenth-century thinking in the philosophy of religion and in theology. This was also one of the lines that came to be important in the linguistic turn of philosophy in the last century. The second line was a return to a more classical metaphysical thinking, characterizing much of analytical philosophy building on some profound traits in logical empiricism. In such a mapping of the last century's philosophy, Wittgenstein and Phillips belong to a branch in the philosophy of language where reflections are rooted in anthropology in the sense of concrete human lives, and not in a conception of an independent objective and outer world of facts, which in philosophy of religion could raise the question of a metaphysical reality that religious language tries to mirror.

It is exactly at this point, I think, that Phillips and Tillich can join hands. For I think it is fair to say that Phillips' writings in the philosophy of religion have circled around problems shaped by philosophers who have tried to make sense of religion on metaphysical, rational and empirical grounds. In relation to these grounds his comment is: 'What we need in religion, as elsewhere, is realism without empiricism.'[5] The main root of confusion lies in the Enlightenment, he suggests:

Instead of Christianity we are offered the categories of the Enlightenment, according to which religious categories as such stand in need of evidence before we can appropriate them with justification. In this way, the authority of religion becomes forgotten – it is hard to know what that authority could ever have been.[6]

Paul Tillich is often thought of as a metaphysician *par excellence* but in my opinion this is a grave misinterpretation of his real intentions. He was, both as a philosopher of religion and as a theologian – two roles he tried to keep apart –, an intellectual eager to come to grips with the modern man's capacity to understand religious language and religious belief.[7] In so doing, he also found that classical metaphysical solutions can no longer apply. We have to find new approaches if we are to make sense of religion in human life. In his discussions he came to use a range of more or less classical philosophical and theological words, with connotations pointing to metaphysical contents. This makes it easy to interpret him as one link in the great chain of metaphysical thinkers. As I intend to show, it is possible to interpret him in another way, a way I think is more in accordance with his own intentions. In order to make sense of the whole of his thinking, I find that Tillich's terminology should be understood as deeply rooted in ordinary human life, an interpretation to which his method of correlation also points.[8] It is fundamental that a key concept for understanding Tillich's use of the concept of Being-itself lies in his talk of 'ultimate

---

5   Phillips, *Recovering Religious Concepts*, p.82.
6   Phillips, *Recovering Religious Concepts*, p.86.
7   See Tage Kurtén, 'Ecstasy – A Way to Religious Knowledge. Some Remarks on Paul Tillich as Theologian and Philosopher', in Nils G. Holm ed., *Religious Ecstasy*, Stockholm: Almqvist and Wiksell International, 1982, pp.253–62, here p.254.
8   See Paul Tillich, *Systematic Theology*, vol. I, Chicago, IL: University of Chicago Press, 1951, pp.62–64.

concern'. Without this anchoring in the concrete human existence, the concept of Being-itself loses all meaning.

Immanuel Kant's influential philosophy of religion contains, according to Joseph Runzo, the idea that God is *noumenal*. And to the extent that God is so, He is inconceivable to the human mind. With his presentation Runzo, though, focuses on the epistemological point of view.[9] Runzo concludes his article with the following remarks concerning realism in religion:

> There are four ways to think about God. We can think about God only as God in Godself. But this seems to lead to the notion of an utterly transcendent, unavailable God. We can take the non-realist path, and thereby avoid the problem of divine transcendence. But as we have seen, however, this raises an even more serious difficulty: why be religious at all, why go beyond humanism? We can claim that God is a real, self-existent being in our experience, but deny altogether that there is a noumenal God. Such a phenomenalist approach also avoids the problem of divine transcendence, but at the cost of giving up the idea that God could exist in Godself, apart from our minds. The fourth alternative is to postulate that beyond the God we confront, there is a self-subsistent noumenal God.[10]

Runzo wants to argue in favour of the fourth solution: 'Faith involves the ultimate commitment that one has indeed confronted God in Godself, a divine reality that is independent of our human minds. And it is the experience and life of faith which bridges the abyss that separates us from an otherwise unavailable God.'[11] As we shall see, Tillich and Phillips do not accept any of these four possibilities. The problem lies in the way the alternatives are formulated by, among others, Runzo.

2. The Main Structure of Paul Tillich's Philosophy of Religion

Paul Tillich is rightly seen as one of the most important theologians and religious thinkers of the last century. To this I would add that he also is a very important philosopher of religion. His importance can be seen in the vast amount of studies and commentaries on his works. I have no intention of getting into a discussion with Tillich interpreters in this essay. I only want to present my own way of reading Tillich. In my doctoral thesis I studied Tillich's way of looking at religious language and his way of doing theology in a comparison with the works by the German Wolfhart Pannenberg and the Swede Anders Nygren.[12] Elsewhere, I have presented some of the main features of Tillich's philosophy of religion in English.[13] I will here summarize my main points made two decades ago, which I still find acceptable.

---

9   Joseph Runzo, 'Realism, Non-Realism and Atheism: Why Believe in an Objectively Real God?', in *Is God Real?*, ed. J. Runzo, Basingstoke: Macmillan, 1993, pp.151–75, here p.154.

10   Runzo, 'Realism, Non-Realism and Atheism', p.171.

11   Runzo, 'Realism, Non-Realism and Atheism', p.172.

12   See summary in Tage Kurtén, *Vetenskaplig teologi och dess samhällsrelation. Presentation och kritisk diskussion av tre metateoretiska modeller.* Åbo: Åbo Akademis Förlag, 1982.

13   Kurtén, 'Ecstasy – A Way to Religious Knowledge'.

In his efforts to reach an intellectual understanding of religious beliefs and religious language, Tillich stands for a solution, the structure of which can already be found in his early work.[14] The leading ideas are almost intact in his late magnum opus *Systematic Theology* vols. I–III.[15] It could be argued that Tillich's term 'Being-itself' points to a referent for a religious language in its talking about God. In that case, however, the term 'reference' is taken in a very special sense. It is not pointing to a certain 'something' in reality outside human beings; a something the religious person would name 'God'. It would also be misleading to see it as an intentional object in a Husserlian sense – although such an interpretation has been given. Every attempt to see the concept of Being-itself as an object seems to fail. Instead, Being-itself must be seen as something implied in every (religious) use of language and possible to grasp only *in* that use, never apart from it. This means, among other things, that an interpretation of Tillich's Being-itself in accordance with classical metaphysical use of 'Being' and of 'Being-itself' is dubious or directly wrong.

The point of saying this is that there is no philosophical way of reaching a 'something' in reality, which could be identified or equated with the 'God' of one or more religions. The position of Tillich at this point is a resounding rejection of human efforts by the help of pure rationality alone, or of rationality and empirical observations, to reach an independent grip of something, which could be seen as an especially religious part of (an outer) reality.

What Tillich is stating, among other things, is that what Being-itself comes to can only be understood as something presupposed in every encounter with reality. Only through our lives *in* reality, can the point of religious language be seen. What Tillich is doing is describing man's situation in the world in order to explain why people have been religious and continue to be so in modernity. The key to the meaning of religious language that he gives us does not lead to a transcendent world of metaphysical objects, but to the world of humankind where God's reality can only be seen in human existence:

> If the word 'existential' points to a participation which transcends both subjectivity and objectivity, then man's relation to the gods is rightly called 'existential'. Man cannot speak of gods in detachment. The moment he tries to do so, he has lost the god and has established just one more object within the world of objects. Man can speak of the gods only on the basis of his relation to them. This relation oscillates between the concreteness of a give-and-take attitude, in which the divine beings easily become objects and tools for human purposes, and the absoluteness of a total surrender on the side of man. The absolute element of man's ultimate concern demands absolute intensity, infinite passion (Kierkegaard) in the religious relation[16]

In discussing the so-called arguments of the existence of God, Tillich states among other things the following:

---

14 See Paul Tillich, *Frühe Hauptwerke, Gesammelte Werke I*, Stuttgart: Evangelisches Verlagswerk, 1959.

15 See Kurtén, 'Ecstasy – A Way to Religious Knowledge'.

16 Tillich, *Systematic Theology* vol. I, pp. 214–15; see also p.218.

The scholastics ... perverted their insights when ... they spoke of the existence of God and tried to argue in favour of it. Actually they did not mean 'existence.' They meant the reality, the validity, and the truth of the idea of God, an idea that did not carry the connotation of some*thing* or some*one* who might or might not exist. Yet this is the way in which the idea of God is understood today in scholarly as well as in popular discussions about the 'existence of God.' ... God does not exist. He is being-itself beyond essence and existence. Therefore, to argue that God exists is to deny him.[17]

Although Tillich is writing here as if he were describing how things are ('God is...'), what he is really saying concerns our use of language, not an ontology independent of our language. In fact, Tillich sees only one important feature in the various arguments for the existence of God. They all express a *question* concerning God, which they somehow find implied in human finitude.[18] Tillich finds it important to emphasize an unconditional element in the experience man has in his encounter with reality. This is what gives the ontological argument its meaning:

The ontological argument ... gives a description of the way in which potential infinity is present in actual finitude. As far as the description goes, that is, as far as it is analysis and not argument, it is valid. The presence within finitude of an element which transcends it is experienced both theoretically and practically ... Neither side has constructed an argument for the reality of God, but all elaborations have shown the presence of something unconditional within the self and the world. Unless such an element were present, the question of God never could have been asked, nor could an answer, even the answer of revelation, have been received.[19]

What Tillich is actually saying is that the presupposition of every religious language lies in the concrete experiences that human being has of life and of the finitude of life. But he goes on and underscores that no existence in reality (the outside world) can be derived from that. It is here he finds that many philosophers of religion have gone astray.[20]

In accordance with the above thoughts, he notices that the Anselmian idea

that God is a necessary thought and that therefore this idea must have objective as well as subjective reality, is valid in so far as thinking, by its very nature, implies an unconditional element which transcends subjectivity and objectivity, that is, a point of identity which makes the idea of truth possible. However, the statement is not valid if this unconditional element is understood as a highest being called God. The existence of such a highest being is not implied in the idea of truth.[21]

As Tillich also rejects the other forms of classical arguments of the existence of a godly reality, he reveals the anti-metaphysical character of his thinking.[22]

---

17 Tillich, *Systematic Theology* vol. I, p.205.
18 Tillich, *Systematic Theology* vol. I, p.205.
19 Tillich, *Systematic Theology* vol. I, p.206.
20 Tillich, *Systematic Theology* vol. I, p.207.
21 Tillich, *Systematic Theology* vol. I, p.207.
22 See Tillich, *Systematic Theology* vol. I, pp.207–10.

In any event, the following quotation can be interpreted in either of two ways. It can be understood as stating an ontology in the sense of stating what 'necessarily exists' because of the way things are – as a comment on the world. It can, however, also be understood as a comment on certain features in our way of using language when we try to place ourselves in the world. The lessons I have learned from reading Phillips make me inclined to understand Tillich in the latter sense – an interpretation I had arrived at before I had read a single line of Phillips. The quotation goes:

> The limits of the ontological argument are obvious. But nothing is more important for philosophy and theology than the truth it contains, the acknowledgement of the unconditional element in the structure of reason and reality. … Modern secularism is rooted largely in the fact that the unconditional element in the structure of reason and reality no longer was seen and that therefore the idea of God was imposed on the mind as a 'strange body'. … The destruction of the ontological *argument* is not dangerous. What is dangerous is the destruction of an approach, which elaborates the possibility of the question of God. This approach is the meaning and the truth of the ontological argument.[23]

In order for us to get a grip on the main structure of Tillich's philosophy of religion some words should be said about his thoughts about religious symbols, and about God-talk as symbolic. To state that everything that can be said of God is symbolic could be interpreted in a classical, metaphysical way, for example in line with Thomas Aquinas's theory of *analogia entis*. Although Tillich himself agrees with this theory I think the key to understanding Tillich at this point lies in his so-called method of correlation. This method implies that a religious language will be meaningful only as far as the religious language of a concrete tradition is rooted in concrete human existence. Only matters important in real human existence can be a means to religious expressions carrying meaning.[24] Consider, for example, the following quotation, where 'revelation' can be taken to mean 'traditional religious formulations':

> A religious symbol *is* true if it adequately expresses the correlation of some person with final revelation. A religious symbol can die only if the correlation of which it is an adequate expression dies. This occurs whenever the revelatory situation changes and former symbols become obsolete.[25]

In sum, according to Tillich, every understanding of a religious language as mirroring reality in a way similar to how scientific language is understood to mirror nature, distorts the very nature of religious language. In addition, it is clear that, according to Tillich, God's reality can only be understood in the concrete lives of religious men and women.

---

23 Tillich, *Systematic Theology* vol. I, p.208.
24 See Tillich, *Systematic Theology* vol. I, pp.59–64, 239–41.
25 Tillich, *Systematic Theology* vol. I, p.240.

3. Phillips' Religious Realism and Its Critics

As we now turn to Dewi Z. Phillips, my claim is not that we meet exactly the same thinking; of course not. But I want to say that both are searching for a solution to the same problem in a similar direction. They both try to catch the meaning of a religious language in a situation in which the attempts to lean in different ways on classical metaphysics seem to miss the point, and where a central aspect of every religious language is in danger of being lost, namely, the character of language being internally related to the user of the religious language.

When Phillips tries to explain his view of the topic of realism–non-realism he writes:

> The realist accuses the non-realist of conflating 'believing' with the fruits of believing. The fruits of believing, the role belief plays in human life, are said to be the consequences of believing. What, then, is 'believing'?[26]

What I think he means is that, in the debate among philosophers concerning realism or non-realism in religion, belief in God is seen as an isolated act which could be stated as: 'I believe/I do not believe in the existence of God.' And this isolated belief is the rationale for a religious life. This means that we have a two-step movement: first, a deliberate (or at least a theoretically recognized) standpoint concerning the reality of God; second, the conscious religious (or non-religious) life which gets its sense from the assumed solution on the question of God's real existence. Atheism is fully understandable in relation to this two-step picture. The atheist denies what the theist maintains. And from their respective first step, their different ways of life can be seen as equally meaningful (as long as there is no final solution to the question whether God really exists or not). What complicates the discussion is the non-realist position of, for example, Don Cupitt, who accepts the two-step picture, denies the reality of God, but nevertheless claims the intelligibility and sense of religious language and religious life.[27]

According to Phillips, these positions are all more or less confused. He says that there is no first step to take at all. The reality of God makes sense only *in* religious life. It cannot be taken as a presupposition that logically and/or in time precedes the life of the believer. If we try to do that then we end up with an empty and nonsensical reality claim. That is what is wrong with most solutions in the realism–non-realism discussion.

Phillips finds that realists fear non-realism (including his own position) because it seems to lead to reductionism.[28] But he shows that it is the other way around: the 'realist's kind of realism' leads to reductionism:

---

26   D.Z. Phillips, 'On Really Believing', in Runzo ed., *Is God Real?*, p.88.

27   Don Cupitt, 'Anti-Realist Faith', in Runzo ed., *Is God Real?*, p.55; see also B. Hebblewaithe, 'Reflections on Realism vs. Non-Realism', in Runzo ed., *Is God Real?*, p.210.

28   See Phillips, 'On Really Believing', p.97.

If the essence of beliefs is not to be found in its so-called fruits, how can God be said to be present in them? *In this way, realism cannot take seriously the central religious conviction that God is at work in people's lives. The reductionism which the realist finds in non-realism is all too prevalent in the realist's account of believing in God.*[29]

Phillips calls attention to Wittgenstein's understanding of pictures in a religious context. Some expressions are non-changeable. Quoting Wittgenstein, he says, 'It says what it says. Why should you be able to substitute anything else?' and he continues:

> Wittgenstein ... is insisting that the whole weight may be in the picture. In that case, the loss of the picture may constitute the loss of what is essential in a belief. When a picture is lost, a truth may be lost which cannot be replaced. This is a far cry from the view of Wittgenstein as a non-realist who sees religious beliefs as expressive attitudes, which have no necessary relation to the object of belief. It is in the use of the picture that the relation of belief to its object is to be understood. It is this use, this method of projection, which the realist ignores. What Wittgenstein is trying to do is not to get the realist to embrace non-realism. Rather, he is trying to get him to look in a certain direction, to our actions and practice, where religious belief has sense.[30]

When realists such as Trigg and Penelhum play by probabilities, and in that sense make religious beliefs relative, Phillips, with the help of Wittgenstein, attempts to point out the absolute character by the religious belief. Again he quotes Wittgenstein's lectures on religion:

> Suppose someone were a believer and said: 'I believe in a Last Judgement.' and I said: 'Well, I'm not so sure. Possibly.' You would say that there is an enormous gulf between us. If he said 'There is a German aeroplane overhead.' and I said 'Possibly. I'm not so sure,' you'd say we were fairly near.[31]

Why do Phillips' critics reject these viewpoints? John Hick, for example, does not accept Phillips' assurance that his position goes beyond the kind of realism that is at stake in the realism–non-realism debate:

> Phillips seeks to conceal these implications [the negative and atheistic implications in non-realism] by professing to be neither realistic nor non-realistic but to occupy a third position. This third position is often hinted at but was never actually produced.[32]

In an article on theological realism and anti-realism, Roger Trigg tries to understand what Phillips is claiming. His picture of Phillips' thought is, however, presented from within his own frame of reference, looking for rational arguments and a possibility of metaphysics. It is hardly surprising that Trigg cannot appreciate Phillips' solution from within this framework. Trigg defines 'realism' in such a way, that the kind of

---

29   Phillips, 'On Really Believing', p.99.
30   Phillips, 'On Really Believing', p.100.
31   Phillips, 'On Really Believing', p.105–106.
32   John H. Hick, 'Belief in God: Metaphysics and Values', in Runzo ed., *Is God Real?*, p.130.

realism Phillips has found in religion is ruled out from the start. A test of the truth of our beliefs must be different from a test of the sincerity of our beliefs, according to Trigg. The latter lies in our action, but the former must be tested against actual reality outside our actions, he says. He also claims that Phillips' view of religious belief is divergent from the understanding religious people themselves normally think they possess.[33] This last objection remains to be shown. But the problem is that it can hardly be shown without an interpretation of the concepts involved and this is exactly what the philosophical dispute is all about.

In an important article, Eberhard Herrmann has tried to analyze the realism debate in more detail. He himself defends a position, which comes close to Phillips' way of thinking. Herrmann refines the key-concept in the debate, taking 'religious realism' in a way that makes room for what he calls 'internal-realism'. I find his contribution a promising attempt to understand Phillips' position in terms that perhaps make it easier to understand and accept for the defenders of religious realism in the debate in question.[34]

One point, however, where I cannot quite follow him is where he argues that Phillips cannot show why a realist could not explain the meaning of 'God exists' independent of any religious practise. This objection presupposes that the problem stated in this way is intelligible. When this is coupled with his acceptance of the realist's distinction between what it means to claim something true in a particular practice and the way we test this truth claim, I see a tendency in Herrmann's argument to find the question of whether God is real or not quite independent of religious beliefs in God, as meaningful, after all.[35] And here I cannot see that Phillips would follow him.

Joseph Runzo (using some of Phillips' early writings) finds that Phillips proposes a non-cognitivist view and that he treats religious language games as inherently exclusionary. Runzo sees no conflict between realism and Phillips' main point that the sense of religious belief is in the role religious beliefs have in people's lives. He continues by claiming that a problem with Phillips' position lies precisely there. Exactly in what sense Phillips could be said to defend a total exclusiveness for religious life is, however, not shown.[36]

These are but a few examples of the many philosophers of religion who have difficulties with Phillips' conception of God and reality. I have exemplified this in order to indicate that Phillips' critics mostly argue from within a framework (of modernity), which is itself the target of Phillips' philosophical attack. As long as this framework is not put in question, Phillips' points cannot be properly understood. And as long as this is the situation, it is important to try to find new ways of

---

33   Roger Trigg, 'Theological Realism and Antirealism', in *A Companion to Philosophy of Religion*, eds. P.L. Quinn and Ch. Taliaferro, Oxford: Blackwell, 1997, pp.213–20, here p.215.

34   Eberhard Herrmann, 'God, Reality and the Realism/Atheism Debate', in *Spinning Ideas. Electronic Essays. Dedicated to Peter Gärdenfors on his 50th Birthday*, http://www.lucs.lu.se/spinning (1999), last accessed 1 July 2007.

35   See Herrmann, 'God, Reality and the Realism/Atheism Debate', pp.56, 58–61.

36   Runzo, 'Realism, Non-Realism and Atheism', in Runzo ed., *Is God Real?*, pp.157ff.

approaching Phillips' thought. My comparison with Tillich is intended to be such a fresh approach.

4. Phillips and Tillich as Internal Realists

In what sense is Phillips' position similar to that of Tillich? Tillich tries to talk about God with the help of the term 'Being-itself'. This is of course a term highly loaded with meanings from the metaphysical tradition. But Tillich's point is that this expression is wrongly understood if it is taken to refer to some highest entity, or in any way to some reality 'out there'. Tillich's difficulties with getting to grips with language in relation to what he apparently wants to say is seen in linguistic experiments like 'the ground of being', 'the abyss' and the like.[37]

According to both Phillips and Tillich, one should not talk of some entity 'out there', to which we refer when we talk about God and which therefore could make religious language and life rational. This does not mean that there is no such entity; or that there is one, for that matter. It means that it is *senseless to think or talk about* some entity existing in that way. They both seem to claim that we do not have any intelligible way of making sense of such talk.

One could argue that Tillich arrives at his Being-itself through a transcendental deduction in a Kantian sense of the world. This means that the starting point is real religious life and real religious language. It is obvious that the concept of God is very much alive in such a context. The reality of God is presupposed in almost every sentence of a religious language. The crucial question, however, is what we mean by 'the reality of God'. When it comes to that question, Tillich tries to avoid those misunderstandings, which, according to Phillips, are being made by most philosophers in the realism–non-realism discussion. Tillich's solution is the concept of Being-itself as a transcendental concept. It contains an idea that is presupposed, for example, in religious life and that, in that context, is often expressed by talking of God. But this idea can only be detected in concrete life and concrete religious language; it is not a presupposition which would make sense outside these concrete contexts. And it cannot be understood as a logical presupposition preceding a religious life.

In order to avoid the kind of position that tries to understand God's reality in isolation from every real human context, Tillich talks about religious symbols. Through Phillips' position we can also learn to see Tillich's idea of religious symbols as a way of avoiding the type of metaphysical questions which occupy the realism debate. Symbols, according to Tillich, are alive only as long as they are in use, which is why he can say that symbols can die. When they no longer make sense, they have lost their position in people's lives.

In this light we can understand Tillich's famous comment on the death-of-God theology: 'How could Being-itself die?' We can understand this comment as his way of saying that there is no point in arguing about the existence of God. To debate whether God exists or ceases to exist (dies) is a totally misleading debate. The only

---

37   See Tillich, *Systematic Theology* vol. I, pp.112ff.

way talk of the death of God (or the existence/non-existence of God) could make any sense is when we discuss the way people do or do not live religious lives in today's world. Gods live and die among human beings. God's reality is internal to religious life.

However, the position so outlined is in danger of reducing God to a social construction and thereby into something relativistic. This is another problematic way of thinking both Tillich and Phillips try to avoid. To avoid this constructivist solution, Tillich employs the concept Being-itself and couples it with 'ultimate concern'. This very concept points to an element, which is necessarily to be found in every human life, Tillich argues. It is not a contingent matter. In this way Tillich avoids getting into mere relativistic constructivism. Human life, as far as we know it, entails an element – 'ultimate concern' – which cannot be removed without changing radically the whole concept of human life.

At this point it sometimes seems to me that Phillips (in some of his later texts) has problems not ending up in a relativist position. For example, in his textbook *Introducing Philosophy* he only talks about his way of philosophically understanding religious language as 'a possibility'. He seems to have lost some of his earlier certainty in stating how we *can* philosophically understand religious language. And with this growing uncertainty, relativism perhaps comes creeping in.[38]

It could be that Phillips, to an extent far beyond Tillich's position, accepts the idea of the modern human world as divided into different sectors, such as politics, morality, religion, science and so on. Phillips would never make any theory of culture out of this: his philosophy is not searching for (philosophical) theories. He tries to get rid of our need to make theories. He does, though, deal with religious language as a language in its own right (*sui generis*). He can therefore see religion fading away entirely as a real possibility. This seems to make it difficult for him to avoid relativism.

However, as far as I can see, Phillips' answer to this would be that this question of relativism makes no sense. As long as we do have religious people among us, religious language continues to puzzle us and to challenge the philosopher to come to terms with it. But if a time comes where there are no religious people in the world (and whether such a moment can ever occur is open to question), religious language will stop puzzling the philosopher.

This said, though, there is also another side to Phillips' texts. In his discussions of reactions and especially of primitive reactions we can find attempts to understand religion as a more or less necessary part of human life – in a way similar to morality being constitutive of human life.[39]

5. Theology and Internal Language

I have tried to show that Phillips and Tillich have in common the idea of internal realism. I will end my essay by showing how this makes sense of their very similar

---

38   D.Z. Phillips, *Introducing Philosophy. The Challenge of Scepticism*, Oxford: Blackwell, 1996, p.165.
39   Phillips, *Wittgenstein and Religion*, pp.113–19.

way of understanding an important trait in theology, namely, the question of the personal involvement of the one doing theological work.

I shall now discuss some features in both Tillich's and Phillips' account of theology in order to make these similarities discernible. Both draw a clear line between philosophy of religion and theology. A philosopher has only his own mind, his ability to make observations of different kinds and his critical thinking on which to lean. Theologians have the task of interpreting and trying to understand a given religious tradition and, according to both our thinkers, they have in some sense to be part of the tradition they try to make intelligible.

Phillips has only briefly discussed theology as an activity in today's world. But he has some remarks on that topic too. Phillips is no theologian. He is a philosopher who has done his main work in philosophy of religion, in ethics and in philosophy and literature. As a philosopher he wants to leave things as they are. He has hinted at what he thinks the task of theology to be. In one of his more recent works he does not talk of theological, but of spiritual criteria in order to distinguish real revelations from false ones. Following St Teresa, he gives two main criteria for deciding on real experiences: Holy Scripture (as a negative criterion) and the spiritual fruits (a practice-oriented criterion).[40] As early as 1963, Phillips stressed an internal relation between theology and religious life and tradition.[41] The criteria of what can sensibly be said about God are to be found within religion. Theology consists of these criteria which, in some way, are intrinsic to religious language. 'As soon as one has religious discourse one has a theology which determines what will be sensible to say and what it will nonsensical to say within that religious discourse without being prior to it.' According to Phillips, systematic theology is to a certain extent a personal matter: 'Theology is personal, since it is based on one's own experience of God. Where the connection between theology and experience is missing, there is a danger of theology becoming an academic game.' Phillips finds that philosophy cannot decide on what are good or bad theological criteria. That is a task for the theologian.[42]

Phillips has also discussed Paul Holmer's book *The Grammar of Faith* with great delight. Among other things, he is happy with Holmer's critique of a range of modern theological endeavours, ranging from rationally and metaphysically oriented ones to pure biblicism.[43] In line with Holmer, Phillips sees a main problem in the tendency to move outside faith. Most theology today is *about* faith, not *of* faith, which Phillips finds problematic. Instead, theology's main task is to be the grammar of faith.[44]

I will not go into all the questions this remark might give rise to, but confine myself to discussing a main point. With the expression 'to be of faith', Phillips touches upon a central conceptual problem in theology today. The problem concerns how to decide what is *of* and *not about* faith. Having discussed this problem elsewhere, my solution is that on the surface theology is about faith. One can require no special properties of

---

40   Phillips, *Recovering Religious Concepts*, p.92.

41   Phillips, *Wittgenstein and Religion*, p.5.

42   Phillips, *Wittgenstein and Religion*, pp.3–7.

43   D.Z. Phillips, *Faith after Foundationalism*, San Francisco, CA: Westview Press, 1995, pp.228–32.

44   Phillips, *Faith after Foundationalism*, pp.232, 234.

a theologian except for a live interest in his or her topic. Although on a deeper level there is a question of some kind of commitment to the faith one is trying to explicate, this commitment cannot be measured in any way and therefore lacks methodological relevance. We will now see that the solution that Phillips and Tillich defend comes close to my idea.

I have pointed to the above features in Phillips' writing in order to underscore how he finds it important that the theologian has an internal relation to his subject. Phillips, however, has not elaborated on this idea very much. I find this idea interesting and of importance for the task of systematic theology. I understand systematic theology as a subject, which tries to understand the Christian tradition in relation to different contexts. Phillips points in the same direction when he talks of the theologian as the 'guardian of the Faith'.[45] Here we can also find some interesting parallels in Tillich's discussions, which I now want to mention.

In his *Systematic Theology*, Tillich describes how he understands the task of the theologian. The most important feature is perhaps that theology, apart from philosophy of religion, is maintained in 'the theological circle'. For Tillich, too, there is an inevitable personal element in a theologian's work. He expresses this in many ways. He couples it with an experience of 'something ultimate in value and being of which one can become intuitively aware'. The experience is rooted in 'a mystical a priori'. He describes this with the expression 'something that transcends the cleavage between subject and object'. The involvement of the theologian makes the enterprise circular. In the theological circle the theologian struggles with his own experiences in relation to his religious tradition. As a churchgoer he takes part in the self-interpretation of the Church. The theologian combines a deliberate (scientific) general method with a concrete tradition and this is done in relation to a specific situation.[46] This could be seen as a way of expressing what 'an internal relation' to the religious faith means.

Tillich makes some important remarks, which helps us grasp what we can expect of a theologian; what criteria a theologian has to fulfil in order to stick to an internal perspective:

> A person can be a theologian as long as he acknowledges the content of the theological circle as his ultimate concern. Whether this is true does not depend on his intellectual or moral emotional state; it does not depend on the intensity and certitude of faith; it does not depend on the power of regeneration or the grade of sanctification. Rather it depends on his being ultimately concerned with the Christian message even if he is sometimes inclined to attack and to reject it.[47]

Tillich's solution concerns a first-person self-understanding of the theologian rather than a third-person perspective on what he or she is doing. This, he thinks, is the solution to the old controversy over a pietistic *theologia regenitorum*.[48] The solution means that the idea of an external, detached and 'neutral' theological enquiry is

---

45   Phillips, *Faith after Foundationalism*, p.238.
46   Tillich, *Systematic Theology* vol. I, pp.9–10.
47   Tillich, *Systematic Theology* vol. I, p.10.
48   Tillich, *Systematic Theology* vol. I, p.11.

a misunderstanding of the nature of religious belief and religious language, and thereby a misunderstanding of what theological thinking consists. It also means that there are no outward ways of deciding when a person has an internal relation to what he proposes. This can only be tested in practice, through the 'spiritual fruits'[49] or 'their verification in their efficacy in the life-process of mankind'.[50]

Precisely what Tillich means by 'being in the theological circle' is not obvious. But I think that this joint presentation of Tillich's and Phillips' ideas helps us to understand it better. Here the relevance of their prior understanding of religious language becomes evident. A religious language talking about an 'object', God, whose reality is internally related to the lives of the religious believers, demands of the person who claims to have some new insights, that he himself is internally related to the language and all that it stands for. As Tillich puts it: the criterion for whether the theologian is in the theological circle is 'the acceptance of the Christian message as his ultimate concern'.[51] This is another way to express the idea of an internal relation.

Tillich finds that this means that there is no first principle in a systematic presentation of theology. All parts of the system belong together.[52] In discussing basic propositions, Phillips puts this same idea as follows:

> We must not forget, once again, that, for Wittgenstein, the basic propositions he discusses in *On Certainty* are not foundations, not prior assumptions. On the contrary, they are held fast by all that surrounds them. The persuasion, if it occurs, will be persuasion in the context of trying to make all that surrounds what is basic come alive; it is, Wittgenstein says, swallowed down with it. This is not a matter of grounding from without. Our beliefs, in this context, are groundless. But it is a matter of elucidating from within. In such elucidation the belief may or may not come alive for the listener. Think of the way we speak of *instruction* in Faith. But what we hear may come alive in different ways.[53]

This is also a thought that finds expression by Tillich, in his idea of the openness of every new (and old) formulation of faith for being accepted *or* rejected; an idea that is also expressed in his 'protestant principle', although Tillich places this in a more theological framework than Phillips. At the same time Tillich also stresses that not much will be changed as long as a tradition is alive – a point he refers to as 'catholic substance'.[54] The idea that most parts in a living faith must not be questioned in a given moment is, I think, also familiar to Phillips.

---

49   Phillips, *Recovering Religious Concepts*, p.92.
50   Tillich, *Systematic Theology* vol. I, p.105.
51   Tillich, *Systematic Theology* vol. I, p.11.
52   Tillich, *Systematic Theology* vol. I, p.11.
53   Phillips, *Faith after Foundationalism*, p.89.
54   Tillich, *Systematic Theology* vol. I, p.37; *Systematic Theology* vol. III: *Life and the Spirit. History and the Kingdom of God*, Chicago, IL: University of Chicago Press, 1963, p.6.

Concluding Remarks

I have shown that Phillips and Tillich have the idea of an *internal* realism in understanding religious language in common. I have also intended to show that they are united in their struggle with the same problem in modernity, the philosophical and theological tendency to separate belief in God from its natural setting. In addition, I have pointed out that their solution leads to an understanding of constructive theological thinking as internally related to the tradition the theologian in question tries to understand. But this internal relation is seen at the same time as something that cannot be fully controlled by the theologian himself or by his academic (or any other) critics.

An interesting question which I have not developed here is to what extent philosophers of religion are bound to have an internal relation to the language they are commenting upon. For example, to what extent can they maintain a detached and neutral approach? Dewi Z. Phillips is himself a paradigm example of a philosopher who is very much committed to his task as a philosopher of religion. I leave open how to interpret this commitment.

Chapter VI

Philosophy and Theology – Too Close for Comfort. A Reply to Tage Kurtén

D.Z. Phillips

1. The Autonomy of Philosophy

At the outset of my reply to Stephen Mulhall, I emphasized my contemplative conception of philosophy in relation to two conceptions of the subject I am trying to avoid (p.29):

> Those who emphasize philosophy's negative task see the philosopher as an underlabourer (to borrow Locke's phrase), who has no subject of his own, but who has a technique for clearing up conceptual confusions on other people's sites. Those who emphasize philosophy's human significance see it as providing a philosophy for living, a guide for human life. The first conception does too little, while the second attempts too much. By contrast, a contemplative conception of philosophy, in seeking to do conceptual justice by the world in all its variety, does so in the sense of philosophy's concern with the very possibility of such a world.

Like Mulhall, Kurtén, too, is tempted to think that my emphasis on philosophical contemplation is a recent one, but, as I said, I perceived it in, and received it from, my teachers at Swansea. What has developed is my appreciation of the importance of this conception, and its centrality in the work of the great philosophers. The issue of the nature of philosophical enquiry is important in discussing Kurtén's comparison of Tillich and myself. I appreciate that he is writing as a theologian. He will appreciate that I am replying as a philosopher.

At the outset of his paper, while correctly identifying my contemplative conception of philosophy, Kurtén also attributes the therapeutic conception to me, saying, 'Philosophy only tries to settle conceptual confusions in our use of language' (p.96).[1] And at the end of the paper, we find him asking 'to what extent the philosopher of religion is bound to have an internal relation to the language he comments on. For example, to what extent can he maintain a detached and neutral approach?' (p.110). Why is there a tension in Kurtén's paper between these different conceptions of philosophy? We find an answer in terms of an historical context

---

1   All quotations from Kurtén are from Ch. V in the present volume, unless otherwise indicated.

which interests him, since he believes that Wittgenstein and I 'are of course children of [our] age, and are to be understood partly in relation to the situation in the history of ideas in which [we] live' (p.96).

The situation we face, according to Kurtén, is one bequeathed to us by Kant's critique of metaphysics. The critique created the conditions of modernity, in which theology in the nineteenth century, and linguistic philosophy in the twentieth century, both took an anthropological turn. Instead of the meaning of things being sought in transcendent ontology, Kurtén tells us, it is now sought (p.97)

> in the sense of concrete human lives, and not in a conception of an independent objective and outer world of facts, which in philosophy of religion could raise the question of a metaphysical reality that religious language tries to mirror'.

Wittgenstein would not agree with these remarks, which lead Kurtén to distinguish between external realism (ontology) and internal realism. The rejection of the former should not be equated with the denial of objective, independent facts. What I am writing these words with is called a pen; what I am writing on is called a writing pad; what the pad rests on is called a table; the table is in a room; the room is in a house and so on. These are all references to objective facts which are independent of me. If we conclude that we can no longer say this, we are agreeing, after all, that the notions of 'objectivity' and 'factuality' *do* depend on the very metaphysics we want to reject. This thought is perpetuated in the distinction between external and internal realism. What we need to recognize is *ordinary* realism.

Tillich and I, according to Kurtén, join hands in the way we meet the challenges of modernity. I want to make clear, at the outset that I, like Kurtén, am not going to get involved in differences concerning the interpretation of Tillich. I am simply going to accept Kurtén's view of him, since I am more concerned with the issues Kurtén wants to raise, then with Tillich. Kurtén sees Tillich as (p.97)

> an intellectual eager to come to grips with the modern man's capacity understand religious language and religious belief. In so doing, he also found that classical metaphysical solutions can no longer apply. We have to find new approaches if we are to make sense of religion in human life.

Would Wittgenstein say that there was a time when metaphysical solutions did work, but that they do not work now, hence the need for new solutions? He would not. For him, metaphysical systems cannot say what they want to say; their words have no application. When he claimed to destroy them, Wittgenstein said that he only destroyed houses of cards.

Wittgenstein's critique is connected with a frequent misunderstanding of my own work. Philosophers such as Terence Penelhum[2] and Roger Trigg[3] are quite happy to see me as a reformer of philosophical realism about religion; a realism which worked once, but does not work any more. To say that philosophical realism never

---

2   Terence Penelhum, *God and Skepticism*, Dordrecht: Reidel, 1983, p.163.

3   Roger Trigg, *Reason and Commitment*, Cambridge: Cambridge University Press, 1973, p.75.

made sense seems to them to be plainly absurd.[4] Like them, Steward Sutherland thinks that what I am doing, as a result, is to provide

> interesting constructions upon or revisions of the Christian tradition rather than as they are apparently offered, descriptions of the most essential or continuing elements of that tradition.[5]

Many other critics could be cited who see my work as religious or theological prescription, rather than as philosophical description.[6] The former view is easier to live with for them, since then I could simply be added to the list of rival interpreters. It is much harder to be told, as I tell my critics: You do not understand my work. I do not want to reform religious language. You may disagree with my conclusions, but you must try to appreciate the character of my investigations. Like Wittgenstein,

> if the place I want to get to could only be reached by way of a ladder, I would give up trying to get there. For the place I really have to get to is a place I must already be at now. Anything that I might reach by climbing a ladder does not interest me.[7]

There are times when Kurtén recognizes this clearly. He identifies my aim, in philosophy, as the difficult one of 'trying to go nowhere';[8] of waiting on the world in all its variety. But what about Tillich? Does he want to go somewhere? Does he try to climb a metaphysical ladder? If so, does Tillich ignore the autonomy of philosophy? In exploring these questions, I am concentrating on what I take to be tensions in Kurtén's paper. Doing so furthers discussion more than a concentration on our agreements, but it is as well to note the latter before examining the tensions.

Kurtén locates important similarities of emphasis in Tillich's theology and Wittgensteinian philosophy of religion. Here are some of them: (a) that the *sense* of God's reality is to be found in religious language (which is quite different from the absurd thesis that, as a result, God is thought to be a linguistic entity! One might as well argue that since we look to language to see *the sense* of the independence of a mountain's existence, it follows that a mountain is a linguistic entity.); (b) that the reality of God is not that of an object or entity, that is, of something which may or may not exist; (c) that the charge of 'non-cognitivism' against religious language comes from reserving the use of 'cognitive' for one kind of discourse which one thereby sublimes; (d) that religious concepts have their meaning in the lives people share.

---

4   See my 'On Really Believing', in *Wittgenstein and Religion*.

5   S. Sutherland, *God, Jesus and Belief*, Oxford: Blackwell, 1984, p.7. See my discussion in 'Religion in Wittgenstein's Mirror' in *Wittgenstein and Religion*.

6   For a recent discussion of them see the early chapters of *Religion and Friendly Fire*. For an oft-repeated claim that my analyses are apologetics in disguise see Kai Nielsen in Nielsen and Phillips, *Wittgensteinian Fideism?*

7   Ludwig Wittgenstein, *Culture and Value*, p.7.

8   See the last chapter of my *Philosophy's Cool Place*.

2. Tillich's Ladder

Kurtén is anxious to maintain that Tillich is not climbing a metaphysical ladder. It is easy to think that he does because of his emphasis on 'Being-itself'; an emphasis which will conjure up similarities with the early metaphysics of the Greeks. Many of the pre-Socratics asked, 'What is the nature of *all things*?' The measure offered in answer to this question was supposed to explain all things, since it was what all things were supposed to have in common. But any particular measure offered faced the unavoidable difficulty that it, too, was open to measurement. But if, as claimed, it was the measure of 'the real', what else was there to appeal to?[9] Tillich, Kurtén shows us, wanted to reject this transcendent notion of 'being'. He was a philosopher of religion as well as a theologian, and he appreciated the logical difficulties in speaking of 'Being-itself'. He saw parallels between these difficulties and the religious idea that God is 'ultimate reality'. This means that 'God', like 'Being-itself', cannot be a particular 'something', open to exploration in terms of a 'something' of another kind. For these reasons, Tillich said that we should look in another direction for an understanding of 'Being-itself': 'The term is not pointing to a certain "something" in reality outside human beings, a something the religious person would name God' (p.99).

On the face of it, that way of putting the matter is difficult. God is certainly not a 'something' among 'somethings', but, surely, his reality is said to be *other than* that of human beings. This is a matter to which we'll have to return. For now, one can concentrate on the fact that Tillich recognizes the futility of a marriage between theology and a transcendent metaphysics. If the place occupied by 'being in itself' in such a metaphysics is vacuous, nothing is achieved by placing God in it.[10] So far, so good, but what is Tillich's alternative? He suggests that 'Being-itself' be understood as a reality rooted 'in the sense of concrete human lives' (p.97). The vital question is whether this is the same emphasis as we find in Rush Rhees' extension of Wittgenstein's work, where he suggests that the intelligibility of things is rooted in the lives people share with each other, in what he called 'the interlocking intelligibility of language'.[11]

In speaking of 'the interlocking intelligibility of language', Rhees is careful to point out that this does not mean that we are all part of one big conversation, or of one big enterprise. He speaks, instead, of a hubbub of voices, some in close proximity to each other, while others pass each other by. There is no voice among them which can be shown to be basic, the one on which all the others depend. Many voices will have strong views on what other voices are saying. Thus, the hubbub cannot be reduced to any kind of theoretical or structural unity. A single voice, say a Christian one, may have *a unified response* to other voices, but that is quite different from the

---

9   See Rush Rhees, *In Dialogue With The Greeks*, vol. I: *The Presocratics and Reality*, Ch. 1, 'All Things'. See also Ch. 1 of my *Philosophy's Cool Place*.

10   See D. Z. Phillips, 'What God Himself Cannot Tell Us: Realism versus Metaphysical Realism', *Faith and Philosophy*, October 2002, and *Religion and Friendly Fire*, Chs. 2–4. See also my reply to Mulhall, Ch. II, section 3 of the present volume.

11   See, again, Ch. II, section 3.

theoretical claim that Christianity reveals the real unity concealed in them all. There is no such unity. Moreover, voices come and go, some prevailing over others at times, but subsiding at other times. Voices may die away, and new ones come to be. This is nothing less than the complexities of human life. A philosopher contemplates this tangled scene, hoping to do conceptual justice by it, whereas a theologian is a voice within it. Tillich is one such voice.

In his attempts to elucidate the Christian message for his time, Tillich is acutely aware of how difficult a task this is in the twentieth century. His efforts make him one of the great theologians of that century. Many give the highest theological accolade to the monumental works of Karl Barth. Barth, in his later work, reached out to the surrounding culture, but he will be remembered, primarily, as the theologian who gave a resounding 'No!' to any attempt to reduce or compromise the challenge of the Christian Gospel. Recalling my reply to Mario von der Ruhr, in Ch. IV, I could say that, for Barth, *the whole weight* is in the Christian picture.[12] He is indeed the guardian of the grammar of the Faith.[13] But what happens in a culture which is increasingly estranged from that grammar? Tillich was acutely aware of that estrangement. It has been said that whereas Barth looked inward to Faith, Tillich looked outward to a culture that was losing its hold on it. His efforts in doing so make him, for some, the greater theologian. The *philosophical* question which has to be asked is whether, despite his best intentions, Tillich climbed a metaphysical ladder in the service of apologetics. I believe he did.

At this point, we need to recall a danger, pointed out by Michael Weston, which may entrap those who turn to language and its historical contextuality, after having abandoned traditional metaphysics. Having given up the notion of a transcendent measure of all things, they turn to their historical situatedness 'to provide the materials for a renewed search for a historically situated measure'.[14] Does Tillich search for such a measure? He does, and claimed to have found it. It is called *ultimate concern*.

In discussing Rhees's reference to 'a hubbub of voices', I said that not only do voices prevail and subside, they also are born and die. This is something Tillich cannot allow as far as 'ultimate concern' is in question. This is a concern which never dies. This is not something Tillich has found out. How could it be? No, he secures the persistence of the concern by metaphysical means; he makes it constitutive of human existence itself. As Kurtén says, 'Tillich finds it important to emphasize an unconditional element in the experience man has in his encounter with reality.' But this 'unconditionality' has no application. It is completely unclear what is being said. Is Tillich saying that it is logically impossible to have human existence in which his 'ultimate concern' is not expressed? Or is he simply saying that, as a matter of fact, it will always be expressed? The latter will not do for him, since, as Kurtén recognizes, his problem is born of a fusion of theological and philosophical concerns. To appreciate these concerns, we must now, as promised, return to my

---

12 See Ch. IV, section 1.

13 See Jeffrey Willetts, 'Karl Barth and Philosophy', University of Wales PhD, 1996.

14 Michael Weston, Review of *Philosophy's Cool Place*, p.262. See also Ch. II, section 1 of the present volume.

earlier quotation from Kurtén. Referring to Tillich's notion of Being-itself, to which the notion of ultimate concern is supposed to be internally related, he says 'The term is not pointing to a certain "something" in reality outside human beings, a something the religious person would name God' (p.99). 'Being-itself' and, hence, 'ultimate concern', then, can only have meaning in the context of the lives people lead. But what *kind* of lives? Kurtén, expounding Tillich, replies (p.105):

> the idea can be detected only in concrete life and concrete religious language, it is not a presupposition which would make sense outside these concrete contexts. And it cannot be understood as a logical presupposition preceding a religious life.

The point could be put like this: the divine is not the presupposition of religious life, but shows itself *in* that life. According to Tillich, the 'showing' takes place via religious symbols, but he admits that the symbols themselves wax and wane (p.105):[15]

> Symbols, according to Tillich's view, are alive only as long as they are in use. That is why he can say that symbols can die. When they no longer make sense, then they have lost their position in the lives of those people.

The consequences of this line of argument roll on with a relentless logic (p.105):

> The only way talk of the death of God (or the existence/non-existence of God) could make any sense is when we discuss the way people do or do not live religious lives in today's world. Gods live and die among human beings. God's reality is internal to religious life.

Kurtén is aware of the dangers of the argument: 'But the position so outlined is in danger of reducing God to a social construction and thereby into something relativistic' (p.106). How does Tillich avoid this?

> To avoid the constructivist solution Tillich makes use of the concept 'Being-itself' and couples it with 'ultimate concern'. This very concept points to an element which necessarily is to be found in every human life, Tillich argues. It is not a contingent matter … Human life, so far as we know it, entails an element, ultimate concern, which cannot be taken totally away without the whole concept of human life changing radically.

By this time, Tillich has climbed to the top of his metaphysical ladder, from which the fall is great. Its beginnings can be seen in the last quotation from Kurtén. On the one hand, ultimate concern is defined as a *necessary* feature of every human life. On the other hand, it is said to be an element in human life as we know it, which is simply a factual claim. Such a claim is insufficient for Tillich's purposes, since it allows for the possibility of a human life without 'ultimate concern', albeit one that will have changed radically. Once *that* is allowed, Tillich would have to allow the possibility of the death of God. But, given Tillich's appreciation of the grammatical insights of the ontological argument, that is something he cannot assent

---

15   I am aware of the controversies surrounding Tillich's discussion of symbols. I am only concerned here with the role it plays in Kurtén's paper.

to. God is not a being that can come to be or pass away. It seems, therefore, that Tillich must stick to the view that 'ultimate concern' is a necessary feature of human existence; something which *cannot* be denied. The problem is that this seems to be little more than arbitrary stipulation on Tillich's part, although he claims that it is not an arbitrary matter. He needs to spell out what kind of necessity he is attributing to 'ultimate concern' in human life.

It isn't clear to me why Kurtén seems to think that Tillich's famous response to death-of-God theology helps in this connection: 'How could the Being-itself die?' All this can mean, given what we have been told, is: 'How can human existence cease to exist?' To which the answer is: by being destroyed or by destroying itself. But putting that obvious objection aside, Tillich has guaranteed the presence of religious life, simply by making all life religious. The problem is that Kurtén has already made a distinction between religious life and non-religious life in insisting that the notion of 'Being-itself' cannot *precede* religious life. But what is the purchase of this point if *all* life is said to be religious? If we are asked to do something if we believe in God, the imperative loses its imperative if *anything* we do meets the requirement.

I appreciate that Tillich was attempting to reach out to a culture for whom the significance of religious language had become eroded, but the concepts he provided, such as 'Being-itself', and 'ultimate concern', are too 'thin' to be substitutes for 'thick' religious concepts, or to sustain religious belief in their absence. And why should a substitution be thought possible? Kurtén seems to quote with approval Wittgenstein's insistence that a religious picture *says itself*. Wittgenstein asked, 'Why should you be able to substitute anything else?'[16] But isn't that what Tillich tries to do? Kurtén does not tell us what he thinks of 'Being-itself', or 'ultimate concern', as such substitutions. Still, we are told that many responded religiously to Tillich's terms. But I think the following question needs to be asked: When that happened, did Tillich's terms create religious sense, or did such sense as they had depend on their being echoes of a religious language far richer than themselves? If one believes the latter alternative to be the case, Tillich's 'ultimate concern', so far from being a necessary feature of human lives, turns out to be the threadbare remains of a well intentioned attempt to maintain religious belief in hard times. For many, Tillich's language created an impression of the need to say something, without providing a successful articulation of what that 'something' was.

Given these criticisms of Tillich, Kurtén would be quite justified in asking where they leave my own work. After all, he thinks that Tillich and I join hands in a common attempt to bring religious belief down to earth from the metaphysical heights at which it cannot breathe. But if I say that Tillich's attempt to avoid what he saw as the threat of relativism and constructivism fails, does it not fail in my own case also? For Kurtén, I hold that 'God's reality is internal to religious life' (p.106). But if that life, as I insist, could be devoid of any trace of religious belief, does it not follow that it is thereby devoid of God's reality? Kurtén offers a view of how I would respond to this problem, but it will not do at all (p.106):

---

16   Again, see the discussion of religious pictures in Ch. IV.

However, as far as I can see, Phillips' answer to this would be that this question of relativism makes no sense. As long as we do have religious people among us, religious language continues to puzzle us and to challenge the philosopher to come to terms with it. But when the moment comes (whether such a moment ever occurs is open) where there are no religious people in the world, religious language stops puzzling the philosopher

The moment alluded to in Kurtén's remarks *cannot* occur for Tillich. Religion does not disappear; it simply goes underground. I, on the other hand, allow that such a moment *could* occur. In that event, am I not committed to saying that God will have died? I do not know whether Kurtén thinks that this *is* an implication of the position he has attributed to me. I certainly think he should. If I accepted his attribution, without qualification, so should I. But I do not. Nevertheless, I am now faced with the task of showing why; of showing why this is one reason why I find his comparison between Tillich and myself, too close for comfort.

3. 'Can God Die?'

Readers will be disappointed if they expect me to answer the question 'Can God die?' with a 'Yes' or 'No', as though a philosopher could resolve the matter for everyone by his arguments. I have argued, elsewhere, that there is no *theoretical* answer to the question.[17] I imagined myself rushing by glass display cabinets in a museum inside which their contents were described as 'Gods of the Upper Nile' and 'Gods of the Lower Nile'. I then posed the question, 'Was I rushing by and ignoring the gods or not?' I do not want to rehearse my arguments here, since my concerns, though related, are rather different. But I ended my paper with comments which *are* relevant to what I want to discuss in closing my reply to Kurtén:

> I spoke of myself hurrying past the relics of dead religions in museums. But, to some extent, I am speaking for myself when I say this. I can give 'dead religions' a purely descriptive use by saying that I mean religions no longer practised. But in saying that I hurry past dead gods, I also show where I stand. After all, many hurry past crucifixes as I hurry past the gods of the Nile. But what would the believers of the dead religions say? They could say that I am ignoring divine realities which judge me for my disrespectful haste. Someone may want to ask: 'Were you hurrying past divine realities? Just tell me straightforwardly, 'Yes' or 'No', without invoking anything spiritual or confessional in your reply.' I have yet to come across a form of that question which makes sense. In other words, the question, 'Where are the gods now?' has no theoretical answer.[18]

Where Tillich is concerned, I feel that, at times, he falls off in attempting to walk the tightrope between theology and philosophy. Theologically, he is trying to address the problems of a culture increasingly estranged from religious language. Philosophically, by making 'ultimate concern' a necessary feature of human existence, he mistakenly tries to show that religious language is everyone's language.

---

17 'Where Are the Gods Now? Time for Judgement', in my *Recovering Religious Concepts*.

18 Phillips, 'Where Are the Gods Now?', p.241.

In my reply to Kurtén, I have to avoid the same mistake. In what follows, therefore, I am simply exploring the question of whether, given my views, a Christian who embraced them would *have* to say, if Christianity disappeared from the face of the earth, that God had died.

Tillich saw, clearly, that God's existence is not contingent. No Christian can say that God may die. Yet, the culture around him seemed to belie this fact. The God who cannot pass away seemed to be passing away in front of his eyes. In fact, Nietzsche had proclaimed that the death of God had already happened, although not even self-proclaimed atheists had appreciated the significance of the event:

> This tremendous event is still on its way, still wandering: it has not yet reached the ears of men. Lightening and thunder require time; the light of the stars requires time; deeds, though done, still require time to be seen and heard. This deed is still more distant from them than the most distant stars – and yet they have done it themselves.[19]

Why should this be the case? James Conant replies, 'God does not all of a sudden, at some point, simply cease to exist. Rather, God *dies*, and his death is a slow business.'[20] This is because God is not a 'something' that can, at any moment, cease to exist. Tillich, Kurtén, and I, would agree. God is Spirit, one that shows itself in the lives of human beings. But what if that spirit ceases to be shown? That, for Nietzsche, as Conant says, is the death of God:

> the overcoming of Christianity for Nietzsche lies not in the disappearance of a certain belief, but in a radical transformation of human existence into an existence no longer informed by Christian practice – no longer shaped by a Christian conception of what is valuable.[21]

What I am asking is: What was open to a theologian, like Tillich, to say, faced by Nietzsche's proclamation? As far as I can see, he had two options: first, he could have denied the possibility of the secular transformation of culture; second, he could have admitted its possibility, but denied that he *had* to say, as a result, that God is dead. As we have seen, Tillich, unfortunately, chose the first option. But what could the second option look like?

It may seem that the reminder that God is Spirit does not meet our difficulties. As I said, in my previous discussion of this matter, critics will remind us of the use of 'spirit' in other connections to bring out how difficult it is, in our context, to deny that God is dead:

> We speak of the spirt of a movement, the spirit of an age, and so on. Yet, when the movement is over and the age has passed, it would be confused to hypostatise their spirit as though it had an independent existence. When a person dies we sometimes say, 'He's gone. The life in him has departed'. Does not a time come when the gods depart, the life goes out of them, leaving their corpses in the museums – the mortal remains of the

---

19 Friedrich Nietzsche, *The Gay Science*, New York: Vintage, 1974, pp.181–82.
20 James Conant, 'Nietzsche, Kierkegaard and Anscombe on Moral Unintelligibility', in *Religion and Morality*, ed. D.Z. Phillips, Basingstoke: Macmillan, 1996, p.262.
21 Conant, 'Nietzsche, Kierkegaard and Anscombe', p.261.

gods? Feuerbach was right: to be serious, theology must be anthropology. The price of this awareness is the admission that religion is relative to the cultural context in which it flourishes and that God has no existence independent of it.[22]

But in speaking in this way, we are thinking of 'existence' as something that comes to be and passes away, whether the existence of an object, or the existence of a movement. But neither Tillich, nor Kurtén, nor I, think of God's existence in these terms. We are speaking of the reality of God, which is said to be a spiritual reality. To speak of it as not existing either before or after a specific time, is to think of it inappropriately in temporal terms. Whenever 'the eternal' appears, it appears as 'the eternal'. Why it should appear at all is, for a believer, a grace to be accepted.[23] As I said in my reply to von der Ruhr, to speculate on *how* it happens is to place 'the eternal' in an inappropriate conceptual category, as though one were trying to get inside the biographical details of what God was up to prior to creation. But 'the eternal' has no biography; God is not a creature among creatures. To speculate what God would be doing, or whether he would exist, if there were no religious believers, is to fall into the same assumptions about God's biography.

Consider a moral analogue. If, stranded in a desert with a friend, a person shared the little water remaining with him, despite the fact that he had a chance of survival whereas his friend did not, many would say that he did a fine thing. He does not survive, so no one knows of his deed. No knowledge of it exists. Does that mean that its moral significance is any less? Surely not. Speaking religiously of the situation, Kierkegaard would have said, 'Though no human being knows what he has done, God knows.'

Part of our difficulty comes from Kurtén's remark, in expounding death-of-God theology: 'Gods live and die among human beings. God's reality is internal to religious life' (p.106). Nietzsche can say that, but not believers in those gods. In Kurtén's remarks, the emphasis is on human beings and their lives. For the believers, the emphasis in their lives is *on God*. When they pray on God to turn away his wrath from them, the point of the prayer is not, 'Don't do that to me', but, rather, 'Don't let me become that'. But we are imagining a time when *no one* believes in God. As I said in my previous discussion, 'The relativist would say that God dies with the demise of this way of thinking.'[24] Kurtén fears the threat of such relativism in my own work, but it is not present there. The language of the eternal, as I said, 'allows the believer to speak of such an eventuality. He would say that the world had turned its back on God.'[25] Alternatively, one might see this as a divine judgement on the world.

Again, I can imagine someone, in the grip of temporality in thinking of God, saying, 'Well, nothing *actually happens* to us, or anyone else, or even the totality of the human race, as a result of not believing in God.'[26] The religious reply would be, 'The worst calamity of all has happened – we and they have lost God!' Tillich's

---

22   Phillips, 'Where Are the Gods Now? Time for Judgement', p.239.
23   See Ch. IV, section 5 of the present volume.
24   Phillips, 'Where Are the Gods Now? Time for Judgement', p.240.
25   Phillips, 'Where Are the Gods Now? Time for Judgement', p.240.
26   See the discussion of this reaction in Ch. IV, section 5 of the present volume.

mistake was to think he could show this *couldn't* happen. What I have attempted to do is to elucidate one religious reaction to the thought that it *could*; a reaction not open to Tillich. Since I want to recognize its possibility, joining my hands with Tillich is, on this matter, at least, too close for comfort.

4. Religion and Culture

In his contribution to this volume, Ingolf Dalferth says, in relation to my work:

> few of those who have praised or criticized his approach in recent years have paid enough attention to the fact that his belief in distinctive religious meanings is only the first part of a more complex view 'that although there are distinctive meanings, these cannot be what they are independent of their relation to other aspects of human life and culture'.[27]

Yet, the connection between religion and culture was emphasized relatively early in my work in a book to which not a lot of attention has been given, namely, *Belief, Change and Forms of Life*.[28] In that work, I addressed the possibility of belief in God, or belief in the God of a specific religion, disappearing entirely from the culture, the possibility that, as we have seen, Tillich seems to resist. I had, in fact, raised the question as early as 1970 in a published version of a BBC Radio Wales discussion with J.R. Jones. I asked the following question:

> if you said that certain modes of moral conduct were to pass away, some people might say that there would be no goodness in the world any more. So why do we not want to say that if these pictures were to die, God dies, as it were, with the pictures?[29]

But in *Belief, Change and Forms of Life* I discussed what I called three comforting theological or religious pictures which sought to deny that such pictures could die in a culture, or that if they did provision is always made for that eventuality. In view of what I take to be Tillich's unjustified optimism, I think it worthwhile to give a reminder of these three illusory sources of comfort, but for detailed examples I must refer the reader to the original work.[30]

I called the first illusory comforting picture *religious individualism*. In describing it, I expressed its core conviction as follows:

> There is a direct relationship between the believer and his personal Saviour. The believer who is saved has certainty in his heart. Whatever happens about him, the heart, the secret place, is safe from such influences.[31]

27　See Ch. IX, p.153 in the present volume.

28　D.Z. Phillips, *Belief, Change and Forms of Life*, Basingstoke and London: Macmillan, 1986.

29　'Belief and Loss of Belief' (with J.R. Jones), in *Wittgenstein and Religion*, pp.128–29. This discussion and the issues I am raising now are related, of course, to my previous discussions in Ch. IV of the present work.

30　Phillips, *Belief, Change and Forms of Life*, see Ch. 5, pp.84–97.

31　Phillips, *Belief, Change and Forms of Life*, p.84.

Having provided various examples, I concluded:

> The limits of intelligibility determine possibilities of speech and thought. This is as true of secret thoughts as of public utterances. So you could not have a longing to be king in a culture where the notion of kingship has no meaning, and no knowledge exists of what it is to be a king in another culture ... For these reasons, we cannot argue that Christianity has a hiding place in man's heart, since if the culture declines, in time there will also be a decline in the thoughts of men's hearts.[32]

I called the second illusory comforting picture *religious rationalism*, and described its core conviction as follows:

> No matter what cultural changes may take place, the validity of religious beliefs is secured by formal arguments which transcend the relativity of cultural contexts ... Such considerations cannot affect the truths of reason where the existence of God is concerned.[33]

I argued against this picture by arguing for its exact opposite:

> So far from it being the formal proofs which give a rational foundation to the beliefs of the faithful, it was the lives of the faithful which breathed into the formal proofs whatever life they had ... the arguments could not survive the demise of ... religious reactions [to the world]. Without the religious responses, the intellectual arguments would be no more than empty shells.[34]

The third illusory comporting picture is the one most relevant to Kurtén's comparison of Tillich and myself. I called it *religious accommodation*, and described its core conviction as follows:

> From the beginning, Christianity responds to the culture surrounding it. Therefore, whatever the changes in our culture, however dark it becomes for certain religious traditions, Christianity can always accommodate the situation by taking on new cultural forms ... Christianity can wear a new culture as it disposes of the previous one like an old garment. The question for Christianity in our day, therefore, is of how to come to a new cultural form which would contain an acceptable *apologia* to meet our contemporary crises.[35]

I argued against this picture by criticizing the analogy between culture and a garment which can be discarded at will. Religious ideas make a contribution to a culture, and that contribution cannot come about as a matter of policy. I said, by way of example concerning excellence in a culture:

---

32 Phillips, *Belief, Change and Forms of Life*, pp.85–86.
33 Phillips, *Belief, Change and Forms of Life*, pp.90–91.
34 Phillips, *Belief, Change and Forms of Life*, pp.91–92.
35 Phillips, *Belief, Change and Forms of Life*, pp.93–94.

Shakespeare, Beethoven and Tolstoy did not give us their work *in order* that we might have something excellent in culture. No, they gave us what they had to give and we found it was excellent.[36]

I argued that religious apologists have much to learn from this conceptual truth:

> The Church cannot speak to the culture in which it is placed by making this a matter of policy. No, it speaks and perhaps the consequences will be good. The Church cannot *decide* to speak with authority in the culture. It speaks and perhaps its voice will be authoritative. Jesus spoke as one having authority, not as one who decided to speak with authority.[37]

So it is with religious leaders, prophets and theologians. They speak and what they say may or may not be authoritative. Tillich spoke in his time. I believe that the issue of whether his voice carried any authority is a matter which divides Christians. My point is that this cannot be made a matter of policy. I went on to say:

> A movement, and a religious movement is no exception, flourishes when people are engaged in its particular concerns, not when they are preoccupied with its maintenance ... But, it may be said, things are falling apart, so why should not the Church be concerned with maintaining the truth. This form of words, in certain circumstances, may be unobjectionable ... Yet the matter must be stated carefully. There is nothing in religion akin to carrying on for the sake of the children in a marriage ... in the case of religion there is no second best once the spirit of faith has departed. One can have integrity in a marriage when love has died, but there is no such thing as integrity in religion when faith has gone.[38]

I go on in *Belief, Change and Forms of Life* to say that my remarks do not support either an *a priori* pessimism, or an *a priori* optimism. But many apologists find my conclusions disturbing because, I suspect, they do possess an optimism of the latter sort. Did Tillich? Does Kurtén? But one must be extremely careful in arriving at one's judgement in these matters, because although a Christian may be obviously optimistic, his optimism may not be of the kind I am criticising *at all*. I'll end by quoting an extended example of how my teacher, Rush Rhees, following Wittgenstein, draws a distinction between different kinds of optimism:

> I will mention ... a remark Wittgenstein made to me after a talk Farrington had given to our Philosophical Society.[39] Farrington[40] spoke on 'Causality in History', in which he advanced some version of the Marxian 'dialectic', with the idea that this shows that in the course of history there is 'progress on the whole'. In the discussion Wittgenstein showed easily enough the incoherence of Farrington's discourse. And when he was walking home with me afterwards he said how he disliked this kind of 'optimism' which was supposed

---

36   Phillips, *Belief, Change and Forms of Life*, p.95.

37   Phillips, *Belief, Change and Forms of Life*, p.95.

38   Phillips, *Belief, Change and Forms of Life*, pp.95–96.

39   Benjamin Farrington, Professor of Classics at Swansea, read a paper on 'Causal Laws and History' to the Philosophical Society in 1943.

40   See Rhees, 'Postscript', in *Recollections of Wittgenstein*, Oxford: Oxford University Press, 1984, p.201.

to result from demonstration (from a theory of history, or of how history must go). 'If a man says 'Certainly things look black at the moment; and if you look at past history, you can find plenty that might lead anyone to be depressed. But in *spite* of all that, I am *still* optimistic.' – then I can admire this, even if I do not agree with him. But if his optimism is just the outcome of a scientific proof – the scientific study of history – then ...' That seemed to Wittgenstein a weak and mealy-mouthed sort of optimism, I think; and one with a sort of smugness to it. It was not really facing the problem it pretended to face; it was painting it over.[41]

I do not think of Tillich or Kurtén as Wittgenstein thought of Marxian dialectic's optimism, but aren't there conceptual parallels to be faced? I can imagine a Christian saying, 'Things certainly look dark, and there is plenty to be depressed about, but I still have hope' – that I can admire. But if someone says, 'I'm optimistic about the future of Christianity because it "points to an element which is necessarily to be found in every human life"' (p.106), then isn't that, too 'not really facing the problem it pretended to face; it was painting it over'?[42]

---

41   Rush Rhees, 'Death and Immortality', in *Rush Rhees on Religion and Philosophy*, ed. Phillips, p.226.
42   Rhees, 'Death and Immortality', p.226.

Chapter VII

A Friend of Demea?
The Meaning and Importance of Piety

Walter van Herck
University of Antwerp

Introduction

In Hume's *Dialogues* Cleanthes is the defender of the well known 'argument from design', an argument which should prove 'the existence of a Deity, and his similarity to human mind and intelligence'. D.Z. Phillips wrote a lot about and against 'the friends of Cleanthes', who get stuck in the tentacles of evidentialism, anthropomorphism and so on. I would like to take the position of one of Cleanthes' opponents, namely Demea, as a starting point for posing some questions in the margins of Phillips' philosophical work. Is he – in declaring himself to be an opponent of Cleanthes – automatically a friend of Demea?

Demea's response to the argument of Cleanthes is rage. 'Good God! cried Demea, interrupting him, where are we? Zealous defenders of religion allow, that the proofs of a Deity fall short of perfect evidence!' What Demea would like is an *a priori* argument – something that would demonstrate the absolute existence of God in an absolute manner. He despises the way in which Cleanthes' argument remains within the boundaries of 'experience and probability' and the imperfect evidence that results from it. His God is a rock, not a probability. In fact one could interpret his cries as saying that anyone who speaks of God in terms of the probable hasn't understood anything about religion. Not without reason he uses the expression 'these extravagant opinions of Cleanthes'. Cleanthes uses words and concepts to speak about God which according to Demea have no place in the vicinity of 'God'. It is an extravagance to use these words and phrases in connection with God. Aren't Demea's remarks in fact grammatical remarks? And doesn't that feature of his interventions make Phillips a potential friend of Demea?

What kind of a man is this Demea? In the *Prologue* he is characterized with the phrase 'the rigid inflexible orthodoxy of Demea'. In *Part I* he reveals himself to be a very pious man who is concerned about the religious education of children. When he points out that students of philosophy must first be introduced to all the subbranches of philosophy before embarking on the complexities of the nature of God, Philo is quick to ask him why he is so late in teaching youngsters the principles of religion. His reply is illustrative:

> It is only as a science, replied Demea, subjected to human reasoning and disputation, that I postpone the study of natural theology. To season their minds with early piety is my chief care; and by continual precept and instruction, and I hope too, by example, I imprint deeply on their tender minds an habitual reverence for all the principles of religion.

Pious as he is, he sees the importance of 'an habitual reverence' in matters of religion. Demea doesn't seem willing to embrace the concept of 'natural religion', which is a new, philosophical type of religion. He leads everything that is said about God back to its habitat of piety and devotion. This is counter the enlightened current and so he is perceived as holding on to orthodoxy in a rigid and inflexible manner. And here is a second feature that may remind us of Wittgensteinian philosophy of religion. Words and concepts are understood in the form of life to which they belong. The importance of 'habitual reverence' is the importance D.Z. Phillips attaches to practices.

The three participants of the dialogue seem to agree that the question of the existence of God and that concerning his nature can be separated. His existence is so certain that there is no need to make it the subject of the debates. His nature however should be the subject of debate: his attributes, his decrees, and his plan of providence. However, it goes without saying that any conclusion about God's nature, which differs radically from the believer's views of God, amounts to the same thing as a straightforward denial of his existence.

When at the end of *Part XI* Philo summarizes his reasoning by saying that 'the original source of all things … has no more regard to good above ill than to heat above cold', Demea soon after draws his conclusions and leaves, on some pretence or other, the company. He is better off absent. For in this way he doesn't have to listen to what is unisono declared by Cleanthes and Philo in *Part XII*. The idea that the controversy between theist and atheist is merely verbal, nothing but a dispute about words and degrees, would have made Demea's ears tingle. Religious faith and trust seem to be reduced here to an opinion about the cause of nature. Another (third) reason for a friendship between Demea and D.Z. Phillips?

Now there are obvious differences between these two, but I would like to postpone the study of the differences a bit. Demea is a pious man who resists the idea of a 'natural religion'. What is piety? Why is it such an unpopular concept today?[1] Is Phillips' philosophy of religion able to cope with the phenomenon of piety? Without pretending to answer these questions, I hope to point to what could be the beginnings of an answer.

1. Attachment and Detachment in Religion

One can find in popular culture a very specific ideal of wisdom. One of the characteristics commonly ascribed to the sage is his ability to see meaning in all

---

1   'Piety', for example, does not appear in the table of contents or in the index of Philip L. Quinn and Charles Taliaferro, eds., *A Companion to Philosophy of Religion*, Oxford: Blackwell, 1997 – this is indicative of the fact that philosophy of religion is to many in the Anglo-Saxon region really 'philosophy of God'.

things, at all times, with all people. Wisdom concerns the inner, not the outer. Unlike us, the sage does not become irritated by the behavior of a careless waiter, or impatient in a traffic jam. On the contrary, even in these situations he is able to see meaning. It is as if he detects a reflection of the absolute in everything. Of course he is not permanently moved, but he remains peaceful with things. This image of the sage has its historical roots, but it is also a cliché: be content with the small and the ordinary.

In the name of this ideal of wisdom the traditional religions are often critized. Instead of conducting people – this is the criticism – to the kernel or the essence of meaning (as described above), they saddle people with the accidental and the accessory. The traditional religions are the champions of the non-essential: one has to know particular texts by heart (the *Our Father*, the *Creed*, etc.), know how to perform certain ritual actions, attend specific services in specific buildings and stick to all kinds of (sometimes absurd) rules. Against this, every rational man should be able to see that 'salvation' is not dependent on knowing certain texts by heart, on burning candles in front of certain statues, on receiving the holy communion, on visiting certain holy places. Is it really necessary to contemplate a tabernacle in order to find meditative rapture, in order to reach salvation? Can't a daily, wondering glimpse at the breadbasket have the same existential effect? For many people who express this criticism, it also follows that it would in principle be possible to do away with all traditional and/or institutional religions and still have religious people around. They would be brought to enlightenment and salvation by contemplating nature, the faces of their fellow men and the most ordinary things. Such a world would even be a better world because all forms of superstition and religious intolerance would be gone.

2. Piety and Superstition

In contrast, the pious person holds on to traditional forms, texts, and actions with great earnestness. In this seriousness he is a potential target for mockery. Not only does he seem to be irrational (Why – for God's sake – take your hat off in church? Does God love you less if you keep it on?), but to this is added that he isn't seen as very religious. He is accused of mistaking the accidental for the essential. He is attached to the cultural and symbolical forms of his religion, when religion should in fact detach people. The wrong road to salvation?

In its earliest meaning 'piety' has to do with honouring your parents (Plato, *Laws*, 717a e). Diogenes Laërtius (III, 83) describes three forms of justice: towards the gods, towards fellow humans and towards the dead. Piety is the first form of justice. Cicero gives the classical definition (*De natura deorum*, I, 116): 'iustitia adversum deos' – in this line he speaks of 'a science of worshipping the gods' (*scientia colendorum deorum*). Piety is therefore in ancient times connected with accomplishing acts of cult. The pious man is very scrupulous in matters of ritual (*akribestata*). Given then his attachment to traditional forms and his scrupulousness concerning worship, it comes as no surprise that piety and superstition are easily associated. An extremely amusing example of this is to be found in Theophrastus'

Characters. The character that embodies superstition (δεισιδαιμονια) is fearful of supernatural powers. He sprinkles himself with holy water before leaving his home; he throws three stones over the road when a weasel has crossed his path; he is always giving his house a ritual cleansing; after each dream he runs to a visionary to inform to which god or goddess he has to direct his prayers.

The concept of piety undergoes several historical changes, beautifully depicted in the *Dictionnaire de spiritualité.*[2] Piety becomes a virtue, even the source of all virtues. The historical tendency is of course towards spiritualization: piety seen as a completely inner practice. Insofar as piety keeps on testifying of a religious attachment to what is outward, material and particular – to specific words, phrases, gestures, pictures and so on – piety is no longer understood. It is easily equated with superstition and with a mercantile conception of the religious life (*do ut des*).

In his *Dictionnaire philosophique* Voltaire writes 'Almost anything that goes beyond the adoration of a supreme being and the submission of the heart to his eternal orders is superstition.'[3] Having reduced religion to deistic opinions it is no wonder that all the rest is to him superstition. Under the same heading of 'superstition' he declares that Christianity was infected with it from the beginning. When Voltaire asks whether there can be a people free of superstitious prejudices, he immediately adds that this question is the same as asking whether there can be a people consisting of nothing but philosophers.[4]

In the same line David Hume writes:

> superstition is a considerable ingredient in almost all religions, even the most fanatical; there being nothing but philosophy able entirely to conquer these unaccountable terrors.[5]

Seeing philosophy as a solid alternative to religion tells us a lot about the underlying notion of religion. To Hume, however, superstition is only one extreme, the other is enthusiasm. In criticizing enthusiasm he acknowledges the importance of 'outward ceremonies and observances':

> When the first fire of enthusiasm is spent, men naturally, in all fanatical sects, sink into the greatest remissness and coolness in sacred matters; there being no body of men among them, endowed with sufficient authority, whose interest is concerned to support the

---

2   A. Méhat, A. Solignac and I. Noye, lemma 'Piété', in *Dictionnaire de spiritualité*, Paris: Beauchesne, 1932–1995, col. 1694–1743.

3   Voltaire, *Dictionnaire philosophique*, Paris: Garnier-Flammarion, 1964, p.357: 'Presque tout ce qui va au-delà de l'adoration d'un Être suprême et de la soumission du cœur à ses ordres éternels est superstition.'

4   Voltaire, *Dictionnaire philosophique*, p.358: 'La superstition née dans le paganisme, adoptée par le judaïsme, infecta l'Eglise chrétienne dès les premiers temps'; p.360: 'Peut-il exister un peuple libre de tous préjugés superstitieux? C'est demander: Peut-il exister un peuple de philosophes?' It is clear that mainly external practices like ritual pose the problem, p.359: 'La secte qui semble le moins attaquée de cette maladie de l'esprit est celle qui a le moins de rite.'

5   David Hume, *Essays. Moral, Political and Literary*, Indianapolis, IN: Liberty Fund, 1985, p.75.

religious spirit: No rites, no ceremonies, no holy observances, which may enter into the common train of life, and preserve the sacred principles from oblivion.[6]

To follow for example Voltaire in his views would involve condemning most religions of the world as superstitious. Furthermore, it would be impossible to draw a distinction between superstition and piety *within* a particular religious tradition. How does Phillips see superstition?

3. Piety, Superstition and Petitionary Prayer

In *The Concept of Prayer* (1965), Phillips tries to make sense of the belief of religious people that prayer must make a difference.[7] In the case of petitionary prayer this means understanding their making specific requests in prayer. In Phillips' view the borderline with superstition is very close.

Phillips seems to define superstition as a causal mistake: to wrongly think that a supernatural cause is responsible for fulfilling the desires made explicit in prayer. Prayer is neither an incantation nor a magical formula. In prayer what one says is of importance, while in an incantation this – in a certain sense – is not true:

> According to such a position, it does not matter from the point of view of *what is said* whether one says one thing or another; what matters is whether what is said *works* or not, that is, whether it brings about the desired end.[8]

Phillips is right of course: when prayer is seen as a way of getting things done, it is a causal mistake. And the orthodox will agree because their God is not an instrument or a means to some further end. Exactly this is what happens, according to Phillips, when one prays for special favours. But how do we know whether a given prayer is a way of getting things done? The criterion to be used here is the relation between the prayer and life. Is this a one-time prayer of an otherwise irreligious or indifferent person? The more this question is answered in the affirmative, the more the likelihood of superstition increases. In the face of death many start to pray, but on Phillips' criterion it isn't even prayer: 'Unless prayers play a certain role in the person's life after the crisis is over, they are not characteristic of the religious role of prayer in the life of the believer. These prayers are far nearer superstition: kissing a rabbit's foot or touching wood.'[9] An anecdote can bring further clarification. A diver who lost his torch while searching a shipwreck, can pray 'O God get me out of this. I'll do anything you want if only you'll let me find my way out.'[10] In analyzing this story Phillips finds two assumptions: (a) that God could intervene to save him, and (b) that God must have a reason for saving him. Isn't it true then that many prayers presuppose the possibility of divine intervention?

---

6   Hume, *Essays*, pp.77–78.

7   D.Z. Phillips, *The Concept of Prayer*, London: Routledge & Kegan Paul, 1965, Ch. 6.

8   Phillips, *The Concept of Prayer*, p.114.

9   Phillips, *The Concept of Prayer*, p.116.

10   Phillips, *The Concept of Prayer*, p.117.

It seems to be Phillips' purpose to deny this. Whenever this possibility is entertained, it follows either that it was not a prayer (but an exclamation), or a case of superstition. For given the fact that the diver dies and given the presupposition of divine intervention, we can follow two lines of thought. The first line is that God had, in this case, no good reasons for saving the diver and that God might have good reasons to save other divers. This leaves us with a rather cruel God. The second line of thought would be to suggest that the diver didn't pray hard enough. If he had, he would have been saved. This line is akin to 'The spell was not powerful enough', and is accordingly superstition.

Now, Phillips has a feel for nuances and knows that the borderline between superstition and true devotion is not razor sharp: 'A prayer does not always reveal by its outward character whether it is rooted in devotion or superstition.'[11] The lighting of a candle, the burning of incense and the offering of flowers to Our Lady can be acts of devotion, but can also be superstition. It all depends on whether or not one believes that things go wrong if one doesn't perform these acts, on whether or not one believes that one is thereby influencing God, Our Lady. The flower offering is not superstitious when it is an act of thanksgiving for, for example, the birth of a child.

Doesn't this mean that according to Phillips there is very little 'petition' in petitionary prayer? A non-superstitious petitionary prayer would according to him be characterized by the following: (a) recognition that things can go either way (and meeting this possibility in God); (b) recognition of one's own helplessness; (c) search for something to sustain one that does not depend on the way things go, namely the love of God.[12]

Such a prayer is mainly an expression of the strength of one's desires and of one's devotion to God. The only reason why the believer doesn't simply pray 'Thy will be done' is that he wants to name the desires that occupy his head and heart. In the superstitious version however one is convinced that God can intervene if he wants to and that by praying it is possible to influence his divine will.

I am not really convinced by this account of petitionary prayer. I think it is one-sided and turns the majority of believers in the world into superstitious people. Convinced of the necessity of using in the philosophy of religion a 'principle of charity', I give the following arguments that may reveal this one-sidedness. There is petition in petitionary prayer and there is nothing wrong with believing in divine intervention.

If the only point of petitionary prayer would be to name the desires that threaten to overwhelm one and to express (and request) devotion to God, then the result would be a completely different type of prayer, something more like: 'Lord, I'm being consumed by my desire that X would be the case, but thy will be done.' In other words, petitionary prayer and prayer about one's overwhelming desires should not be taken as identical.

Another questionable move is, I think, to dig for presuppositions where ordinary people do not suppose or presuppose anything. Petitionary prayer seems to presuppose

---

11 Phillips, *The Concept of Prayer*, p.118.
12 Phillips, *The Concept of Prayer*, p.120.

the possibility of divine intervention. But divine intervention in itself entails a cruel God who intervenes in some cases and not in others. Thus, petitionary prayer does not presuppose divine intervention; when it does, it is superstition.

But sometimes people pray without having a theology or metaphysics of prayer. In a variation on Wittgenstein's words, one could say that 'people do this [pray] and then feel satisfied'. Religious devotion is not in search of coherence. Prayer and what people say about it are not meant to be developed in all kinds of directions. If this were a principle to go by, one should not be allowed to speak about, again following Wittgenstein, 'the eye of God', because this entails that God has eyebrows, can get cataract, has a body and so on. Part of learning a religious language-game is learning how one may or may not develop utterances, metaphors and ideas. In the same vein Phillips says that we cannot tell God something he didn't know when we ask him for something specific in prayer, because that would not be in accordance with the notion of an all-knowing God whom people say they venerate. But as William James points out, God is endowed with metaphysical attributes such as 'infinite' (and in this line also all-knowing) by philosophers and ordinary men alike. When we look at their religious practices (like petitionary prayer), however, we find that these practices are not in accordance with the metaphysically professed beliefs: 'I feel bound to say that religious experience, as we have studied it, cannot be cited as unequivocally supporting the infinitist belief ... Partial and conditional salvation is in fact a most familiar notion.'[13] Why would what a believer says about his practices be assigned more authority than the practices themselves?

So, the notion of divine intervention should not be dropped in a description of prayer because it entails incoherent propositions. In fact, the view that any implication of divine intervention in prayer is superstition sounds more like a theological decision rather than a philosophical description. To begin with, not every specific request made to God or a saint must be seen as a reduction of God or saint to the level of a means to an end. People ask me favours all the time, and though some people make me feel used, I do not feel used all the time. Why should it be impossible to influence the divine will?[14] More importantly, whatever one answers to the last question, it must be noted that it is a theological question (not for a philosopher to decide, as Phillips so often tells his audiences).

I would like to bring this criticism of Phillips' views of petitionary prayer and superstition into a broader historical perspective.[15] I have already drawn attention to the fact that since the twelfth century there is a tendency to see piety as concerning only the inner self. Before that time piety and spirituality were much more

---

13 William James, *The Varieties of Religious Experience*, ed. M.E. Marty, Harmondsworth: Penguin, 1985, pp.525–26.

14 'Influence' does not of course mean 'compelled'. See C.S. Lewis, 'The Efficacy of Prayer', in C.S. Lewis, *Essay Collection. Faith, Christianity and the Church*, ed. L. Walmsley, London: Harper Collins, 2000, pp.238–39: 'For prayer is request. The essence of request, as distinct from compulsion, is that it may or may not be granted. ... God always hears and sometimes grants our prayers.'

15 See also Brian R. Clack, 'D.Z. Phillips, Wittgenstein and Religion', *Religious Studies* 31 (1995), 111–20, and Phillips' reaction, 'On Giving Practice its Due – a Reply', *Religious Studies* 31 (1995), 121–27.

associated with outward (moral, symbolical, sacramental) actions. This is reflected in the Catholic view of superstition. Traditionally, in Catholicism, superstition has a specific, fourfold meaning: (a) improper worship of the true God; (b) idolatry or offering Divine worship to beings other than God; (c) divination or trying to extract from creatures what only God knows; (d) vain observances or magic and occultism. It should be noticed that unlike in Phillips' approach, superstition has here to do with a specific class of actions. Phillips focuses on the inner: on the intentions and convictions of the actor. Does he make a causal mistake? Does he think that God can intervene? Does he think that he can influence God's will?

This brings us back to the popular view I spoke about in the beginning of this paper: the kernel of religion is or should be purely spiritual. We know where people got this idea. They got it from the Enlightenment thinkers: religion is all about convictions and sentiments concerning God, the afterlife and morality. The rest (traditions, rituals, devotions) is excess luggage. Although William James stands in this enlightened current with his highly individualistic and emotional view of religious experience, he also went against the tide in his emphasis on the importance of the notion of divine intervention. It is to his criticisms of the enlightened distortions of religion that we now turn.

4. Crass and Refined Supernaturalism

In a brief postscript to *The Varieties of Religious Experience. A Study in Human Nature* (1902) William James makes a distinction between naturalists (for whom everything is to be explained in natural, even material terms) and super-naturalists (for whom the natural order does not have the last word).[16] Within the class of supernaturalists, he further distinguishes between the 'crasser' and the 'more refined' variety. The refined supernaturalists, which according to James includes most philosophers, deny that the supernatural can in any way interfere with the course of events in the natural world: the world of the ideal never bursts into the phenomenal world at particular points. In contrast to this, the crasser variety, which has a large following among the uneducated 'admits miracles and providential leadings and finds no intellectual difficulty in mixing the ideal and the real worlds together by interpolating influences from the ideal region among the forces that causally determine the real world's details'.[17]

Because he is convinced that through interrelation with the Ideal, new forces are released into the world, James classes himself among the crasser type. The refined type yields too much ground to naturalism, for every particular fact can be explained at the phenomenal level. The *super*-element only comes into view with reference to the totality. The world *as a whole* is a supernatural fact, not the particular events which fill the world.[18] The smallest unit within which the Absolute can operate is

---

16   James, *The Varieties of Religious Experience*.
17   James, *The Varieties of Religious Experience*, pp.520–21.
18   Under the heading refined supernaturalism, James had in mind idealists such as F.H. Bradley. For a comparison of James and Bradley in this respect see T.L.S. Sprigge, 'Refined and Crass Supernaturalism', in *Philosophy, Religion and Spiritual Life*, ed. M. McGhee,

the world in total, while our limited minds feel that every change for the better must happen *in* this world at specific moments. James writes: 'In this universalistic way of taking the ideal world, the essence of practical religion seems to me to evaporate.'[19] For the refined supernaturalist there is, for instance, no point in prayer. If we don't like the way things are, then we should have spoken up earlier and prayed for a different world before this one came into being. James calls himself a crass supernaturalist because the idea that no single particular of experience can change its complexion as a result of God's existence is to him quite preposterous. Yet this is the central tenet of refined supernaturalism: 'It is only with *experience en bloc*, that the Absolute maintains relations. It condescends to no transactions of detail.'[20]

The crasser form of supernaturalism, which is what in fact the vast majority of simple believers really subscribe to, has within it the notion of partial and conditional salvation and even a disguised sort of polytheism. In defending this crasser form James feels himself alone 'like a man who must set his back against an open door quickly if he does not wish to see it closed and locked'.[21] In other words for James there was a cause worth fighting for: on no account must the door be closed.

The line that James is taking brings to mind the way David Hume put it in the eighteenth century. According to Hume, humankind is not in the first place led to religious worship through rational contemplation of the uniform laws of nature. For the religious person it is precisely the irregularities, the sudden turn of events that are primary. '[A]n animal, complete in all its limbs and organs, is to him an ordinary spectacle, and produces no religious opinion or affection', but 'a monstrous birth excites his curiosity, and is deemed a prodigy. It alarms from its novelty; and immediately sets him a trembling, and sacrificing, and praying.'[22] Hume too is suggesting that crass supernaturalism plays the more important part. Supernatural incursions that manifest themselves in wondrous happenings score higher on the religious scale than the unchanging regularity of nature. It is only in philosophical circles that the eternal constancy of the natural order is seen as a pointer to God.

The distinctions made (between crass and refined supernaturalism, between supernatural intrusions and a fixed order of things) correspond to what in the Christian tradition is referred to as particular and general providence. God cares for humankind not only by giving his creation order and regularity; at the same time he provides for all the particular events in a human life that he endows with a meaning that is only open and apparent to him. If we translate James's and Hume's concerns into Christian terminology, then their point is the importance of particular providence. The door that must not be closed is the door of crass supernaturalism, of particular providence, of a divine order, which shines through the history of each

---

Cambridge: Cambridge University Press, 1992, pp.105–25. See further by the same author *James and Bradley: American Truth and British Reality*, Chicago, IL: Open Court, 1993.

19   James, *The Varieties of Religious Experience*, p.521.
20   James, *The Varieties of Religious Experience*, p.522.
21   James, *The Varieties of Religious Experience*, p.523.
22   David Hume, 'The Natural History of Religion', in *Hume on Religion*, selected and introduced by R. Wollheim, Collins, The Fontana Library, 1963, p.35.

person. It is, that much should be clear, the door that piety uses all the time. Is it the front entrance or is it only a suspendable, redundant back door?

5. Piety and Religious Language

In the mind of many intellectuals, piety is a secondary phenomenon. It concerns attachment to the outward, material forms, actions, symbols, and so on, of a religion. Contrary to what Phillips says, even in prayer one is attached to these words in this particular sequence. The words of the *Our Father*, of the *Creed* cannot be varied at random.[23] That is why a look at religious language from the perspective of piety may help us further.

In a classical formulation of the problem of religious language it concerns the quest for a middle course between univocity and equivocity. If words and phrases mean exactly the same in a religious context as in a non-religious context, then the divine is taken down. If those words and phrases mean something completely different in a religious context, we in fact do not know what we are saying in religious contexts. It is not difficult to recognize the cliffs of anthropomorphism in the first alternative and the cliffs of agnosticism in the second.[24]

The presupposition of much philosophizing about religious language is that it is, in an important sense, always secondary or derivative language. B. Tilghman describes what I mean here as follows:

> The reason for this, I suggest, is that our understanding of the language of religion is derivative from our understanding of the language in which we talk of other people. We must know what it is to talk to another person before we can understand what it is to talk to God and we must understand what it is for something to be the handiwork of a man before we can understand the world as the handiwork of God.[25]

Many predicates that are used to describe God are also used to describe people. The examples that one analyses and tries to explain in the study of religious language are mostly of the following types:

Examples:
(a) God is good.
(b) God is wise.
(c) God is king.
(d) God is shepherd.

What is striking, is that the discussion is concentrated on predicates for God (*God-talk*) and that it concerns always – whether this religious discourse is literal language

---

23   See Catherine Pickstock, 'Asyndeton: Syntax and Insanity. A Study of Revision of the Nicene Creed', *Modern Theology* 10 (1994), 321–40.

24   Wim A. de Pater, *Analogy, Disclosures and Narrative Theology*, Leuven: Acco, 1988, p.35.

25   B.R. Tilghman, 'Isn't Belief in God an Attitude?', *International Journal for Philosophy of Religion* 43:1 (1998), p.25.

(as in the examples (a) and (b)) or figurative (as in examples (c) and (d)) is quite immaterial – predicates which also have an extra-religious use. God is good and wise, but people are good and wise too (or can be). The application of these concepts to God presupposes a familiarity with their so-called ordinary use, as Tilghman remarks in the above quotation. Theories of religious language therefore generally explain how the ordinary or profane use is linked to the derivative, religious use. The doctrine of analogy for example says that both uses are not identical but connected. I.T. Ramsey tried to indicate something similar with his concept of disclosure.

There remains however a question as to the way in which the speaker is able to make this step from the ordinary, profane use to the religious, derivative use of these terms. The speaker must have some clue about or some sensitivity for the religious quite apart of this secondary talk, otherwise the transposition from the profane to the religious would not appeal to him. In answering this question the part played by a religious language, which is non-derivative, seems to me crucial. It concerns a portion of the religious vocabulary, which is often neglected in philosophy of religion. This non-derivative religious language consists in words and expressions, which have no other but a purely religious use. This discourse is religious although it is mostly not about God. The following examples from the Catholic tradition may clarify what I have in view:

> *ablution* (cleansing of chalice and fingers by the priest),
> *absolution* (prayer at the bier in remission of sins),
> *alb* (white linen vestment with long sleeves),
> *Low Sunday* (first Sunday after Easter),
> *beguine*,
> *Capuchin, chrisma, tonsure, complines, confiteor, consecration*[26]

Although these words may be derived from non-religious terms, they are used exclusively within religion (as opposed to such terms as 'good', 'wise', 'king' and 'shepherd'). They all concern liturgical objects, acts or vestments such as the liturgical year, ecclesiastical architecture, religious orders and their ways of life, ecclesiastical authorities and institutions. In sum: they all concern the most material, tangible aspects of religion. This language is exclusively religious and represents a symbolical and tangible universe in which the body is central: one bows and kneels in front of the altar, strides through the nave, smells the incense, sings the psalms in the choir, enters the holy place. Cerebral, speculative words such as grace, redemption, predestination and eschatology are not prototypical of this primary religious language.

In this connection it is perhaps relevant to quote Andrew Greeley who makes a distinction within Catholicism between 'the high tradition' and 'the popular tradition', between – which is the same – 'prosaic' and 'poetic Catholicism'. The first is what one learns in schools; it is cognitive, propositional and didactically presented. The

---

26 This is a random list from *Katholiek Woordenboek [Roman Catholic Dictionary]*, Amsterdam/Brussels: Thomas Rap, 1996 (1st edn. 1987). Other traditions would easily yield a similar set of examples.

second is what a child learns from its parents, friends, neighbours and relatives even before he or she goes to school. It is practical, imaginative, experiential and narrative. The high tradition is to be found in theological libraries, in institutional documents. The popular tradition can be found in the rituals, the arts, the music, the stained glass, the devotional practices and the stories of the ordinary church folk. Now poetic Catholicism is primary in an important sense: 'Anyone who thinks *homoiousios* is more important to ordinary folk then the Madonna and her child is incurably prosaic – besides being wrong.'[27]

> None of the doctrines is less true than the stories. Indeed, they (i.e. the doctrines, wvh) have the merit of being more precise, more carefully thought out, more ready for defense and explanation. But they are not where religion or religious faith starts, nor in truth where it ends.[28]

The language of poetic Catholicism is a more accessible religious language. Religious education doesn't start with 'seeing meaning in suffering', with 'feeling accepted by God' or the like. The surmise that there is a more basic level is justified; it is the level at which one is introduced in the space-time continuum of religious objects, activities, festivities etc. What shows itself here is the primacy of piety.

6. Recognizing the Religious Aspect of Reality

In an article from 1977 Peter Winch expressed the following view: 'we first become acquainted with religious uses of language in becoming familiar with a particular religious tradition'.[29] In so doing we arrive, according to him, at concepts which can be applied outside our own tradition. Someone who knows for example what a 'pious Catholic' is, is not in need of additional instruction concerning the meaning of a 'pious Jew' or a 'pious Muslim'. Winch thinks it is no coincidence that these concepts are of a practical nature. These concepts are even responsible for the universal applicability of the term 'religion'. We only give a religious interpretation of concepts we encounter for the first time, if we can see that they are linked to this devout behaviour or to these pious acts. The universal applicability of the term 'religion' is not based on the universal presence of particular religious ideas or concepts of god and gods. The non-derivative religious language that I have brought up is intimately linked with the devotional, ritual practices about which Winch writes. The acquisition of this non-derivative religious language is (therefore) the precondition for the religious transposition of secular, profane language.

This is in accordance with what Wittgenstein says in *On Certainty* (§ 476): 'Children do not learn that books exist, that armchairs exist, etc. etc., – they learn

---

27   Andrew Greeley, *The Catholic Imagination*, Berkeley, CA: University of California Press, 2001, p.78.

28   Greeley, *The Catholic Imagination*, p.4.

29   Peter Winch, 'Meaning and Religious Language', in *Reason and Religion*, ed. Stuart Brown, Ithaca, NY: Cornell University Press, 1977, pp.193–221; also in *Contemporary Classics in Philosophy of Religion*, eds. Ann Loades and Loyal D. Rue, La Salle, IL: Open Court, 1991, pp.349–75. The quotation is taken from the latter publication, p.350.

to fetch books, sit in armchairs, etc.'[30] The child that is raised in a religious culture learns first and foremost religious practices. In connection with these it learns the non-derivative language of its religion: the names of the rooms it enters, the vestments it sees, the feasts it celebrates and so forth. The correct comprehension of the 'derivative' or the more speculative language that is used later on is dependent on this practical initiation. The transposition that has to be performed with primarily profane concepts as love, friendship, goodness or kingship – in order to understand the religious uses of these terms –only has significance against the background of this practical feel for what religion is all about. A child that never entered a sacred space, that was never introduced to any devotional practice (and has no notion whatsoever of such practices), that has no words to speak about the world of piety, devotion and worship, would – when receiving an explanation of the word 'God' for the first time – not be able to think of anything except a kind of physical principle (creation) or a character from a fairytale (a judge). A child that visits a church with its grandparents, that learns to name things there and says a prayer in the light of a candle has – in this hypothesis – learned more and something far more important, than the child that hears about 'Jesus is my friend' in the classroom. My point would be that the religious dimension of this Jesus-friendship can only dawn on a child as a result of the aforementioned initiation into piety. If 'Jesus is my friend' contains the 'derivative' concept of friendship, this entails that one has to have prior knowledge of the source domain from which it is derived (one must know what it means that Joey is a friend), but also of the target domain to which it is to be derived. If this target domain is wholly unknown, then 'Jesus is my friend' can make but an infantile impression.

Religious language is more than 'lifted' ordinary language. My pointing to the existence and the scholarly neglect of a non-derivative religious language is an attempt to show that there is a world of objects which is right from the start invested with religious meaning – a world that can be identified without having recourse to prior profane or secular functions. Someone who wants to understand 'Christ is shepherd' must be familiar with pastoral country life, but in order to understand 'prayer', 'altar' and 'Low Sunday' no such dependency is required.

To me all these reflections suggest that to find religious meaning at a tabernacle is – so to speak – the precondition for finding a religious meaning in more ordinary things (such as the breadbasket) and events. Someone unable to find religious meaning in what is sacred, will not even know what to look for in the trivial.

Concluding Remarks

In a world without the traditional and/or institutional religions such a possibility would have vanished. As Phillips wrote in another context, it is impossible to long for a king in a country where the concept of kingship is unknown. Religious life and language are the touchstones of a conceptual inquiry. When a familiarity

---

30 Ludwig Wittgenstein, , *Über Gewißheit / On Certainty*, eds. G.E.M. Anscombe and G.H. von Wright, Oxford: Blackwell, 1979, p.62.

with religious practices is lost or when they are only experienced in a perverted or distorted way, then no touchstone is left.[31] So Phillips' way of doing philosophy of religion needs to be supplemented in my opinion with an historical interest in religious practices and devotions or with an anthropological interest in the culture of religion.

Pious people are liable to be accused of superstition. They are attached to the material, particular or even singular forms of their religion. Phillips does not often refer to this basic level of the 'material world of religion'. The religious language game is to him much more characterized by words as 'grace', 'thanking', 'sin', 'renunciation', 'forgiving'. In my recollection there is no reference at all to the importance of this material world of faith in the whole of *The Concept of Prayer*. Perhaps it is a typical Catholic thing or it is typically Catholic to stress this dimension, as does Andrew Greeley:

> Catholics live in an enchanted world, a world of statues and holy water, stained glass and votive candles, saints and religious medals, rosary beads and holy pictures. But these Catholic paraphernalia are mere hints of a deeper and more pervasive religious sensibility which inclines Catholics to see the Holy lurking in creation.[32]

But then: is not Catholicism also religion?

Let us return to our opening question: Is D.Z. Phillips a friend of Demea? Can he account for piety and its cruciality? There is certainly an obvious difference between Phillips and Demea. Demea speaks and reacts as a believer, while Phillips means to speak and react as a philosopher. In *Faith after Foundationalism* Phillips calls the philosopher of religion 'a guardian of grammar'. 'Philosophy leaves everything where it is and simply endeavors for clarity concerning it; the primary language of faith and theology included.'[33] Philosophy is not piety.

Since Phillips has motives other than those of Demea for his reactions to Cleanthes, I do not think we can call him a friend of Demea. 'A friend of a friend of Demea' sounds more appropriate. But being an amicable man it would not come as a surprise when Phillips would use the motto 'any friend of yours, is a friend of mine'.

---

31   See D.Z. Phillips, *Faith after Foundationalism*, p.245: 'I am talking of the primary language of faith losing its meaning because it gradually ceases to be available to people: the well becomes poisoned at the source.'

32   Greeley, *The Catholic Imagination*, p.1.

33   Phillips, *Faith after Foundationalism*, p.249.

Chapter VIII

Philosophy, Piety and Petitionary Prayer – A Reply to Walter van Herck

D.Z. Phillips

1. Why Demea Departed

Most readers of Hume's *Dialogues Concerning Natural Religion* would say that he presents Demea as an inferior character to Philo and Cleanthes. Demea, appalled at the arguments of Cleanthes from the outset, and realizing, late in the day, that he has been hoodwinked by Philo, makes his excuses, shakes the dust from under his feet, and departs at the end of Part XI of the *Dialogues*, leaving Philo and Cleanthes to argue over what he regards as their skeletal conception of the Faith. For their part, neither Philo nor Cleanthes have really listened to Demea as a partner in the discussion. He is regarded as a rigid, inflexible defender of orthodoxy, who has not earned his place at the philosophical table. No one is sorry to see him depart. By contrast, Walter van Herck argues that, in Demea, Hume created a character of greater significance then he realized and that the reasons for his departure merit close philosophical attention. Moreover, he finds similarities between those reasons and my own work in the philosophy of religion.

At first, the comparison between myself and Demea may seem a surprising one. After all, Demea seeks an absolute proof of God's existence in the ontological argument, and no Wittgensteinian philosopher of religion would seek that. On the other hand, Van Herck suggests that Demea can be seen as appreciating the *grammatical* insights the argument affords, namely, that God cannot be regarded as a being who may or may not exist. That is an interest in the argument shared by Wittgensteinians.[1] While their aim is not to defend orthodoxy, Wittgensteinians claim to be doing justice to the grammar of religious belief. This claim has disturbed evidentialists and Reformed epistemologists who *do* see themselves as defenders of that orthodoxy, and who accuse Wittgensteinians of distorting it. But the accusers are themselves accused of such distortion by Thomists, who regard their views as no more than a modern blip enjoying a temporary success.[2] So the contemporary

---

1   See Norman Malcolm, 'Anselm's Ontological Arguments', in Norman Malcolm, *Knowledge and Certainty*, Englewood Cliffs, NJ: Prentice-Hall, 1963, pp.141–62, and D.Z. Phillips, *Religion without Explanation*, Oxford: Blackwell, 1976, Chapter 10.

2   See Brian Davies, 'Letter from America', in *New Blackfriars: Essays in Memory of Gareth Moore* 84 (July/August 2003). For further Thomistic critiques see the essays of Brian Davies, Gyula Klima, James Ross and David Burrell *Whose God? Which Tradition?* eds. D.Z. Phillips and Mario von der Ruhr, unpublished. In my introduction, 'God and Grammar', I

philosophical scene is rather different, in that respect, from the relations between Hume's characters. But there are also similarities.

Evidentialists confess their frustration at trying to argue with Wittgensteinians,[3] while Reformed epistemologists comfort themselves with the thought that they are a small circle convincing no one but themselves.[4] One gets the impression that few would regret it, if, like Demea, the Wittgensteinians were to depart, and let philosophers get on with the real discussion. Unlike Demea, however, the Wittgensteinians stay around, urging their disconcerting message on their reluctant listeners. They do not offer new theories for old. That would have been welcomed. Instead, they tell philosophers to stop doing the *kind* of thing they are doing. Hardly a message which could expect a welcome![5] One is telling people who regard themselves as protectors of the Faith that they are damaging it, and, that, as a result, religion becomes the victim of their friendly fire.[6]

Van Herck would like to call me a friend of Demea, but, instead, ends up calling me a friend of a friend of Demea's. There are two reasons for this modification. First, our motivations are different. Demea's spring from a reaction to the dishonouring of piety he sees in Philo and Cleanthes, while my motivation is rooted in philosophical considerations. Second, as we shall see later, he believes that, in certain aspects of my work, I forget Demea's lessons, and thus cease to be his friend in those contexts. Nevertheless, Van Herck sees important similarities between us, and I believe he is correct in doing so. Four may be noted as central.

First, neither Demea nor I think that one can determine whether there is a God by assessing probabilities according to criteria shared by believers and non-believers alike. Even if the probabilities come down on the side of belief, a merely probable God would not do justice to the grammar of the God of Faith.

Second, a dispute over whether the cause of nature is divine or not, does not do justice to the notion of a creator. In the dispute between Philo and Cleanthes, it is shown to be simply a matter of opinion, or even a purely verbal issue.

Third, and most important, is the agreement between Demea and myself concerning the relation between philosophy and piety. The practices of piety are not answerable to a canon of rationality laid down by philosophy. Rather, philosophy should wait on piety to do conceptual justice by it. For Demea, this is a matter of paying due regard to religious habits of reverence as found in specific religious traditions. For Wittgensteinians, it is a matter of making 'practice' central in a consideration of religious belief. If we leave religious practices out of consideration, we are left with Hume's 'true religion'. This 'true religion', the bare idea of an author of nature, is not, as some have thought, the necessary substratum of faith,

---

have tried to set the scene regarding the philosophical significance of the charges and counter-charges regarding philosophy and Christian orthodoxy.

    3   See Richard Swinburne, 'Philosophical Theism', in *Philosophy of Religion in the 21st Century*, eds. D.Z. Phillips and Timothy Tessin, Basingstoke: Palgrave, 2001, pp.3–20.

    4   See Nicholas Wolterstorff, 'Reformed Epistemology', in *Philosophy of Religion in the 21st Century*, eds. Phillips and Tessin, pp.39–63.

    5   See D.Z. Phillips, 'Philosophy and Theological Castles', Ch. 7 of *Contemporary Conceptions of God*, ed. Cyril G. Williams, Lewiston, NY: Edwin Mellen Press, 2003.

    6   See D.Z. Phillips, *Religion and Friendly Fire*, Aldershot: Ashgate, 2004.

the existential and propositional presupposition of piety, but, rather, the emaciated remains of a religious language devoid of substantive content.[7]

Fourth, Demea and I agree in opposing the conception of rationality said to be the opposite of pious practices, attained without the unnecessary baggage associated with them. This is the wisdom of the sage (p.127):

> every rational man should be able to see that 'salvation' is not dependent on knowing certain texts by heart, or burning candles in front of certain statues, on receiving the holy communion, on visiting certain holy placed. Is it really necessary to contemplate a tabernacle in order to find meditative rapture, in order to approach to salvation?

According to the advocates of rational wisdom, the same existential, beneficial effects can be obtained through it without recourse to any religious tradition. As a result, Van Herck tells us (p.127):

> it would in principle be possible to do away with all traditional and/or institutional religions and still have religious people around. They would be brought to enlightenment and salvation by contemplating nature, the faces of their fellow men and the most ordinary things. Such a world would even be a better world because all forms of superstition and religious intolerance would be gone.

Because of these four important similarities, one can see why Van Herck is tempted, though he does not succumb, to call me a friend of Demea.

2. Departing from Demea?

Why can't Van Herck call me a friend of Demea's without qualification? It is because of questions he wants to pose in what he calls, modestly, 'the margins of [my] philosophical work' (p.125). In fact, his questions are far more central then that, and deserve serious attention. He asks (p.126):

> What is piety? Why is it such an unpopular concept today? Is Phillips' philosophy of religion able to cope with the phenomenon of piety? Without pretending to answer these questions, I hope to point to what could be the beginnings of an answer.

Given the similarities already noted between Demea and myself, Van Herck would be hard pressed to show a *general* tension between his views and my philosophy of religion. In fact, his claim is far more specific, namely, that there is a tension between Demea's views, and my treatment of petitionary prayer in Chapter 6 of my first book, *The Concept of Prayer*.[8] On that basis, he concludes that being opposed to Cleanthes[9] does not make me an automatic friend of Demea.

---

7   See D.Z. Phillips, 'Is Hume's "True Religion" a Religious Belief?', in *Religion and Hume's Legacy*, eds. D.Z. Phillips and Timothy Tessin, Basingstoke: Macmillan and St. Martin's Press, 1999, pp.81–98.

8   London: Routledge and Kegan Paul, 1965; paperback Oxford: Blackwell, 1981.

9   See, for example, Chapter 2: 'Hume's Legacy', in my *Religion without Explanation*, and 'The Friends of Cleanthes', in *Recovering Religious Concepts*.

I depart from Demea, in my account of petitionary prayer, according to Van Herck, because I am attracted, ironically enough, given my general position, to the rational conception of wisdom, not as it is employed by secularists, but by rationalists who want to hold on to the notion of the supernatural. Like them, Van Herck argues, I distinguish between refined supernaturalists and crass supernaturalists. William James elucidates the difference as follows (p.132):

> The refined supernaturalists ... deny that the supernatural can in any way interfere with the course of events in the natural world: the world of the ideal never bursts into the phenomenal world at particular points. In contrast to this, the crasser variety, which has a huge following among the uneducated 'admits miracles and providential leadings and finds no intellectual difficulty in mixing the ideal and real worlds together by interpolating influences from the ideal region among the forces that causally determine the world's details'.[10]

Deism and refined supernaturalism have nothing to do with the piety of specific religious traditions, tending to equate it with superstition. It is their impoverished view of reverential practices that makes Demea depart from them. Van Herck's claim is that he would also depart from my account of petitionary prayer. This claim, however, needs careful attention. It is important to be clear about the senses in which I do *not* depart from Demea, even in the restricted context of petitionary prayer.

Van Herck says, 'For the refined supernaturalist there is ... no point in prayer' (p.133). The first thing to note is that he does not accuse me of saying that. Second, Van Herck is not saying that I, like the refined supernaturalists, think that the particular practices of religious traditions are superstitious. As Van Herck says, for such people, it is impossible 'to draw a distinction between superstition and piety within a particular religious tradition' (p.129). By contrast, he says of me (p.130):

> Phillips has a feel for nuances and knows that the borderline between superstition and true devotion isn't razor sharp ... The lighting of a candle, the burning of incense and the offering of flowers to Our Lady can be acts of devotion, but can also be superstition.

Third, Van Herck agrees with me that no account of prayer is acceptable which makes God an external causal instrument to attain one's ends. Using God as though he were a lucky charm would be a clear case of doing so. The charm, in some unknown causal way, is supposed to guarantee that no harm will befall one. People's lives are full of superstitions of this kind, some traditional, others highly personal. The belief that crossing knives at a table will lead to a quarrel falls into the first category. Believing that a dispute will be settled one way or another by the number of times a light-cord swings against a wall, falls into the second category.

When superstitions are religiously damaging, they are usually the result of misplaced analogies. Think of the superstitious belief that sins can be washed away like dirt. Go into the holy river dirty at one end, and come up clean at the other. Swallow the wafer and be automatically cleansed of sin. The Roman Catholic Church has inveighed against mechanistic views of the Mass. Are we not told that

---

10 James, *The Varieties of Religious Experience*, p.521.

'he who eateth or drinketh unworthily heaps coals of fire on his head'? One can touch the magic charm, or swallow the magic wafer, whether one is unworthy or not: if it works it works. One's relation to them is purely external. One's relation to lighting a candle, or to saying 'Hail Marys' or 'Our Fathers' may be just as external, as may the injunction to perform these deeds – 'Say twelve and the slate's clean'. How exactly?

Fourth, Van Herck seems to agree, most of the time, that no account of petitionary prayer is satisfactory in which God is thought of as a more powerful version of ourselves. 'The liker the better', as Cleanthes would have it. Such a God is thought to have the power to bestow good or ill on us. It's up to him. Naturally, we would prefer him to bestow good, and that is what we ask him to do in our prayers. Sometimes he gives us what we want, and, sometimes, apparently, he does not. Faith on this view, is believing that appearances deceive us and that, in the end, we get what we want. According to Van Herck, I am not alone in thinking that this is an unsatisfactory view of prayer (p.129):

> the orthodox will agree because their God is not an instrument or a means to some further end … The criterion to be used here is the relation between prayer and life

I have argued that the above view of prayer makes moral nonsense of God. One of the main lessons of the Book of Job is to illustrate this nonsense when an attempt is made to correlate answers to prayers with the moral character of the petitioner. I asked whether we are to tell the mother whose son has not returned from war, that she did not pray hard enough. What sort of God would insist that she had to pray at all? Philosophers argue that God has to allow the evils in unanswered prayers, because of a greater good that cannot be achieve without them. But they forget that their God is supposed to be morally perfect! This God had blood on his hands.[11]

Having condemned this account of prayer on the whole, Van Herck makes two curious observations in defence of it. First, to get round the problem of the instrumental conception of God he says, 'People ask me favours all the time, and though some people make me feel used, I do not feel used all the time' (p.131). This comment does not get around the external relation envisaged between the supplicant and God. Neither does it meet the kind of difficulties I have noted, which arise once one raises the question of what reasons are given for refused requests. The analogy invoked by Van Herck is surprising, given his admiration for Demea, since it is the kind of response one would expect from Cleanthes. He seems to have forgotten, for the moment, that Demea rejected not only the skeletal 'true religion' of Philo, but also the disastrous anthropomorphism of Cleanthes. Van Herck argues, later, that ordinary language is transformed when applied to God, via distinctive *religious* meanings. The problem with his proposed analogy is that no such transformation is evident.

The second attempt Van Herck makes to avoid the difficulties I have raised for instrumental conceptions of prayer, is equally unsatisfactory. He says (p.131):

---

11   See Part I: 'Our Problematic Inheritance', in my *The Problem of Evil and the Problem of God*, for a much fuller discussion of objections such as these.

> Religious devotion is not a search for coherence … So the notion of divine intervention should not be dropped in a description of prayer because it entails incoherent propositions.

That simply will not do. Van Herck has argued that rationalistic rejections of petitionary prayers do not do justice to their grammar. They are thought to be incoherent only because they are misunderstood. But here Van Herck seems to be saying that the rationalists are right after all. Petitionary prayer *does* entail incoherencies, but all we should say is, 'Don't worry about it!' This is the weakest form of pragmatism and, on reflection, I do not believe Van Herck would want to stick with it. There is also the danger of condescension in this view. Are those who practise the religion supposed to be aware of the incoherencies, or is this knowledge only possessed by intellectuals? If so, do the intellectuals think that the believers are not up to hearing the news? Alternatively, do the believers know, but pass on responsibility to the intellectuals? I do not think Van Herck would be happy with either eventuality. Think of Miguel de Unamuno's scathing denunciation of such attitudes, which I mentioned in Chapter IV in replying to Mario von der Ruhr (see p.84).

In this section, I began by mentioning Van Herck's view that I have departed from Demea in my account of petitionary prayer. But in what way? All I have done so far is to eliminate four ways in which this might have been said to happen. These are issues on which Van Herck and I are agreed: prayer is not pointless; all specific religious traditions cannot be said to be superstitious; prayer cannot treat God as a lucky charm; requests to God are not requests to a being whose power is simply an extension of our own. True, Van Herck equivocates on this last issue, but I regard the two ways in which he does so as slips that he himself would want to rectify.

None of this shows that my account of petitionary prayer does not deviate from Demea. What it does show is that I do not do so in any of the four ways discussed in this section – and Van Herck agrees.

3. Prayer and Practice

What does Van Herck want to insist on in relation to petitionary prayer? The answer can be found in the distinction between refined and crass supernaturalism which we have already noted (see p.142). He wants to insist that petitionary prayers clearly belong to the latter. They are prayers which make specific requests, and those who pray them believe that God could intervene to grant them. William James called himself a crass supernaturalist. Van Herck tells us, for a very good reason: 'Because the idea that no single particular experience can change its complexion as a result of God's existence is to him quite preposterous' (p.133). To repeat what we have said already, the crass supernaturalist

> finds no intellectual difficulty in mixing the ideal and real worlds together by interpolating influences from the ideal region among the forces that causally determine the world's details.[12]

---

12   James, *The Varieties of Religious Experience*, p.521.

Why, then, do philosophers, including myself, insist on finding intellectual difficulties in petitionary prayer? Van Herck's reply is that we do so, because we insist on attributing to believers metaphysical, physical, or theological theories which they simply do not indulge in (p.131):

> But sometimes people pray without having a theology or a metaphysics of prayer. In a variation on Wittgenstein's words one could say that 'people do this (i.e. praying) and then feel satisfied' ... Prayer and what people say about it is not meant to be developed in all kinds of directions ... Part of learning a religious langue game is learning how one may or may not develop utterances, metaphors and ideas

Van Herck's observation is extremely important, and I want to devote this section of my reply to bringing out why it is relevant to Van Herck's dissatisfaction with my account of petitionary prayer.

Let us imagine someone who thought that all rituals had implications concerning a theory about means-ends causal relations. In that event, he is likely to hold that burning an effigy must entail a causal theory (albeit a confused one) about how doing so can harm the intended victim. Wittgenstein criticizes this in a way Van Herck would approve of, namely, by denying that any such theory need be involved.

> Burning an effigy. Kissing the picture of a loved one. This is obviously *not* based on a belief that it will have a definite effect on the object which the picture represents. It aims at some satisfaction and it achieves it. Or rather, it does not aim at anything; we act in this way and then feel satisfied.[13]

Notice that, at first, Wittgenstein is tempted to replace a material means-ends relation, with a psychological means-ends relation, but quickly corrects himself. In this case, the act is not performed in order to causally harm the other, or in order to achieve psychological satisfaction. It is itself an expression of anger. Should we, for that reason, say that nothing happened? Of course something happened – anger is expressed.

It may be said that the above example casts no light on petitionary prayer where, very often, what is requested has to do with something independent of the person praying. In that case, let us change our example of a ritual. What if a person is cursed in a public ritual? The dreadfulness of the curse may be such that the person cursed is broken by it – to be cursed among one's people. A person may die as a result. Of course, to understand this what one needs is not a theory, but the significance of the curse. Wouldn't such a ritual bear out Van Herck's insistence that in cases such as this, 'there is a world of objects which is right from the start invested with religious meaning' (p.137)? I repeat: his point is an important one, since here we have examples of 'something happening' without any suggestion of the presence of the kind of theories for which philosophers criticize them.

Van Herck has his own 'world of objects' in mind, which belongs to what he calls 'poetic Catholicism': 'one bows and kneels in front of the alter, strides through the nave, smells the incense, sings the psalms in the choir, enters the

---

13 Wittgenstein, 'Remarks on Frazer's *Golden Bough*'.

holy place' (p.135). Van Herck's point, however, is of more general philosophical significance. His argument is that what he calls 'prosaic Catholicism' is secondary, and that 'poetic Catholicism' is primary. Philosophers tend to reverse this relation, suggesting that 'prosaic' matters, propositions, metaphysical theories, etc, are the foundation on which the 'poetic' depends, that the propositional logically precedes practice. Thus, any successful critique of those propositions and practices becomes a successful critique of practice at the same time. Van Herck sees Demea and myself as resisting these far-reaching assumptions, so common in contemporary philosophy of religion, and he agrees that it is essential to do so. Speaking of 'prosaic' and 'poetic' Catholicism, he says (p.135),

> The first is what one learns in schools, it is cognitive, propositional, and didactically presented. The second is what one learns from parents, friends, neighbours and relatives even before one visits a school. It is practice, imaginative, experiential and narrative. The high tradition is to be found in theological libraries, in institutional documents. The popular tradition can be found in the rituals, the arts, the music, the stained glass, the devotional practices and the stories of the ordinary church folk.

Van Herck agrees with Andrew Greeley when the latter says:

> None of the doctrines is less true than the stories. Indeed they (i.e. the doctrines, wvh) have the merit of being more precise, more carefully thought out, more ready for defense and explanation. But they are not where religion or religious faith starts, nor in truth where it ends.[14]

It is important here to distinguish between the metaphysical theories and propositions that distort religious practice, and the systematic theology which is internally related to it. In the latter context, the above comment by Greeley is too sharp. In my second published paper in English, I discussed an analogy between logic and language, on the one hand, and theology and religious practices on the other.[15] As soon as one has language, one has its logic at the same time, which shows itself *in* the language. To learn the language is, at the same time, to learn what can and cannot be said. Similarly, as soon as one has religious practices, no matter how rudimentary, one has a theology which shows itself *in* them. This is why Wittgenstein referred to theology as grammar. Systematic theology is a refinement of this relation, but there is always, at its best, a dialectical relation between reflective theology and practice, each reacting and counter-reacting to developments which occur in each other.

It is in this context that Van Herck expresses dissatisfaction with what I say about petitionary prayer. In this instance, I, too, he thinks, have reversed the relation between 'the poetic' and 'the prosaic'. Worse, I have not only made theological concepts primary in the way to be avoided, but I have aligned these to philosophical theories which are simply not present in the devotional practice of petitionary prayer. On the basis of such philosophical presuppositions *whenever* a special request is made in prayer, or when 'a prayer is a way of getting things done' (p.129), I jump

---

14   Greeley, *The Catholic Imagination*, p.4.
15   See my 'Philosophy, Theology and the Reality of God', in *Wittgenstein and Religion.*

to the conclusion that God is being conceived of in an instrumental way, and that the prayer is superstitious. Similarly, he thinks that acts of piety, such as lighting a candle are superstitions for me, if it is said that 'something will go wrong' if they are not observed. In short, my account of petitionary prayer belongs to the assumptions of refined supernaturalism, rather than to the realities of crass supernaturalism. As a result, I cannot give an account of how the complexion of a particular experience is actually changed by God's actions in response to petitionary prayer. Where the relation between God and real events is concerned, I cannot account for the way in which they mix 'by interpolating influences from the ideal region among the forces that causally determine the world's details' (see p.132). The practice of petitionary prayer shows what this interpolation comes to.

Van Herck's general position is like that of Mario von der Ruhr in Chapter III: both concur, on the whole, with my methods in the philosophy of religion, but believe that, in some specific cases, I am not true to them. I am not, as I claim, describing religious practices conceptually, but prescribing practices of which I approve. Von der Ruhr thinks that this may be true of my discussion of belief in life after death, whereas Van Herck thinks it is true of my discussion of petitionary prayer. For Van Herck, these are theological issues '(not for a philosopher to decide, as Phillips so often tells his audiences)' (p.131). Van Herck's point is correct, as far as it goes, but it does not address the fact of philosophical puzzlement. What if someone *is* puzzled by the phenomena of petitionary prayer? Is nothing to be said to him? There is little point in simply repeating utterances and deeds from 'poetic Catholicism', since it is these that have created his puzzle. Surely, in such circumstances, conceptual elucidation is called for, not by substituting theories for practice, but by bringing out the kind of life the practice has. I take it that Van Herck is not opposed to this. His point is that, in relation to petitionary prayer, I have not done it well.

At this point, the reader would expect me to be able to compare my account of petitionary prayer with that of Van Herck, but that is something I cannot do, because he does not provide one. In this respect, he shares an unfortunate similarity to Demea: he departs too soon, instead of pressing ahead with the discussion. It is not enough to tell those who are puzzled about petitionary prayer, that others find no difficulty at all. What Van Herck does succeed in doing is to point out the roads we should not take, and to indicate, *the general direction* in which we ought to travel. But he does not travel very far in that direction himself. Perhaps that is what he meant, after all, by saying, at the outset, that he does not pretend 'to answer these questions', but hopes to provide 'what could be the beginnings of an answer' (p.126). But, in replying, I assume I am expected to go further.

4. Prayer as 'The Practice of the Presence of God'

In Chapter III, Mario von der Ruhr's discontented Catholic suspected that I denied that anything actually happened if one believed in life after death. As we have seen, Van Herck thinks that I deny that anything actually gets done in petitionary prayer, that the complexion of an experience can be causally changed as a result of it, or that something could go wrong if we do not observe devotional practices. But I do not deny *any* of these things. What I have disputed is what some philosophers have said about these notions. I have said that they have distorted their grammar. But, of course, if I am not to depart because of that, as Demea did, I must now try to elucidate the grammar that I claim is being distorted.

Let me begin by emphasizing something about which Van Herck would surely agree, namely, that believers hold that their prayers should be acceptable to God. One might say that believers pray under the eye of God. Following Wittgenstein, Van Herck says that no one who speaks of the eye of God feels committed, thereby, to go on to speak of his eyebrows, the possibility of getting a cataract, toenails, entrails, and so on. Why not? Because talk of living under God's eye has a natural home in religious language, whereas the other matters do not.[16] To hope that one's prayer is acceptable under God's eye, is to hope that God's will is expressed *in* one's prayer. Would Van Herck agree that this is as true of petitionary prayer as of any other? It is important to maintain his own emphasis on the fact that such prayers are acts of devotion, as all prayer is supposed to be. That is why Brother Lawrence called it 'the practice of the presence of God'. In other words, a prayer is only a prayer when it is offered in the right spirit; indeed, it is the exercise of that spirit. That is why Mark Twain's Huck was correct in saying, 'You can't pray a lie'. The prayer cannot reach God because there is nothing of God *in* it. Isn't that the point of Simone Weil's saying that only God can talk to God?

I agree with Van Herck that 'Religious life and language are the touchstones of conceptual enquiry' (p.137), but I do not think that his account of liturgical practices will do as such a touchstone. He speaks, sometimes, as though the form of such practices will of itself yield its sense for us. In Chapter IV, I spoke of pictures which say themselves, but I did not mean to suggest that they do not need a wider context in order to do so. A picture of the crucifixion may say itself, but in order to show that it is deeper than another, I'd need a surrounding religious culture in order to do so. What is more, it would be foolish to try to confine the religious spirit to the formalities of that culture, even to a particular text, such as the Our Father. Tolstoy's cautionary tale 'The Three Hermits' illustrates why.[17] A bishop is told of three hermits who live together on an island, and who are reputed to be holy men. He visits them, and finds that the only prayer they every pray is, 'Three are ye, three are we, have mercy upon us!' The bishop is amused at their prayer:

'You have evidently heard something about the Holy Trinity,' said he. 'But you do not pray aright. You have won my affection, godly men. I see you wish to please the Lord,

---

16   But what of Mormons? My former Mormon students, now teachers of philosophy and theology, tell me that their initial reaction is to say that talk of God's eye *does* entail talk of eyebrows, since God has a physical body. But when I go on to ask about the colour of the eyes, or the length of the eyebrows, I am told that those questions are inappropriate. So one is unsure about the grammar of 'physical body' in this context. I gather this is a topic of lively contemporary debate in Mormonism.

17   In the account that follows I am simply repeating what I said in *The Concept of Prayer*, pp.60–61.

but you do not know how to serve him. That is not the way to pray; but listen to me, and I will teach you.'[18]

The bishop manages to teach them the Lord's Prayer by getting them to repeat it after him time and time again. At last, satisfied that they know it, he departs. That night, when the ship is far from land, the three hermits are seen running on the water, and they cry out to the bishop,

> 'We have forgotten your teaching, servant of God. As long as we kept repeating it we remembered, but when we stopped saying it for a time, a word dropped out, and now it has all gone to pieces. We can remember nothing of it. Teach us again.'

The Bishop crossed himself, and leaning over the ship's side, said:

> 'Your own prayer will teach the Lord, men of God. It is not for me to teach you. Pray for us sinners.'[19]

To think that liturgical form guarantees a meditation of sense, would fall foul of what Wittgenstein called a magical view of signs; the idea that the sign yields its sense immediately. A logical view of signs, on the other hand, concentrates on the place the sign occupies in our discourse. Van Herck's concern, it might be said, is with the place of the actual petitions in the discourse of petitionary prayer. Does anything actually happen in them? Isn't my account of them too cerebral, and not down to earth? For me, Herck argues (p.130):

> Such a prayer is mainly an expression of the strength of one's desires and of one's devotion to God. The only reason why the believer doesn't simply pray 'Thy will be done' is that he wants to name the desires that occupy his head and heart. In the superstitious version however one is convinced that God can intervene if he wants to and that by praying it is possible to influence his divine will.

Clearly, Van Herck cannot leave matters there, since, like me, he wants to distinguish between religious and superstitious notions of petitionary prayer. Indeed, his whole case rests on allowing a non-superstitious account of a belief in divine intervention as a result of prayer. I would say that in order to give such an account, petitionary prayer must be seen, not as an attempt to influence the will of God, but as an attempt to participate in it. After all, I am still assuming that Van Herck wants to avoid the difficulties in the accounts of prayer I discussed in section 2 of my reply.

The reason why Van Herck finds my account of petitionary prayer unsatisfactory is because he sees it as a form of refined supernaturalism. When I emphasize 'the unchanging will of God', over against the actual requests of believers, Van Herck sees this parallel to 'the whole' of refined supernaturalism which never leads to anything actually happening in the particularities of peoples lives. But is this so? Let us look again at words by Kierkegaard which I used in the course of my analysis:

---

18   Leo Tolstoy, 'The Three Hermits', in *Twenty-three Tales*, Oxford: Oxford University Press, 1960, p.198.
19   Tolstoy, 'The Three Hermits', p.201.

A hasty exploration could assert that to pray is a useless act, because a man's prayer does not alter the unalterable. But would this be desirable in the long run? Could not fickle man easily come to regret that he had got God changed? The true explanation is therefore at the same time the one most to be desired. The prayer does not change God, but it changes the one who offers it.[20]

If we concentrate, as I suspect Van Herck does, on the reference to 'the unchanging God', there is a chance of missing the fact that Kierkegaard is insisting that *a change comes about in the person who prays*. But wasn't it this that Van Herck thought was missing in my analysis: a reference to something happening? Furthermore, if we remember that to pray is to practise the presence of God, we are referring to a change which God brings about. Indeed, whenever a prayer participates in the life of God, God has intervened, in that respect, in the life of the person who prays.

Van Herck does not mention the fact that I gave three examples in *The Concept of Prayer* of prayer as participating in the life of God.[21] The first example concerned petitionary prayers for a deeper relationship with God. Here, there is an internal relationship between what is requested and the prayer, since the prayer itself is a spiritual exercise, an attempt to wait on God. Luther confessed that he had failed to pray on a single occasion without distraction. The second example I considered, was that of a request by a believer for the prayers of his fellow believers within a community. Here, too, the internal relation I speak of is in evidence through the sustaining spirit of the community. Theologically, it is called the fellowship of the Holy Spirit. In my third example, that internal relation seems to be absent, since it concerned the prayers of the faithful for the conversion of the world. Yet, its absence is illusory, since once again the point being made is extremely important, namely, that spiritual transformation can only come through spiritual means. This is because God's only omnipotence is the omnipotence of love – that is a grammatical remark.

The grammar of omnipotence is extremely important in discussing the kind of petitionary prayers which Van Herck concentrates on, namely, those that affect the material aspects of life such as food, health, one's loved ones and so on. I was so concerned to avoid the misunderstandings of these prayers, discussed in section 2 of this reply, that the positive account was not as full as it ought to have been. Deeply accountable for the misunderstandings of these prayers is the widespread assumption that God's omnipotence means the ability to do anything which is describable without contradiction. In fact, there are millions of actions, so describable, including the foulest imaginable, that cannot be ascribed to God. It is not that God *could* do these things, but chooses not to, but that it makes no sense to talk of God in this way.[22]

In 'God is love' the 'is' is not one of predication, but of identity. It fixes the conceptual parameters within which God is to be thought of. Thus creation is not thought of as a demonstration of power, but an act of self-emptying love, in which something other than God, namely, human beings, are allowed to exist. Yet, there is sorrow mixed with love in creation, since the good things, the blessings of life,

---

20 Kierkegaard, *Purity of Heart*, pp.44–45.
21 *The Concept of Prayer*, pp.124–28.
22 For a discussion of this misconception see Chapter 1: 'Logic and Omnipotence' and Chapter 2: 'Logic and God's Will' in my *The Problem of Evil and the Problem of God*.

can also be the source of the greatest pain. When a request in a petitionary prayer is fulfilled, God answers it because God is in it, if it is received as his gift. Van Herck asks whether this changes anything, whether something actually happens. The answer is that a gift is given; what would otherwise be a coincidence or good fortune is transformed into a grace. If we ask what difference it makes, one has only to think of how receiving a day as a gift affects the conception of a day, gratitude for it, and an answerability, at its end, for how it has been spent. Life itself can be seen as such a gift. In this context, when what is asked for comes about, it always comes about in God whose gift it is.

But what of those desires that are not fulfilled? There is a religion of lies that is big business, and misuses the gift of life conceived in the way I have described. It tells people that all their dreams will come true. And when they do not, year after year, they are told that they will in God's good time. This religion of false consolation hides the precariousness of the gift of life, the fact that terrible things happens to human beings. Not much attention is paid to the prayers said *after* it is all too clear that what was requested in prayer *is not going to happen*. These are prayers said to a Saviour who was acquainted with grief, and whose mother, for good reason, is called, Our Lady of Sorrows. God's compassion in moments such as these, the fellowship of suffering, again changes things; not by ensuring that they do not happen, but in changing one's conception of what is happening – that it does not render love and compassion pointless. But the most extreme of circumstances are those when life visits human beings with such affliction that it destroys a sustaining faith. What is left then? The only answer which is not a lie is: the story of what happened to such as these. At the heart of Christianity is such a story – the story of a crucified God. In the Garden of Gethsemane, he makes his petitionary prayer; he asks that if it be possible, this cup should pass from him. It was not granted. But he asked, at the same time, that God's will be done. On the Cross, however, even the possibility of saying *that* is taken from him, as he cries out, asking why God has abandoned him. What is left? *His story*. The story being what it was, even if no one remembered him, God can be said to remember him. Why? *Because God is in his story*. In fact, for Christians, the story is the story of God.[23]

I hope Van Herck will recognize that I am not indulging in an etherealization of life. I am referring to actual events in the daily routines of people's lives, and how they face them in God. Perhaps the outcome of my reply is not what Van Herck was expecting when he asked me his important question. But if the grammar of the petitionary prayers I have been talking about is paid the grammatical attention due to it, then, to use Van Herck's language, we can see what is meant by saying that *something happened* to people who said these prayers, that things were changed for them, and that the very complexion of their experience of joys and sorrows was transformed by their belief in God's existence. And if, as I have argued, God can be

---

23 I am acutely mindful of how briefly I have stated this most important aspect of my reply to Van Herck. What preceded it was necessary to create the space in which it could appear. But an adequate expression of it could not be contained in a greater extension of this reply. My attempt at a much fuller discussion can be found in Part II: 'A Neglected Inheritance' of my *The Problem of Evil and the Problem of God*, pp.147–275.

said to be in the belief, the complexion of their experience can be said to be changed by God. Nor am I going to haggle over whether one can say that it was caused by God. What is important is not the word, but its use. No one who has understood what I have been saying would think that the grammar of 'a change of complexion caused by God' is remotely like the grammar of 'his change of complexion was caused by the fever'. What does the change caused by God look like? That is what I have been talking about all along in this reply.

Chapter IX

Religions in a World of Many Cultures: Conflict, Dialogue, and Philosophical Contemplation

Ingolf Dalferth
University of Zurich

Philosophy of religion, as D.Z. Phillips has taught us for years under changing headings, is best understood and practised as 'hermeneutics of contemplation'.[1] Its aims are neither apologetic nor in principle critical of religion. Rather it seeks to keep the insights and to avoid the pitfalls of both sides by rescuing 'atheism, as much as belief, from distortions of itself'.[2] Its main concern is 'with doing justice to possibilities of religious sense'[3] by understanding religions in their own terms. For Phillips is convinced that there are distinctive religious meanings, neither in general to be criticized nor in principle in need of justification, but a constant source of wonder and amazement, and hence an unceasing occasion for philosophical contemplation.

However, few of those who have praised or criticized his approach in recent years have paid enough attention to the fact that his belief in distinctive religious meanings is only the first part of the more complex view 'that although there are distinctive religious meanings, these cannot be what they are independent of their relation to other aspects of human life and culture'.[4] Religions exist not *in vacuo*, but in cultures. They do so because it is people who are religious (or not religious), and people live their lives in complex human cultures. This is why understanding religions in their own terms is not a matter of moving in closed circles of religious meanings but requires us to take their relations to other aspects of human life and culture into account, including their relations to other religions. To understand religions in their own terms is to understand the role they play in human life and culture.

This is an endless task, for a number of reasons. We know religion only through religions, and religions not independent of cultures. But there are cultures such as ours in which many different religions exist so that it is impossible to understand any religion without taking its relations to other religions into account. And there

---

1   Phillips, *Philosophy's Cool Place*; Phillips, *Religion and the Hermeneutics of Contemplation*.
2   Phillips, *Religion and the Hermeneutics of Contemplation*, p.4.
3   Phillips, *Religion and the Hermeneutics of Contemplation*, p.325.
4   Phillips, *Religion and the Hermeneutics of Contemplation*, p.25.

are religions such as Judaism, Christianity or Islam which exist, or have existed, in many different cultures so that understanding any one of them becomes a very complex issue indeed. For how do these religions, in their own terms, relate to other religions in a common culture, or to different cultures in a world of many religions, or to different religions in a world of many cultures? Conflict and dialogue, change and toleration are obvious issues at stake here. Has a contemplative philosophy of religions anything interesting to contribute to these questions? To contemplate these questions, and some possible answers, I begin with some simple but important truths, first about culture, then about religion.

1. Culture

For the present purpose, I suggest we define culture not normatively ('high culture' vs. 'common' or 'popular culture') but descriptively: In the broadest sense possible, culture is that aspect of human common life 'which is socially rather than genetically transmitted.'[5] Six points are important here.

First, culture is relative to a group or community.[6] Human beings differ from other primates by having a culture. In this sense '[c]ulture is the defining mark of human life.'[7] But what does it involve? According to recent research in cultural anthropology, the possibility of culture is based on the human cognitive capacity to identify with the other, to distinguish between one's own perspective and the perspectives of others, and to understand the intentions of others as being different from one's own. This capacity of taking the place of the other enabled human beings to develop ways of social and cultural learning in communities. And this, we are told, made all the difference: Whereas biological progress is tied to slow genetic mutation in individuals, humans have sped up the process of evolution by learning in communities.[8] Human communities have developed reliable means of storing and transmitting knowledge in a generation-transcending way. 'Culture' is the summary term for this communal capacity and activity.

Second, since culture is always a culture of ..., it varies with social group or community. Whereas all and only human beings have culture, not all human beings

---

5   Anthony O'Hear, 'Culture', *Routledge Encyclopaedia of Philosophy*, London: Routledge, 1998, pp.746–50, here p.746.

6   Some well known definitions of 'culture' miss this point, for example, Leslie A. White, *The Science of Culture*, New York: Farrar, Straus and Giroux, 1949: 'Culture is the name of a distinct order, or class, of phenomena, namely those things and events that are dependent upon the exercise of a mental ability peculiar to the human species, that we have termed symbolling [i.e., the invention and use of symbols]. It is an elaborate mechanism, an organization of ways and means employed by a particular animal, man, in the struggle for existence and survival.'

7   Kathryn Tanner, *Theories of Culture. A New Agenda for Theology*, Minneapolis, MN: Augsburg Fortress, 1997, p.25.

8   Michael Tomasello, *The Cultural Origins of Human Cognition*, Cambridge, MA: Harvard University Press, 1999.

have the same culture. Culture comes in the plural, and not every culture is everyone's culture.

Third, cultures are trans-individual, but they are not based on agreement. 'Agreement' is a way of overcoming differences by argument and decision, and 'consensus' is an achievement in the light of opposing opinions or positions. But a culture comprises what we take for granted and what goes without saying, and that is not based on agreement. What we take for granted is neither coherent nor consistent, nor accepted by all nor acceptable to everyone in the same way. It is often riddled with inconsistencies and the source of disagreement as much as of agreement. Before we can even begin to agree, or disagree, about anything, we live our lives in the light of the tacit assumptions and highly inconsistent beliefs of our world and culture. They may (and need to) be questioned, but not all at once. And it is an open question, which of them will be accepted by whom and to what extent when made explicit.

Fourth, it follows that cultures are not dependent on social consensus. Participants in the same culture do not necessarily hold common beliefs and sentiments or behave and act in the same ways. Cultures are not principles of social order that are binding for all their members. As human constructions they form the basis for conflict as much as they form the basis for shared belief and sentiment. They provide common orientation, but they do not enforce identical behaviour.

Fifth, cultures are products of historical process, and they are contingent. They have been made by human beings, and they are constantly being changed by them. Every culture could have been otherwise, and just as communities differ, so do cultures. There is to this day no 'global culture' worth that name; there are only particular cultural traditions,[9] some of which have universal aspirations and define global standards, which they expect others to accept. Other cultures often reject those standards because they have not been involved in formulating and disseminating those views, values and standards. For, as a rule, a culture only incorporates what it can appreciate in its own perspective as a possible future for itself. Whatever it cannot see as a possible continuation of its own legacy and tradition, it will not accept but reject, and insist on being different.

Sixth, cultures are adaptable to changing contexts because they are internally differentiated. There are not only differences among cultures, there also are differences within cultures. Cultures are not internally consistent wholes; rather they include their own alternatives and have their own internal principles of change. Thus every culture is pregnant with other cultures, and every given state of a culture is in transition to a variety of possible others. In some of these possible futures religion plays a role, in others it doesn't; and which will be the case, depends on how religion makes its present felt in a given culture.

---

9   Living traditions are communities with a (particular) culture of symbolic communication, social organization and generation-transcending learning, but there is no TRADITION in capital letters because there is no community of communities that includes all and everyone.

2. Religious Pluralism

There are obvious similarities between cultures and religions. Just as culture exists only in cultures, so religion – whatever we mean by the term – exists only in religions. And just as cultures display a luxuriant diversity of beliefs and practices, so do religions. Religious pluralism is a fact, and it can take many different forms, both within and among cultures. There are cultures with a single or a dominant religion, and there are other cultures that are composed of many different religions. Again, there are pluralist religious cultures that superimpose a civil religious structure on religions (Roman religion; Varro's tripartite division of mythical, political and natural theologies). And there are other religiously pluralist cultures, which refrain from organizing or evaluating the plurality of religious and non-religious views and ways of life (Western culture; distinction between private and public life).

Attempts at reducing religious plurality to a single religious outlook or a common core of all religious convictions have not only failed in fact but fail in principle. This is borne out by all the major accounts of religion that are commonly discussed. Thus reductive naturalism claims that religious beliefs about a transcendent reality are all false. Exclusivism, whether doctrinal or soteriological, holds that only one religion (one's own) is true and offers an effective path to salvation, whereas all others are believed to be false and to lead astray. Inclusivism claims that although one religion (one's own) contains the final truth, others contain approaches or approximations to it. And pluralism holds that 'a single ultimate religious reality is being differently experienced and understood in all the major religious traditions; they all, as far as we can tell, offer equally effective paths to salvation or liberation'.[10]

All four options fail to convince because they assume something that cannot be shown to be true, that is, that all religions are false (naturalism); that only one religion (one's own) is true (exclusivism); that one religion (one's own) contains the final truth of all religions (inclusivism); that all religions are about the same ultimate reality (pluralism). None of these views can convincingly be argued and defended on neutral and universal grounds. Rather reasonable people can, and do, reasonably disagree on these issues. Moreover, each of these convictions holds a much-oversimplified view of religion. Religions are much too diverse and multifaceted, both within and among themselves, to be judged and evaluated in such a global and indiscriminate manner. A religion may involve, on the one hand, strands that are acceptable to a culture (but not to others) and, on the other hand, strands that go contrary to some deeply held convictions of that culture (but not of others). There never is a one-to-one match between a religion and a culture but always agreement as well as disagreement.

Thus a religion may cease informing a culture by becoming either too distant or too adaptive to it. It may be on the wane because it has become too foreign or too familiar. The first is well known, but the second is not always taken seriously enough. A religion may become unable to relate to other cultures, or to a changing cultural situation, by concentrating too exclusively on those (rational or mystical,

---

10   Philip L. Quinn, 'Religious Pluralism', *Routledge Encyclopaedia of Philosophy*, London: Routledge, 1998, pp.260–64, here p.260.

doctrinal or ritual) strands that are acceptable to a given culture while divesting itself of everything that runs against the grain of that culture (e.g. Modernist Protestantism and Catholicism). Being too successful in a culture can do as much harm to a religion as losing all appeal to its cultured despisers.

3. Religions and Cultures

What is important to note, therefore, is that religions relate differently to culture. This is true of different religions in different cultures but also of the same religion in different cultures (Christianity in antiquity and modernity) and of a particular religion in a particular culture (Christianity in Britain).

Moreover, whereas all religions have some impact on a culture, not all religions carry their own culture with them. Some religions are intrinsically allied to a culture; they cannot be transplanted into another cultural context without being seriously weakened or destroyed. Other religions are vehicles of a particular culture because they are tied to a holy language, a book or a ritual practice that is part and parcel of a specific cultural tradition.

Again, there are religions which proselytize because they are not tied to a particular culture (such as Christianity); and there are others which proselytize because they are part of a particular culture which they seek to disseminate (such as Islam). The Christian faith, for example, is not tied to a particular culture but a way of transforming, modifying, improving (in some respects), and of ending (in other respects) certain strands in a culture. It is not a 'religion of a book' but has always existed only in translations. Throughout its history it has attracted interest precisely because of its critical distance to the cultural matrix of the time. This is why it has been able to give direction to a culture and to engage critically with its own and other cultural traditions.

A religion's engagement with a culture results in a particular configuration: a combination of its religious ends with the particularities of the cultural matrix in which it operates. These configurations change over time, and just as sometimes a culture cannot live up to the developments of a religion (witness the rise of Christianity in antiquity) so a religion may fail to keep up with the changes in a culture. That is why it is important for a religion to relate critically to a culture, to distinguish between itself and the cultural matrix in which it operates; otherwise it will be too directly involved in the rise and fall of that culture. On the other hand, as a living religion it must relate to a culture. It is always a meaningful question to ask how a culture has been changed by a religion, and how a religion has been changed through engagement with that culture.

There is no single answer to these questions because there is no single role that religions play in a culture. Religions are not means to a particular cultural end. If they serve a purpose in culture or society, they do so because of what they are and not the other way around. If a religion was nothing but its function in a culture, another could replace it without loss. But that is not how things are. So, in a very important respect, whether a religion continues or not depends on that religion itself. It keeps going when its interests are strong and it succeeds in (being) convincing. But the motivation must lie within the religion itself, not merely in its cultural surroundings. If it has a message to live by, it will engage in transmitting it. If not, it won't make an impact.

Religions do not all serve the same end but there is an actual diversity of religious ends. If differences between religions are to be overcome (and this does not seem to be necessary everywhere, in each case and in every respect) they are not overcome by concentrating on what religions share in common, but on what divides them. A worldwide agreement between religions, for example, will hardly take the form of agreement on common content (on what we all share), but rather on irreducible differences (on the ways in which we differ). But then what must be explored is the distinctive contribution a religion makes to the direction of human life and the resolution of human conflict within and among cultures. Since there is no general answer to this question, it has to be explored and answered in each particular case.

4. Deep Conflict

This is particularly difficult where a religion identifies with a culture or cultural tradition. Exploring the religion becomes indistinguishable from exploring a particular culture. But if religions were themselves dictated by cultural forces, it would appear that they could have no decisive direction to provide to their cultures.[11] What we normally find, therefore, are differences between the value orientation of a religion and a culture.

These differences can be the source of deep conflict between religions and cultures. Deep conflict arises from conflict of underlying value orientations that are taken for granted in a religion and in a culture. Where disagreement cuts that deep, where it concerns not merely particular values or styles of life but underlying background convictions, progress can only be made, as some argue, if all parties involved accept the contingency of their religious and cultural orientations. Whatever they are, they could have been otherwise. Yet isn't this precisely why what they are, is so important to them? The difficulty is not that religious believers are asked to accept the contingency of their religion and yet believe that it provides reliable ('true') orientation in life, indeed a better and more reliable orientation than any rival religion or world view. This, or something like this, is a well known problem in many areas of human life, and we know how to handle it. The religious difficulty is viewing religions in this way at all, that is, as options that we rationally choose because they look more likely to achieve certain ends, or to achieve them better, than any other religious or non-religious alternative. This is not how believers relate to their religion, at least not normally and in traditional religions.

However, we live in a pluralistic culture today, and sociologists keep reminding us that the 'pluralistic situation is, above all, a market situation'.[12] A 'religion', Peter Berger argues, 'can no longer be imposed, but must be marketed'.[13] But

---

11 See S.M. Heim, *Salvations. Truth and Difference in Religion*, Maryknoll, NY: Orbis Books, 2001, p.199.

12 Peter Berger, *The Social Reality of Religion*, Harmondsworth: Penguin, 1973, p.142.

13 Berger, *The Social Reality of Religion*, p.148.

this alternative is neither convincing nor compelling. A religion like Judaism, for example, survives neither by being 'imposed' nor by being 'marketed as an option' but by the way it is lived and practised and handed on in a particular community from one generation to another.

And as in this case, so in many others: Whether and how a religion continues are questions that each religion has to answer for itself, in its own terms and by its own practice. It will not normally see and present itself as a mere option among others but as a way and a view of life that has to be understood and appreciated in its own terms. If a religion 'meets the challenges of others purely in terms of pragmatic accommodation what is distinctively its own will be lost'.[14] Religions are forms of life and practice that seek to provide orientation in life. This requires more of them than meeting the challenge of a given culture. They must point beyond it and critically engage with a culture with the aim of transforming it in the light of their objectives. At the end of the day a religion survives not by being successfully marketed but by being practised as a way of life that convinces by the orientation it provides and by the example of those whose lives it informs and transforms.

5. Transformative Contemplation

If religions aim at change and transformation, is this also true of philosophy of religion? Philosophy of religion does not pursue the same end as religion, only in a rational, less confused or more defensible way. It contemplates (explores, describes, analyzes, imaginatively reconstructs) religious orientations, but it does not itself provide any religious orientation. It talks about religions, but it is not itself a move within a religion, or a better alternative to it.

Many philosophers have made this point, most prominently Wittgenstein, R. Rhees and D.Z. Phillips: Philosophy leaves everything as it is.[15] It has no message for anyone, and *a fortiori* not a religious message. Its task is to contemplate religion, not to meddle with it, and to 'contemplate possibilities of sense is different from advocating those possibilities, or of finding a faith to live by in them'.[16] Philosophy of religion is not to be mistaken for a rational substitute of religion and philosophers should stop the futile and misguided attempts to replace the alleged confusions of religions by more rational constructions of their own, or to provide us with a message to guide us in life.[17] This ruins philosophy, plays into the hands of religious sceptics,[18] fails to improve religion, and doesn't help to sort out conflict, to say nothing of deep conflict, between religions.

But then why engage in philosophy of religion at all? What has been said so far cannot be the whole story. Wittgenstein, for one, 'never saw philosophy as an

---

14 Phillips, *Religion and the Hermeneutics of Contemplation*, p.269.

15 Wittgenstein, *Philosophical Investigations*, §124.

16 Phillips, *Religion and the Hermeneutics of Contemplation*, p.5.

17 Phillips, *Religion and the Hermeneutics of Contemplation*, p.318.

18 See Lance Ashdown, *Anonymous Skeptics. Swinburne, Hick, and Alston*, Tübingen: Mohr-Siebeck, 2002.

exercise in quietism'.[19] He claimed that philosophy leaves everything as it is, but he also encouraged a certain way of looking at things, and he clearly thought that this way is philosophically more appropriate than other ways.

This does not imply that there is an appropriate way of looking at religions, a way which Phillips has restated as 'contemplation'. There is no such thing as 'the appropriate view of religion', or 'the only adequate way of doing philosophy'. Sometimes philosophy's task is contemplation and description, at other times criticism, polemics, imaginative invention, apologetics or direction. The way in which we philosophize depends on the questions that trouble, confuse or provoke us. Contemplation is often but not always the appropriate way to respond. But it is not a monolithic activity, and we can do different things through philosophical contemplation. Sometimes it can help us to see what was mistaken in our understanding (or misunderstanding) of a religion. Sometimes it may deepen and confirm our previous understandings. And sometimes it may open our eyes to something we hadn't noticed before. Philosophical contemplation can have different effects: dispel illusions, clarify problems, correct mistakes, change opinions, suggest improvements or confirm views. But it does have effects, not in changing what it contemplates but in changing those who contemplate.

The whole point of doing philosophy, as M. Jamie Ferreira has rightly pointed out, is to be 'working on oneself, and ultimately working on oneself is a matter of changing one's way of seeing things'.[20] Philosophers may indeed be well advised to aim merely at contemplating the world, not at changing it. They contemplate possibilities of sense even when they think about the actualities of life. They do so by placing the actual against the backdrop of the possible and explore the many ways in which what happens to be the case could have been otherwise. Their experimental thinking does not change the world, but it changes them so that they see the world, and their own place in it, differently. Philosophical contemplation is an exercise in transformation – self-transformation.

So why do we start philosophizing, about religion or anything else? Not because we decide to do so, but because we cannot help it. We are confused by what we see, or think we see, in a religion. We cannot understand why others believe what they do, or why they don't believe what we take to be self-evident, or believe what to us looks very strange or quite unacceptable. Not only Locke had occasion to wonder why 'religion, which should most distinguish us from beasts, and ought most peculiarly to elevate us, as rational creatures, above brutes, is that wherein men often appear most irrational and more senseless than beasts themselves'. Why are so many believers 'led into so strange opinions, and extravagant practices in religion, that a considerate man cannot but stand amazed at their follies, and judge them so far

---

19   M. Jamie Ferreira, 'Vision and Love: A Wittgensteinian Ethic in *Culture and Value*', in *Grammar and Grace: Reformulations of Aquinas and Wittgenstein*, eds. Jeffrey Stout and R. MacSwain, London/New York: SCM/Macmillan, 2004. See M. Jamie Ferreira, 'Normativity and Reference in a Wittgensteinian Philosophy of Religion', *Faith and Philosophy* 18 (2002), 443–64.

20   Ferreira, 'Vision and Love: A Wittgensteinian Ethic in *Culture and Value*'.

from being acceptable to the great and wise God, that he cannot avoid thinking them ridiculous, and offensive to a sober good man'?[21]

Perhaps we are more amazed about Locke than about what he was amazed about. But there are plenty of reasons to be confused, amazed or wondering about religion. Unless we are, we won't philosophize, and while we are, we cannot stop philosophizing. We seek to overcome our own confusions by contemplation, but we cannot tell how it will be possible or whether it can be achieved. We contemplate what we cannot understand or what makes us wonder. But unless we ourselves engage in contemplation, we cannot gain anything from philosophy. Philosophical problems cannot be solved by proxy. What others have thought, or said, or written may guide our reflection or provoke our contemplation. But we have to reflect and contemplate it ourselves if we want to overcome our confusions and find answers to our questions. Philosophy is *Selbstdenken*, as Kant has summed up the enlightenment tradition, not because we have no other topic to think about than ourselves, but because we ourselves have to do the thinking if philosophical contemplation is to have any point. *Sapere aude* is a philosophical injunction which each has to follow by herself or himself, in contemplating religion as much as in any other matter.

Philosophy of religion, as all philosophy, is contemplation. It contemplates problems provoked by religions. Not just any problems a religion may pose, and not the problems others may have, but those we have. So we have to do the contemplating. We contemplate what amazes us, why it amazes us, and why it doesn't amaze others. And in doing so we find ourselves engaged in transformative contemplation – transformative not by changing the religions we contemplate, but us who contemplate them.

6. Differences and Conflicts

We live in a world of many religions with many different ends. But actual religious differences are not a root evil that needs to be overcome in each and every case. No one will deny that there are differences between a Muslim, a Buddhist and a Christian that are not in practice reconcilable. But even if in some respects religious differences amount to value conflicts, value conflict is not necessarily something to be resolved or avoided. It is not a form of inconsistency within a single coherent system. Yet only inconsistency, not conflict, needs avoiding, at least with respect to ideas, beliefs, values and sentiments.

Moreover, conflict among religions, or between religions and culture, cannot be contained by attempting to integrate all differences into a rich and more comprehensive whole. Even within one and the same society we do not need a common (or the same) 'sense of the whole' in order to live peacefully together but legal, political and juridical structures that enable us to live together in the light of irreconcilable differences.[22] The stability of culturally and religiously diverse societies does not depend on a common ideology or on any shared ethical tradition

---

21 John Locke, *Essay Concerning Human Understanding*, Bk. IV, chap. XVIII, para. 1.

22 See I.U. Dalferth, 'Paradigm Lost. From the Sense of the Whole to the Sense of the Presence of God', in *Religion in a Pluralistic Age. Proceedings of the Third International*

but on legal, political and juridical institutions that function independently of any particular religion, worldview, ideology or morality.[23]

This is not to say that we should never seek to remove conflicts in values. But both individuals and communities are capable of tolerating a considerable amount of value conflict in their personal and communal affairs. So we must be careful. It is not prudent to try to sort out what doesn't need to be sorted out to solve a particular problem. We may even create conflict by trying to reconcile differences that do not, or need not, lead to conflict here and now. Moreover, ways of life such as religions are not systems of belief that stand and fall with being consistent in every possible respect. So insisting on principles and consequences without regard for the particularities of a given situation may do more harm than good. Nobody will deny that peacemaking among religions is desirable and good. But in times of peace, attempts at peacemaking may create conflict rather than help to avoid it. Not every difference is a conflict that needs to be solved, and not every conflict stands in the way of peaceful co-existence.

So we must pay attention to the particularities of a situation, both in our private and public lives. In private life, inconsistency is intolerable only when we recognize conflict among our own value commitments, not when ours differ from those of others.[24] Only in the context of public policy formation may it become necessary to sort out value conflicts among different religious orientations.

But for this we need no common agreement on some shared fundamental values or a common view of the good life. All we need for peaceful co-existence are legal, political and juridical structures that enable us to live together with different value orientations. This implies institutions that have the right and power to sort out conflicts between us in ways that have been accepted as acceptable by all parties involved, and hence justify the use of legitimate coercion if necessary. That is, when conflict arises that needs sorting out we must, in the last resort, be able to fall back on justified ways of coercion that have been accepted, for whatever reasons, by the parties involved independently of the particular conflict at stake. Commitment to law, not a common morality or a shared ethical code is what is needed for peaceful co-existence. And that commitment may be justified in a plurality of ways, religious and non-religious, not merely by public reasons that are not connected to any particular religious or ethical tradition and which any rational citizen would accept.

7. Dialogue

This is why dialogue among religions is important but not enough. Dialogue is not a way of solving conflicts or of overcoming differences but of identifying and clarifying them. It falls short of decision. Dialogue may prepare the way for it, but it

Conference on Philosophical Theology, eds. D.A. Crosby and Ch.D. Hardwick, New York: Peter Lang, 2001, pp.21–48.

23   See for a similar argument Robert Audi, *Religious Commitment and Secular Reason*, Cambridge/New York: Cambridge University Press, 2000, esp. Ch. 3.

24   Isaac Levi, *The Covenant of Reason. Rationality and the Commitments of Thought*, Cambridge: Cambridge University Press, 1997, p.237.

cannot end a conflict. This is true of dialogue among individual believers as much as it is of dialogue among official representatives of religious traditions.

Moreover, dialogue is never 'inter-religious' in the sense of being a comprehensive meeting of religions in all their respects. On the contrary, dialogue is always particular and specific, not holistic and general; it is local and not independent of the particularities of a situation; and it is not always effective in the same way. Dialogue among individuals of different religious or cultural traditions may for instance change a believer's system of beliefs and values (that is, effect individual changes of outlook and orientation). But for the whole religious community a dialogue becomes effective only if its results are officially received and accepted according to the agreed procedures of the community in question. And while this may occasionally be a way of overcoming past conflicts among religions, it rarely helps to avoid or to resolve actual conflict.

What we need, therefore, is not only dialogue among religions but also public debate that paves the way towards decision. In conflicts of value orientation (among religions or among religions and cultures) we must sort the defensible from the unacceptable in public debate, and this is not something to be left to the religions alone.

What is defensible cannot be decided in advance but will only show in the actual process of making both these differences and their grounds publicly accessible and debatable. Some of these may turn out to be unacceptable to all or most of us for a variety of reasons. Some may be acceptable to some but not be live options for others. And some may turn out to be of much wider interest and relevance than we had expected. Clarifying defensible differences in public debate, therefore, is a means of improving both one's own religious tradition and one's understanding of others. And knowing in which respect one is different, and why, and how others react to it, and why, is a prerequisite for peacefully co-existing in religiously and culturally diverse societies.

What we need, therefore, are not common religious convictions but agreement on public procedures of debate, defence, contest and decision-making that enable people with different interests, moral codes and views of the good life to live together without using physical or mental force to sort out their differences.

Our societies are comprised of an increasing number of citizens who lack a common religious background and history. This fact by itself is no reason to worry about imminent culture wars or global clashes of civilizations. But to contain the potentially destructive effects of religious diversity, we must learn to appreciate, not merely what we hold in common, but what makes us differ, and perhaps irreconcilably so. Tolerance is the cement of our societies. But the crucial respect is for persons, not beliefs, moral codes, or practices. We must find out what constitutes the irrevocable otherness of the other, that is, his or her religious identity, and in the last resort, this otherness is to be found, not in what we share, but in what distinguishes us.

The promising route to take in dealing with religious diversity, therefore, is (a) to make publicly accessible what lies at the heart of religious convictions and traditions and (b) to construct rules, rights[25] and institutions of justified coercion to deal with problems provoked by those differences without expecting these rules to lead to global consensus or a common view of life. After all, common convictions are no guarantee against conflict. On the contrary, even where there is a lot in common (such as in the Christian Churches), it is often precisely what is shared in common which is the basis of conflict. Here as elsewhere it is not what is believed but the way it is believed which decides on the rationality of these beliefs and the defensibility of the corresponding moral codes and ways of life.

But there is no valid reason why all rational beliefs and defensible views should have to be part of the same more encompassing whole. Different religious beliefs may be reasonable for different persons for different reasons without being part of some larger whole. This admission is not to give in to relativism. Just as there are no beliefs that are not beliefs of someone, so there are no reasons that are not reasons for someone. But there are well grounded beliefs that are false (for example, scientific beliefs), there are ill grounded beliefs that are true, and there are incompatible beliefs that are well grounded for different persons, although one of them must, or all of them may, be false.

Yet the problem is not merely one of the compatibility or incompatibility of beliefs. Religious beliefs are intimately bound up with ways of life and practices, and just as one cannot love everyone at once in the same way, so a person cannot seriously engage in a plurality of religious activities at the same time. What is at stake here is not the logical incompatibility of opposing religious beliefs, but the factual impossibility of living more than one life at once. In this respect we have no choice. We live in one way, and thereby exclude other ways. We may change our way of living, and constantly do. But this doesn't alter the basic situation. We live only one of the lives that we might and could have lived. Life is a series of decisions many of which depend on decisions taken by others, and we cannot know in advance whether what we choose, or find ourselves to have chosen, will turn out to be right. So we must seriously entertain the possibility that we may be wrong and the other right. And this, some have argued, is one of the main and most compelling reasons for us to practise toleration.

8. Toleration

Toleration, as I. Berlin has argued, 'implies a certain disrespect. I tolerate your absurd beliefs and your foolish acts, though I know them to be absurd and foolish'.[26] This is quite different from genuine respect. Genuine respect differs from both contemptuous toleration and pseudo respect in that I genuinely entertain the other

---

25   'Human rights are historical constructions, not natural kinds', as John Clayton has rightly pointed out ('Common Ground and Defensible Difference', in *Religion, Politics and Peace*, ed. L.S. Rouner, Notre Dame, IN: University of Notre Dame Press, 1999, p.27).

26   Isaiah Berlin, *Four Essays on Liberty*, London/New York: Oxford University Press, 1969, p.184.

view as a serious possibility. If I really take it seriously, I must be prepared to change my convictions.[27]

This attitude is sometimes but not always appropriate. Our '[b]eliefs ... are resources of deliberation. We use them as a standard for assessing propositions with respect to serious possibility.'[28] We do not change or drop that standard at will, and hence we cannot accept each and every other belief as a serious possibility.

That is to say, we must distinguish between the etiquette of debate and controversy and the ethics of controversy. Etiquette may require me to I pick my words carefully and to keep my views to myself if not asked. But the ethics of controversy demand of me that I do not pretend to take another view seriously if I am not prepared to entertain the serious possibility of changing my own views in the light of it. And I can only entertain such a possibility seriously if I respect the authority of the one who propounds the view in question and/or see the point of that view as being important and a serious candidate for consideration in the area under discussion.

For example, if someone tells me that I am a product of a virgin birth,[29] I do not show the non dogmatic open-mindedness that is rightly cherished in our societies if I pretend to take this view seriously by assigning it some (weak or very weak) probability rather than dismissing it out of hand. In everyday life as much as in the academy we have a moral obligation to call a stick a stick. If I really follow my convictions and act on that which I am sure to know, that's what I ought to do.

'But doesn't everyone deserve to get a serious hearing?', some may ask. Sure, but I am not obliged to accord everyone a serious hearing on every issue. I may pretend do so, but I am not seriously engaging with a view unless I am prepared to modify my own convictions. The 'views of the competent ought to be taken seriously – at least concerning matters about which they are competent.' But on issues concerning which they lack authority, 'we have no obligation to take them seriously'.[30] And on matters which we know we know better, we must accept that '[c]ontemptuous toleration is sometimes preferable to sceptical respect'.[31] The respect we owe others does not imply that we have to respect their wrong views. Wrong views may be tolerated, but not respected, and toleration does not oblige us to respect, or pretend to respect, what we know to be wrong. This is true in everyday life as much as in religion, as D.Z. Phillips rightly points out: 'Nonsense remains nonsense even if we associate God's name with it.'[32] We tolerate it, but we are not obliged to take it seriously.

Similarly, 'although it would be wrong to impose a legal ban against the publication of creationist views, there may not be good enough reasons to take them seriously or to encourage their dissemination'.[33] Not all agree. Even if we are not obliged to open our minds to dissent without good reasons, aren't we obliged not merely to tolerate

---

27 Levi, *The Covenant of Reason*, p.241.
28 Levi, *The Covenant of Reason*, p.244.
29 Levi's example.
30 Levi, *The Covenant of Reason*, p.251.
31 Levi, *The Covenant of Reason*, p.251.
32 Phillips, *Belief, Change and Forms of Life*, p.13.
33 Levi, *The Covenant of Reason*, p.252.

but to encourage and support the dissemination of dissenting views?[34] Not, I think, as a general rule. The positive desirability of proliferating dissenting ideas and of taking them seriously has to be justified in each case.

All this is also true with respect to religions. Here as elsewhere an open mind is one thing, an empty mind another. To give every view the same hearing or to take it to be just as important (or unimportant) as any other is to refrain from assessing it and to fall prey to what Isaac Levi has called the scepticism of the empty mind. But we never start from scratch. We all live in particular historical settings with contingent preferences for some views, values and goals rather than others. Those preferences are not completely arbitrary but reflect past or present experiences of our communities that we would be ill advised to ignore. In a changing world we need to assess them critically in order not to fall prey to prejudice, error and delusion. And in order to do so we have developed criteria such as justice, goodness, freedom and equality. But we cannot transcend our contingent situations altogether. Our ideas of justice, goodness, freedom, equality are tied up with specific experiences, practices and background assumptions of our culture. Their content and force can only be illumined and assessed against that background, and they lose their point and persuasive power when they become divorced from the wider cultural tradition to which they belong.

Now whereas ideas such as justice or equality provide good reasons for having an open mind for the views of others, they do not justify pretending to have an empty mind. We need to have good reasons for opening our minds up so as to entertain seriously the dissenting religious or non-religious views of others:

> The mere presence of disagreement is not such a good reason. If it were, it would equate toleration and respect for the views of dissenters. Since there will be a dissenter for virtually every substantive view, advocates of toleration who conflate it with respect for the views of dissenters must be urging upon us the skepticism of the empty mind.[35]

And whatever the dialogue between religions and cultures hopes to achieve, this cannot possibly be one of its objectives.

---

34 Levi, *The Covenant of Reason*, p.252.
35 Levi, *The Covenant of Reason*, p.3–4.

Chapter X

Philosophy, Theology and Cultural Conflicts – A Reply to I. Dalferth

D.Z. Phillips

1. Culture and No-Through Roads

Ingolf Dalferth recognizes that, in relation to religion, the hermeneutics I am concerned with is not the hermeneutics of suspicion, or the hermeneutics of recollection, but the hermeneutics of contemplation. My work certainly does not belong to the first kind of hermeneutics, the reductive task of showing that religious beliefs are either false, nonsensical, or amount to no more than 'morality touched with emotion'.[1] Neither does it belong, despite the opinion of many that it does, to the second kind of hermeneutics, to the attempt to recall, for our culture, a purer form of religious belief, purged by the fires of criticism.[2] In being concerned with the hermeneutics of contemplation, with the relation of language to reality, it involves doing conceptual justice to the world in all its variety.[3] It is this last conception of philosophy that I argued for in Chapter II in my reply to Stephen Mulhall, responding to what I took to be his difficulties in locating philosophy's 'cool place'.[4] I shall not repeat those arguments here.

Faced with the complexities of cultural conflicts, the last thing a contemplative philosophy tires to do is to reduce them to a feature they all have in common, or to suggest that, despite appearances, underneath them is a common form waiting to be made explicit. Dalferth and I agree that the conflicts are real conflicts, that the differences are real differences. This is as true of religious differences as of any other.

Theological reactions to religious differences have also been diverse. Exclusivism says that only one religion is true. Other religions are to be judged in the light of the opportunities they have had to believe in it. Inclusivism, too, says that there is only one true religion, but some other religions are acknowledged as approximations to it. Pluralism holds that the major religions are different cultural expressions of the

---

1   See Kai Nielsen's arguments in Kai Nielsen and D. Z. Phillips, *Wittgensteinian Fideism?*.

2   See the work of Paul Ricœur, for example.

3   See my *Religion and the Hermeneutics of Contemplation*.

4   For an elucidation of this conception see my *Philosophy's Cool Place*.

same fundamental reality. They are equally valid as paths to salvation. Each of these reactions inherits difficulties, as does the reductive analysis of religion.

The major difficulty for reductive naturalism, which I have emphasized again and again in my work, is that it succeeds because it is highly selective in the practices it targets. Its criticisms are often merited, but then, in its craving for generality, it imposes an alien grammar on major forms of religion.[5]

A serious difficulty for exclusivism, is the presentation of impressive examples of faith from other religions; I mean impressive *on its own terms*. Faced with these, an exclusivist has to say that no matter how impressive the spiritual fruits may be, they are growing on the wrong religious tree. Such a reaction leads to difficulties of great severity. For example, it would be difficult for a Christian exclusivist to deny that the words 'Jesus saves' mean very different things within Christianity. But if the same words can have different meanings, why can't different words have the same meaning? 'By their fruits ye shall know them.' Thus, it may be possible to see Christ in the Buddha, or to see the Buddha in Christ. If truth is denied, even when spiritual parallels are recognized, truth seems to be reduced to displaying the right label. But in Christianity itself, in the story of the Last Judgement, the labels are exposed for the empty things they are. Those who have professed Christ's name, without showing his spirit, are told to depart, while those who have shown his spirit, but have not professed his name, are welcomed. Exclusivism, then, seems to face the difficulty of a plurality of shared spiritual realities, even though they do not all share the same name.

Inclusivism does recognize that the same spiritual truths may be found in religions other than one's own. The criticism it has to face comes in the suggestion that there are spiritual truths, other than those of one's religion, from which there is something to learn. They are not mere approximations to one's own.

Pluralism may express its view of world religions in at least two different ways. The first of these states that no religion has a complete revelation of God. Each is a cultural manifestation of a God who transcends them all. This God cannot be worshipped, since any form of worship would simply be another manifestation of the God who transcends it. Pluralism sees different religions as paths to the same salvation. But how can this be known if God is transcendent? Pluralism's answer is that this is a reasonable assumption, given the similar spiritual character of the lives of the deviant in different religions.

The second form of pluralism, argues that the world religions have something to learn from each other. The reality of the divine is shown in a synthesis of the values found in them. God transcends any particular religion, not by being metaphysically transcendent, beyond the possibility of worship, but by including in his nature a spectrum of spiritual values which goes beyond those expressed in any one religion.

The second kind of pluralism, like the first, has to face the charge that it is selective in its choice of religions. Religious values would exhibit differences were it not for such selectivity. It can be argued, however, that the first kind of pluralism

---

5   For my criticisms of different forms of reductionism, see my *Religion and the Hermeneutics of Contemplation*.

is the second in disguise. It would like to be thought of as an example of Kant's metaphysical distinction between the noumenal and phenomenal realms. In reality, it is born of a theological desire for harmony of a kind exemplified by the second form of pluralism. Kantianism is simply used as a pragmatic device, to subserve the theological judgements made prior to its deployment.

In thinking of a religion as the incomplete expression or description of a reality which transcends it, pluralism runs into confusions concerning the relation of language to reality. It treats language as though it were a description of reality. We may describe states of affairs, accurately or inaccurately, when we speak, but the language in which we do so is not itself such a description. Consider a simple example: one person may describe a material as blue, while another person describes the same material as green. Their beliefs about the colour of the material contradict each other. But they agree on the meaning of 'blue' and 'green'. Without the agreement in meaning, there could be no disagreement about the fact of the matter. But the meanings are not themselves descriptions of realities, of 'blueness' and 'greenness', existing in some special realm. This confuses the meaning of a name with the bearer of the name. As Wittgenstein says,

> It looks to us as if we were saying something about the nature of red in saying that the words 'Red exists' do not yield a sense. Namely that red does not exist 'in its own right'. The same idea – that this is a metaphysical statement about red – finds expression again when we say such a thing as that red is timeless, and perhaps still more strongly in the word 'indestructible'.[6]

When we turn to religious beliefs, it is extremely easy to forget these fundamental lessons about language and reality. We think that the conceptual parameters of a religion are pointers towards a reality they cannot reach.[7] But the logical point is that the language shows us what is meant by divine reality, including what is meant by saying that 'it is beyond mortal telling'. The latter phrase is the language of praise, not an epistemic report on the failure of that language. One doesn't bypass language because it cannot capture transcendence. What 'transcendence' means is shown in the language in which it is expressed. The memory of 'transcendence' is not transcendent. By contrast, the notion of 'transcendence' in pluralism, cuts the notion off from the living religions in which it has its sense. It is not required by pluralism of the same kind, which says that the divine is found in different ways in different religions. Whether the inter-religious comparisons are conceptually accurate is another matter, which would have to be looked at case by case.

I have reason to believe that, in general, Dalferth would agree with the observations I have made so far, although he does not discuss them in the way I have done. His appreciation of the logical issues involved shows itself in his reaction to the complexities of our culture, and in his discussion of the conflicts within it. I have said already that he regards these conflicts are real. If difficulties between

---

6   Ludwig Wittgenstein, *Philosophical Investigations*, Oxford: Blackwell, 1958, Part I, para. 58.

7   I refer again to my interesting discussion with John Edelman on this issue. See Ch. IV, p.82, n.19 of the present volume.

religion and other cultural movements are to be addressed at all, he says that it
is not by ignoring differences, but by recognizing them. Culture is not a seamless
garment. That is no neat fit between the activities within it. One should not assume,
therefore, that religion is at home in it. Its tasks may be related critically to its cultural
surroundings. Given these cultural facts, Dalferth asks what contribution religion
can make to a culture in which conflict is evident.

At the beginning of his discussion, Dalferth identifies some 'no-through roads'
which I agree should be added to those I have already mentioned. Given conflict
between religions, the religions involved cannot be regarded as options between
which we can choose at will. This notion of an isolated, autonomous choice, does
not explain what would inform such a choice, or what the situation of the person
making it is supposed to be. It does not do justice to the phenomenon of conversion,
to situations in which someone may be genuinely torn between different religions, or
to situations in which a person struggles with belief and unbelief. There is certainly
no way out of religious conflicts by turning to the 'market' considerations which
once attracted Peter Berger. To simply adapt one's beliefs to trends in 'the cultural
market' is not to have genuine beliefs at all. It is an avoidance of the discourse in
which real conflicts occur.[8]

I agree with Dalferth's views about these 'no-through roads', which neither
theology nor philosophy should be tempted by in their discussions of cultural
conflict. As we shall see, the extent of my agreement with him does not end there.
But we also have our disagreements. Some of these begin to emerge when Dalferth
seeks to characterize my philosophical reaction to cultural conflict, and when he
expresses his own reaction to contemplative philosophy.

2. Describing Philosophies and Philosophizing

Dalferth recognizes that contemplative philosophy does not transform one's life in
the way religion can (p.159):

> It contemplates (explores, describes, analyzes, imaginatively reconstructs) religious
> orientations, but it does not itself provide any religious orientation. It talks about religions,
> but it is not itself a move within a religion, or a better alternative to it.

This recognizes the distinction between the philosophical and the personal that I
argued for in my reply to Stephen Mulhall.[9] Dalferth emphasizes its importance in
the work of Wittgenstein and Rush Rhees, as well as in my own (p.159):

> It has no message for anyone, and *a fortiori* not a religious message. Its task is to contemplate
> religion, not to meddle with it, and to 'contemplate possibilities of sense is different from
> advocating those possibilities, or to finding a faith to live by in them'.[10] Philosophy of
> religion is not to be mistaken for a rational substitute for religion and philosophers should
> stop the futile and misguided attempts to replace the alleged confusions of religions by

---

8   See Ch. 11 of my *Religion and the Hermeneutics of Contemplation*.
9   See Ch. II, section 2: 'The Philosophical and the Personal' in this volume.
10 Phillips, *Religion and the Hermeneutics of Contemplation*, p.5.

more rational constructions of their own, or to provide us with a message to guide us in life.[11]

Dalferth points out that if one is committed to philosophy, one does not decide to philosophize. One does so because one cannot help it. No one can philosophize for us. We have to contemplate for ourselves. Sometimes, Dalferth makes this point in a way that could be misleading. Wanting to say that we must make philosophical problems our own, he says: 'not the problems others may have, but those *we* have' (p.161). This may obscure the fact that an important element in philosophical contemplation is wonder at the fact that others have the problems that they do, and that they find answers to them in the way they do. This is not wondering how they could have *those* problems, or settle for *those* answers, as distinct from *our* sense of the problematic, and the answers *we* have arrived at. Rather, it is letting their problems and answers be themselves; seeing that human life can be like that. Dalferth's way of putting the matter threatens to lose the distinction between the personal and the philosophical he and I want to maintain.

Dalferth says that appreciating my contemplative conception of philosophy (p.160)

> does not imply that there is an appropriate way of looking at religions, a way which Phillips has restated as 'contemplation'. There is no such thing as 'the appropriate view of religion'.

If Dalferth is making the obvious point that a contemplative, philosophical interest in religion is not the only kind of interest one can have in it, who would disagree with him? There are all sorts of interests other than philosophy and theology, interests which are historical sociological, anthropological and so on. But Dalferth also says that there is no such thing as 'the only adequate way of doing philosophy' (p.160). This may seem to express a commendable humility, until we ask from whose mouth the statement is supposed to come.

Dalferth's remark can be seen as purely descriptive, in which case it becomes innocuous. There are many different schools of philosophy. Who would deny that? Sometimes, in different cultures, or at certain historical periods in one's own, one may be inclined to speak of different conceptions of the subject, such that what *doing* philosophy amounts to is different. I mean, for example, traditions in which one studies influences and counter-influences in the thought of 'the wise', but without criticism. Or again, think of disputations where a departure from tradition, or a contradicting of a verse from Scripture, would, itself, be a sufficient ground for rejecting an argument. Putting such differences aside, I am concerned with the history of Western philosophy which is essentially critical. Take away the critical discussion and there would be no philosophy. In this context, saying that there is no adequate way of doing philosophy is, therefore, problematic. Ways of philosophizing are no more options than religions are. Take away the striving for an adequate way

---

11 Phillips, *Religion and the Hermeneutics of Contemplation*, p.318. In this connection see Ch. II, section 1: 'The Lure of a Philosophy for Living' in the present volume.

of philosophizing, and one takes away the motivation for philosophizing. As Rush Rhees says,

> It is interesting that we should take different views about philosophy, although such differences are common enough. Philosophers have almost always found that their discussions were in large part about what philosophy is ... I do not think this is an accident; I think that if one reflects on philosophical discussions one can see why it is so and always will be.
>
> There are certain problems which have come up again and again from the time of the early Greeks right down to the present; and I should maintain that the other problems generally centred round them.[12]

The problems have to do with language and the world, what it means to say something, what kind of account can be given of reality; in short, the fundamental problems of philosophy. It is in struggling with these questions that philosophers form different conceptions of what they are doing. In that struggle they are related critically to each other. So while philosophizing, they are not related to fellow philosophers merely historically or descriptively. They want to see things clearly; to do conceptual justice to them. To say that there is an adequate and appropriate way of philosophizing is to recognize the spirit of that enquiry. This is not to say, absurdly, that this spirit is only to be found in one philosopher. Further, a philosopher may find it in those he disagrees with, if only because they deepen his understanding of the extent of the problems and difficulties that have to be faced.

In reaching certain conclusions, the philosopher will, of necessity, be rejecting others in the course of arriving at them. Thus, he cannot simply look on warring conclusions and activities as an array of approaches one is free to choose from. Contemplative attention to the world is not one option among many for those philosophers who pursue it. Thus, they will find Dalferth's words problematic when he says (p.160):

> Sometimes philosophy's task is contemplation and description, at other times criticism, polemics, imaginative invention, apologetics or direction. The way in which we philosophize depends on the questions that trouble, confuse or provoke us. Contemplation is often but not always the appropriate way to respond.

The crucial point to note is that contemplative philosophy emerges, not from problems that happen to trouble or confuse us, but from the fundamental problems of philosophy. As Rhees said, how those problems are treated is internally related to our understanding of the kind of problems they are. Contemplative philosophy about religion, for example, does involve criticism and imaginative invention, but not apologetics. It would argue that the apologetic character of much of contemporary philosophy of religion is a major weakness in it. It cannot therefore, say, that apologetics is simply another way of doing philosophy of religion. When

---

12   Rush Rhees, 'The Fundamental Problems of Philosophy', in Rhees, *Wittgenstein and the Possibility of Discourse*, p.viii.

contemplative philosophers imagine other ways of doing things, as Wittgenstein does, to better understand our own, Dalferth says (p.160):

> Their experimental thinking does not change the world, but it changes them so that they see the world and their own place in it, differently. Philosophical contemplation is an exercise in transformation – self-transformation.

True enough, but as Dalferth pointed out, this transformation is not like religious transformation. It is what a philosopher does with the fundamental problems of philosophy, what he does with them, that determines the character of his self-transformation.

3. Contemplating Differences

In the remainder of his paper, Dalferth reflects on what measure should be taken when faced by conflicts arising from moral and religious differences in our culture. He places great emphasis on legal and political measures that he thinks are needed. At first, these concerns may be thought to take us far away from contemplative philosophy, but this is not so. That philosophy is deeply concerned with what it means to say that we are in the world which, in turn, obviously includes our lives in society. Contemplative philosophy raises the central question of the nature of society; of what kind of intelligibility the notion has.[13] Its treatment of this question has a direct bearing on Dalferth's reflections.

Social contract theory is an attempt to elucidate the concept of society. An attempt is made to emphasize the rationale of social life, in terms of the psychology of the individual. We are asked to imagine that human beings used to exist in a pre-social environment, a state of nature, in which they were constantly at war with each other. The self-interest of the individual is not advanced in this condition, since his will is constantly being threatened by the will of others. It is therefore in the interest of every individual to enter into a social contract in which he agrees to live in a society with his neighbours. Why should he accept the constraints and coercion involved in doing so? The answer is that while no individual gets all that he wants, he gets *more* than he acquired in the state of nature. What matters, for our present purposes, is not whether social contract theory is meant to be an historical or conceptual analysis, but the conceptual assumptions contained in it.

Social contract theories face serious logical difficulties. They are supposed to show us what the very possibility of social life and agreement comes to. That possibility is said to be lacking in a state of nature, hence the agreement to enter into a social contract. But that agreement shows that the possibility of consensus is already presupposed. By agreeing to enter the contract, the people exhibit a consensus which the contract is supposed to create for the first time. Moreover, the notion of a contract has its sense *in* a social context, and cannot, therefore, be the prior condition of such contexts. What these criticisms show is that social existence does not depend on, and cannot be analysed in terms of, the *prior* consent of individuals.

---

13   See Peter Winch, 'How is Political Authority Possible?'.

The above analysis does not make the notion of political consensus unimportant. This is not a prior agreement to make political judgements of various kinds, but an agreement which shows itself *in* the political judgements people are prepared to make. Clearly, these judgements vary, as do the conceptions of political authority expressed in them – allegiance to the monarch, obedience to the elders, respect for parliamentary democracy and so on. We cannot ask whether these forms of authority are themselves reasonable, since, for those who adhere to them, they constitute what counts as authoritative reasons. If one does want to use the word 'unreasonable' to describe challenges to such authority, which have, of course, occurred, it is important to note that the idea of what is unreasonable is itself rooted in a rival political conception of authority.[14] The dispute is between rival political ideas, not between ideas as expressions of a common rationality by which they can be assessed.[15]

The relevance of this brief excursus into political philosophy is that it bears directly on what Dalferth wants to say about moral and religious conflicts in our culture. The further extent of my agreement with him, which I referred to earlier, can be seen in the way many of his comments fit in well with the critique of social contract theory. At other times, however, his remarks are either in tension with, or fall foul of, that critique. A contemplative philosophy will want to distinguish between these. In the remainder of this section, I shall note six points, made by Dalferth, which accord well with what I have been saying.

First, Dalferth points out that 'value conflict is not necessarily something to be resolved or avoided. It is not a form of inconsistency within a single coherent system' (p.161). This being the case, a set of values cannot be criticized for failing to cohere with such a system. There is no such system. A society or a culture is certainly not such a system.

Second, it follows from the first point that whatever resolution of moral and religious differences may come to, the task is not 'to integrate all differences into a rich and more comprehensive whole' (p.161). The notion of society or culture as such a whole is confused.

Third, applying these lessons to religious differences, Dalferth concludes that 'there is no valid reason why all rational beliefs and defensible views should have to be part of the same more encompassing whole' (p.164).

Fourth, in Dalferth's extremely important recognition that, in our discussions with each other, in our criticisms and counter-criticisms (p.166),

> we never start from scratch. We all live in particular historical settings with contingent preferences for some views, values, and goals rather than others. These preferences are not completely arbitrary but reflect past or present experiences of our communities that we would be ill advised to ignore.

If anything, Dalferth's point needs a stronger statement. The phrase 'contingent preferences' is too weak an expression for the traditions and their values in which

---

14   See the discussion in Ch. II, section 1 of the present volume.

15   Interestingly, slavery is a limiting case. This is because the denial of freedom is so radical that it is seen as the denial of the possibility of having a point of view which can be expressed in discussion with others.

people may be rooted. Perhaps it is this choice of phrase which leads Dalferth to call the rootedness 'not completely arbitrary'. But why should it be called 'contingent' or 'arbitrary' at all? That might apply to thoughtless preferences, hence my misgivings too about the use of 'preference' in this context. What would 'non-contingent' or 'non-arbitrary' rootedness mean, given Dalferth's use of the terms? I do not see what meaning they could have. But, in that case, I do not see how this use of 'contingent' or arbitrary' can mean anything either.

Fifth, Dalferth makes an extremely important distinction between an open-mind and an empty mind (see p.166). It is an intellectualist fantasy to think that intellectual enquiry entails that everything and anything may be open to question. In any context, there will be matters that simply do not arise, and we would not know what it would mean to raise them.[16] It is too weak to say, as Dalferth does, that we would assign these matters a low degree of probability. The point is that neither we, nor the person asking the question, would understand what is being said. I am thinking of examples such as the following. A scientist may be asked whether the results of an experiment are premature. It might be pointed out that other considerations need to be taken into account before they are accepted. These may lead the scientist to revise his conclusions. But if the scientist is asked why he should rely on experimentation at all, what could he say? What is being asked? I may be asked whether, on a visit to China, I visited a certain city, and I may give the wrong answer. But what if I am asked whether I know that I am writing these words now with a pen, in the sun-lounge of my home in Wales? Wouldn't it be insane to check whether I am? I mean: what would 'checking it' be? The question does not arise.

Is it different with religion? A believer may wonder whether he is answerable to God for something he has done; that is, he wonders whether it is a sin or not. But suppose someone asked him whether he was answerable to God for anything. What could he say? Not: 'Yes, *because* he is my Creator', since to call God 'Creator' already acknowledges that answerability. But the sceptic may be asking, 'Why do you think like that at all?' If the believer finds himself adopting the question, he is not trying to answer it within a coherent system of beliefs shared by believers and unbelievers alike, but beginning to lose hold of his very conception of God. This is why it is important to emphasize, as Dalferth has, that all questions are not questions within a single, coherent system, and that all changes are not mere readjustments within such a system. Losing one's religious belief is not such a readjustment.

Sixth, with respect to actual religious conflicts, Dalferth is admirably pragmatic about what can or cannot be done, what methods can be used, what it makes sense to aim for, and what the consequences are likely to be. He emphasizes the foolishness of thinking that all eventualities can be foreseen before dialogue, attempts to solve conflicts, or settling for them, even begin.

In the six ways I have noted, I take Dalferth to be in agreement with what I have said about social and cultural movements, and especially about the way the values they express show themselves in the judgements of their adherents. Interwoven with

---

16 See D.Z. Phillips, Ch. 17, section II: '"No Last Word" – An Intellectualist Fantasy' in Kai Nielsen and D.Z. Phillips, *Wittgensteinian Fideism?*.

the six points I have noted, however, are other ways of talking in which, it seems to me, Dalferth departs from the insights of his own remarks.

4. Subliming Our Concepts

In the previous section, I noted six ways in which Dalferth discusses conflicts in our culture with which I agree. This is not to assume, of course, that Dalferth would necessarily agree with the way I have presented them. In the present section, however, I want to note a further six points in Dalferth's discussion which, it seems to me, are at variance with those I have already ascribed to him. In these latter six, he seems to be guilty of subliming the concepts to which he appeals.

First, Dalferth wants to point out that peaceful co-existence in a society does not depend on a resolution of religious or moral conflicts, and that it is a confusion to think that it does (p.161):

> The stability of culturally and religiously diverse societies does not depend on a common ideology or any shared ethical tradition but on legal, political and juridical institutions that function independently of any particular religion, worldview, ideology or morality.

What Dalferth does not emphasize, in these remarks, is that the stability he refers to does reflect an agreement in political values of the kind I discussed in the previous section of this reply. My point is not to disagree with these values, but to point out that an agreement in values is involved. Dalferth, on the other hand, is tempted to turn stability and peace into limiting concepts, by which particular social and cultural conditions can be assessed. In this way, the concepts are sublimed. Dalferth says, 'Nobody will deny that peacemaking among religions is desirable and good' (p.162). What is the status of that remark? Is it meant to be a factual remark, or a theological or religious recommendation? If it is meant to be factual, it is plainly false, as evidenced in history and contemporary events. If it is a theological or religious recommendation, it comes from a specific tradition – 'Blessed are the peacemakers'. Further, if the values are seen as legal and political, as Dalferth seems to view them, it is important to recognize that they express priorities that cannot simply be taken for granted as though they were limiting concepts.

Second, Dalferth's desire to make peace and stability limiting concepts, can be seen in his claim that society could not 'go on' without them. This is connected with his claim that 'Tolerance is the cement of our societies' (p.163). That sounds like, 'Tolerance is what holds societies together, and they could not go on without it'. But this view runs into insuperable difficulties, even on his own terms. This is because, as we shall see, Dalferth also wants to speak of toleration as something which may be absent; as an ideal towards which we ought to strive. But, in that case, how are societies 'going on' in the meantime? Dalferth can give no coherent account of this, since, on his view, they lack the 'cement' to hold them together. By subliming the notions of peace and stability he obscures what he knows only too well, namely, that certain militant, proselytizing religions, may prefer conflict to peace in the pursuit of their ends. The societies in which they breed conflict do not fail to 'go on'. That is how they *do* go on – through conflict. Dalferth is taking for granted certain views about the relations between religion and the state, which are themselves the expression of the values of a tradition. One need only think of conflict between the advocates of a secular or an Islamic state. Again, the point is not to disagree with Dalferth's values, but to point out that his subliming of them prevents him from acknowledging the other values which are in conflict with them. Perhaps Dalferth only intends his comments to be related to a specific cultural situation. The problem is that in talking in the way he does, he gives the impression that he is talking of limiting conditions for any society or culture. That is why I accuse him of subliming specific political concepts and allegiances. In doing so, he is in danger of falling foul of his own warnings against subsuming differences within the 'whole' of an alleged single, coherent system.

Third, the tendency to sublime certain concepts increases when Dalferth elucidates what he means by 'tolerance'. He recognizes that someone who values peace and stability may, nevertheless, exercise tolerance of a very minimal kind. One does not interfere with the neighbour, but one does not have much to do with him either. This need not be the kind of toleration which, according to Isaiah Berlin (p.164),

> implies a certain disrespect. I tolerate your absurd beliefs and your foolish acts, as though I knew them to be absurd and foolish'. This is quite different from genuine respect.

Putting aside the claim to know that the neighbour's views are absurd and foolish, there may be more to this minimal toleration than Dalferth allows. It tolerates others in giving them space to get on with their lives. It may be more realistic, and, in some ways, less dangerous than the toleration he advocates, namely, a respect for others which obliges one to take their views seriously, to enter into discussion with them, and so on. But whatever of this, my only point, at the moment, is to show that Dalferth is far from showing that the latter kind of toleration is the 'cement' of society, and that society could not 'go on' without it.

Fourth, I think that there is a further sublimation of concepts when Dalferth elaborates on what he means by 'readiness to enter into discussion with others' (p.165):

> the ethics of controversy demand of me that I do not pretend to take another view seriously if I am not prepared to entertain the serious possibility of changing my own views in light of it. And I can only entertain such a possibility seriously if I respect the authority of the one who propounds the view in question and/or see the point of that view as being important and a serious candidate for consideration in the area under discussions.

In the sixth feature of Dalferth's reflections on conflict of values that I noted in the previous section, I commended his pragmatic approach to what could be said or done about them. Here he sublimes the 'serious possibility of changing one's view', by making it the *sine qua non* of 'taking another view seriously'. I do not see why they have to be equated in this way. Whether we are talking about a change of view about one's religion, or the more radical change of religion, Dalferth places 'readiness to change' as a serious possibility, far too early in his analysis. What is the prior condition, surely, is the readiness to listen, and the attempt to understand. This will bring one to an appreciation of the seriousness of the view, and of how it could go deep for a person. *As a result* of what one sees, one may or may not change one's views. To place 'readiness to change' at the *outset* of a discussion, not only seems unreal, but also gives the misleading impression that one's present convictions must be regarded as provincial or hypothetical at best, or, at their worst, tentative and fragile. But this does not do justice to the opening stages of inter-religious dialogue.

Fifth, I find tensions between what Dalferth says about inter-religious dialogue, and occasions where he says one has 'to sort out value conflicts among different religious orientations' (p.162). Speaking of dialogues, Dalferth says that they rarely resolve conflicts. Rather, they help us to see where our differences lie. But, now, in sorting out these differences, Dalferth says that all we need 'are legal, political and juridical structures' (p.162). These, apparently, 'need no common agreement on some shared fundamental values or a common view of the good life' (p.162). But when we ask what these structures give us, we are told that they enable us 'to live together with different value orientations' (p.162). This is not to sort out conflict between different religious orientations, only to live in peace despite them. But the institutions are said to promise more. They are supposed to be (p.162):

> Institutions that have the right power to sort out conflicts between us in ways that have been agreed as acceptable by all parties involved, and hence justify the use of legitimate coercion if necessary.

These expectations make sense where keeping the peace is concerned, but how does one sort out conflicts of value by coercion? It may be said that this is what happens when cases are resolved in the civil courts. But in what sense? Of course, those who win in court really do win, and those who lose really do lose. But the losers express disappointment with the verdict, which shows that their values have no changed. So in what sense is the conflict *in values* sorted out? It makes no sense to speak of *that* conflict being resolved by coercion. Things 'move on' legally and politically, but, as Dalferth says all one needs for this is 'Commitment to law, not to a common morality or a shared ethical code' (p.162).

Sixth, Dalferth is not content to say, as I do, that readiness to abide by legal decisions itself shows a certain agreement in judgments. He wants to give that readiness a further foundation. He says that it is based, though not merely, on 'public reasons that are not connected to any particular religious or ethical tradition and which any rational citizen would accept' (p.162). Dalferth's last phrase adds nothing, but reverses the logic of the commitments involved. The citizen Dalferth envisages does not accept the reasons and justifications because they are rational. Rather, it is these reasons and justifications which, for the citizen, constitute what is to count as 'rational'.

5. Retrospective

In section 1, I mentioned far-reaching agreements between Dalferth and myself regarding conflicts and differences in a culture. We agree on some philosophical 'no-through roads' in discussing them. In section 2, I discussed the connection between these dead ends and a contemplative conception of philosophy. In section 3, I showed the connection between this conception of philosophy and issues concerning the possibility of social existence, the kind of intelligibility it has. I emphasized that people do not agree to commit themselves to values. Rather, their agreements show themselves in the values they have. In this section, too, I noted six features of Dalferth's reflections on cultural conflicts which I take to be in accord with the point of view exemplified earlier in the section. In section 4, I pointed out another six features of Dalferth's reflections which are interwoven with those discussed in the previous section. In these, it seems to me that he sublimes certain concepts in ways which obscure moral and religious conflicts in a culture.

It may seem, that when we turn to practical issues of conflict resolution in a culture, a contemplative conception of philosophy has little to say to them. Hopefully, my engagement with Dalferth's essays shows this is not the case.

Chapter XI

Philosophy of Religion in a Pluralistic Culture

Henk Vroom
Vrije Universiteit, Amsterdam

One of the rituals of the biannual conferences of the European Society of the Philosophy of Religion was for D.Z. Phillips to interrupt a debate on the precise definition of a religious term by posing some unanswerable questions. One of the honorable members proposed a definition of a concept such as revelation, reconciliation, eternal life, prayer or divine nature, or even indicated the percentage of the probability that Jesus has been risen from the grave bodily and literally, and Phillips would stand up to explain that belief in resurrection is on a different order from things that can be counted in percentages of probability. He would explain that that the resurrection, if true, depends on trust in God, that Paul himself did not share a belief in a resurrection of people in the form they take here and now (indeed it would not help much if such a resurrection would occur), and that a revelation of God made people dumb or blind, or made them fall silent and take their shoes from their feet, or change their whole way of life. So, in this way Phillips would change the subject to religion and move away from those neat but superficial forms that allow themselves to be analyzed as if they were clearly and distinctly definable. His point converges on the Barthian point that what people sometimes say about surgeons is valid also for some philosophers and theologians: the operation was a success, but the patient is dead. Sometimes philosophers of religion look like pathologists: they analyze bodies to learn about biological systems but do not bother about the experiences of living persons. What Phillips wants to do is to show the real life of religion, its unsurpassable depth and unfathomable heights, and the real nature of religious stories and uses of language.

I remember one such discussion during one of our conferences in which some of us showed worries about the inconsistency of theism to the point of making it improbable to believe at all. In response, Phillips made up some odd stories in order to show that consistent theism is not the point at issue; rather, it is the experience people have of standing before God, naked and vulnerable, and then falling silent, and afterwards trying to utter some words to their friends about what has happened, which they cannot do very precisely. We made a joke out of it, thinking how God, the Omniscient and Almighty One, asked Adam and Eve after they had eaten the disastrous apple contemptuously offered to them by the snake: 'Where are you, Adam?' To which the 'the human being', Adam, should have answered: 'But you know where we are, because you are the infinite, everlasting, imperishable highest being, who knows all things and, therefore, knows that we hide ourselves behind this tree.' Put simply, the hiding of Adam and Eve had no point at all. Phillips' theme is that philosophy of religion loses its subject during its journey. People try to elucidate religious concepts, but do not in this way help people to understand what religion is about, and so are in danger of bringing people to the conclusion that religion is not true – because it is inconsistent and cannot be fully formulated in clear philosophical theories.

From my formulations it will be clear that I largely agree with this position. Thus any questions that I may have concerning Phillips' ideas are to be interpreted as discussions within one family in the circle of philosophers of religion. I should add immediately that a critique of some schools of philosophy, that they use the analytical apparatus in an incorrect way, does not imply that 'we' do not analyze. Philosophy is an effort to understand reality as it really is – beyond the things that we can establish by empirical methods. As Phillips stresses, philosophy is not after quasi-empirical facts, but something that lies beyond the empirical method. So conceptual analysis is not a continuation of empirical research by other means, but thinking about what cannot be established by empirical descriptions. It can truly be said of religion (but not only religion) that 'if there were evidence, this would in fact destroy the whole business'.[1] What we do is to contemplate phenomena in reality and try to describe them. Phillips tries to locate the area in which religion lives and, from the time of *The Concept of Prayer* onwards, to circumscribe the attitude of prayer and religion, the part it plays in life, and the way in which it gets its real meaning – instead of explaining religion, which would make philosophy of religion into a descriptive, 'scientific' study of religion. Phillips tries to show what religion really is: the real religion, amid all kinds of mediocrity, hypocrisy and superficiality. Look and see, he says, following Wittgenstein.

Now the question that we have to face is on whose authority Phillips claims to tell us what religion really is. Writing on the ideas of truth in various religious traditions, I once chose as a definition for the idea of truth (as far as concerns beliefs and theologies): 'what indicates how things really are'. Actually, this convenes with Augustine's definition: 'quae ostendit id quod est', with the addition of the word 'really'.[2] 'Really' points to the claim of religions that the truth about life and transcendence is not what people usually say, but what has to be found elsewhere, in a place that is deeper, more mysterious, and often less convenient. Because truth in religion requires a change of mind, conversion, obedience and meditation play a role. Religious treatises speak about 'awakening', 'freedom of spirit', 'inspiration' and liberation but it is another form of freedom than the European Enlightenment hoped for – first and foremost a freedom of the self and the new, manmade authorities that in modern culture have replaced the authorities of Church and State that the Enlightenment thinkers wanted to remove. There exists a gap between how we often experience reality – Marxists

---

1   Wittgenstein, *Lectures and Conversations on Aesthetics, Psychology, and Religious Belief*, p.56.
2   See my *Religions and the Truth*, Grand Rapids, MI/Amsterdam: Eerdmans/Rodopi 1989, p.357, 238.

and Buddhists alike would say in an estranged state of mind – and reality as it really is. Phillips wants to look and see, and describe religion as it really is. Therefore, we cannot escape the question of on whose authority he speaks. Has he had a private revelation about true religion and the real nature of the divine? Or is he perhaps a sort of theologian who takes a stance and confesses: 'Here I stand and I cannot do otherwise'? Do not philosophers defend their own views as 'the true religion', 'the true agnosticism', 'true mysticism' or whatever – and therefore become just as little subject to control as people who defend their views on the basis of religious experience or revelation? Therefore, if philosophy of religion cannot be the effort to give precise definitions of religious concepts but tries to show things as they really are, does not the philosopher dress himself with the yellow robe of guru? Whose experiences does he describe – whose real prayer, real sacrifice and trembling before the real God? All these questions lead to the question: what is the task of philosophy of religion in a pluralistic age?

In order to deal with this complicated issue, I will distinguish several academic disciplines and try to locate philosophy of religion among the other ways to study religion. We will compare them with Phillips' idea of philosophy and its Cool Place. He advises us to be content 'to show what is involved in speaking a language' and not to try to know how things should be done otherwise.[3] Philosophy contemplates how things are. The difficult role of the philosopher is not to be a citizen of any community of ideas: 'that's what makes him a philosopher', as Wittgenstein says (compare PCP p.59). This approach has been called quasi-religious because of his wonder at the fact that the great problems of philosophy existed at all, but this wonder is at a far distance from a religious stance that sees the world as the work of God (PCP p.61). Philosophy serves no other goal then to look and see, and show what 'belief', 'agreement' and 'disagreement' really are (PCP p.99). Philosophy is not apologetics. In order to better understand Phillips' view of philosophy, I will compare it with various branches of theology and religious studies. I will define theology as broadly as possible as all thinking within world view traditions, secular or religious – this may seem a little unusual and perhaps baffling for some secular thinkers, but the normal rhetoric of 'theology versus philosophy' hides from the fact that many secular thinkers are related to atheist, agnostic, humanist, neo-Marxist, naturalist, or 'liberal' schools of thought. In a global and pluralistic culture the old Western distinction between philosophy and theology must be rethought; there are many theologies and many philosophies, with or without naturalist or 'cosmic' traits and with or without all kinds of ideas of transcendence. So we will take Buddhist thought, Hindu thought, Confucian though, Christian thought, naturalist thought, socialist thought, 'liberal' thought, atheist thought and so on, as different schools of 'theological ideas' in order to distinguish them from Phillips' idea of philosophy. Naturally, the patterns of participation differ from tradition to tradition. Naturalist thinkers are organized in other kinds of networks from Roman Catholic seminary professors, but the same applies to many Buddhist and Protestant professors as well. Not all of them have

---

3   Phillips, *Philosophy's Cool Place*, p.52. Henceforth cited parenthetically in the text as PCP.

established relations with religious communities but they all think, in their own way, within and from the perspective of a worldview tradition, whether secular or not. They are a 'member' of one or perhaps two of those 'communities of ideas'.

Phillips' position is not a theological one; as a philosopher he claims not to belong to any community of ideas. So he claims that one school of philosophy – his school – does not have its own ideas about reality but describes what is going on in the various schools that defend their ideas of reality. Now, on this very point Phillips is in the company of one other community that speaks about religion and claims not to belong to one of the religious communities – maybe personally but not professionally: the community of the scholars of religious studies. Therefore, Phillips has to mark the difference between his philosophical description of what goes on in religious uses of language and a description found in religious studies, especially when this description involves an effort to understand the nature of the religious use of language.

For that reason in the section 1 we will start with the commonalities and eventual differences between the Cool Place of contemplative philosophy and religious studies. In section 2 we will consider the other side of the problem and see whether Phillips really does not make moves that make him a kind of theologian, because he is a member of one school of ideas and not of another. In the third section we will suggest a further possibility, related to religious studies again, in which people do not only describe religious phenomena, but try to understand them as well. If Phillips really has found his Cool Place and is not a theologian, is he not a scholar of religion in that case? In the last section we return to the question of what place, if any, is left for philosophy of religion.

1. Religious Studies

Philosophy of religion and theology cannot do without religious studies. What I will do in this section is, first, show that philosophical analysis without study of the vocabularies of the various religious traditions is meaningless and, second, describe the difference between what Phillips wants to do and the distanced place of the students of religious studies.

If a philosopher of religion analyzes the meaning of a concept in an attempt of clarification, it would be irresponsible not to take into account the results of biblical, or Buddhist, et cetera, scholarship. How can we clarify the ideas of incarnation, avatar, Last Judgement, humanum, nature, karma, reincarnation and rebirth, soul, atman, jiva, anatman, without learning the meaning of these terms in the context of the various traditions? Could we really clarify the idea of incarnation without the study of the biblical stories about the virgin birth, the relation between God and humankind or the stories of the Fall and sin? Or the idea of an avatar without reading about Vishnu's descents into the earthly world in order to help people live and learn to loosen their ties with an unjust and filthy world? What is the meaning of maya if it is isolated from an Advaita Vedanta philosophy or from a quite different school of theist Hindu thought? Words have no meanings on their own. Religious pictures of God have their meaning within a 'religious world' and are related to practices and experiences – as Phillips has stressed in a paper on 'Presuppositions, Pictures and Practices'.[4] Words have their meaning in a meaningful circulation within human communities. Therefore, the meaning of words cannot be elucidated without reference to the communities from which they stem. Naturally, everybody may take a word from another community, for example, reincarnation or humanity, and propose from his or her own perspective a clear and consistent meaning for that concept, but terms belong to fields of ideas and are part of practices such that their meaning fades away without those surroundings. 'Meaning' is not an platonic idea or something in the air that we might grasp and bring to earth; rather, words have their meanings in contexts and are related to practices. We have to learn those meaning within these horizons and cannot start our clarifications from isolated ideas.[5]

The same argument applies to the history of religious ideas in the various schools of thought. When we start reading histories of Hindu, Buddhist, Humanist, Jewish, or Christian thought, it becomes evident that thinkers in these traditions have wrapped their heads around difficult emotional and intellectual questions that arise within their traditions. For example, Buddhists have asked themselves: What is the relation between meditation and analysis? In response to the question 'If Brahman is one, how can we pray to so many gods?', Advaita thinkers have decided that it is wise to surpass all images of the divine. In this vein some Hindus call themselves atheists. Others have defended the idea that the divine is the ground of being and at the same time the God to whom human beings can pray and carried on century-long discussions concerning how both 'roles' of the divine could be combined and understood. Buddhists have quarrelled since time immemorable over how it is possible for people not to have a soul or enduring entity and be reborn again according to 'their' karma. Christians had lengthy discussions among themselves about how Jesus could be divine (and infinite) and human (and finite) at the same time.

If the ideas of a tradition are not so clear or if some beliefs seem to be incompatible, then time and again their relation will have been discussed in the history of that tradition. Therefore, philosophical analysis of religious concepts without a deeper knowledge of those traditions does not make sense. It is not clear how people can try to clarify ideas from a tradition without studying their background and complex network of meaning that is foundational for it. In this sense, philosophy of religion is dependent upon exegesis and the history of Christian, Humanist, Buddhist ideas. If philosophers of religion neglect the vocabularies of a tradition and begin making their own distinctions, then they easily miss the point of the beliefs of a tradition. Conceptual analysis has to take into consideration the network of ideas, concepts

---

4   Paper read at the Conference of the European Society of the Philosophy of Religion, Cambridge, 6–9 September 2002.

5   See also Patrick Sherry, *Religion, Truth and Language-Games*, London: Macmillan, 1977, who speaks about concepts as part of complex conceptual schemes, p.107, and stresses, with Wittgenstein, the surroundings of concepts, pp.6–7. See on concepts my 'The (Ir)rationalism of the Theistic Concept of God', in *Post-theism. Reframing the Judeo-Christian Tradition, Festschrift Han Adriaanse*, eds. H. Krop *et al.*, Leuven: Peeters, 2000, pp.223–36.

and practices of the traditions it studies. Therefore, it cannot meaningfully loosen the ties to the various areas of religious studies in which people try as well as they can to look and see and to describe things as they are.

Nevertheless, this is not the Cool Place of the philosophical reflection upon religion that Phillips has in mind. In religious studies people describe rituals and translate and explain texts from Tibetan, Arabic, Persian, Hebrew or other languages. The methods in religious studies vary from sociological to literary and historical methods. Scholars try to be as neutral as they can. In religious studies people can describe and explain texts, but what Phillips has in mind is metatheory: understanding what it is to be a religious text or ritual or idea. This contemplative philosophy has to learn from religious studies but its task is to remind people of the real nature of the real religion, which is not so easy to describe objectively and surely not so easy to understand. That goes beyond religious studies. You could explain – or at least pretend to explain! – the broad variety of biblical texts on reconciliation without really knowing what 'reconciliation' is. It is not impossible to write about meditation and the need to become detached without meditating yourself on the question of whether you are yourself attached and estranged. Religious studies can be interesting and scholarly without, in a way, being about the real religion. In this sense the contemplative philosopher that Phillips wants to be is not another member of the community of students of religious studies.

However, this view has a price. If he does not describe facts that everybody can observe and prove, then his 'objectivity' and neutrality is at stake. The next floor in the building of the academic study of religion is the discipline that confesses openly not to be neutral, and allows people to rethink their confessional heritages – be they Humanist, Buddhist, Christian or whatever else – and disagree with people from other traditions. So could it be that Phillips and his comrades are theologians in disguise – or wolves clothed as philosophical sheep?

2. Systematic Theology and Dialogue between Philosophies

Thinking within and about one's tradition

So we have to consider the nature of theology, not as religious studies in departments of theology, but as reflection on the beliefs and practices by people who in one way or another take part in a worldview tradition. This worldview is not confined to religion. As has been said before, the term 'theology' is best understood to cover expressions such as Buddhist thought, Islamic and Jewish theology, Humanist thought, and naturalist schools of philosophy. Whatever the differences between them are, it is the reflection upon the insights of the tradition in which one stands or with which one sympathizes. Such theologies are as diverse as the pluralism between and within traditions. Merging of traditions is a normal phenomenon, as for example the merging of Western European Christianity and Enlightenment thought and in East-Asian countries the merging of Buddhism with Confucianism.

The borderline between 'neutral' and 'confessional' studies is not a sharp one. Because everyone reads and interprets phenomena within the horizon of a culture and is influenced by some school of thought, each person's view of life will in one way or another influence the results of his or her study of religious text, beliefs, and rituals. One's own understanding of reality – cultural and religious – plays a role in the interpretation of texts as well, especially if exegesis reaches deeper levels and explains texts more broadly. On the textual level, a Greek aoristus is an aoristus and a reference to Kyoto a reference to Kyoto. On more complex levels of interpretation, however, the interpreter has to find her own way, because she has to weigh various elements in the texts, and this inevitably leaves more possibilities for her own views and cultural luggage to come into play. What is the symbolic meaning when an old text refers to Benares or Jerusalem? Such differences in the interpretation may even result in discussions on the exact reading of a text, the meaning of specific sentences or conjectures. Thinkers differ widely on biblical or early Buddhist anthropology, the nature of maya, or the nature of nature. This sort of debate implies that in the activity of theology some areas are actually religious studies, such as large parts of the sociology and psychology of religion, exegesis of holy scriptures (Veda, Qur'an) or other classical texts, the history of a tradition and description of the thought of classical thinkers of these traditions. Neutrality is not as easy as that, however, since time and again more 'confessional' and contemporary cultural elements play a role. In Christian dogmatics people may describe and interpret Aquinas, Luther and Barth, in Islamic thought Al-Farabi, Al-Ghazali and Iqbal, but at the very moment that they try to learn from their subject they start thinking for themselves – and who can rethink without posing his own questions and doing his own thinking? It is important to discern these levels in religious studies and 'theology'. In a book on Ramanuja, the author can say that every scholar will see that Ramanuja says X and Y, and in the same study the same author can defend the view that people can learn X from Ramanuja. These practices take place on two different floors in the building of academic studies, although the interpretation that the authors have given of X could be made on the staircase in between.

From now on we will concentrate on systematic theology: dogmatic theology, theological ethics, ecumenical theology, fundamental theology and philosophy of religion, or at least part of what many philosophers of religion do. Theological work in dogmatics and ethics is primarily inner-confessional. People ask themselves: what can we as ... justifiably say about ...? One asks oneself what a Buddhist should say honestly about euthanasia and human identity, the origin of evil, Buddha nature and so on. We can express this by saying that the first public of dogmatic theology are colleagues in one's own tradition. We might refine this in two respects. First, often people argue not as Buddhist, Christian, Humanist, etc., but, for instance, as Zen, Pure Land, Catholic, Lutheran, Advaita, Liberal or Socialist humanist. The public to which people direct themselves varies – that is one of the main points that I want to make in this contribution. Second, even if a Catholic theologian writes with Catholic colleagues in mind, her study can be read by Protestants or Muslim theologians as well. Public communities are no longer separated wholes. Nevertheless, the question a person asks within a community is how as a Zen master and philosopher he can understand and explain Great Death and Great Life, samara *sive* nirvana, or as a Christian that Christ is the image of the invisible God, or as a Muslim that the Qur'an is the revelation of God, and so forth. The questions that we have we can formulate within our more specific tradition (for example, Welsh Congregationalism) or within broader traditions (revival Protestantism/Protestantism/Christianity). Some ideas we will defend as Reformed, some as Protestant, and some very basic ones as Christian – or Muslims or Naturalists – in general. Such is the case in other traditions as well. Christian ecumenical studies is a comparative confessional area in which Christians of various denominations discuss different interpretations of Christian faith. This view implies that time and again we have to look and see which discussions people have and who their partners in those discussions are and on what level of commonality they speak. Now it is clear that Phillips' contemplative philosophy does not want to be a confessional theology in any sense of the word. So let us climb another staircase and reach the floors above confessionalism, where people live who look for broader communities and some even for wider reflective equilibria.

Thinking in dialogue with people of other worldview traditions

Now we reach the departments of fundamental theology and philosophy of religion. Philosophers of religion do various things. The students of philosophical theology often study one tradition and try to clarify the ideas of this tradition; according to our definition of theology, their studies are not philosophical but theological: their public are their fellow members of their traditions – although people within other traditions can buy their books and read them. Because they think from within the community of a certain worldview tradition, they practise theology. Philosophical theology is a branch of systematic or dialogical theology.

Fundamental theology (*Fundamentaltheologie*) has its origin in the justification of specific Christian beliefs. Traditionally, natural theology had as a task to prove the existence of God, and fundamental theology the plausibility of the teaching of the Church, that is to say, of those doctrines that are given in special, biblical revelation. So it is an in-between floor between confessional theologies and general human dialogue, between debates within one family and those between all families. Nowadays fundamental theology comprises both reflection on theology as a field of studies and apologetics, often called theological dialogue with thinkers of other worldviews, in short, dialogical or comparative theology. Because on this floor people from all kinds of worldview traditions have their rooms, this really is another public, including people from a broad variety of backgrounds.

In comparative (or dialogical) theology, people ask themselves what they can believe honestly when they compare beliefs from their own tradition with beliefs from other worldview traditions. They take account of other people and of themselves as well. These thinkers should not be misunderstood as attempting to prove the truth of their beliefs in a neutral way – as if a position above all parties were possible, a view without a horizon that sees from all perspectives at the same time. Therefore, what many scholars feel an urge to do in a pluralistic global culture is to give an account, that is, make deliberations and arguments and indicate why they think that some of the basic beliefs of their tradition are right and, what should not be forgotten, what can be learned from their neighbours. Worldview traditions do not give full accounts, whether naturalist or religious, of reality as a whole. Worldviews point out basic beliefs that help direct human lives. They are fragmentary and do not usually claim to provide insights into all aspects of life or, if they do so claim, have not yet succeeded.[6]

This comparative and dialogical theology is theological in the sense that in accounting for his or her religious position, and in comparing it with that of thinkers in other traditions, the scholar learns from those traditions.[7] Some may argue that Islam is more plausible than Christianity, or that Judaism, Christianity, and Islam are more plausible than Naturalism or Humanism. A Buddhist example of such an approach is the publications of Masao Abe, who explains Zen thought in comparison to Christian theology.[8] Such studies direct themselves to a public from both traditions, while people from other traditions can read them as well.

The question is whether a position such as Phillips' is theological. His position is clearly not on the confessional floor, but as a philosopher he would also not like to have his office on the dialogical level, given that he wants his Cool Place to be outside or above any school of thought and community of worldview ideas – in a sense, on the top level of the building. Therefore, we have to climb another staircase. Yet we have to be conscious of the fact that on this higher level with its broad perspective and all thinkers, irrespective of their beliefs, as a public, we do not have the possibility to judge which moralities and philosophies of life are best. Just as moral philosophy is not a guide for life but an analysis of what morality is and how people are moral, philosophy of religion cannot tell people what to believe but tries to understand what people do if they do believe, what worldviews are (either secular or religious) and how they are related (or do not relate).[9] As Phillips says, quoting Peter Winch: 'philosophy can no more show a man what he should attach importance to than geometry can show a man where he should stand' (PCP p.43).

Nevertheless, it could well be that on further analysis the price is higher than Phillips has realized – geometry is not philosophy, after all, and has its empirical place on the same level as religious studies – but we shall see. Phillips does not want to decide which religion is true, but to point out what really happens in religious language. Without this word 'really', we would have to descend several levels in the elevator and join the sociologists in order to enquire what people actually do in religion. Research in sociology and cultural anthropology can tell us what people do believe, how they practise their religion, and what they say about it. They look into the facts of the philosophies of life, and philosophy cannot do without such actual knowledge of traditions, but neither can it judge

---

6   On traditions as configurations of basic insights, see my *Religions and the Truth*, pp.321–43. An example of such a dialogue between a naturalist philosopher and Christian thinkers on the conclusiveness of a naturalist or theistic position and the limitations of purely rational argumentation: Hendrik Hart, Ronald Kuipers and Kai Nielson, eds., *Walking the Tightrope of Faith*, Amsterdam/Atlanta, GA: Rodopi, 1999.

7   See for example John B. Cobb, Jr., *Beyond Dialogue*, Philadelphia, PA: Fortress Press, 1982; his phrase 'and coming back changed' became well known.

8   See Masao Abe, *Zen and Western Thought*, ed. W.R. LaFleur, Basingstoke: Macmillan, 1985, and the collection with discussions: John Cobb and Christopher Ives, eds., *The Emptying God*, Maryknoll, NY: Orbis, 1990.

9   Compare Phillips, *Philosophy's Cool Place*, in a discussion of Annette Baier and Martha Nussbaum on moral philosophy, pp.124, 132.

which philosophy of life is the true one, because such a judgement would meet with the objection that Moses could not answer: 'Who made you a ruler and judge over us?'[10] There is a remaining question, however, that cannot be solved by sociological and anthropological research: how can we understand the phenomenon of worldviews and their relations? The theory of religion (and worldviews) cannot be dealt with on the floor where the empirical facts are processed. The description is a preparation that lets the believers speak for themselves, as Paul Ricœur says, while the philosopher for the time being accepts their motivations and intentions. The philosopher recollects these experiences and opinions, not in their original naivety, but 'neutralized' in the sense of 'as if'. 'In this respect phenomenology is a symbolic and sympathizing recollection.'[11] We do not only gather a multitude of examples of phenomena and compare similarities and differences, but we want also to *understand* the phenomena of morality and religion at a deeper level. So far, Phillips is in the good company of these continental philosophers.

3. Phenomenology of Religion

The twentieth century has seen the birth, the rise and the fall of a new field of religious studies: the phenomenology of religion. Widengren says in his introduction to the phenomenology of religion that phenomenology tries to give a summarizing description of the wide variety of religious phenomena; as such it is a systematic complement of religious studies.[12] This goal differs from Phillips' goal because Phillips does not want to try to summarize all kinds of religious phenomena: prayers from the Batak, the Samen, the Inuit, twice-born North-Americans, clerics in the Vatican, imams in Afghanistan and sadhus in Benares. He tells Nussbaum not to harmonize different ways to act morally and as a philosopher tries to understand what people do instead of prescribing what they should do. Different perspectives on reality have to be taken as different views of individuals and groups. 'Human life can be like that': people act differently and believe various things (PCP p.146–47). However, it is not as easy as that to reject the idea that Phillips is perhaps a kind of phenomenologist. For what is the point in such a summary, as Widengren seems to suggest? What do we learn from such a survey and comparison of holy buildings, holy persons, holy books? The aim of a serious field of academic study as religious studies and comparative religion(s) cannot just be to provide the student with a survey like a tour through a museum. In one room we find an exposition of holy scriptures and in another the statues of priests, prophets, imams, gurus and popes. 'Look and see': 'Human life can be like that'! That makes a collection, but an academic study aims at more, at insight and understanding. What kind of insight can this study provide? As complicated as his answer has been, Gerardus van der Leeuw was more penetrating. His is one of the monumental works of the phenomenology. He says that

---

10   Exodus 3:14.

11   Paul Ricœur, *The Symbolism of Evil*, trans. by Emerson Buchanan, San Francisco, CA: Harper and Row, 1967, Introduction §3.

12   G. Widengren, *Religionsphänomenologie*, Berlin: de Gruyter 1969, p.1.

phenomenology aims at an understanding of the essence of the phenomena, or, more precisely, that phenomenology aims to penetrate through the abundance of religious forms to the essence of the phenomena as the prayer, the holy person and so on. Thus, he did not write about the concept of prayer in order to show what the kernel of prayer is, but described many forms of prayer and prayer-like phenomena and tried to understand what was going on.[13] We can understand the reasonableness of his procedure: compare descriptions of several religious traditions, select phenomena that seem to fulfil comparable functions; compare those phenomena closely; and then try to determine the real meaning of the phenomenon (in the midst of much superficiality, hypocrisy and misunderstanding). The point at stake is the word 'real'. We could also say: look and see what its real meaning (or essence) is.[14] This is the kind of thing people want to know: not just what happens, but the real meaning of things, for example, 'What are we doing when we pray?',[15] and 'What is the real function of religious figures?' Van der Leeuw was sure that we cannot circumvent the normal questions that we all have after visiting the museums and reading the books of religious studies, and he believed that it was possible to answer these questions, at least partly.[16] If we read all these surveys of religious phenomena, we look for a deeper understanding, and that suggested the terminology of 'phenomena'. Van der Leeuw begins his epilogue of his *Phänomenologie der Religion* with an explanation of the idea of phenomena:

> Phenomenology looks for the phenomenon. The phenomenon is what shows itself ('was sich zeigt'). This says three things: 1) it is something; 2) this something shows itself; 3) it is a phenomenon by showing itself. However, this showing-itself stands in relation to that which shows itself as well as in relation to the person to whom it is shown. Therefore, the phenomenon is not a pure object, neither the object, the true reality which essence just is hidden behind the appearance of the (many) phenomena. That is the teaching of some schools of metaphysics. However, with a phenomenon we do not point to something that is just subjective ... The phenomenon is an object related to the subject and a subject

---

13 Actually I formulate it in a somewhat challenging way by writing 'prayer' with its reference to Phillips' *The Concept of Prayer*. Van der Leeuw has sections on community, marriage, convenant, church, nation and humanity, soul (several), sacrifice, sacrament, service, divination, holy times, festivals, holy places, holy word. Gerardus van der Leeuw, *Phänomenologie der Religion*, Tübingen: Mohr, 1933, 'Epilegomena', pp 634–59 (E pp.671–95). Numbers in the text are from this original edition of the work; page numbers preceded by 'E' are from the English translation by J.E. Turner, *Religion in Essence and Manifestation. A Study on Phenomenology*, trans. by J.E. Turner, London: George Allen and Unwin, 1938.

14 Remember such twentieth-century titles as: *The Essence of Christianity, ... of Judaism*, and typologies such as 'religions of the law', 'religions of salvation'.

15 See Vincent Brümmer, *What Are We Doing When We Pray? A Philosophical Inquiry*, London: SCM, 1984 – but who are 'we'?

16 Just as conservators of museum departments will make sure that their exhibitions are representative and typical and allow for some understanding. The same applies to documentaries.

related to the object. ... The phenomenon is not produced by the subject; ... its whole essence lies in its showing itself, showing itself to 'somebody'.[17]

This is a fascinating exposition. Van der Leeuw is right in that instances of the 'same' kind awaken in us questions as to their nature, and what such phenomena reveal about existence and their meaning in life, and how they relate to other phenomena in life. Or, as the Dutch philosopher Theo de Boer has said, how we can map the various domains of reality, history, nature, individuality, society, culture, morality, religion, art.[18] Van der Leeuw speaks about the various domains of religious life and its 'phenomena'; he looks and sees their superficial and serious forms and tries to understand them. In the articulation of the school of the phenomenological philosophers, he says that from the multitude of comparable phenomena a phenomenon arises which shows itself impressively to the attentive student of religious studies. But Van der Leeuw draws back from saying that the essence is a real thing, or, for instance, that the various prayers of all different 'we's' and religions have the same essence or idea behind the variety of their forms because he does not postulate a something, an idea or form or other kind of being in or behind the varieties of religious experiences and practices of prayers. He wants simply to study everything as it shows itself – could we not say – in its Cool Place? In the end, in his view, the phenomena behind the multitude of what is going on (in my words) hang in the air as a 'between' between scholars and their variegated materials.

It is much easier to criticize this position than to reformulate the truth behind the phenomenological position – its Cool Place. Today everybody can easily mention some of these objections. Who tells us what the essence in the phenomena is? That is subjective. How can empirical research go behind what it sees empirically? Do not bring different things under one heading, but let the 'hubbub of voices', which includes our own voices, be left as it is.[19] Half a century later, scholars of religion wanted to stop looking for essences and learned to be content with describing individual forms of religion and sometimes comparing one with another, without drawing phenomenological (or philosophical) conclusions that could not be substantiated by empirical facts. So the successors of the phenomenologists of religion took their books and moved to the lower floor of religious studies, linked more directly to the basement of the building.

That may be what most of them thought, but the retreat to descriptions implies that the academic question of explanation can be answered only in terms of the social sciences. In such a way only the influences behind the forms of religion can be explained, and not the nature of religion, because every explanation of the nature of religion would inevitably be another description of an essence. Every statement about prayer, honest holiness and authentic religious texts goes beyond

---

17   Van der Leeuw, *Phänomenologie*, pp.634–35, my translation from the German. The English translation uses 'to appear' and 'appearance' for 'sich zeigen' and 'das Sich-zeigen' which is one-sided because 'das Sich zeigen' involves both the phenomenon and the phenomenologist. My use of 'to show' which is stronger than 'to appear' expresses this.

18   Theo de Boer, *Langs de gewesten van het zijn*, Zoetermeer: Meinema, 1996, p.7.

19   See PCP p.85; also pp.74–75 where, against those who always plea for dialogue, Phillips says that in certain situations it is wise not to talk to strangers.

a neutral stance. Van der Leeuw could admit this more easily because he did not want to do religious studies proper. He wants – and I feel that he could have expressed himself in such a way had he known the later philosophical work of a certain Austrian philosopher who lived mainly in England – to look and see, and to leave everything as it is. Phenomenology of religion, Van der Leeuw says, is not philosophy of religion, but it can be a preparation for philosophy. But then, we should ask, what is philosophy of religion? According to Van der Leeuw, philosophy of religion wants to 'move' its findings by means of a dialectical movement of the spirit (*Phänomenologie der Religion*, p.651; E p.687). If we do not accept his dialectical conception of philosophy, given that since the decline of the Frankfurter Schule the mainstream of modern philosophy has dropped the idea that philosophers should not interpret the world but change it, the question arises whether contemplative philosophy is not akin to phenomenology of religion. Phenomenology of religion comes close to what Phillips wants to do: not change the world by its reflections, leave everything as it is and just point out how phenomena really are. Both positions, phenomenology of religion and contemplative philosophy, are very close indeed. Phillips will answer that he does not want to describe a phenomenon in or behind the variegated reality, not the morality but the ways in which people are moral, not the religion but the ways in which people are religious. He allows for what I like to call a real pluralism that does not fail to acknowledge the differences and does not disregard the alternity; that is his principle.[20]

With this thought in mind it is not so easy, however, to locate Phillips. On which floor is he located: religious studies, phenomenology or on a higher level such as philosophy? His Cool Place is difficult to find. He himself says that it is a difficult or even painful position, because the philosopher should not try to interfere with his subject (see PCP p.19). He quotes Rush Rhees who says that the philosopher should try to understand which questions arise in human lives, not in order to answer them and take them away, but 'to understand human thinking and human investigation and human life; to understand how they arise in, and in one sense belong to, our thinking about questions that we ask and answer. This goes with contemplation of the ways in which people think and inquire' (PCP 58–59). Phillips' idea of philosophy is at odds with Van der Leeuw's idea of philosophy of religion and much closer to his phenomenology. In Wittgenstein's view, philosophy is not for anything.[21] Nevertheless, it will be for understanding, and does not this idea of philosophy come very close to the phenomenology of religion? Phillips has a

---

20   '[T]here can be disagreements not simply within moral perspectives but between moral perspectives', PCP, p.162; *passim*. The same is valid for worldview traditions, as I have recently stressed in *A Spectrum of Worldviews. An Introduction to Philosophy of Religion in a Pluralistic World*, trans. by Morris and Alice Greidanus, Amsterdam/New York: Rodopi, 2006. The main argument of the present contribution can be found in shortened form as a conclusion of the treatment of different 'types' of worldviews, pp.290–98.

21   See PCP, p.63. See also Wittgenstein, *Philosophical Investigations*, vol. I, p.126: 'Philosophy simply puts everything before us, and neither explains or deduces anything. Since everything lies open to view there is nothing to explain. For what is hidden, for example, is of no interest to us.'

problem. He has three options: First, he may simply describe the multitude of ways in which people are moral and religious. That is a branch of descriptive religious studies (sociology of ethics and religions, and other disciplines that claim to leave everything as it is). Second, he might say that he wants to understand what people really do when they really pray or engage in other religious practices. However, he is then making judgements concerning good and bad prayer. He does not change anything, not because it is not implied in his view that philosophy should improve understanding and practice, but because people like listening to bishops and television preachers more than to philosophers – if they understood what they were doing when they prayed, they could change and, in a sense, this change would be the philosopher's doing. If that is not what Phillips wants, he joins the phenomenologists of religion. I would prefer to say that phenomenology of religion tried to find a middle way between religious studies and philosophy of religion. Indeed, if you take stances about the 'real' and the 'typical' in religion, then it is better to call it philosophy of religion, and if you do not, then what you are doing is descriptive religious studies. Thus, in answer to the quote of Rush Rhees I would say that the description of what people do believe is religious studies and the effort to understand what really is going on in religions and world views is philosophy. And that is the third option. If we stretch option two, because we take phenomenology of religion as philosophy of religion, the question at stake is: what is the difference between Phillips' contemplative philosophy of religion and religious studies?

4. Philosophy of Religion

Phillips' approach looks like Theo de Boer's description of the task of philosophy quoted earlier: to describe the structures of the various domains of reality, to explore different kinds of experiences, and eventually to judge out false pretensions, if one area of life transgresses its responsibilities and passes the borderline into other domains of reality. This task requires the philosopher to look into the particulars within the various domains. For religion this implies that the philosopher immerses her- or himself in religions (in the plural), otherwise the understanding of 'religion' will be one-sided and built upon prejudices. The implication is that philosophy of religion is not possible other than in a pluralistic context. This conclusion agrees with Phillips' many references to the real pluralism in moral and religious matters. Phillips himself clarifies the task of philosophy in the following way (PCP 35–36):

> When a philosopher tries to be clear about the character of a scientific hypothesis, he is not doing science, himself testing the hypothesis as a scientist would. The philosopher, it might be said, is keeping the scientific hypothesis at arm's length. A philosopher may also try to be clear about the character of the response Christianity calls for. In doing so, he is neither making nor rejecting the response himself. He keeps them at arm's length. Further, to avoid certain confusions, he may want to bring out the differences between responding to a proposed scientific hypothesis, and responding to the challenge of Christianity. Here he is keeping both responses at arm's length, and bringing out the conceptual difference between them. As a philosopher, he may see that the religious challenge is such that it

demands more of him as a person, but whether he responds or not does not have a bearing on the philosophical enterprise.

I think that this view corresponds very much indeed to the views of the phenomenologists of religion and the school of phenomenological philosophy discussed earlier. What Phillips tries to see when he holds his subject at arm's length are not the various ways in which billions of people have their worldviews, but the structure and meaning of 'being religious' or 'having ideas about life', and 'doing scientific research' or 'explaining classical texts' or even the real challenge of Christianity! That indeed is theology or philosophy and not religious studies, and it requires knowledge of actual religious phenomena and of theological discussions. Phillips rightly stresses the plurality and rejects an easy essentialism, but also wants to get insight in religion, morality, science and so forth. There is a tension between his accent on descriptions of various cases and his wish to understand domains of life, including the real challenges of Zen, Advaita, Naturalism. Such an understanding requires insight into the variety of religious experiences and prayers, and goes far beyond mere description.

My main reservation concerning this view of philosophy is Phillips' claim that philosophy is neutral. I do not believe that at all. Therefore, I will rephrase it differently. Inevitably, the work of Western philosophers is 'Western'; of secularized Christians, secularized-Christian; of twice-born Christians, and so forth. We cannot escape our culture and the worldview traditions that have formed our thinking so far. The philosophical enterprise will be coloured by somebody's stance on religion. That is not necessarily a question of belonging to a tradition, because sometimes a 'stranger' sees better, but often it is, and in all cases it is a question of interest, sympathy and affinity with life as it seen by other traditions rather than just membership or belonging. The difference between a religious or, in general, a position from the perspective of a worldview, and such a philosophical position is that in the last case we are convinced to speak as human beings and not 'just' as Buddhists, naturalists, and so on. The difference is what we think our public should agree with. As said before, we can speak within a tradition, but there are 'truths' with which we think that everyone will agree, or would agree with if only they had the right knowledge and expertise. As a (certain kind of) Christian I may think that everybody could see and believe that the world is not without its own meaning and end, and therefore is creation but I know that not everybody shares this belief, and I can see reasons why they do not. So on the level of theology and inter-religious dialogue, I can hold my views as plausible and accept plurality. However, in some matters I do not accept this plurality, for example, equality between human beings, worldwide solidarity and justice, and the idea that religious traditions have much in common but deep differences as well. I do not think that the cognitive side of religious truth can be considered apart from its spiritual, experiential and moral side, but some of these insights we find generally true – and we would not like to accept that their truth requires a kind of conversion. The line between what we defend in dialogue and these truths is thin; nobody is neutral or has a confessional and a neutral part in himself. For example, a person holds ideas about the world as a cosmos, creation or maya at arm's length, tries to understand them, compares them and is aware that he or she shares one of these views. That implies a truth claim, that is, the claim that insight is on the level of interreligious dialogue. Some other ideas that we defend we do not argue for as 'believers' in one or another tradition because we thinks that they are true for all believers of all worldviews – and we do so knowing that the sociologists will tell us that such an agreement is not an established fact at all. Therefore, statements about 'religion as such' and about certain aspects of human life and reality are ideas that we think should be accepted as true by all people, irrespective of cultures and worldviews.

Therefore, the differences between religious studies, dogmatic theology, comparative and dialogical theology, and philosophy of religion can be explained with reference to the communities within which and to whom we direct ourselves. Philosophers not only want to clarify domains of life and their mutual relationships, the nature of worldviews, but also to defend some insights that they think that nobody could deny. This practice requires the distance from traditions that Phillips characterizes as a 'Cool Place'. I think what Phillips is doing when he 'philosophizes' is showing religion as it really is and defending his views independent of his confessional position, and trying to let the phenomenon 'impress itself' upon those who care.[22]

---

22   The point is not that such philosophical positions are neutral, but that we claim that we have those ideas not because of our further convictions but because of our being human. This claim implies for philosophy (and not only philosophy of religion) that scholars should have much more knowledge of other worldview traditions than only some Western traditions. The line between inter-worldview dialogue and philosophy is very thin because a Zen philosopher will argue that the insight that the world ultimately is *shunyata* is generally true, and a Muslim that everyone can see that world has been created on purpose, and the Naturalist that everything is conditioned within the whole web of natural causality. Nevertheless, the claims differ: I may ask a naturalist for what good reason he grants human beings special value (critical dialogue), and I may defend that human beings have a special status (a general statement and, although some worldviews do not share that idea, therefore not neutral).

Chapter XII

Philosophy's Radical Pluralism in the House of Intellect – A Reply to Henk Vroom

D.Z. Phillips

1. Any Room at the Inn?

I began my replies in this volume by trying to answer a philosopher's doubts about my contemplative conception of philosophy. Stephen Mulhall argued that anything it is said to achieve, can be achieved equally well by the underlabourer conception of the discipline, in which philosophy is the technique of clearing up conceptual confusions on sites of other people. Moreover, Mulhall argues, when we consider the human significance of philosophy, the kind of clarity it beings to our lives, it is difficult not to see it in relation to other intellectual movement of equal significance. Once we do this, it ceases to be feasible to regard philosophy as an autonomous enquiry.

Now, as I come to my last reply to the critiques in this volume, I find myself faced, once again, with questions about my conception of philosophy, only, this time, from a multi-faceted perspective of the study of religion. In reply to both, I want to insist on the autonomy of philosophy, and on the distinctiveness of its central problems – problems about the relation of language to reality, what it means to say anything, and the sense in which we are 'in the world'. It would be reasonable for Vroom and readers to expect me, therefore, to begin with an elucidation of 'Philosophy's Cool Place'. There is little point in saying that I have done so elsewhere,[1] because it is this effort which has led Vroom to the questions he puts to me. Nevertheless, I do have a problem at this point in the volume, namely, that I do not want to repeat what I have said already in reply to the other critiques. I have made a further attempt, in this volume, to provide further elucidations of my contemplative conception of philosophy. To avoid repetition, I must crave Vroom's and the readers' indulgence, in asking them to take these elucidations as a background to my discussion of Vroom's questions. The most helpful course of action, from my point of view, would be to ask readers to re-read the relevant sections of my replies which go to make up the background. I am referring to Ch. II, section 3: 'Beyond Language-Games'; Ch. IV, section 1: 'Pictures and Logic'; Ch. VI, section 1: 'The Autonomy of Philosophy'; Ch. VIII, section 1: 'Why Demea Departed'; and Ch. X, section 1: 'Culture and No

---

1   See my *Philosophy's Cool Place*.

Through Roads', and section 2: 'Describing Philosophies and Philosophizing'. This makes it obvious that Vroom's questions, in one form or another, have been with us all along. He, like others, wants to know what place there is, if any, for contemplative philosophy in the House of Intellect.

At first, Vroom gives the impression that he and I are part of a family who have taken up residence in that House. He agrees with me that there is a need to bring words back to their natural homes, including religious homes, from the construals that philosophers have put on them.[2] He says: 'Thus any questions that I may have concerning Phillips' ideas are to be interpreted as discussions within one family in the circle of philosophers of religion' (p.182). Perhaps the fact that Vroom and I are nearer to each other than we are to many philosophers of religion we could mention, has led to this over-familiarity on his part, since major differences would have to be overlooked to place us in the same family. For example, by the end of his paper we find him saying, 'My main reservation concerning this view of philosophy is Phillips' claim that philosophy is neutral. I do not believe that at all' (p.195). Take neutrality away, however, and one takes away the contemplative character of philosophy at the same time. It seems to me that Vroom makes the recognition of my neutrality unnecessarily difficult for himself, partly because of his extremely wide ranging use of the word 'philosophy'. He says (p.183):

> In a global and pluralistic culture the old Western distinction between philosophy and theology must be rethought; there are many theologies and many philosophies ... So we will take Buddhist thought, Hindu thought, Confucian though, Christian thought, naturalist thought, socialist thought, 'liberal' thought, atheist thought and so on, as different schools of 'theological ideas' ... but they all think, in their own way, within and from the perspective of a worldview tradition, whether secular or not. They are a 'member' of one or perhaps two of those 'communities of ideas'.

Vroom admits that this broadest of definitions of 'theology' is somewhat 'unusual and perhaps baffling for some secular thinkers' (p.183). I have to admit that it is baffling for me too. What we need is more attention to particulars, in this context, rather than the proliferation of even more general 'generalities'. Fortunately, Vroom's discussion does not proceed in terms of them. They serve the limited purpose, however, of being contrasted with Wittgenstein's conception of a philosopher whom, he insists, is *not* a member of any community of ideas. In that case, where is he? 'What is the task of philosophy of religion in a pluralistic age?' (p.183). Given Vroom's view that the task is not a neutral one, what are his conclusions regarding it? At the end of his paper, he suggests that although a philosopher cannot escape from his 'culture and the worldview traditions that have formed [his] thinking thus far' (p.195), the audience he addresses is wider than the community of ideas to which he, inevitably, belongs. The philosopher may 'want to clarify domains of life and their mutual relationships, the nature of worldviews', but he also wants 'to defend some insights that [he thinks] nobody could deny' (p.196). To do this, Vroom tells us, 'requires the distance from traditions characterized by Phillips as a Cool Place'

---

2   In this respect, the titles of two of my recent books speak for themselves: *Recovering Religious Concepts* and *Religion and Friendly Fire*.

(p.196). But to do *what*? Vroom's answer is not at all clear to me. The ambiguity is not resolved for me by Vroom's final conclusion (p.196):

> I think that what Phillips is doing when he 'philosophizes' is showing religion as it really is and defending his views independent of his confessional position, and trying to let the phenomenon 'impress itself' upon those who care.

On this view, what room exists for the contemplative philosopher in the House of Intellect? A number of answers seem possible, but none without difficulty, given Vroom's arguments.

First, is Vroom saying that, regardless of my or anyone else's confessional position, I can show, what religion really is, by displaying insights no one would deny? The difficulty in ascribing this view to Vroom, is that he denies that I am looking for the essence of religion, or that I have some neutral method of arriving at that essence.

Second, is Vroom saying that what I am doing is to make my confessional position clear to others, and endeavouring to make their confessional positions clear to myself, so that I can say, 'This is what religion is really like down my way', and 'I see what religion is really like down your way'? On this view, anyone should be able to appreciate anyone else's confessional position. But, if so, what does Vroom mean by saying that this is regardless of my confessional position? Wouldn't the elucidations, again, be a form of neutrality?

Third, is Vroom saying that regardless of the fact that I am inevitably confined to my own confessional position, this is all I can make clear for anyone; to whoever happens to care? I can only show what religion really is down my way, and that is all anyone else can do too. That is why, presumably, Vroom says that I 'philosophize' rather than philosophize.

Fourth, is Vroom saying that despite the plurality of confessional religions, there are some insights, concerning equality and justice, for example, that no one can deny, which are independent of all varieties of faith?

At various times, we shall see, Vroom gives us reason to accept *any* of these readings. Does the fact of so many possible readings indicate that Vroom himself is unclear about what he wants to say, or that I am missing what he wants to say? In an attempt to get clearer on these questions, let us look at Vroom's comparisons between contemplative philosopher and other residents in the House of Intellect. Of one thing I am sure, namely, that at no time is Vroom aware of how radical is the pluralism which has to be recognized if one allows full occupancy to contemplative philosophy in the House of Intellect.

2. Contemplative Philosophy and the Inn's Residents

The first group of residents with whom Vroom wants to confront the contemplative philosopher of religion, are the practitioners of religious studies. He tells us that they are to be found on the first floor (better called 'the ground floor' for these purposes). Why is that? Vroom's answer is simple: philosophy and theology cannot do without religious studies. But is this true? After all, to say that philosophy and theology predate religious studies in an understatement, to put it mildly. So how did they get along without it? Furthermore, as Vroom says, 'methods in religious studies vary from sociological to literary and historical' (p.186). But, surely, he knows as well as I do how those methodologies can themselves be guilty of conceptual confusions, and exhibit, at times little understanding of the religious practices they purport to be studying.[3] Neither the philosopher, nor the theologian, would be wise simply to accept what they are told, simply because it occurs under the name of religious studies. Furthermore, there is a tendency in religious studies to omit an essential feature of religions, of which theology and contemplative philosophy must take account. As Vroom says, in religious studies, 'Scholars try to be as neutral as they can' (p.186). They pride themselves on their neutrality, since it is taken to be what distinguishes them from theologians. But, often, what is neglected, is the challenge and claim religions make on human lives. Without these challenges and claims, the religions would not be what they are. Theology is internal to the religion which makes the claim. It could be called its guardian. Contemplative philosophy, in giving an account of different religions, must do so in a way that includes their challenges. That is why its task is so difficult. I am not denying, of course, that an account of a religion in religious studies may be such that it also gives a lively portrayal of its challenge. Neither, in criticizing confused methodologies in religious studies, am I denying the possibility of insightful ones, or the possibility that religious studies may give us insights into religious practices by raising questions which are not asked in the practices themselves. All I am questioning is Vroom's bold claim about the dependence of philosophy and theology on religious studies.

Vroom's claim, I believe, is a confused version of a quite different one, namely, that theology and philosophy are dependent *on religion*. The same is tautologically true of religious studies. In fact, it is odd to say that theology is *dependent* on religion, since it is internally related to it. What about philosophy of religion? Clearly, if one is puzzled about the grammar of religious concepts, one must pay attention to the practices in which they have their natural home. Surely *that* is the point on which Vroom wants to insist when he says, 'If philosophers of religion neglect the vocabularies of a tradition and begin making their own distinctions, they can easily miss the point in a tradition's beliefs' (p.185). But the tradition being referred to here is the traditions of a religion, not the traditions of religious studies. Similarly, when Vroom speaks about the various discussions which take place within the traditions of different religions, he is obviously correct in saying that to understand those discussions, philosophers must pay attention to the concepts of the religions in question. Again, philosophers should not speak of religion in general terms, ignoring the variety covered by that term. Wittgenstein admired William James for noting the varieties of religious experience within the same religion, not to mention the religions of the world.

Vroom does want to maintain, however, that there is a difference between contemplative philosophy and religious studies. He says that while, in religious studies, 'people can describe and explain texts … what Phillips has in mind is meta-theory: understanding what it is to be a religious text or ritual or idea' (p.186). But

---

3   For numerous examples see my *Religion and the Hermeneutics of Contemplation.*

contemplative philosophy is not a matter of theory at all, let alone meta-theory. Wittgenstein says that it must be content with *description*, but this term has a special meaning in his thought. That meaning is obscured when Vroom says that the task of contemplative philosophy 'is to remind people of the real nature of the *real* religion (p.186). That makes it look as though, having looked at religions, philosophy, in a meta-theoretical way, tells you which, if any, is the real thing. That reverses the philosophical emphasis, which is that it is by waiting on religious practices that philosophy reminds you of the reality (that is, the intelligibility), that is there to be described. But 'description' here does not mean what it does in religious studies. It is not a matter of giving an historical account, or a sociological survey, of religious practices. 'Description' means showing the logical space occupied by concepts in religion. It is a matter of 'description', rather than explanation, because philosophy does not add anything to religious practices. Reminders concerning their logic become necessary because of a tendency to be confused about them. Moreover, the confusions that may occur are connected with the central questions of philosophy. In what sense does religion *say* anything? How does it tell us anything about the world? In what sense can it be called true or false? What considerations enter into answering these questions one way rather than another? Vroom says of my attempts to answer such questions (p.183):

> Phillips wants to look and see, and describe religion as it really is. Therefore, we cannot escape the question of the authority on which he speaks. Has he had a private revelation about true religion and the real nature of the divine? Or is he perhaps the sort of theologian who takes a stand and confesses: 'Here I stand and I cannot do otherwise'? Do philosophers not defend their own views as 'the true religion', and 'the true agnosticism', 'true mysticism' or whatever and remain just as unaccountable as people who defend their views on the basis of religious experience or revelation? … Whose experiences does he describe – whose real prayer, real sacrifice, trembling before the real God?

In the light of what I have said, my answers to these questions should be obvious. *I do not speak with authority*. The authority is *in the religion* we are reflecting on, not in any private revelation or confessional stand of my own. What we have to wait on is the actual application religious language has. How is that application to be made conceptually explicit? The answer is, through discussion and examples. It is also through discussion that confusions are revealed; a discussion which shows that in the confused accounts of religion, the words offered have no application, even thought those who propound them think that they do. As for philosophers defending their positions self-assertively, this is simply avoidance of the discussion which is the lifeblood of philosophy. The difficulty, however, comes from the fact that getting philosophers to engage in a certain kind of discussion, is itself a philosophical achievement. I have referred to the frustration of some philosophers when they come into contact with it.[4] As Wittgenstein says, he is not trying to get people to believe what they do not believe, but to *do* what they will not do.

At this point, Vroom takes us to the next floor of the House of Intellect where the confessional theologians dwell. He does not linger long there, because he recognizes

---

4   See my *Religion and Friendly Fire*, Ch. 1.

that such theologians, as their name implies, are internally related to their various confessional traditions. Vroom says, 'Now it is clear that Phillips' contemplative philosophy does not want to be a confessional theology in any sense of the word' (p.188).

Proceeding to the next floor, Vroom introduces us to dialogical theologians who reflect on the context of world religions. These reflections are not independent of the religions concerned, but are, rather, *varied* responses to the question of what they can learn from each other, responses to what they take as basic and what not: what is right or wrong. The results of such reflections, Vroom tells us (p.188),

> do not give full accounts of ... reality as a whole ... They are fragmentary and do not usually claim to provide insights into all aspects of life or, if they do so claim, have not yet succeeded.

Vroom does not tell us what might be meant by 'reality as a whole', but in any case, Vroom realizes that a contemplative philosophy cannot be identified with any substantive point of view arrived at by dialogical theologians. This is because, on its view (p.189):

> Just as moral philosophy is not a guide for life but an analysis of what morality is and how people are moral, so philosophy of religion cannot tell people what to believe but tries to understand what people do if they do believe, what worldviews are (either secular or religious) and how they are related (or do not relate).

It is obviously time to move on again, this time to a floor on which there was considerable coming and going in the twentieth century, but where Vroom thinks the closest similarities to my work can be found. I refer to the phenomenology of religion. Unfortunately, I am at a considerable disadvantage here, since I am not acquainted with the works to which Vroom refers. I want to make it clear, therefore, that my general comments are based entirely on what I find in Vroom's paper.

There seems to be some ambiguity in the aims of the phenomenology of religion. On one view, it reflects on the variety of religious practices, be it prayer, ritual, or whatever, in order to arrive at the essence of prayer, ritual, or whatever is being reflected on. This would be similar to Wittgenstein's view in his 'Lecture on Ethics', or *The Blue Book*, where examples are meant to give you what is the typical form of what is being discussed. An alternative view of the phenomenology of religion, draws back from identifying real prayer, or real ritual with the essence of those activities, and, instead, lets the different examples be themselves. This is near to my aim, Vroom argues, of showing these examples 'in a Cool Place', without meddling with them. This would be similar to the advance made by Wittgenstein in *The Brown Book* where, although he speaks of different ways of doing things, they are no longer thought of as different ways of doing the same thing.

Having said this, however, Vroom comes full circle, and wonders, once the search for an essence is abandoned, how the survey of particular examples is any different from the surveys of religious studies, something I addressed at the outset of this section of my reply in emphasizing the special meaning of 'description' in contemplative philosophy (see p.201).

To the end, Vroom thinks that there is 'a tension between [my] account of descriptions of various cases and [my] wish to understand domains of life' (p.195). On the other hand, he thinks I allow for what he wants to call a *real pluralism*. I wonder, however, to what extent Vroom recognizes that the pluralism recognized by a contemplative philosophy is more radical than anything he envisages. For Vroom, pluralism seems to be itself an attitude to other possibilities which one may or may not have. For example, despite his relation to his own basic religious beliefs, Vroom says of believers in other religions, 'I can hold my views as plausible and accept plurality' (p.195). With respect to 'questions of equality between human beings, worldwide solidarity and justice', on the other hand, he says, 'I do not accept that plurality' (p.195). Clearly, here, 'pluralism' is itself a moral or religious attitude, exercised in some cases, but withheld in others. In this matter, Vroom is speaking for himself, expressing his own moral/religious position.

He recognizes, however, that philosophy, in some sense, is concerned with insights that ought to be available to all who pay a certain kind of attention to the world. His ambiguous conclusion about my philosophy of religion, however, seems to show that he is unclear about what the sense is. My claim is that we see it in Wittgenstein's conception of philosophy. I have been trying to show this, in different ways, in my replies to the critiques in this volume. It is an attempt to show how contemplative attention to the world can and should lead to the conclusion, 'Human life can be like that'. Vroom asks, 'What is the task of philosophy of religion in a pluralistic age?' The short, but unsatisfactory reply is, 'The same as that of philosophy'. A more satisfactory answer, to which I shall try to attend, is to show how radical pluralism is the fruit of contemplative philosophy.

3. Philosophy and Radical Pluralism

An early form of pluralism may tempt us to be content with saying that reality is made up of a number of activities, each with its own distinction between the real and the unreal. We are then likely to look for the rules, in each case, which determine how the distinction is to be drawn. But, then, we want to ask from whence such rules get *their* authority.

It is important to appeal to rules when the meanings of words are in dispute. We may teach a child the rule for the use of a certain word, and we shall want to know whether the child has mastered it. But talk of rules does not fit so well when we think of what we say to each other in conversation. Does the conversation proceed according to rules, and do we speak of mastering it? It seems that it is not the rules which give meaning to our lives, but our lives which give meaning to the rules.

But what account are we to give of these lives? Since rules vary, we may think it natural to speak of them as a collection of practices which have their own criteria of intelligibility. But this suggestion creates problems of its own. If each practice has an autonomous intelligibility, what account are we going to give of the intelligibility of language, since all the practices occur in the same language? One cannot say that each practice constitutes a different language.[5]

We have seen the futility of looking for a common form to cover all discourse. Wasn't I tempted to say, 'to cover all forms of discourse'? But, then, our question becomes: what makes all the forms of discourse, discourse? It is tempting to reply that this is shown in the features of the practices. True, no one feature can be found in them all, but different features resemble each other, some features being present in some comparisons, while others are introduced in other comparisons, with some of the previous features dropping out. This is a structural explanation of language. An explanation in terms of features, which make language language. We seem to be back at the suggestion that our lives depend, for their intelligibility, on features of discourse which make it possible. Language is governed, not by one form, but by many.

What structural explanations ignore is the dialogical character of language. This does not mean that we are always in a dialogue; but that without dialogue, how we take what is said to us, the weight we give to our expressions in innumerable ways and the bearing these things have on each other, it is difficult to see what could be meant by the intelligibility of discourse. It is not that forms of language, recognizable as such, can be seen to have features in common, but that without their bearing on each other in the lives of people who speak the language, they would not be recognizable as language in the first place. It has been said that to imagine a language is to imagine a form of life. This does not mean that a sociological discernable form of life determines the possibility of language. Rather, it means that what we say to each other, the bearings of things on each other, the ways in which things are taken, our songs and dances, our literature, our humour, our varied social movements, religion and anti-religion, and so on, *show* the form of life we have. It cannot be summed up in a single sociological account, though a good novelist or dramatist may portray segments of it, as will a good historian.

Philosophical contemplation engages with this big question about the possibility of discourse. As we have seen, however, consideration of this question will lead to a recognition of differences, the hubbub of voices, in which some may be close to each other, while others may be separated by great distances. Philosophical contemplation of this sense of radical pluralism is essential if discussions of the nature of reality are to be rescued from confusion. In this radical pluralism, we find the different relations between religions we have mentioned. Philosophical contemplation of them, which gives attention to this radical pluralism, is very different from theological pluralism.

Theological pluralism is a specific attitude to world religions. It advocates respect for them, for example. They are called different paths to the same God. To earn this respect, and to be called 'a path to God', theological pluralism insists on a spiritual affinity between the religions it praises. Theological pluralism has no

---

5   Here we are returning to issues raised in my first response to Mulhall in discussing the inadequacy of the analogy between language and games. See Ch. II, section 3.

interest in doing conceptual justice to religions, no matter what their character. It is essentially theologically selective.[6] Radical pluralism is not.

We would look in vain, in theological pluralism, for any discussions of religions in which human sacrifice is central. Such rituals are likely to be dismissed as primitive, superstitious practices; as understandable, but mistaken attempts to appease supernatural powers, in an effort to ward off the terrible in human life. Radical pluralism does not deny the possibility of rituals which fit this description. What it resists is the general thesis that this is all human sacrifice *can* amount to. The thesis misses the possibility that what gives rise to such terrible rituals is precisely that – awe at the terrible. The rituals are an expression of that sense. Our predominantly utilitarian culture can only see in such rituals attempts to ward off the terrible. It finds difficulty in seeing how the terrible in human life can be seen as a sacrament. Philosophical contemplation does conceptual justice to such rituals by recognizing them as part of the radical pluralism of human life. It involves seeing how human life can be like that.

In recognizing radical pluralism, philosophical contemplation endeavours to let the world be itself in all its variety. It allows the hubbub of voices and their diverse relations to each other to be themselves. For this very reason, it is extremely easy to misunderstand the recognition of radical pluralism in a number of ways.

First, the recognition of radical pluralism can be confused with an advocacy of quietism, as though it were saying, 'Live and let live'. True, philosophical contemplation, though it will address what it takes to be philosophical confusion, is not a method for settling disputes between people. But this is because it wants those disputes, and the ways of settling them, along with failures to settle them, to be themselves. To rescue them from the shadow-play they may become at the hands of philosophy, radical pluralism, so far from ignoring criticism, allows it to be itself, and restores it to its proper place. It recognizes the character of inter-religious criticisms. It is by appreciating them that the philosopher comes to recognize that the variety of values cannot be cashed into a common coinage to be assessed by philosophy for their value. The clash is between real values. One cannot get 'behind' them, as it were, to find a standard to determine which values are of value. Any standard selected will be a further value which can be contested by adherents to others. Contemplative philosophy reaches these conclusions, not by ignoring criticism, but by recognizing its character.

Does this mean that, in this radical pluralism, there is simply a clash of conflicting values, but no place for change and development in people's lives? Not at all. In the first place, although it has to be recognized that what is regarded as a higher or lower form of religion is a personal matter, people change their minds in a number of ways. For example, people may change when an aspect of a religion they had not noticed before is brought to their attention. It may destroy or erode an allegiance, or it may create or begin a new one. The religion one adheres to may have consequences one had not recognized. Events in people's lives may bring them to, or take them away, from a certain kind of religious allegiance. This scene of religious 'coming' and 'going' is allowed to be itself when radical pluralism is recognized. That 'coming'

---

6   See the discussion in Ch. X.

and 'going' will be falsified, however, if the various visions of the good and truth are not included in the elucidation of religions, since without those visions, the demands they make on human life, the religions would not be what they are.

Second, the recognition of radical pluralism may be confused, not with quietism, but with a relativism which argues that since philosophy cannot be an adjudicating measure between religions, it must hold that all religions are equally valid. Such a view is self-contradictory, since having argued that philosophy does not posses the measure by which religions are to be assessed, it proceeds to measure them by saying that they are all equal. To conclude that things are equal is obviously one possible outcome of measurement. Having denied measurement, relativism of this kind proceeds to employ it. Furthermore, from whose mouth is the judgement of equality supposed to come? Even allowing for such a judgement, it would simply be another view of religions, not an external measure of them.

Third, the recognition of radical pluralism may lead one to suppose that, since the equality of religions cannot be established, the notion of 'truth' in these contexts must be jettisoned. A new external account can be sought, one which neither philosophy nor theology can provide. This can be recognized, it is argued, if one realizes how, even in allowing for the hubbub of voices in radical pluralism, an intellectualized picture of that hubbub is being imposed on it. Even if we say that some voices are at a distance from each other, the picture presented is still too easy: a picture of human beings in conversation, even if some are not talking to each other. What this leaves out is the presence of power and coercion in human life. The vital question is: who owns the conversations? Are there not conversations which pass others by marking them as those who are not allowed to speak, as those who are denied a voice? Language, on this view, is simply a clash of readings of human life, in which power and possession are the central issues. Since philosophy and theology, wittingly or unwittingly, have been manifestations of power, they cannot provide the external account of the radical pluralism we need to understand. This external account is to be provided by the social sciences, whose categories are suited for our purposes. They allow us to go below the surfaces to the hidden dynamics of society. We are taught the importance of suspicion. Things are not what they seem. To recognize coercion, oppression and exploitation, is, at the same time, to recognize the justifying strategies of our surface language which hide these realities from us.

The recognition of radical pluralism ignores the coercive elements referred to at its peril. On the other hand, it will resist replacing one general account of that plurality by another. If philosophy needs to be toppled from a throne it thought it occupied, it is not in order to make room for the social sciences to sit on it. Contemplative philosophy gives us reason to be suspicious of metaphysical suspicion. For philosophy, nothing is hidden. It restores a conceptual trust in surfaces, in the sense that it brings into view all the possibilities of coercion and oppression which, rightly, cannot be excluded from the picture. These possibilities, however, with their references to unconscious motivation, power struggles, oppressive and possessive forms of discourse, the need for liberation, etc., etc., all refer to the phenomena of distortion and evasion. These notions, however, are themselves parasitic on some conception of something being distorted or evaded. Without that contrast, one could give no account of what is happening. To eliminate all reference to truths people adhere to, would, at the same time, eliminate the possibility of accusations of distortion, power-seeking and exclusions of voices from a discourse. The dialectical relation between these terms is all-important. The social sciences, in their various forms, have pointed out connections and implications in social movements which the participants in them may not have recognized. But these become additional features of the radical pluralism philosophy contemplates, along with the plurality of reactions to these hitherto-unrecognized implications and consequences when they are made explicit. The social sciences must do justice to those features of human life they are interested in, since the point of their endeavours, surely, should be to lead to a better understanding of that life. Their procedures are answerable to it. Thus, what they can teach us must be there to be seen. What they do not offer is a language whose terms reveal the hidden dynamics of human life, such that this language can be seen as giving the real account of *all* that happens. The recognition of radical pluralism resists the tyranny of methodology. For example, to point out how religion can be an instrument of oppression or liberation is one thing. To suggest that religious concepts can be reduced to the terms of a power struggle is another. The distinctive contribution of religious concepts in teachings and practices must also be recognized. The recognition of radical pluralism preserves the dialectical relations between these different factors, including the recognition that, in those relations, the reactions of people are hugely different. The social sciences, like philosophy, cannot provide a language which offers *the* mode of understanding for human affairs. Rather, they should wait on the language which is there to be contemplated in the stream of human life.

Fourth, it may be said that the contemplative philosophy being envisaged is unreal because no person can live it. Perhaps this is what Vroom wants to emphasize in saying that one cannot escape one's particular tradition, etc. Thus, the radical pluralism I keep referring to is beyond our reach for a very obvious reason: the person who claims to be a contemplative philosopher is a human being who has a life to live. In that life, he or she will be called on to show where they stand on various issues. Inevitably, they will embrace certain values and reject others, be drawn to certain movements and interests, and away from others. In short, life is not an exercise in contemplation. To invite someone to indulge in it is, at best, an invitation to a schizophrenic existence. How is this challenging criticism to be met, if at all?

Contemplative attention to radical plurality is not a retreat from life, a lack of interest in the fray, but a certain kind of interest in human life, born of wonder at it. The misuse of 'disinterested' as 'uninterested', in American parlance, is unfortunate. To be disinterested is not to have no interest in things, but to be gripped by an interest of a certain kind; an interest in doing conceptual justice to the world in all its variety. Comparisons have been made between the philosopher's interest and that of a dramatist staging a play involving characters in conflict with each other, a conflict which may end in tragic irreconcilability. The dramatist is not interested in resolving that conflict (the familiar weakness of didactic literature), but in showing it to us, so that we may understand it. The dramatist's interest is in giving a faithful account of that segment of human life. Similarly, though inspired by the different questions of their subject, contemplative philosophers are engaged in the enormously difficult task of being conceptually faithful to the world. One's own values, which may be held very strongly, may well get in the way of seeing points of view which are other than one's own. One's own values may get in the way of the moral demands of philosophical enquiry.

Doesn't this mean that philosophical values, after all, are being said to transcend other values, and held to be superior to them? No, it does not. We are referring to the moral demands of philosophical enquiry itself, in the kind of attention one is asked to pay to the world. It asks that conceptual justice be done to it. For example, it asks that recognition be given to values other than one's own; to recognize that they are not distortions of one's own, or expressions of a flight from one's own. It asks one to recognize that people's values really are their values. Such a recognition is not peculiar to philosophy. Without it, no great literature or history would be possible. In philosophy, as I have tried to show, the call for contemplative attention to the world is internally related to the sense in which the subject is concerned with the nature of reality.

Fifth, it may be said that there is a conceptual impediment to the task of contemplative philosophy, in that it cannot do justice to certain forms of moral or religious single-mindedness. This single-mindedness, it is argued, cannot be included in the radical plurality said to be contemplated, without distorting what such single-mindedness amounts to. How is this said to come about?

The contemplative philosopher, it is argued, characterizes the single-minded person as simply seeing one aspect of a situation. By contrast, the contemplative philosopher, in contemplating radical pluralism, sees aspects of the situation which the single-minded person does not see. Inevitably, the impression is given that the single-minded person's limited understanding is enhanced by the fuller understanding of the philosopher. The single-minded person sees a part, while the philosopher sees the whole.

The trouble is, so the argument continues, that this whole picture begs the question by mischaracterizing the single-mindedness in question. The philosophical description of that single-mindedness need not be accepted by the person who exhibits it. He or she will deny that they are simply seeing one aspect of a situation. They are simply seeing things as they are. A recognition of radical pluralism, by its very nature, it is said, cannot do conceptual justice to this single-mindedness.

I believe that this argument is confused. Part of the difficulty comes from characterizing the single-mindedness as 'seeing an aspect' of things, with the inevitable suggestion that the person is blind to other aspects of the situation. In this way, single-mindedness is said to suffer from 'aspect blindness', and the single-minded person would be right to protest. Matters are different if one were to substitute 'meanings' for 'aspects'. It remains true that single-minded people may be blind to certain religious meanings other than those they embrace. But this can no longer be characterized as being blind to possibilities *for them*; or being blind to the totality of a situation which is theirs. This is shown by the fact that if the other meanings were recognized, this need not lead the single-minded person to say, 'Now I recognize aspects of my situation I failed to recognize previously.' He or she may say, 'I utterly reject the meaning of faith you are offering me.' The only change would be that he or she now understands what they reject, whereas, previously, they were blind to it.

The single-minded person may not simply stick to the view of things embraced, but also claim that there are no other meanings. This is to advance a philosophical thesis, which can be shown to be confused. What is being run together is the question of the existence of possibilities of meaning, and the question of whether those meanings are possible *for me*. The recognition of possibilities of religious meanings is quite consistent with saying that they are not possible for me. Elucidation of such possibilities is wider than personal appropriation. Further, the recognition, called for in contemplative philosophy, is not an indulgence in abstract possibilities, but a recognition that, for some people, human life is like that.

Where does that leave the situation? First, it is simply a fact of the matter that some people are simply narrowly blind to possibilities of meaning which others embrace. For obvious reasons, such people will not be able to give radical pluralism the kind of attention demanded by philosophical contemplation. That contemplation, however, will be able to do justice to the conceptual character of that single-mindedness which is blind to other possibilities of meaning. Second, the single-minded one may make the confused philosophical claim that other possibilities of religious meaning do not exist. This may come about through the confusion of thinking that recognition of these possibilities would involve embracing them, at least as options, for oneself. The 'children of light', recognizing other religious meanings, may still call those who embrace them 'children of darkness'. This is one reaction philosophical contemplation would recognize, among quite different reactions to discovering new religious meanings. The plurality of reactions, their disagreements and agreements, are part of the radical pluralism philosophy contemplates.

Sixth,[7] and finally, it may be said that there is a limit to philosophical contemplation, not in the single-mindedness of those who would have difficulty in practicing it, but in the conditions of human existence which no one can escape. There will be moral, religious or psychological limits beyond which any enquirer will be unable to recognize what is presented. How much weight is to be given to this point? Some ways of giving it weight can mislead us about the nature and scope of philosophical contemplation.

It is certainly true that philosophical contemplation does not ask one to be superhuman, to deny the conditions of one's existence. That would be meaningless, and therefore cannot be presented as a limitation to be overcome. On the other hand, questions do arise about how one conceives of the conditions of existence, since this will have a direct bearing on what one takes to be the scope of philosophical contemplation. Clearly, it will not do to limit the contemplation to that which wins one's assent, and which one may advocate. But some have argued that in extending one's contemplation beyond that circle, one must still be able to lay claim to what one recognizes, even if it is not something one would advocate oneself. Laying claim to it is said to mean, seeing the possibility of engaging the adherents to the values in question in serious conversation. That possibility, it is said, is not present when most of us are confronted by Nazism. What would it mean to see in Himmler a possible partner for conversation? My sense of the human, it is said, rules that out.

---

7   I am grateful to my Claremont colleague, Patrick Horn, for discussion which improved my reaction to this objection to contemplative philosophy.

The limiting of contemplation to what I can meet in conversation does not capture its possible philosophical scope. In fact, that limit seems close to the danger of seeking a new unity of form for the situation. There is the danger that what appears to be radical openness, turns out to be the degree of openness which a certain liberalism will allow, but no more. Why did Wittgenstein, in insisting that Göring had a certain kind of ethic too, think that philosophers need to be reminded of that fact? A woman had protested to Göring that what the Nazis did was unjust. He replied, 'Justice is what we do.' Why do we need to be reminded of that? I think that it is to silence a certain attitude, namely, one that seeks to demonstrate openness within the bounds of a familiar morality. If that morality itself advocates a certain kind of openness, as liberalism does, for example, it becomes all the harder to distinguish between it and what I mean by philosophical contemplation. If one is impressed by the minute and subtle explorations of a Henry James, one needs to put alongside it the larger than life figures of a Flannery O'Connor, and the perverse speech of a Nathanael West.

Again, in religious contexts, can I only contemplate child sacrifice, the worship of Dourga or Moloch, head-hunting, if I can go some distance in conversation with them? In many cases, that would be a singularly unwise endeavour to pursue. This is not to deal in abstract possibilities. These spaces have been occupied, but conversations with the occupants may not go far, and, in some cases, may fail to begin. When we said earlier that language makes sense if living makes sense, that living involved a hubbub of voices, some close to each other, others separated by a great distance. Conversations move around each other, and some pass each other by. But these encounters, or lack of encounter, will not be the same for everyone. So far from attempting to transcend these conditions in philosophical contemplation, they are an important part of what philosophy contemplates. Moreover, we do not need exotic examples to illustrate the point. In professional relationships, such as those in academia, and in personal relationships, such as those between husband and wife, parents and children, people may find that they can't really talk any more. This indeterminacy in human understanding is again an important object of philosophical contemplation.

Given what I have said about distances, and breakdowns in conversation, is there any point in still talking about the unity of language in such circumstances? Why talk of unity in the midst of such discord? Doesn't such talk do violence to the radical pluralism of accord and discord in human life? Not necessarily, since a certain conception of unity may be necessary if we are to do conceptual justice by the situation. If language were a collection of discrete games, it need not matter much if you do not play the game I play. But the distances between our words and practices are not of that kind. They are real distances in the lives of people which, as we know, can have tragic or terrible results. Questions concerning whether such distances are avoidable or not, admit of no simple answer. Why that should be so is a topic which is itself one for philosophical contemplation. I cannot embark on a discussion of it here,[8] but it should be clear that where it leads us undoubtedly, or collectively, cannot be laid down in advance.

---

8   See D.Z. Phillips, 'Mastery, Indeterminacy and Conversation', in *Wittgenstein and Philosophical Psychology*, Festschrift Lars Hertzberg, eds. Christoffer Gefwert and Olli

As my responses to the rewarding critiques in this volume come to an end, additional questions arise, as usual in philosophy, which would take us beyond our present concerns (at least, in *this* chapter). Throughout the discussions we have been concerned, in the main, with issues concerning the philosophy of religion, its character and place in the House of Intellect. But in Chapters III and VII, Mario von der Ruhr and Walter van Herck, respectively, mention believers who are not overly concerned with the House of Intellect, but seek to dwell in a house not made with human hands. Von der Ruhr asks whether these latter should trouble themselves overmuch with what the philosophers are saying, and Van Herck reminds us that they are certainly not philosophizing themselves. Doesn't more need to be said about the relation between philosophers and such believers? In contemplative philosophy one can speak of a growth of understanding, and of the fact that a person learns and develops as a person in that way. Doesn't someone miss much by staying within a single confessional belief? On the other hand, the confessional believer may say that if the contemplative philosopher does not believe in God, what is missed is the most important thing of all, the pearl of great price. What is to say about this contrast? There is more to be said,[9] but, for the moment, sufficient unto the day are the responses thereof.

Lagerspetz, Åbo: Åbo University Press (forthcoming).

    9   I have *begun* to reflect further on this matter in Patrick Horn and D.Z. Phillips, 'Religion and Cultural Completeness', in *Kritik von Religion*, ed. Dalferth and Grosshans.

In Retrospect

D.Z. Phillips

The first thing I want to do in these introductory remarks is to thank Stephen Mulhall, Mario von der Ruhr, Tage Kurtén, Walter van Herck, Ingolf Dalferth and Henk Vroom, for the time and attention they have devoted to aspects of my work. I have named them in the order in which I have replied to their critiques. That the order suggested itself to me quite naturally, shows that the critiques raise issues which are closely related to each other, each one leading naturally to the questions discussed by the next. This is indeed a fortunate feature of the critiques, given that they were written independently of each other. The critiques I have been fortunate enough to receive are not exercises in point-scoring. They are written by philosophers and theologians who are generally sympathetic to my work, but who ask probing questions about my contemplative conception of philosophy which have occurred to many readers. This in itself shows that I needed to say more about these issues, and I am grateful for the opportunity of doing so.

To begin with Stephen Mulhall was an easy choice to make, since he, more than any of the others, raises serious questions about my very conception of contemplative philosophy. Deeply influenced by Wittgenstein, as I am, he does not think that conception can be sustained by a reading of his work. He argues that anything I attribute to contemplative philosophy, can be found in an underlabourer conception of the subject, whereby it is seen as a method for clearing up conceptual confusions on the sites of other people. Given the clarity in living, thus attained, philosophy is brought into an inevitable relationship with other intellectual movements in our culture. Mulhall holds that this makes it difficult to regard philosophy as the autonomous discipline I take it to be, or to insist, as I do, on the importance of distinguishing between 'the philosophical' and 'the personal'.

Mario von der Ruhr, while sympathetic with my contemplative conception of philosophy, addresses a worry that has been a major feature of reactions to my work. If, following Wittgenstein, I say that philosophy 'leaves everything where it is', wouldn't one expect an assent among my audience, especially religious believers, to the elucidations I provide? But, as von der Ruhr points out, too often for comfort, the opposite has been the case. Indeed, in some quarters, my views would be deemed heretical. Am I, then, as many have accused me of doing, prescribing rather than describing religious belief? Von der Ruhr does not commit himself, in general terms, on this issue, but presses me about my discussion of belief in an afterlife which, in the opinion of many critics, brings these issues to the fore.

Tage Kurtén's critique raises interesting questions about the relation of Wittgenstein's philosophy to theology. He recognizes the contemplative character of my work, and its attempt to 'go nowhere' and let everywhere be itself, but he is also attracted by a therapeutic conception of the subject. This latter conception is attractive to a theologian because, naturally, he has to face the problems of modernity and post-modernity in communicating Christianity in a culture which is increasingly estranged from its language. In this context, Kurtén compares my work with that of Paul Tillich, and there are interesting similarities. Nevertheless, there are tensions if too close a liaison is sought. I explore this tension in a radical way, by asking whether Tillich can, as a contemplative philosopher must, envisage human life without a belief in God.

Walter van Herck recognizes clearly the major difference between my Wittgensteinian philosophy of religion, and the apologetics which dominates contemporary philosophy of religion. He puts this in dramatic form by suggesting that, like Hume's Demea, I depart from their company. This comparison may have its drawbacks, but, in any case, Van Herck's main complaint is that I have not emulated Demea enough in the account I give of the practice of piety. This is particularly evident, he believes, in the account I give of petitionary prayer. Along with my account of life after death, petitionary prayer is the other example quoted most often by critics to show that my conceptual elucidations do not leave everything where it is.

In the last two critiques of the collection, the concern of the authors is with the place of philosophy of religion and theology in a complex culture, in which conflicts and tensions are all too evident. Ingolf Dalferth and I agree that many responses to this situation are, philosophically, 'no-through roads'. He is tempted to say, however, that philosophical contemplation is not enough, as he turns to consider the practicalities of conflict-resolution. Tensions in what he says about such 'resolutions', however, show that so far from being irrelevant to such practicalities, philosophical contemplation is deeply informative about the intelligibility, or otherwise, of our conceptions about 'what is to be done'.

With the last critique, we turn full circle, since Henk Vroom brings us back to examine, once again, what I mean by a contemplative conception of philosophy. What floor, if any, does it occupy in the House of Intellect? He compares it with the tasks of religious studies, confessional theology, dialogical theology and the phenomenology of religion. As in my reply to the first critique, I still insist on the autonomy of philosophy in the House of Intellect; an autonomy which shows us a pluralism more radical than most philosophers and theologians are prepared to contemplate.

I am grateful to Andy F. Sanders whose idea it was to have me answer these critiques, and, as always, to Helen Baldwin, Secretary to the Department of Philosophy at Swansea, for preparing my handwritten replies for publication.

Bibliography

Abe, Masao, *Zen and Western Thought*, ed. W.R. LaFleur, Basingstoke: Macmillan, 1985.

Ashdown, Lance, *Anonymous Skeptics. Swinburne, Hick, and Alston*, Tübingen: Mohr-Siebeck, 2002.

Audi, Robert, *Religious Commitment and Secular Reason*, Cambridge/New York: Cambridge University Press, 2000.

Augustine, *Confessions*, trans. by R.S. Pine-Coffin, Harmondsworth: Penguin, 1976.

Berger, Peter, *The Social Reality of Religion*, Harmondsworth: Penguin, 1973.

Berlin, Isaiah, *Four Essays on Liberty*, London/New York: Oxford University Press, 1969.

Brümmer, Vincent, *What Are We Doing When We Pray? A Philosophical Inquiry*, London: SCM, 1984.

Catechism of the Catholic Church, New York: Doubleday, 1995.

Cavell, Stanley, *Must We Mean What We Say?*, Cambridge: Cambridge University Press, 1976.

——, *The Claim of Reason*, Oxford: Oxford University Press, 1979.

——, *The Senses of Walden: An Expanded Edition*, San Francisco, CA: North Point Press, 1981.

——, 'On Wittgenstein', *Philosophical Investigations* 24:2 (2001), 89–96.

Clack, Brian R., 'D.Z. Phillips, Wittgenstein and Religion', *Religious Studies* 31 (1995), 111–20.

Clayton, John, 'Common Ground and Defensible Difference', in *Religion, Politics and Peace*, ed. L.S. Rouner, Notre Dame, IN: University of Notre Dame Press, 1999.

Cobb, John B., Jr., *Beyond Dialogue*, Philadelphia, PA: Fortress Press, 1982.

——, and Christopher Ives, eds., *The Emptying God*, Maryknoll, NY: Orbis, 1990.

Cockburn, David, 'Critical Notice of Rhees' *Wittgenstein and the Possibility of Discourse*', *Philosophical Investigations* 25:1 (2002).

Conant, James, 'On Putting Two and Two Together', in *Philosophy and the Grammar of Religious Belief*, eds. Timothy Tessin and Mario von der Ruhr, London: Macmillan, 1995.

——, 'Nietzsche, Kierkegaard and Anscombe on Moral Unintelligibility', in *Religion and Morality*, ed. D.Z. Phillips, Basingstoke: Macmillan, 1996.

——, 'Philosophy and Biography', in *Wittgenstein: Biography and Philosophy*, ed. James C. Klagge, Cambridge: Cambridge University Press, 2001.

——, 'On Going the Bloody *Hard* Way in Philosophy', in *The Possibilities of Sense*, ed. John H. Whittaker, Basingstoke: Palgrave, 2002.

——, 'What "Ethics" in the *Tractatus* is *Not*', in *Religion and Wittgenstein's Legacy*, eds. D.Z. Phillips and Mario von der Ruhr, Aldershot: Ashgate, 2005, pp.16–50, 85–129, 39–88.

Cupitt, Don, 'Anti-Realist Faith', in J. Runzo ed., *Is God Real?*, Basingstoke: Macmillan, 1993, pp.45–55.

Dalferth, I.U., 'Paradigm Lost. From the Sense of the Whole to the Sense of the Presence of God', in *Religion in a Pluralistic Age. Proceedings of the Third International Conference on Philosophical Theology*, eds. D.A. Crosby and Ch.D. Hardwick, New York: Peter Lang, 2001, pp.21–48.

Davies, Brian, 'Letter from America', in *New Blackfriars: Essays in Memory of Gareth Moore* 84 (July/August 2003).

——, Gyula Klima, James Ross and David Burrell, in *Whose God? Which Tradition?* eds. D.Z. Phillips and Mario von der Ruhr, unpublished.

De Boer, Theo, *Langs de gewesten van het zijn*, Zoetermeer: Meinema, 1996.

Denham, Alison, 'How Long Can You Stay Cool at the Dance?', *Times Literary Supplement*, 23 June 2000.

Drewermann, Eugen, *Kleriker* (Munich: DTV, 1991).

——, *Worum es eigentlich geht. Protokoll einer Verurteilung*, Munich: Kösel-Verlag, Random House Group, 1992.

——, *Discovering the God Child Within*, New York: Crossroads, 1994.

Edelman, John T., 'Pointing Unknowingly: Fantasy, Nonsense and "Religious Understanding"', *Philosophical Investigations* 21 (1998), 63–87.

Eldridge, Richard, *Leading a Human Life*, Chicago, IL: University of Chicago Press, 1997.

Ferreira, M. Jamie, 'Normativity and Reference in a Wittgensteinian Philosophy of Religion', *Faith and Philosophy* 18 (2002), 443–64.

——, 'Vision and Love: A Wittgensteinian Ethic in *Culture and Value*', in *Grammar and Grace: Reformulations of Aquinas and Wittgenstein*, eds. Jeffrey Stout and R. MacSwain, London/New York: SCM/Macmillan, 2004.

Fleming, Richard, *The State of Philosophy*, Lewisburg, PA: Bucknell University Press, 1993.

Gould, Timothy, *Hearing Things*, Chicago, IL: University of Chicago Press, 1998.

Greeley, Andrew, *The Catholic Imagination*, Berkeley, CA: University of California Press, 2001.

Hadot, Pierre, *Philosophy as a Way of Life*, ed. Arnold Davidson, Chicago, IL: University of Chicago Press, 1995.

Hart, Hendrik, Ronald Kuipers and Kai Nielson, eds., *Walking the Tightrope of Faith*, Amsterdam/Atlanta, GA: Rodopi, 1999.

Hebblewaithe, Brian, 'Reflections on Realism vs. Non-Realism', in J. Runzo ed., *Is God Real?*, Basingstoke: Macmillan, 1993.

Heim, S.M., *Salvations. Truth and Difference in Religion*, Maryknoll, NY: Orbis Books, 2001.

Heine, Heinrich, *Religion and Philosophy in Germany. A Fragment*, trans. by John Snodgrass, New York: State University of New York Press, 1986.

Herrmann, Eberhard, 'God, Reality and the Realism/Atheism Debate', in *Spinning Ideas. Electronic Essays. Dedicated to Peter Gärdenfors on his 50th Birthday*, http://www.lucs.lu.se/spinning (1999), last accessed 1 July 2007.

Hick, John H., 'Belief in God: Metaphysics and Values', in J. Runzo ed., *Is God Real?*, Basingstoke: Macmillan, 1993, pp.130–32.

Holland, Roy F., *Against Empiricism*, Totowa, NJ: Barnes and Noble, 1980.

Horn, Patrick, and D.Z. Phillips, 'Religion and Cultural Completeness', in *Kritik von Religion. Zur Aktualität einer unerledigten philosophischen und theologischen Aufgabe*, eds. I.U. Dalferth and H.-P. Grosshans, Tübingen: Mohr-Siebeck, 2006.

Hume, David, 'The Natural History of Religion', in *Hume on Religion*, selected and introduced by R. Wollheim, Collins, The Fontana Library, 1963.

——, *Essays. Moral, Political and Literary*, Indianapolis, IN: Liberty Fund, 1985.

James, William, *The Varieties of Religious Experience*, ed. M.E. Marty, Harmondsworth: Penguin, 1985.

Kierkegaard, Søren, *Purity of Heart*, London: Fontana, 1961.

Knippenberg, W.H.Th., and F. Oudejans eds., *Katholiek woordenboek*, Amsterdam/Brussels: Thomas Rap, 1996.

Kurtén, Tage, *Vetenskaplig teologi och dess samhällsrelation. Presentation och kritisk diskussion av tre metateoretiska modeller*. Åbo: Åbo Akademis Förlag, 1982.

——, 'Ecstasy – A Way to Religious Knowledge. Some Remarks on Paul Tillich as Theologian and Philosopher', in Nils G. Holm ed., *Religious Ecstasy*, Stockholm: Almqvist and Wiksell International, 1982, pp.253–62.

——, *Grunder för en kontextuell teologi. Ett wittgenstienskt sätt att närma sig teologi i disussion med Anders Jeffner*, Åbo: Åbo Akademis Förlag, 1987.

Lacy, Allen, *Miguel de Unamuno: The Rhetoric of Existence*, The Hague: Mouton Press, 1967.

Levi, Isaac, *The Covenant of Reason. Rationality and the Commitments of Thought*, Cambridge: Cambridge University Press, 1997.

Lewis, C.S., 'The Efficacy of Prayer', in C.S. Lewis, *Essay Collection. Faith, Christianity and the Church*, ed. L. Walmsley, London: Harper Collins, 2000.

Locke, John, *Essay Concerning Human Understanding*, Bk. IV, chap. XVIII, para. 1.

McGinn, M., *Sense and Certainty: A Dissolution of Scepticism*, Oxford: Blackwell, 1989.

Malcolm, Norman, 'Anselm's Ontological Arguments', in Norman Malcolm, *Knowledge and Certainty*, Englewood Cliffs, NJ: Prentice-Hall, 1963, pp.141–62.

——, *Wittgenstein – A Religious Point of View?*, Ithaca, NY: Cornell University Press, 1994.

Méhat, A., A. Solignac and I. Noye, lemma 'Piété', in *Dictionnaire de spiritualité*, Paris: Beauchesne, 1932–1995, col. 1694–1743.

Minar, Edward, Review of Richard Eldridge, *Leading a Human Life*, *Philosophical Investigations* 23:1 (2000), 73–81.

Monk, Ray, 'Philosophical Biography: The Very Idea', in *Wittgenstein: Biography and Philosophy*, ed. James C. Klagge, Cambridge: Cambridge University Press, 2001, pp.3–15.

Mounce, H.O., 'The Aroma of Coffee', *Philosophy* 64:248 (1989), 159–73.

Mulhall, Stephen, *Stanley Cavell: Philosophy's Recounting of the Ordinary*, Oxford: Clarendon Press, 1994.

——, *Inheritance and Originality*, Oxford: Clarendon Press, 2001.

——, Review of Phillips, *Philosophy's Cool Place*, *Philosophical Quarterly* 51:202 (2001).

Nielsen, Kai, and D.Z. Phillips, *Wittgensteinian Fideism?*, London: SCM Press, 2004.

Nietzsche, Friedrich, *The Gay Science*, New York: Vintage, 1974.

O'Hear, Anthony, 'Culture', *Routledge Encyclopaedia of Philosophy*, London: Routledge, 1998, pp.746–50.

Pater, Wim A. de, *Analogy, Disclosures and Narrative Theology*, Leuven: Acco, 1988.

Penelhum, Terence, *God and Skepticism*, Dordrecht: Reidel, 1983.

Phillips, D.Z., *The Concept of Prayer*, London: Routledge and Kegan Paul, 1965.

——, *Death and Immortality*, London and Basingstoke: Macmillan, 1970.

——, 'Religious Beliefs and Language Games', *Ratio* 12 (1970), 26–46; also in *The Philosophy of Religion*, ed. B. Mitchell, London: Oxford University Press, 1971; and in D.Z. Phillips, *Wittgenstein and Religion*, Basingstoke: Macmillan, 1993.

——, *Religion without Explanation*, Oxford: Blackwell, 1976.

——, *Belief, Change and Forms of Life*, Basingstoke and London: Macmillan, 1986.

——, *Interventions in Ethics*, Albany, NY/London: SUNY Press/Macmillan, 1992.

——, 'On Really Believing', in J. Runzo ed., *Is God Real?*, Basingstoke: Macmillan, 1993.

——, *Wittgenstein and Religion*, Basingstoke: Macmillan, 1993.

——, Review of Richard Fleming, *The State of Philosophy*, *Philosophical Investigations* 19:4 (1994).

——, *Faith after Foundationalism*, San Francisco, CA: Westview Press, 1995.

——, 'On Giving Practice its Due – a Reply', *Religious Studies* 31 (1995), 121–27.

——, *Introducing Philosophy. The Challenge of Scepticism*, Oxford: Blackwell, 1996.

——, Review of Timothy Gould, *Hearing Things*, *Philosophical Investigations* 22:4 (1999), 349–53.

——, 'Is Hume's "True Religion" a Religious Belief?', in *Religion and Hume's Legacy*, eds. D.Z. Phillips and Timothy Tessin, Basingstoke: Macmillan and St. Martin's Press, 1999, pp.81–98.

——, *Philosophy's Cool Place*, Ithaca, NY, and New York: Cornell University Press, 1999.

——, *Recovering Religious Concepts*, Basingstoke: Macmillan and St. Martin's Press, 2000.

——, *Religion and the Hermeneutics of Contemplation*, Cambridge: Cambridge University Press, 2001.

——, 'On Wittgenstein', *Philosophical Investigations* 24:2 (2001).

——, 'Winch and Romanticism', *Philosophy* 77:300 (2002), 261–79.

——, 'What God Himself Cannot Tell Us: Realism versus Metaphysical Realism', *Faith and Philosophy* (2002).

——, 'Philosophy and Theological Castles', Ch. 7 of *Contemporary Conceptions of God*, ed. Cyril G. Williams, Lewiston, NY: Edwin Mellen Press, 2003.

——, *Religion and Friendly Fire*, Aldershot: Ashgate, 2004.

——, *The Problem of Evil and the Problem of God*, London: SCM Press, 2004.

——, 'An Audience for Philosophy of Religion?', in *Philosophy of Religion for a New Century. Essays in Honour of Eugene Thomas Long*, eds. J. Hackett and J. Wallulis, Dordrecht: Kluwer Academic Publishers, 2004, pp.133–46.

——, *From Fantasy to Faith*, 2nd edn., London: SCM Press, 2005.

——, 'The Case of the Missing Propositions', in *Readings of Wittgenstein's 'On Certainty'*, eds. Danièle Moyal-Sharrock and William H. Brenner, Basingstoke: Palgrave, 2005.

——, 'Mastery, Indeterminacy and Conversation', in *Wittgenstein and Philosophical Psychology*, Festschrift Lars Hertzberg, eds. Christoffer Gefwert and Olli Lagerspetz, Åbo: Åbo University Press (in press).

—— ed., *Can Religion Be Explained Away?*, London: Macmillan, 1996.

—— and Mario von der Ruhr eds., *Religion and Wittgenstein's Legacy*, Aldershot: Ashgate, 2005.

Pickstock, Catherine, 'Asyndeton: Syntax and Insanity. A Study of Revision of the Nicene Creed', *Modern Theology* 10 (1994), 321–40.

Quinn, Philip L., 'Religious Pluralism', *Routledge Encyclopaedia of Philosophy*, London: Routledge, 1998, pp.260–64.

——, and Charles Taliaferro, eds., *A Companion to Philosophy of Religion*, Oxford: Blackwell, 1997.

Rhees, Rush, *Without Answers*, ed. D.Z. Phillips, London: Routledge, 1969.

——, ed., *Ludwig Wittgenstein: Personal Recollections*, Oxford: Blackwell, 1981.

——, *Recollections of Wittgenstein*, Oxford: Oxford University Press, 1984.

——, *Rush Rhees on Religion and Philosophy*, ed. D.Z. Phillips, Cambridge: Cambridge University Press, 1997.

——, *Moral Questions*, ed. D.Z. Phillips, New York: St. Martin's Press, 1999.

——, 'On Wittgenstein IX', *Philosophical Investigations* 24:2 (2001), 153–62.

——, *In Dialogue with the Greeks*, vol. I: *The Presocratics and Reality*, and vol. II: *Plato and Dialectic*, ed. D.Z. Phillips, Aldershot: Ashgate, 2004.

——, *Wittgenstein and the Possibility of Discourse*, ed. D.Z. Phillips, 2nd edn., Oxford: Blackwell, 2005.

Ricœur, Paul, *The Symbolism of Evil*, trans. by Emerson Buchanan, San Francisco, CA: Harper and Row, 1967.

Ruhr, Mario von der, 'Is Animism Alive and Well?', in *Can Religion Be Explained Away?*, ed. D.Z. Phillips, Basingstoke: Macmillan and St. Martin's Press, 1996, pp.26–45.

Runzo, Joseph, 'Realism, Non-Realism and Atheism: Why Believe in an Objectively Real God?', in *Is God Real?*, ed. J. Runzo, Basingstoke: Macmillan, 1993, pp.151–75.

Sherry, Patrick, *Religion, Truth and Language-Games*, London: Macmillan, 1977.

Sprigge, T.L.S., 'Refined and Crass Supernaturalism', in *Philosophy, Religion and Spiritual Life*, ed. M. McGhee, Cambridge: Cambridge University Press, 1992, pp.105–25.

——, *James and Bradley: American Truth and British Reality*, Chicago, IL: Open Court, 1993.

Sutherland, S., *God, Jesus and Belief*, Oxford: Blackwell, 1984.

Swinburne, Richard, 'Philosophical Theism', in *Philosophy of Religion in the 21st Century*, eds. D.Z. Phillips and Timothy Tessin, Basingstoke: Palgrave, 2001, pp.3–20.

Tanner, Kathryn, *Theories of Culture. A New Agenda for Theology*, Minneapolis, MN: Augsburg Fortress, 1997.

Thomas, R.S., *Collected Poems 1945–1990*, London: Dent, 1993.

——, 'Priest and Poet', *Poetry Wales*, Spring 1972.

Tilghman, B.R., 'Isn't Belief in God an Attitude?', *International Journal for Philosophy of Religion* 43:1 (1998).

Tillich, Paul, *Systematic Theology*, vol. I/III, Chicago, IL: University of Chicago Press, 1951/1963.

——, *Frühe Hauptwerke, Gesammelte Werke I*, Stuttgart: Evangelisches Verlagswerk, 1959.

Tolstoy, Leo, 'The Three Hermits', in *Twenty-three Tales*, Oxford: Oxford University Press, 1960.

Tomasello, Michael, *The Cultural Origins of Human Cognition*, Cambridge, MA: Harvard University Press, 1999.

Trigg, Roger, *Reason and Commitment*, Cambridge: Cambridge University Press, 1973.

——, 'Theological Realism and Antirealism', in *A Companion to Philosophy of Religion*, eds. P.L. Quinn and Ch. Taliaferro, Oxford: Blackwell, 1997, pp.213–20.

Van Antwerp, Eugene I., 'An Abstract of a Dissertation on St. Augustine's *The Divination of Demons and Care of the Dead*', Washington, DC: Catholic University of America Press, 1955.

Van der Leeuw, Gerardus, *Phänomenologie der Religion*, Tübingen: Mohr, 1933. English translation, *Religion in Essence and Manifestation. A Study on Phenomenology*, trans. by J.E. Turner, London: George Allen and Unwin, 1938.

Van Huyssteen, J. Wentzel, *Alone in the World? Human Uniqueness in Science and Theology*, The Gifford Lectures 2004, Grand Rapids, MI/Cambridge: Eerdmans Publ. Company, 2006.

Voltaire, François-Marie Arouet, known as, *Dictionnaire philosophique*, Paris: Garnier-Flammarion, 1964.

Vroom, H.M., *Religions and the Truth*, Grand Rapids, MI/Amsterdam: Eerdmans/Rodopi 1989.

——, 'The (Ir)rationalism of the Theistic Concept of God', in *Post-theism. Reframing the Judeo-Christian Tradition, Festschrift Han Adriaanse*, eds. H. Krop *et al.*, Leuven: Peeters, 2000, pp.223–36.

——, *A Spectrum of Worldviews. An Introduction to Philosophy of Religion in a Pluralistic World*, trans. by Morris and Alice Greidanus, Amsterdam/New York: Rodopi, 2006.

Weil, Simone, *Letter to a Priest*, London: Routledge and Kegan Paul, 1953.

——, *Gravity and Grace*, London: Routledge and Kegan Paul, 1963.

Weston, Michael, *Kierkegaard and Modern Continental Philosophy*, London: Routledge, 1994.

——, Review of *Philosophy's Cool Place*, *Philosophical Investigations* 23:3 (2000).

White, Leslie A., *The Science of Culture*, New York: Farrar, Straus and Giroux, 1949.

Widengren, G., *Religionsphänomenologie*, Berlin: de Gruyter, 1969.

Willetts, Jeffrey, 'Karl Barth and Philosophy', University of Wales PhD, 1996.

Williams, Rowan, 'Looking for Jesus and Finding Christ', in *Biblical Concepts and Our World*, eds. D.Z. Phillips and Mario von der Ruhr, Basingstoke: Palgrave, 2004, pp.141–52.

Winch, Peter, 'Moral Integrity', in Peter Winch, *Ethics and Action*, London: Routledge and Kegan Paul, 1972.

——, *The Idea of a Social Science*, 2nd edn., London: Routledge, 1990.

——, 'Meaning and Religious Language', in *Reason and Religion*, ed. Stuart Brown, Ithaca, NY: Cornell University Press, 1977, pp.193–221; also in *Contemporary Classics in Philosophy of Religion*, eds. Ann Loades and Loyal D. Rue, La Salle, IL: Open Court, 1991, pp.349–75.

——, 'Picture and Representation', *Tijdschrift voor filosofie* 49:1 (1987).

——, *Trying to Make Sense*, Oxford: Blackwell, 1987.

——, 'Response', in Norman Malcolm, *Wittgenstein – From a Religious Point of View?*, Ithaca, NY: Cornell University Press, 1994, pp.95–132.

——, 'How is Political Authority Possible?', *Philosophical Investigations* 25:1 (2002), 20–32.

——, 'Lessing and the Resurrection', in *The Possibilities of Sense*, ed. John H. Whittaker, Basingstoke: Palgrave, 2002, pp.182–203.

Wittgenstein, Ludwig, *Philosophical Investigations*, trans. by G.E.M. Anscombe, Oxford: Blackwell, 1953.

——, *Tractatus Logico-Philosophicus*, London: Routledge and Kegan Paul, 1961.

——, *Lectures and Conversations on Aesthetics, Psychology, and Religious Belief*, ed. Cyril Barrett, Oxford: Blackwell, 1966, reprinted 1970.

——, *Über Gewißheit / On Certainty*, eds. G.E.M. Anscombe and G.H. von Wright, Oxford: Blackwell, 1979.

——, *Culture and Value*, Chicago, IL: University of Chicago Press, 1990.

——, 'Remarks on Frazer's *Golden Bough*', Ch. 7 of *Wittgenstein: Philosophical Occasions*, eds. J. Klagge and A. Nordmann, Indianapolis, IN: Hackett, 1993.

Wolterstorff, Nicolas, 'Reformed Epistemology', in *Philosophy of Religion in the 21st Century*, eds. D.Z. Phillips and Timothy Tessin, Basingstoke: Palgrave, 2001, pp.39–63.

Index

a priori 58, 108, 123, 125
Abe, M. 189
absolute 9, 14, 23, 32, 37, 99, 103, 125, 127,
    132, 133, 139
academic disciplines 183, 188, 190
Advaita 184, 185, 187, 195
afterlife 61–2, 75, 79, 87–9, 147, 213
    character of 65
    pictures of 61
    see also eternal life
agnosticism 134
agreement 33, 113, 155, 156, 158, 162, 163,
    169, 170, 173, 174, 175, 176, 178,
    179, 183, 196, 209
Al-Farabi 187
Al-Ghazali 187
alternity 193
analogy 24, 25, 51, 101, 135, 142, 143
analysis 3, 8, 56, 57, 60, 62, 64, 68, 173,
    182, 184, 185
Anscombe, E. 43
anthropology 97, 112, 120, 138, 154, 187,
    189, 190
anthropomorphism 125, 134, 143
apologetics 3, 4, 9, 41, 57, 115, 153, 160,
    172, 188, 214
Apostles 65, 91
Aquinas, T. 101, 187
argument, religious 55–7
arts 18, 21
Ashdown, L. 18n.
atheism 35, 56, 57, 58, 59, 102, 126, 183, 185
attention, contemplative, philosophical 3, 9
    22, 23, 38, 39, 40, 43–4, 46, 48, 57,
    139, 141, 142, 162, 172, 198, 203,
    207, 208, 209
attitudes 65, 79, 80, 84, 85, 88, 203, 210
Audi, R. 162n.
audience 198, 213
Augustine 74, 83, 84, 87, 182
Austin, J.L. 18
authority 6, 18, 25, 26, 66, 97, 123, 128,
    165, 174, 182, 183, 201, 203
autonomy 5, 6, 7–8, 29, 32, 35, 113, 170,
    197, 203, 213, 214

awe 205; *see also* wonder
Ayer, A.J. 42, 46

Baier, A. 189n.
Baldwin, H. 214
Barth, K. 115, 187
Beethoven, L.van 123
'Being-itself' 95, 97–8, 99, 100, 105, 106,
    114, 116, 117
Belief, Change and Forms of Life 9, 121,
    123
believers 7, 8, 60, 73, 74, 76, 77, 83, 121,
    144, 145, 158, 160, 163, 175, 196,
    203, 213
    and philosophical confusion 48, 67, 78
    and prayer 120, 148, 150
    reactions of 60–63
    thoughts and actions of 64
Berger, P. 158, 170
Berlin, I. 164, 177
biography 37, 45, 46, 120
de Boer, T. 192, 194
Brown Book, The 202
Brümmer, V. 191n.
Buddhism 183, 184, 185, 186, 187, 189

catechism 55, 56, 63, 64, 80–81, 87, 93
Catholicism 8, 62ff., 70, 79, 83, 84ff., 132,
    135–6, 138, 142, 183
    poetry of 136, 145–6
    theology 187
Cavell, S. 3, 21, 23–6, 27, 29, 30, 31, 32–6
change 9, 22, 30, 62, 133, 150, 151, 154,
    155, 157, 159, 160, 165, 177, 178,
    182, 193, 205
character, 37, 38, 51
choice 164, 168, 170, 175
Christ 8, 61, 62, 89, 168
    Ascension 68, 71–2, 74, 81
    Cross 66, 91, 151
    Resurrection 63, 64, 65–6, 68, 85, 86,
        87, 89–90, 91
Christianity 26, 33, 71, 88, 89, 96, 97, 115,
    119, 122, 124, 128, 133, 151, 183,

185, 186, 187, 188, 189, 194, 195,
     214
  and culture 154, 157
  exclusivism 168
Christians 4, 5, 22, 195; *see also* believers
Church 123, 182, 188
Cicero 127
clarity 3, 19, 22, 37, 43, 44, 46, 47, 49, 50,
     96, 138, 197, 213
Cleanthes 125, 126, 138, 139, 141, 143
Cobb Jr., J.B. 189n.
Cockburn, D. 52, 54
coercion 164, 178, 206
co-existence 162, 176
coherence 16, 131, 144, 161, 174, 175, 176,
     177
commitment 4, 6, 50, 98, 108, 162, 159
common view 161, 162, 163, 164, 167, 172,
     174, 176, 178, 195, 204
community 32, 150, 154, 163, 184, 185,
     187, 188, 189, 196
comparative religion 190, 191, 192; *see also*
     theology
compartmentalism 38
Conant, J. 3, 21–3, 25, 26, 27, 29, 30, 31,
     36–42, 45–6, 119
concepts 3, 7, 15, 16, 19, 24, 57, 113, 117,
     126, 173, 207, 208
  profane 137
  religious 135, 136–7, 181, 182, 184, 185
  subliming of 176–7, 179
concrete existence 98, 101, 105, 112, 114,
     116
condescension 83, 84, 144
confessional claims 195, 196, 199
conflict 10, 154, 155
  cultural 167, 170, 173ff., 179
  political 173–4
  religious 164, 169–70, 174–5, 176, 179
  resolution of 163–4, 176, 178
  value 161, 162, 174, 177, 178, 205
Confucianism 183, 186

confusion, philosophical 2, 20, 22, 29, 33, 35,
     39, 54, 96, 97, 111, 159, 161, 169,
     176, 197, 200, 201, 204, 205, 209, 213
  and language 14–15, 17, 19
  and religious belief 61, 62, 65, 66, 67,
     69, 75, 78, 80, 87
  and way of life 41, 43, 47, 48
  Wittgenstein and 23, 36, 58

consensus 155, 164, 173, 174; *see also*
     agreement
constructivism 106, 116
contemplation 2, 30, 35, 36, 49, 159, 160,
     161, 171, 183, 213
  critique of 4, 19, 32
  hermeneutics of 153, 167
  of language 53
  and life 193
  limits of 209–10
contemplative philosophy of religion 2–3,
     10, 13, 14, 21, 34, 38, 40, 54, 67,
     170, 171, 173, 193, 194, 213
  aim of 3 5, 29, 111, 159, 183, 186
  and radical pluralism 203–11
contingency 155, 158, 166, 174, 175
controversy 177
  etiquette of 165
conversation 13, 16–17, 25, 26, 27, 35, 51,
     52, 53, 114, 203, 206, 209, 210; *see
     also* dialogue; discourse
conversion 170, 182, 195
correlation, method of 101
cosmos 7, 41, 195
creation 7, 18, 66, 77, 137, 150, 195
creationism 165
criteria 23, 24, 32, 59, 107, 166, 203
  internal 3, 6, 9, 59, 108
criticism 4, 32, 34, 127, 153, 160, 167, 171,
     172, 174, 205
culture 6, 7, 9–10, 26, 32, 118, 119, 121–4,
     138, 148, 153, 168, 170, 187, 195, 198
  and conflict 155, 167, 170, 173ff., 179
  definition of 154–5
  and religions 153–4, 156, 157–8
Cupitt, D. 102

Dalferth, I.U. 3–4, 10, 121, 167, 169–70ff.,
     214
death 63, 66, 85, 88, 89, 92, 129
  of loved ones 61, 62, 64, 87
'death of God' 105–6, 116, 117, 118–21
debate 187, 188; *see also* dialogue; public
     debate
Degenhardt, J.J. 72, 73
Demea 125–6, 138, 139, 140–41, 142, 143,
     144, 146, 147, 148, 214
Denham, A. 30, 31
description 4, 6–7, 60, 62, 78, 80, 113, 147,
     154, 160, 171, 190, 191, 192, 193,
     194, 195

special meaning of 201, 202
design, argument from 125
detachment 59, 108, 111, 127
devotion 130, 131, 144, 146, 148; *see also*
    piety
dialectical movement 193, 207
dialogical theology 188–9, 196, 202, 214
dialogue 2, 16, 19, 20, 26, 27, 33, 58, 154,
    162–4, 166, 175, 178, 188, 204
    inter-religious 195, 196
    unity of 17, 21, 25, 53
    see also conversation; discourse
differences 190, 193, 195, 204
    and conflict 161–2
    cultural 155, 167, 170, 177, 178
    religious 158, 161, 163–4, 167, 168,
        170, 172, 173, 174, 177, 178
disagreement 45, 60, 67, 74, 77–8, 83, 155,
    156, 158, 166, 169, 183; *see also*
    differences
discord 11
discourse 75, 113, 135
    intelligibility of 204
    possibility of 2, 3, 10, 13, 19, 25, 27,
        50, 204
    modes of 18, 20, 21, 25, 26
    unity of 17, 18, 20, 26, 53, 114, 214, 215
    see also conversation; dialogue
divine intervention 8, 129–31, 132–3, 144,
    149
divinity 76, 185
doctrines 55, 68, 136, 146, 188
Drewermann, E. 59, 67, 68–74, 80–84
Drury, M. O'C. 47

ecumenical studies 188
education 125, 136–7
Egypt, ancient 71
Eicher, Professor 68ff., 80, 81, 90
Eldridge, R. 34
elucidation, conceptual 2, 5, 7, 8, 56, 64,
    109, 147, 197, 199, 206, 209, 213,
    214
Emerson, R.W. 33, 34
empiricism 82, 97, 99, 192; *see also* facts
emptiness 14, 15, 23
'empty mind' 166, 175
encounter 99, 100, 115, 210
ends, religious 157, 158, 161, 176
Enlightenment 96, 97, 132, 161, 182, 186
enquiry 58–9, 108, 175, 208

enthusiasm 128
epistemology 98
equality 195, 199, 203, 206
equivocity 134
essence 192, 199, 202
essentialism 195
eternal life 5, 6, 8, 63, 92
    belief in 78–9
    confused ideas of 79
    and survival after death 85–6, 88
eternity 61, 65, 93
    concept of 92, 120
    pictures of 6, 8, 60–61, 75, 93
    see also eternal life
ethics 3, 23, 25, 32, 33, 39, 41, 42, 44, 46,
    49, 120, 143, 190, 203, 208, 210
    of controversy 165, 177
    see also theological ethics
European Society of the Philosophy of
    Religion 181
evidence 70, 72, 81, 97, 125, 182
evidentialists 125, 139, 140
exclusivism 156, 167, 168
existence 99, 100, 117, 120; *see also*
    concrete existence
existentialism 9, 55, 99
experience 76, 91, 100, 107, 131, 132, 133,
    181, 183, 185, 190, 195, 200
explanation 37, 53, 192, 201, 204
external relation 143, 206

facts 56, 59, 72, 76, 77, 82, 112, 116, 182,
    190, 192
faith 55, 59, 63, 86, 98, 107, 143
falsity 75, 76, 107, 156, 164
family resemblances 15, 16, 51
Farrington, B. 123
Ferreira, M.J. 160
Feuerbach, L. 58, 120
fideism 54
finitude 34, 100
Fleming, R. 34
folklore 70, 71
forms of life 3, 4, 16, 17, 20, 21, 26, 27, 32,
    35, 39, 40, 43, 56, 59, 64, 126, 159,
    162, 164, 204
Frazer, J. 42–3
freedom 182
Frege, G. 45
Fulda, Archbishop of 68–72, 80, 81, 90

games 15, 16, 17, 51, 52, 72, 210; *see also* language-games
Gealy, W. 91
gift 9, 66, 69, 151
God 9, 24, 32, 37, 48, 49, 69, 70, 76, 88, 131, 134, 135, 175, 181
    and afterlife 61, 92, 93
    arguments for existence of 99–100, 105–106, 125, 126, 139, 188
    communion with 93
    nature of 126
    and pictures 77
    and pluralism 168
    and prayer 142, 143, 148, 150
    question concerning 100, 101
    reality of 5, 102, 105–106, 113, 114, 120
    see also 'death of God'
Goering, H. 210
Gould, T. 34
grace 120, 135, 138, 151

grammar 8, 15, 17, 20, 27, 54, 56, 57, 62, 72, 73, 75, 125, 139, 144, 151, 152, 200
    differences 21, 62
    distortion of 148
    'eye of' 148
    of faith 107
    surface 78
    and theology 146
    violations of 14, 23
Greeley, A. 135, 138, 146
'ground of being' 105, 185

Hadot, P. 42
Heidegger, M. 13, 24
Heine, H. 55, 56, 59, 68, 74, 80, 83
Hellenistic philosophy 40–41, 42
Herck, W. van 5, 7, 139, 140, 141ff., 147, 211, 214
hermeneutics 3, 6, 7, 9, 10, 153, 167
Herrmann, E. 104
Hick, J. 103
Himmler 209
Hinduism 183, 184, 185
history 4, 7, 21, 81, 90, 91, 115, 124, 155, 185, 200, 201
Holland, R.F. 34, 70
Holmer, P. 107
hope 61, 62, 65, 87, 92, 124, 148
Horn, P. 209n., 211n.
human beings 26, 27, 31, 100, 120, 154,

173, 195
human life 7, 9, 10, 26, 29, 35, 85, 89, 92, 97, 99, 100, 106, 115, 129, 159, 181, 193, 207
    and discourse 204
    judgement of 61, 79, 88
    and rules 203
    see also concrete existence; forms of life; living
human sacrifice 205
humanism 98, 183, 185, 187, 189
Hume, D. 40, 56, 125, 128, 133, 139, 140
Huyssteen van, J.W. 8n.

Ideal 132, 133, 144, 147
identity 100, 150, 163
illusions 121–2
images 65, 93, 185; *see also* pictures
imagination 32, 204
imaginative invention 4, 160, 172
immortality 61, 62, 65, 67
    evaluative view of 79, 80
    see also afterlife; eternal life
impartiality 57–8, 60
Incarnation 63
inclusivism 156, 167, 168
inconsistency 161, 162, 174, 181, 182
infinity 100, 131
insights 196, 199, 200, 203
institutions 162, 164, 176, 178
instrumentalism 5, 35, 143, 147
intelligibility 53, 75, 114, 203–204
intercourse *see* conversation; dialogue; discourse
internal relations 39, 40, 42, 43, 44, 89, 107, 108, 109, 110, 111, 120, 150
Introducing Philosophy 106
ipso facto 58, 70, 71
Iqbal, M. 187
Islam 154, 157, 177, 187, 189

James, H. 210
James, W. 8, 132–3, 144, 200
Jeffner, A. 95
Job 143
John's gospel 72, 73
Jones, J.R. 121
Judaism 154, 159, 189
justice 127, 166, 195, 199, 203

Kant, I. 96, 98, 105, 112, 161, 169

karma 184, 185
Kierkegaard, S. 1, 3, 7, 8, 21, 26, 31, 36, 50, 87, 93, 96, 99, 120, 149–50
Kurtén, T. 5, 7, 9, 111–12ff., 124, 213–14

Laërtius, D. 127
language 6, 7, 27, 50, 100, 111, 146, 172, 181, 184, 197, 204, 206, 207, 210
  concept of 19
  contemplation of 53
  dialogical character 204
  as a family 15, 16, 51
  interlocking intelligibility of 53, 75, 114
  ordinary 2, 15, 19, 20, 135, 137, 143
  and philosophical confusion 14–15
  and puzzles 51–2
  and reality 76, 169
  structure 204
  as technique 31
  unity of 2, 15, 17, 18, 20, 21, 25, 26, 51, 53, 210
  see also language-games; religious language
language-games 2, 15, 17, 20, 25, 51–2, 54, 104, 131, 145
Last Judgement 77, 80, 87, 88, 103, 168, 184
law 162, 173, 176, 178
Leeuw, G. van der 190–93
Lessing, G.E. 90
Levi, I. 166
liberalism 183, 210
life after death *see* afterlife; *see also* eternal life
linguistic philosophy 54, 112
literalism 82
literature 24, 25, 200, 204, 207, 208
liturgical objects 135, 149, 150
living 29, 30, 31, 34, 35, 36, 39, 42, 48, 53, 64, 65, 116, 193; *see also* forms of life; human life
Locke, J. 29, 32, 33, 160–61
logic 45, 50, 51, 146, 169, 201
  of pictures 77
love 63, 65, 86, 91, 93, 123, 130, 137, 151
  God's 5, 6, 66, 67, 127, 150, 164
Luther, M. 150, 187

magic 132, 150
Marx, K. 58
Marxism 182, 183

material forms *see* outer actions
mathematics 21
meaning 6, 7, 11, 82, 101, 112, 127, 137, 145, 169, 182, 184, 185, 189, 209
  religious 153, 208
  and rules 203
means-ends relation 145
meditation 182, 185, 186
metaphor 73, 74, 82
metaphysical theism 1
metaphysics 9, 14–15, 32, 56, 96, 97, 101, 112, 114ff., 169
meta-theory 4, 186, 200–201
methodology 57, 96, 200, 207, 213
Michelangelo 77
miracles 69
modernity 96–8, 99, 104, 110, 112, 157, 182, 214
Monk, R. 45
moral philosophy 41, 46, 189
moral reactions 44
morality *see* ethics
Moses 190
motivation 5, 140, 158, 160, 172, 190, 206
Mulhall, S. 2, 29–30ff., 48, 51, 52, 53, 54, 167, 197, 213
  and Cavell 32–6
  and Conant 36–8, 46–7
mystery 93
mysticism 73
myth 71, 74, 82

natural religion 126
naturalism 132, 133, 156, 168, 183, 195
nature 127, 133, 140, 141, 173
Nazism 209, 210
neutrality 2, 4–6, 7, 21, 26, 29, 30, 108, 110, 111, 186, 187, 198, 193, 195, 196n., 198, 199, 200
Nielsen, K. 30, 31
Nietzsche, F. 58, 119, 120
non-believers 48, 76, 77, 140, 175
non-cognitivism 104, 113
non-realism 95, 98, 102, 103, 105
noumenal realm 98, 169
Nussbaum, M. 190
Nygren, A. 98

objectivity 100, 105, 112, 116
O'Connor, Flannery 34, 87, 210
O'Hear, A. 154n.

omnipotence 67, 150
ontological argument 100, 101, 116, 139
ontology 9, 100, 101, 112, 116, 139
open-mindedness 165–6, 175, 210
oppression 206, 207
optimism 123–4
ordinary life 14, 97, 127, 131, 133, 135, 137, 141

Pannenberg, W. 98
passions 2, 3, 14, 21, 27, 49, 50, 99
de Pater, W.A. 134n.
Paul 8, 63, 65, 73, 89–90, 91, 181
Peace 162, 176, 178
peacemaking 162, 176
Penelhum, T. 103, 112
personal factors 2, 3, 5, 6, 21, 23, 36–50, 57–60, 65, 107–109, 170, 171, 183, 187, 199, 207, 208, 209, 213
petitionary prayer 5, 6, 9, 129–31, 141–52, 214
    aims of 129, 142–4, 147–51
phenomena, concept of 191–2
phenomenology of religion 4, 58, 98, 190–94, 195, 202–203, 214
Phillips, D. Z.
    and petitionary prayer 129–31, 141–52
    and phenomenology 190, 193–4, 195, 202, 214
    philosophical aims 1, 159, 181–2, 183, 186, 189, 190, 193–4, 196, 197ff., 213
    and piety 141
    and realism 102–5
    and reductivism 79–80, 84, 167
    response of believers to 60–61, 77–9, 211, 213
    self-description of 13
    and sensitivity 57–9
    and theology 5–6, 59–60, 107–108, 184, 188, 189
    and Tillich 95–6, 97–8, 105–10, 112, 117–18
Philo 125, 126, 139
philosophers 21, 22, 26, 75, 83, 97, 102, 107, 110, 140, 145, 146, 159, 181, 182, 194
    lives of 31, 32, 37–8, 45–6, 207
    motivation of 160–61, 171, 172
    need for impartiality 57–8
    and truth 183, 196
Philosophical Investigations (Wittgenstein) 15, 16, 17, 20, 47

philosophical problems 14, 21, 23, 31, 36, 40, 63, 161, 171, 183, 197
philosophical theism *see* metaphysical theism
philosophical theology 3, 6, 56, 188
philosophies of life *see* worldview traditions
philosophy 3, 4, 83, 93, 96, 97, 118, 125, 128, 138, 159–60, 193, 195
    'cool place' 2, 6, 13, 19, 23, 29, 30, 183, 184, 186, 189, 192, 193, 197, 198, 202
    deficient concept of 13, 14, 19, 29
    excessive concept of 13, 14, 20, 29
    and life 22, 207–208
    method 14–15, 17, 20–21, 171–2, 181–2, 183
    modern and ancient 41
    negative task 2, 14, 18, 29, 111
    passionate version 2–3
    and personal difficulties 23, 36–50
    and piety 140
    and religious argument 56–7
    therapeutic conception of 2, 29, 30, 31, 35, 50, 54, 75, 111, 213–14
    underlabourer role 2, 29, 46, 111, 197, 213
    value of 14, 20, 29
    see also philosophy of religion
philosophy of logic 6, 7, 10
    aims of 153
philosophy of religion 1, 3–5, 7, 97, 107, 193, 214
    aims of 157, 159–61, 170–73, 181–2, 183, 186, 187, 188, 189
    and confessional theology 201–202
    and dialogic theology 202
    and phenomenology of religion 202–203
    and religious studies 184–6, 199–202
    see also contemplative philosophy of religion; philosophical theology
Philosophy's Cool Place 2, 13, 20, 22, 23, 29, 33, 36, 40, 53, 197
Pickstock, C. 134n.
pictures 14, 15, 103, 117, 121–2, 148, 185
    of eternity 6, 8, 60–61, 93
    logic of 77
    and propositions 50
    and reality 75–7
    religious 76, 80, 82
    and representation 64
piety, 126, 127–32, 141, 142, 147

and petitionary prayer 129–32
and philosophy 140
poetry of 136, 145–6
and religious language 134–6
and superstition 128ff.
Plato 13, 17–19, 25, 31, 41, 127
pluralism 9–11, 183, 186
and conflict resolution 163–4
radical 10–11, 202, 203–11
of religions 9, 156–7, 167–8, 168–9, 194
theological 10, 204–205
poetry, and piety 136, 145–6
polemics 4, 160, 172
political institutions 162, 178
politics 32–3, 173–4, 176, 177
positivism 56, 57, 68, 74, 81
possibility 2, 3, 10, 15, 19, 25, 27, 50, 76,
    101, 106, 111, 159, 160, 165, 173,
    203, 204, 205, 206, 209
practices 146, 147, 192, 203, 204, 210; *see
    also* religious practices
prayer 120, 130–31, 133, 134, 144, 148,
    150, 182, 190, 191, 194, 202; *see
    also* petitionary prayer
prediction 61, 79, 85, 86
prescription 7, 113, 147, 213
pre-Socratics 13, 17, 18, 25, 114
presupposition 20, 26, 56, 91, 100, 105, 116,
    130, 134, 141, 146, 173, 185
primitive peoples 43–4, 190
'principle of charity' 130
probability 125, 165, 175, 181
proof 70, 72, 81, 122, 125, 139
propositions 50, 51, 56, 59, 146
    as pictures of reality 75–6
proselytizing 157
Protagoras 18
'protestant principle' 95, 109
Protestants 183, 188
providence 9, 126
    particular 133–4
psychoanalysis 24, 25, 26, 33
public debate 163, 165
purity 3, 14, 38, 39, 49, 50

quietism 10, 30, 31–2, 160, 205
Quine, W. 46
Quinn, P.L. 104n., 126n., 156n.

Ramsey, I.T. 135
rationality 55–6, 99, 141, 142, 178

'real' 189, 191, 192, 194, 201
realism 2, 10, 73, 82, 95, 97, 98, 102–5
    external 112
    internal 9, 104, 105–106, 110, 112
    ordinary 9, 112
    and reductionism 102–103
    religious 98, 104
reality 9, 18, 19, 25, 26, 50, 53, 54, 114,
    202, 203
    of God 5, 102, 105–106, 113, 182, 191, 192
    objective 99
    and pictures 75–7
    and truth 182, 183
redemption 89, 91
reductionism/reductivism 8, 37, 46, 73, 74,
    75, 79–80, 82, 84, 102–3, 116, 156,
    167, 168
reference 80, 99
reflection 22, 32, 48, 60, 93, 96, 186, 188
reform 5, 6, 7, 82, 112, 113
Reformed epistemologists 139, 140
relation 99
relationships 210
relativism 10, 103, 106, 116, 118, 120, 164, 206
religion 200
    death of 118
    and life 106, 115, 181, 182
    and rational argument 55–6
    see also phenomenology of religion;
        religions; religious beliefs;
        religious language; religious
        practices; religious studies
religions 4, 127
    and cultures 9–10, 153–4, 156, 157–8
    pluralism of 156–7, 168
    'religious accomodation' 122
religious beliefs 3, 7, 35, 48, 50, 54, 79, 175
    and argument 56
    and conflict 164
    and culture 122
    hermeneutics of 167
    and life 64
    reductive analysis of 75
    and philosophy 78, 83
    realism/non-realism debate 102–105
    see also believers
religious fantasies 87
'religious individualism' 121–2
religious language 3, 6, 9, 48, 56, 57, 82,
    98–9, 100, 106, 113, 117, 118, 148,
    184, 201

derivative 134–5, 137
method of correlation 101
non-derivative 136, 137
reform of 113
use of 102
religious life 1, 7, 22, 48, 59, 64, 78, 102, 104, 105, 106, 107, 116, 117, 120, 128, 137, 148, 192
religious people 101, 106, 118, 127, 141, 153; *see also* believers
religious practices 3, 7, 8, 126, 131, 137, 138, 140, 146, 147, 185, 194, 200, 201, 202
criticism of 127
outer forms 127, 135
poetic element of 136, 146
'religious rationalism' 122
religious studies 6–7, 8, 183, 184–6, 187, 190, 191, 192, 193, 194, 196, 199–201, 202, 214
renunciation 66
representation, perspicuous 1, 2, 19, 20, 21, 41, 45, 53
respect 57, 164, 165, 166, 174, 177
resurrection 61, 63–4
revelation 181, 183
Rhees, R. 1, 6, 8, 14, 16, 18, 20, 25, 27, 31, 34, 39–40, 41, 43–4, 46, 51, 52, 53, 54, 67, 75, 84, 159, 170
on afterlife 65–6, 87–9, 92
on optimism 123–4
on philosophy 172, 193
Ricoeur, P. 190
rituals 43, 44, 127, 128, 132, 135, 136, 145, 202, 205
Romanticism 26, 33
Ruhr, M. von 7, 8, 75, 76, 78, 79, 80, 83, 87, 93, 114–15, 147, 211, 213
and Drewermann 81–2
rules 15, 16, 52, 53, 164, 203
Runzo, J. 98, 104
Russell, B. 39, 44–6

sacrament 205
Sanders, A.F. 214
salvation 127, 131, 133
Sartre, J.P. 24
scepticism 18, 25, 31, 71, 73, 81
Schopenhauer 58
science 4, 8, 21, 23, 67, 70, 72, 74, 194
Scripture 65, 66, 72, 93, 107

exegesis 68, 73, 80, 187
secularism 5, 101, 119, 183, 198
self-knowledge 22, 23, 34, 96, 108
self 41, 64, 91, 100, 131, 161, 182
self-reflection 22, 96
self-transformation 4, 160, 173
sense 6, 7, 49, 52, 53, 117, 159, 160
sensibility 47
Shakespeare, W. 123
Sherry, P. 185n.
sincerity 104
single-mindedness 208–209
social contract 32, 173, 174
social sciences 206, 207
society 158, 161, 173, 174, 176, 177, 192, 206
sociology 7, 187, 189, 190, 194, 196, 200, 201, 204
Socrates 13, 25, 31, 83, 92
Son of God 71
sophists 18, 25, 83
soul 61, 63–4, 79, 89, 93, 185
speech 14, 16, 17, 21, 27, 33, 51, 122
concept of 19
see also 'to say something'; *see also* utterances
Spinoza 40
spirit 119–20, 148, 150, 168, 193
'spiritual fruits' 107, 109, 168
spirituality 107, 131, 132
stability 10, 161, 176, 177
Stoicism 41
stories 136, 146, 151, 181
subjectivity 100, 192
'subliming' 10, 54, 75, 176–7, 179
substitutions 117
suffering 151
supernaturalism 8, 10, 128, 129, 142, 144, 147, 149, 205
crass and refined 132–4, 142, 144, 147, 149
superstition 70, 74, 78, 127ff., 138, 141, 142
Catholic view of, 132
see also petitionary prayer
survival after death 85–6, 88; *see also* afterlife; eternal life
suspicion 206
Sutherland, S. 113
symbols 71, 73, 82, 95, 101, 105, 116, 134, 135, 187, 190
Szabados, B. 30, 31–2

Tanner, K. 154n.
Tessin, T. 140n., 141n.
Thales 18
theism 3, 8, 9, 181
theologians 4, 5, 55, 57, 83, 97, 107–108,
    115, 123, 183, 184, 185, 200, 201
theological ethics 187
theology 1, 3–8, 9, 56, 59–60, 97, 98,
    107–109, 114, 184, 195, 198, 213,
    214
  academic discipline 183, 187–90
  comparative/dialogical 188–9, 196, 202,
    214
  confessional 188, 201–202, 214
  dogmatic 187, 196
  ecumenical 187
  fundamental 187, 188
  grammar of 146
  natural 188
  and pluralism 168, 169
  systematic 107, 108, 109, 146, 187
  see also theologians; theological ethics
Theophrastus 127
theories 9, 96, 106, 145, 146, 147, 182, 201
Thomas, Apostle 72–3, 81
Thomas, R.S. 8, 91–2
Tilghman, B. 134–5
Tillich, P. 9, 112, 124
  and existence of God 99–100
  and metaphysics 112, 114–18
  and Phillips 95–6, 97–8, 105–10,
    117–18, 214
  and philosophy 113, 118
  and religious language 98–9, 100, 109
  and symbols 101, 105, 116
  and 'theological circle' 108–9
time/temporality 92, 93, 120
'to say something' 14, 16, 17, 19, 20, 27, 33,
    46, 50, 51, 52, 117, 148, 172, 197,
    201, 204
toleration 10, 154, 162, 163, 164–6, 176,
    177
Tolstoy, L. 148
Tomasello, M. 154n.
Tractatus (Wittgenstein) 39, 46, 49, 50, 51,
    52, 75–6
traditions 5, 25, 33, 101, 108, 109, 110, 140,
    141, 171, 183, 195, 200
  Catholic 135–6
  cultural 155, 158
  ideas of 185–6

theological 187–8, 189
  see also worldview traditions
transcendence 34, 98, 99, 115, 168, 169,
    182, 183
transformation 119, 143, 150, 159, 160, 173
Trigg, R. 103–104, 112
truth 10, 18, 75, 76, 100, 104, 156, 164, 168,
    183, 195, 196, 206
  definition of 182
Twain, M. 148

'ultimate concern' 95, 99, 106, 108, 109,
    115, 116, 117, 118
Unamuno, M. de 84, 144
unconditionality 99, 100, 115
understanding 9, 10, 31, 32, 35, 58, 101,
    193, 194, 195, 210
univocity 134
utterances 14, 23, 51, 56, 65, 84, 122, 131,
    145, 147

values 33, 62, 79, 80, 108, 168, 179, 208
  agreement in 176
  conflicts of 158, 161, 162, 174, 177,
    178, 205
  personal 208
Virgin Birth 63, 68–71
voices, hubbub of 10, 34, 53, 114–15, 192,
    204, 205, 206, 210
Voltaire 128
Vroom, H.M. 4, 5, 7, 8, 197ff.

Weil, S. 1, 8, 66, 67, 74, 85, 148
West, N. 210
Weston, M. 32, 115
White, L. 154n.
Widengren, G. 190
Williams, Rowan 90
Winch, P. 1, 8, 15, 34, 41, 47, 50, 53, 64,
    66–7, 74, 76, 84, 85, 86, 89–90, 91,
    136, 189
wisdom 126 7, 141, 142
Wittgenstein, L 1, 2, 4, 6, 41, 58, 84–5, 87, 89,
    95, 96, 109, 112, 113, 136, 169, 170,
    183, 193, 198, 200, 201, 202, 210
  and contemplation 30, 35, 36
  deficient view of 13, 14–20, 29
  and language 16–17, 19
  and living 22–3, 35
  philosophical difficulties 39
  philosophical method 14–15, 20, 96

and philosophy of religion 159–60
and pictures 75–7, 103, 117
and prayer 131, 145
and quietism 31–2
reactions to 13, 29, 30
and religion 48–50
sensitivity of 47
and theology 213
transgressive view of 13, 20–27, 29
Wittgensteinians 21, 27, 29, 139, 140
wonder 6, 13, 20, 35, 40, 42–3, 49, 96, 171, 183, 207
words 2, 14, 15, 16, 17, 18, 19, 20, 25, 34, 50, 52, 80, 86, 112, 125, 126, 128, 181, 198, 201, 210

and meaning 168, 169, 184–5
and piety 134, 135
and rules 203
world 7, 29, 30, 99, 100, 101, 132–3, 172, 197, 205, 208
world-pictures 35
worldview traditions 186, 188–90, 195–6, 198
worship 44, 48, 127

Zen thought 187, 189, 195, 196n.

Printed in Great Britain
by Amazon

35384327R00137